Kayhan Delibas is Lecturer and Professor of Sociology in the Department of Sociology at the Adnan Menderes University Aydın-Turkey. He is also Research Associate in the School of Anthropology and Conservation at the University of Kent.

'Kayhan Delibas provides a unique study of the roots of Muslim politics in Turkey. Based on extraordinary direct observation, he offers compelling evidence that the imbalances resulting from a fragmented party system, urbanisation, and neoliberal economic restructuring provided the main impetus to grassroots activism. This is thus a powerful explanation for the rise of religious-leaning political movements in an avowedly secularist republic, as well as a much-needed rebalancing of perspective in the often ideologised debates over political Islam generally.'

James Piscatori, Professor of International Relations, School of Government and International Affairs, Durham University

'An essential contribution to our understanding of the everyday workings of political Islam. An exemplary case study.'

Frank Furedi, Emeritus Professor of Sociology, School of Social Policy, Sociology and Social Research, University of Kent

'**Kayhan Delibas** has written an important book. He takes political Islam seriously and seeks to move beyond the simplistic accounts which place ideology as the central driver of a social movement. Without ignoring the ideological imperatives inherent in Turkey's political Islam, he demonstrates how rapid economic and demographic changes to urban Turkey, like Ankara, and by extension other parts of the Muslim world, like Tehran, have resulted in an increased perception of isolation from mainstream politics ... Clearly a book to read for anyone concerned with security in the Middle East and the broader Muslim world.'

Stephen M. Lyon, Senior Lecturer, Department of Anthropology, Durham University

THE RISE OF POLITICAL ISLAM IN TURKEY

Urban Poverty, Grassroots Activism and Islamic Fundamentalism

Kayhan Delibas

I.B. TAURIS
LONDON · NEW YORK

Published in 2015 by I.B.Tauris & Co. Ltd
6 Salem Road, London W2 4BU
175 Fifth Avenue, New York NY 10010
www.ibtauris.com

Distributed in the United States and Canada
Exclusively by Palgrave Macmillan
175 Fifth Avenue, New York NY 10010

Library of Modern Turkey: Volume 10

ISBN: 978 1 78076 565 5
eISBN: 978 0 85773 800 4

A full CIP record for this book is available from the British Library
A full CIP record is available from the Library of Congress

Library of Congress Catalog Card Number: available

Printed and bound by CPI Group (UK) Ltd, Croydon, CR0 4YY

FSC
www.fsc.org
MIX
Paper from
responsible sources
FSC® C013604

CONTENTS

LIST OF FIGURES AND TABLES

Figures

Tables

ACKNOWLEDGEMENTS

It is simply not possible to thank all of the hundreds of people who in one way or another contributed to this project. I can only name a few of the many WP/VP activists who generously offered help on the ground during my research. While doing fieldwork in Ankara I was assisted by many rank-and-file members of the Virtue Party, which later closed down and split into two parties: Sadet Partisi (Happiness Party; HP) and the Adalet ve Kalkınma Partisi (Justice and Development Party; AKP), which has been ruling Turkey since 2002. Throughout the whole project all sorts of help was invaluable, but especially when doing fieldwork in what was uncharted territory to me. I would like to thank Professor Oya Akgönenç, MP; İsmail Alptekin, founding chairman of the Virtue Party; and his assistant Metin Karadağ. Metin Karadağ provided me with much-needed access to the network of grassroots activists in Ankara. In Ankara's sub-districts Mamak and Keçiören, I met hundreds of grassroots activists, party members, supporters and local people in their neighbourhoods, and of course it is literally not possible to thank to all of them by name. Perhaps, however, I can name a few activists and politicians, such as Ahmet Tunç, Mehmet Bayır and Veysel Hoca from the WP/VP's Mamak local organisation committee. Also many thanks to Cemil Çiçek, MP (currently speaker of the Turkish Parliament), İdris Erdoğan, Nizam Demir and Süleyman Çadır from Keçiören local organisation committee; along with many others, these people were most helpful during the fieldwork.

Over the years, many people have inspired me in this project. Discussions with Professor Frank Furedi and the late Professor Paul Stirling helped me better formulate my views on several aspects of this project. I would like to express my thanks to Professors Sencer Ayata, MP, Chris Pickvance, H. Russell Bernard and Mike Fischer for their invaluable support throughout this research.

Furthermore, several friends and colleagues have read the drafts of this book. I owe special thanks to my good friends Dr Adam Burgess, Dr Steve Lyon and Sean Ireton. I would also like to thank Maria Marsh, Middle East Editor of I.B.Tauris Publishers, for her support and patience with this project, and Allison McKechnie who read the whole manuscript meticulously, prevented many typographical errors and made valuable suggestions.

I would also like to state my greatest thanks to my parents, Kurban and Kadriye, who always encouraged and trusted me. Far and above all, I am most grateful to my wife, Yeter Delibaş, and my daughters, Emek Gökçe Fidan Delibaş and Ekin Gül Delibaş, for their generous support, encouragement, patience, energy and loving care over the years. Without them this book would never even have gotten off the ground, let alone been completed.

This book is dedicated to my parents, Kurban and Kadriye Delibaş.

PREFACE

This book is the product of over a decade's work on political Islam in Turkey. It is based on extensive fieldwork among the grassroots activists of the pro-Islamist WP/VP (Welfare Party, later the Virtue Party) in Ankara (in 1999 and 2000) and it has been revised, updated and rewritten, taking into consideration the significant changes that have occurred since then. The book is the first of its kind to focus on the sociological causes and dynamics of the rise of political Islam in Turkey. To do so it concentrates particularly on urban poverty, grassroots activism and the rise of political Islam from the mid-1990s to the early 2000s. The objective of the book is to offer an explanation, based on empirical data, for the rise of Islamic fundamentalism in Turkey and, by extension, across the Muslim world. Compared to the existing literature on political Islam, my book explores the structural conditions in which an Islamic movement emerged and became popular in Turkey, a non-Arab Muslim country that has had a modernist state apparatus since the 1920s.

This study offers an in-depth and empirically based analysis of the rise of political Islam and Islamic movements in Turkey and by implication in the contemporary Middle East. Since the 1980s, the unprecedented rise of Islamic movements across the Muslim world has been the subject matter of a growing academic literature. It can be said that the ongoing upheavals (started in Tunisia in 2010) and consequent revolutions in countries like Egypt, Yemen, Libya and many others have been the most visible sign of the rising power of political Islam. The Arab Spring represents one of the most significant transformative events since the revolution in Iran. Perhaps it would not be wrong to suggest that what the Arab Spring represents for the region is almost equal to what the American or French revolutions represented in the past.

Most work on political Islam explains the phenomenon as the result of religious-based ideology. While it is true that Islamist movements are strongly anti-West and seemingly anti-modernist (or rather, anti the hegemony of the Western formulations of the cultural programme of modernity and its impacts on Muslim societies[1]) they are not the root causes of the Islamic fundamentalist revivalism. Rather, the revivalism is the result of alienation stemming from painful neoliberal restructuring programmes and rapid urbanisation during the 1980s when oil prices fell. Tehran's population tripled from 3 to 9 million between 1970 and 1990 (Roy, 1994). And similar increases were seen in Turkey too: the major cities encircled by *gecekondu*s (shanty towns) were where the WP/VP gained most of its electoral support.

Another point we need to acknowledge is that Islamist movements also emerged as the only vibrant major opposition to the New World Order and the neoliberal economic policies of the 1990s. The strongest point of this book is the empirical component of it. It is unique in its approach to the subject matter.

I will be arguing throughout that political Islam has been the most active and influential political and social force in Turkey since the mid-1990s. As anticipated, political Islam has gained an increasingly influential role in socioeconomic, political and cultural life, coming to power in the 2002 elections (Ayata, 1993). Employing party politics and using the conventional electoral process, political Islam chose a democratic and peaceful strategy to become a prominent political actor. In fact, in the early days, the rise of political Islam seemed to contradict all predictions of the modernist, secularist paradigm. After all, this was happening despite one and a half centuries of modernisation, Westernisation, and strictly guided secularisation policies. Although much of the fear that the WP/VP and Justice and Development Party

(Adalet ve Kalkınma Partisi, hereafter AKP) would undermine the democratic secular regime and lead the country to a backward Sharia regime turned out to be unfounded, it has become powerful enough to dominate government since 2002, and established anti-democratic authoritarian rule when it consolidated its power and was elected for the second time in 2007.

In Turkey, political Islam was represented by the pro-Islamic Welfare Party during the 1980s and until 2001. Since 2001, the movement has been represented by the AKP, which won a landslide victory in the general elections of 2002. Under the decade-long rule of the AKP, Turkey has witnessed transformative changes. This book is a qualitative case study, based on long-term participatory observation among grassroots party activists in Ankara. It explores the structural conditions in which an Islamic movement emerged and became popular in Turkey.

The Major Changes and the Current Situation Regarding Political Islam in Turkey

Since this book is a long-term account of the rise of political Islam, which originally started in 1997, it would be useful to inform readers on political developments in Turkey since the late 1990s, especially aspects that have changed drastically since the research was carried out, and also to describe the current situation regarding political Islam.

These are as follows:

- **28** June 1996: Necmettin Erbakan, the leader of the pro-Islamist WP, became Turkey's first Islamic prime minister (1996–1997). The WP formed a coalition government with the centre-right True Path party. This Islamist-led government sparked strong opposition across the political spectrum and Turkey's powerful military actively engaged to undermine the pro-Islamist government. Within a year there was a military intervention, a 'post-modern coup' as it was named, and this so-called '28 February

(1997) process' forced the Islamist-led coalition government to step down.

- 16 January 1998: The Islamist Welfare Party, the largest party at the time, was banned by the Constitutional Court for 'activities against the secular regime'. The court also banned the leader of the WP, Necmettin Erbakan, with six other MPs, from politics but did not rule against the WP's (more than 150) other MPs. The court announced its written verdict on 23 February 1998.
- In preparation for the court's decision to close the WP, former Welfare deputies had created the Virtue Party (17 November 1997). It replaced the WP on 25 February 1998. Almost all (150 out of 158) of the WP's MPs in the parliament and mayors across the country joined the VP so it became the largest political party in parliament.
- The parliament voted for early elections. In the elections of 18 April 1999 the VP passed its first hurdle with minor losses. Its share of the vote eroded from 21.4 per cent in 1995 to 15.41 per cent (109 seats in the assembly) in 1999. The VP did better locally than nationally. At the local level it took 17 per cent of votes and, more importantly, the VP retained the Istanbul and Ankara municipalities (*Milliyet*, 20 April 1999). This means that by and large voters had been happy with the VP's municipalities but at a national level voters wanted to avoid any further confrontation with the secular establishment (Alpay, 1999).
- 18 June 2001: The Virtue Party was closed down by the Constitutional Court, accused of being the focus of anti-secularist activities. This closure further increased the long-standing division within the VP between so-called 'traditionalists' or the 'grey-haired' and the 'progressives'. The division emerged before the WP closed down but it became most visible in the first and last general party congress of the VP on 18 May 2000. At that congress for the first time ever there were two candidates for the leadership: Recai Kutan, the acting leader, who had been appointed by Erbakan, and challenging him, Abdullah Gül (later president of the Turkish Republic), the representative of the 'progressive' group. To the surprise of many, Mr Gül received 42 per cent of the vote from

party delegates. After the congress the split grew, and after the Constitional Court's decision this group started to establish their party under the leadership of ex-Istanbul Mayor Recep Tayyip Erdoğan (prime minister since 2003).

- Divisions within the Islamist party grew, and out of the Virtue Party came two different parties under different leaderships: the Saadet Partisi (Happiness Party; HP) founded by the 'traditionalist' conservative wing of the National View movement. The HP had 48 MPs in parliament. The second party was the AKP, founded by the 'progressive' wing, a new generation of Islamist politicians under the leadership of Recep Tayyip Erdoğan. The AKP had 52 MPs in parliament.
- In 1999 two large earthquakes hit western Turkey with thousands killed and injured. The failure to respond rapidly undermined the government's credibility. Damage from the quakes was later estimated at USD 10–25 billion and over 17,000 were reported killed.
- Turkey experienced a very severe economic crisis in November 2000 and again in February 2001. These crises deepened the ongoing political crisis and destroyed the already weak public trust and credibility of the three-party coalition government headed by the frail Bülent Ecevit of the centre-left Democratic Left Party.
- In early general elections held on 3 November 2002, the newly established pro-Islamist AKP won a landslide, with 34.2 per cent of the votes. This was the first time since the 1990s that any party had been in a position to govern alone. In these elections the centre-left Republican People's Party (RPP) won 19.4 per cent, the centre-right True Path Party 9.5 per cent, and the nationalist National Action Party 8.3 per cent. It meant that all three members of the coalition government lost heavily and two of them did not enter parliament at all. This election was a key turning point in Turkish politics. Although the AKP received 34.2 per cent of votes, due to the electoral regime it received nearly 65 per cent of the seats in parliament.
- 24 April 2007: Turkey's foreign minister, Abdullah Gül, was named as the ruling party's candidate for the presidency, a decision that would maintain continuity in EU reforms but failed

to resolve a fight between the country's secular and Islamist camps. The election for president was perhaps the most important development since the AKP came to power. The struggle between sceptical secular circles, military and government entered a new phase when government announced its candidate as Abdullah Gül. After a long battle and a referendum, Gül was elected president.

- 22 July 2007: In the general election, the AKP won by a wide margin, gaining 47 per cent of the vote. The AKP secured its majority and gained 341 out of 550 seats in the parliament. The pro-secular Republican People's Party (RPP) won 21 per cent of the vote.[2]
- 12 June 2011: In the general election the ruling AKP won for the third time since 2002, with 46.4 per cent of the vote. The centre-left RPP gained 20.8 per cent and the nationalists 14.2 per cent. It was yet another sign of consolidation of the AKP as a system party.

CHAPTER 1

POLITICAL ISLAM IN TURKEY: GRASSROOTS ACTIVISTS AND THEIR EFFECT ON THE RISE OF PRO-ISLAMIC PARTIES

Introduction

The aim of this book is two-fold. First of all, I wish to explore the underlying causes of the unprecedented rise of political Islam in Turkey. In other words, to shed light on why and how the pro-Islamist Welfare Party tripled its share of votes between 1987 and 1995 from 7 per cent to 21 per cent at general elections, which later paved the way for the pro-Islamist AKP government in 2002. Second, I aim to find out what effect grassroots organisations and activism had on the WP/VP's unprecedented electoral success in the 1990s.

There is no doubt that one of the most important developments of the 1980s and 1990s was the emergence of fundamentalist movements all around the world. Not surprisingly Turkey, a predominantly Muslim country, was no exception to this religious revivalist trend. From the early 1980s onwards, political Islam had an increasingly influential role in the country's socioeconomic, political and cultural life (Ayata, 1993, p. 65). In the early 1990s it was argued that this revival of Islamic fundamentalism would change Turkish society (see

Şaylan, 1992, p. 127). In fact, this development contradicted predictions of a modernist, secularist paradigm that envisaged secularisation as imminent and the role of religion in politics diminished forever. What was more mysterious for many was the fact that political Islam became one of the main political forces in Turkey despite one and a half centuries of modernisation, Westernisation and strictly guided secularisation policies.

The Historiography of the Rise of the Turkish Islamist Movement: The 1990s

The pro-Islamist Refah Party (the Welfare Party, WP) became the biggest mass political party within a relatively short period of time. The Welfare Party increased its share of the vote from 9.8 per cent in 1989 to 19.1 per cent in the 1994 local elections, a turning point in Turkish political history. For the first time in over 70 years of the secular republic, many of Turkey's major cities including Istanbul and Ankara, the capital of the secularist republic, faced the reality of having Islamist mayors. This was a devastating shock for the militant secularist elites – chiefly the military and bureaucratic elites, liberals, social democrats, and the Westernised strata of society. The modernised, Westernised and secular elements of Turkish society felt under siege. They felt threatened by Islamic fundamentalism, which is often associated with 'extremism', 'irrationality', 'intolerance' and 'religious bigotry' and, since 11 September 2001, with international terrorism.

The results of the general elections held on 24 December 1995 showed that the WP was strengthening its power. It attained 21.4 per cent of the total vote and gained more seats (158 out of 550) than any of the mainstream secularist parties.[1] This time the general election heightened the tension between *laicists* (secularists) and Islamists (fundamentalists) to a degree where the Islamic-led government was forced to resign after just 11 months in office. However, the resignation of Necmettin Erbakan, the leader of the WP, on 28 February 1997, following what some commentators have called a postmodern coup was not the end but the beginning of another chapter in a long and exhausting battle between secularist military and bureaucratic elites and the Islamic WP.[2] Not only was the Welfare Party, the largest party in the country, being closed down by the supreme court, but Erbakan and six other MPs were banned from politics as well.

In response to the rise of political Islam, the military elite that dominated the National Security Council (NSC) needed to redefine its 'security concept'. After fifteen years fighting with the Kurdistan Workers Party (PKK), political Islam was elevated to the number one internal threat to the secular republic. From then on, virtually all of the monthly NSC meetings focused on the *şeriat tehdidi* – the threat of Islamic fundamentalism – assessed the latest *irticai* (fundamentalist) activities of various Islamic groups, and worked on plans for their eradication. 'If necessary, our fight against the fundamentalist threat will continue for one thousand years', declared one of the leading army generals.[3] The process of 28 February continues. It has laid the foundations for the pacification of political Islam. Leading figures such as Erbakan, the creator and leader of the Welfare Party; Recep Tayyip Erdoğan, the ex-mayor of Istanbul (for many the future leader of political Islam); Şevket Kazan; Hasan Mezarcı; Şükrü Karatepe, ex-mayor of Kayseri; and many others, have been banned from politics.

In addition to internal concerns, the rise of political Islam in Turkey caused a considerable degree of disquiet in the capital cities of Turkey's Western allies. *New York Times* journalist John Darnton (1995) wrote:

> For years a strategic ally in the containment of Soviet Communism, Turkey has now become a bulwark against dictators, terrorists and Islamic radicals ... Now, with conflicts multiplying in Azerbaijan and elsewhere, the east conjures up danger as well as riches. Turkey is recasting itself as a buffer state and as a bulwark, only this time against revolutionary Islam.

After noting Turkey's strategic position during the Cold War as a buffer state against Soviet Communism, Darnton pointed out the new threat to the West by referring to the comment by Willy Claes (ex-secretary general of NATO) that 'fundamentalism posed as big a threat to the West as Communism once did'.[4] There is nothing new in Willy Claes' point of view. It has been widely shared by many influential Western intellectuals but the importance of his view comes when NATO is taken into account. When NATO began to view Islamic fundamentalism as the biggest threat to the West, Turkey, as one of the key NATO members, had a new role as a buffer zone against political Islam. Richard Holbrooke (assistant secretary of state at that time), another high-ranking diplomat in the US administration in the 1990s, assessed the regional situation as 'the most volatile portion of the world today'. And he added: 'We haven't paid enough attention to Turkey.'[5] Returning to the situation in Turkey, Darnton argued that, 'The fundamentalist rise is already very real. The Welfare Party, a militant Islamic group, has taken control of local governments in Ankara, Istanbul and other municipalities (ibid.).'

In his article, Darnton highlights three important points: first, Islamic fundamentalism is the new threat to the West; second, Turkey as a bulwark was and will continue to be crucial for Western interests; and third, Islamic fundamentalism is a real threat in Turkey as well. Therefore, it is a security concern for the West itself.

Why is the rise of political Islam so important? First of all, because of the embedded tension between the modernist, secularist elite representing the 'centre' and anti-secular Islamic groups representing the 'periphery'. Turkey is a predominantly Muslim country established from the ruins of the Ottoman Empire in 1923 as a modern and secular republic. The Turkish revolution led by modernist, secularist elites changed everything from the alphabet to the dress code. The most challenging step was the abolition of the Sultanate and the Caliphate, the supreme religious authority of Islam. This was a daunting task, opposed by the conservative religious elite and various sections of society. Since the 1920s the secularist elite have always seen Islam as a major obstacle to Turkey's modernisation and a serious threat to political authority (Toprak, 1987, p. 218; see also Göle, 2000, pp. 63–4).

Roots of the 'Centre–Periphery' Divide

The importance of the rise of political Islam in Turkey comes partly from the nature of the main political cleavage in Turkey. Şerif Mardin argues that: '"centre–periphery" relations provide a good explanatory scheme to comprehend Turkish politics' (1973, pp. 169–91). In the same vein, Nur Yalman points out that during the 'beneficent period of 1838–1877, Ottoman society was divided into two *kulturkamps*' (1973, p. 152). This duality continued until the 1960s. Since then new elements have been added to the equation, such as class and ethnic dimensions. But the divide of secular/anti-secular is still one of the most important aspects of the Turkish polity. For this reason the unprecedented rise of political Islam has caused sharp polarisation – a deep political crisis, widespread panic, anxiety and fear, as well as escalating the tension between the modernist secularists and the Islamist camps in Turkey.[6]

Few other problems, since the 1920s, have challenged the Turkish secular establishment as political Islam did. The Kurdish nationalist movement from 1984 is perhaps the only other fundamental challenge that Turkey faced throughout the 1990s.

Since the mid-1990s the rise of religious movements in general and political Islam in particular has been one of the most commonly discussed subjects in the mass media and various academic disciplines (Benin and Stork, 1997, p. 8; Munson, 1995, pp. 151–66; Sidahmed and Ehteshami, 1996, p. 2). This extraordinary interest is, on the one hand, due to dramatic changes that came about with the end of the Cold War and the proclamation of the New World Order. The collapse of the former Socialist bloc and the diminishment of its mighty military machinery left the US as the single super power. This was a major shift in international politics – a power vacuum that had to be filled. At this historical juncture, Islam, with its one billion adherents spread out across the globe, appeared to constitute the most pervasive and powerful transactional force in the world (Esposito, 1995, p. 4). On the other hand, there has been an increasing politicisation of Islam as an assertive alternative politics across the Muslim world. Furthermore, there have been a series of events, such as attacks on Western embassies, hijackings and hostage-takings, and violent acts by some Islamist groups. Most importantly, the bombing of the World Trade Centre in 1993 and the events of 11 September 2001 triggered massive media coverage of Islamic fundamentalism.[7]

However, the rise of political Islam cannot be investigated in isolation as a regional or localised phenomenon because it is closely connected with political and socioeconomic developments taking place on a global scale (Bina, 1994, p. 3). This is true in the case of the WP in Turkey as well. The rise of the WP/VP from a movement to a mass political party was closely connected with globalisation of neoliberal economy policies and the implementation of restructuring policies by the IMF and the World Bank in Turkey.

Islamic Fundamentalism: A Problematic Categorisation?

The categorisation of political Islam as Islamic fundamentalism was, by and large, one of the results of the end of the Cold War. Was there a new phenomenon called 'fundamentalism', or rather a shift in sociology's conceptualisation? It appears that the conceptualisation of 'fundamentalism' has been heavily influenced by the discourse of the New World Order, a sociopolitical trend that dominated the 1990s. Many of the extremist forms of politics that are today labelled fundamentalism could have been called extremism, fanaticism, Buddhism or Islamism in the past, but today are called fundamentalism only because of ideological shifts taking place on a global scale. The proclamation of 'the end of history' and claims about 'the universalisation of Western liberal democracy as the final form of human government' explicitly excluded many non-liberal or non-Western ideologies and government types.[8] It is this presumption that has allowed the labelling of non-Western or non-liberal politics or ideologies as 'fundamentalist'.

Like many sociological concepts, the concept of fundamentalism has been rather problematic. The application of this concept to Islam has generated widespread criticism among scholars. It is argued that this concept is neither descriptive nor explanatory (Campo, 1995, pp. 167–94). The concept originated with the American Protestant fundamentalist movement that emerged in the 1920s. Fred Halliday (1995b, p. 399) points out that there are some problems with applying the term 'fundamentalism' to Muslim movements. Also, Nikki Keddie (1986, cited in Halliday 1995b, p. 399) suggests that '"Islamist" instead of "Islamic fundamentalist" is probably the most accurate concept for this movement'. The discourses of Islamic fundamentalism are diverse. The most permanent discourses shaped by Western commentators tend to view these sociopolitical movements as religious fanatic groups with a unique and rigid agenda of restoring a seventh-century-style Islamic society in the twenty-first century.

Political Islam is often regarded as a major threat to the stability of the Middle East, and therefore to Western interests in the region (Esposito, 1995, p. 4). For some writers like Huntington (1994) and Lewis (1990) Islamic fundamentalism is not just a threat to Western interests but a threat to Western civilisation too. In effect, it has become the Green Menace that replaced the Red Menace of the Cold War era (Esposito, 1995, p. 5).

The discourse on political Islam among Western commentators and academics has some parallels with the discourse on political Islam in Turkey. The one exception is the emphasis given to secularism/anti-secularism and modernity/anti-modernity, which are well-known elements of Western discourse. In Turkey the central focus of the debate is on the threat of 'Islamic fundamentalism' to the modern, secular, democratic republic and the principles of Atatürk.[9]

Furthermore, 'Islamic fundamentalism' for many scholars is equated with 'terrorism', 'extremism', 'intolerance', 'irrationality' or 'the Green Menace'.[10] These claims are not all unjustified exaggeration or accusations or the product of imaginative minds of external/Western observers. Some of the worst terrorist attacks, such as the 11 September attacks, several plane hijackings, the Dahran bombing in Saudi Arabia and other terrorist attacks (in London, Istanbul, Madrid, etc.) have been staged or orchestrated mainly by Al-Qaeda and some other Islamist terrorist groups. These have conjured up the idea of a global 'fundamentalist' *jihad* (holy war) against the West in the eyes of the Western public. But the issue of terrorism is something that cannot be confined to a particular religion or region. There are groups from all religions, nationalities, ethnic backgrounds or political persuasions that choose terrorism as a way of doing politics. In other words, there is nothing in terrorism exclusive to Islam.

In addition, there are many other problems with the categorisation of Islamic fundamentalism. Labelling political Islam as 'extremism', 'fanaticism', 'fundamentalism', 'intolerance' or 'irrationality' does not help sociologists grasp the conditions in which these movements emerge and develop. On the contrary, it has led area specialists, sociologists, public policymakers and politicians to a misleading conclusion about the realities of these Islamist groups. Viewing them as nothing more than 'irrational', 'fundamentalist', 'intolerant' movements automatically makes them an enemy of tolerance, democracy and the Western way of life. More importantly, the actions of these groups are the symptoms, but the prime objective of social science is to find out the *root causes*, the driving forces of these Islamist movements, rather than simply looking at the bare symptoms and launching security policies that have themselves become part of the problem associated with these movements.

The use of the term 'fundamentalism' can be criticised for four serious defects: taxonomic error, taxonomic imprecision, polemical distortion and ideological mobilisation (Campo, 1995, p. 172). Its usage is arbitrary in many ways. It is often accusatory, especially in the media; Juergensmeyer (1993, p. 4) has said the term is 'pejorative'. It implies that these movements are 'an intolerant, self-righteous and narrowly dogmatic religious literalism'. He points out that 'the term reflects our attitude toward other people more than it describes them ... To call someone a fundamentalist suggests that he or she is motivated solely by religious beliefs rather than by broad concerns about the nature of society and the World' (Juergensmeyer, 1993, p. 4).

Edward Said and Eduardo Campo are sharply opposed to the use of the term 'fundamentalism' in relation to Islamic movements:

> 'Fundamentalism' as employed in the description and explanation of developments in contemporary Muslim societies ... contends that rather than referring to an objective set of phenomena, this concept has been created to serve as a key element in European and American hegemony discourses about these societies in order to subordinate and control them. This means that it is of little explanatory value; does not facilitate rendering modern amalgamation of religion and politics more intelligible (Campo, 1995, p. 165; also see Said, 1993, p. 310).

Campo's and Said's concerns with the term 'fundamentalism' are twofold: first, they question the objectivity of the concept. Second, the conceptualisation of Islamist movements as fundamentalist is a deliberate attempt by the West to subordinate and control Muslim societies.

There are some other observers who approach the problem from a different perspective. Frank Furedi (1995, pp. 18–19), for instance, argues on the one hand that the uncritical acceptance of the term 'fundamentalism' by Western conservative, liberal and radical commentators is indicative of an erosion of intellectual criticism among the Western elite. On the other hand, for him, the fundamentalist label provides a moral and cultural condemnation of millions of people in one part of the world.

Categorisation of fundamentalism indicates a value judgement rather than an objective definition of this phenomenon. For this reason, instead of using 'Islamic fundamentalism' I prefer to use other terms such as 'political Islam'.

Existing Research

When my research began, very little had been done on grassroots organisations and grassroots activism in Turkey. I noticed immediately that the Turkish literature on political parties and the party system was weak, and on party organisations and membership it is almost non-existent. One of the first empirical studies on political participation and local party organisation was undertaken by Ayşe Güneş Ayata (1984). She studied the local party organisations of the Republican People's Party in the early 1980s in two Turkish towns. Another empirical study was done by the Türkiye Ekonomik ve Sosyal Etüdler Vakfı (TESEV; Turkish Economic and Social Studies Foundation) in 2000. The survey was carried out among 782 of what the researchers called 'effective party workers' of all six parties who were active in the parties' executive committees in 36 district capitals. Despite its empirical chapter on 'effective party workers', due to its broad scope (i.e. covering all political parties) and sampling problems it falls short in providing a detailed analysis of party activism in Turkey.

There was another study by the Türkiye Sosyal Ekonomik Siyasal Araştırmalar Vakfı Veri Araştırma (TÜSES; Turkish Social Economic Political Research Foundation, 1999) which focused on the social structure and the voters of political parties in Turkey. This study is not directly concerned with party activists but rather with the voters. Also, Ergun Özbudun's (2000) book contains a chapter in which he deals with parties and party systems in Turkey. There were a few other works on this topic but none of them covered party organisations and membership in detail.

Because of this limited body of literature on grassroots politics, I used Halliday's (1995a) 'contingent'[11] approach in my study, taking grassroots activism as an independent variable. Among the few studies on grassroots activism, the focal point of this book, I have benefited considerably from Seyd and Whiteley (1992) and Whiteley, Seyd and Richardson (1994), both studies on grassroots which provided a model for my research.[12]

As stated previously, Islamic movements have long been on the rise across the Muslim world. Since the early 1980s the apparent increase of Islamic fundamentalism has been one of the most debated phenomena in media and academic circles. Different approaches have been developed to explain what these movements are and why they have been rising. Through an extensive literature review I have identified four different approaches. The Turkish literature also by and large confirms this pattern.

The Main Approaches to Political Islam

Political Islam as a Threat to the West

The most common view among Western scholars regards political Islam as a threat to the West. The most important proponents of this approach are Huntington (1994) and Lewis (1990). Both scholars are very influential in American intellectual and policy circles and have determined the parameters of the discourse on Islamic fundamentalism (Esposito, 1995, p. 195). It is assumed that Islam poses a three-dimensional threat: political, civilisational and demographic. Huntington, in his famous article and his book *The Clash of Civilisations?*, argued that most important conflicts will occur between cultures: 'The fault lines between civilisations are replacing the political and ideological boundaries of the Cold War as the flash points for crisis and bloodshed' (1994, p. 22). For Huntington, today, the differences between civilisations are more profound than the differences between ideologies and political regimes. He states increased interaction between civilisations, increased consciousness of civilisations and awareness of civilisational differences have increased the possibility of a clash between them (ibid., p. 25). Huntington argues that one of the consequences of modernisation is that local identities disappear, but that gap has been filled by religion. Islamic fundamentalism emerges as a process of 're-Islamisation' of the Middle East (ibid., p. 26). For him this re-Islamisation or Islamic fundamentalism, and many other non-Western cultures, present a great challenge with their ambition and resources to shape the world in a non-Western way.

Huntington specified a 'Confucian–Islamic' alliance that 'emerged to challenge Western interests, values and power'. He concludes: 'a central focus of conflict for the immediate future will be between West and several Islamic–Confucian states' (ibid., pp. 45–8). Given Huntington's influence, his article provided a solid ideological base for many commentators.[13]

In a similar vein, Lewis views the Islamic world as an entity that has 'deeply rooted rage' towards the West, and especially towards the US as the leader of the Western world (1990, p. 195). Lewis begins by saying that 'there is no Cuba, no Vietnam, in the Muslim world, but there is a Libya, an Iran and a Lebanon and an increase of hostility raises alarm bells for the Americans' (ibid., 1990, p. 195). For him, the hostility of Muslims towards the West becomes a 'rejection of Western civilisation', and because Islamic revivalist leaders describe their enemies as the enemies of God, this hostility and rejection of Western civilisation will persist for a long time.

The common point that Huntington and Lewis, both very authoritative intellectuals, make is an immediate conflict between Islam and the West. Both view this conflict through a historical lens as a continuity of aggression, hatred, violence or irrationality of Islamic fundamentalism towards the West or Christianity.

Political Islam as a Threat to Modernisation and Secularisation in Turkey

There are many parallels between the 'threat to the West' approach in the West and some of the Turkish approaches to political Islam in Turkey. They share some common elements, such as fear of the Islamic fundamentalist threat, anxiety and panic. The rise of the WP in the mid-1990s generated a shockwave across the political spectrum – from extreme leftists to liberals, from ordinary people to high society. The panic, fear and anxiety were coupled with disbelief and dismay that an Islamic party could gather so much popularity in a strictly guided secular society in such a short time. It was a devastating blow that shattered the 70-year dream of a truly modernised, Westernised and secularised Turkish society.

The majority of Turkish radical secularist intellectuals view political Islam as a threat to the Kemalist project of modernisation, Westernisation and secularisation. They argue that Islamic fundamentalists are the biggest threat to Atatürk's *laik* (secularist) republic, democracy, nationalism and the enlightenment of Turkish society.[14] According to Ekşi, (1995, p. 9):

> [Islamic fundamentalists] want to put dynamite on the foundations of the secular and democratic republic. The most visible characteristic of [Islamic] movements is that they seek to change the lifestyle of women completely. In many Muslim countries such as in Afghanistan, Egypt and Algeria women are forced to cover themselves, to wear *highab*. Even the rights that were given thirty, forty years ago have been taken away from them.[15]

The extent of the panic and fear felt by radical secularists and some liberals was best illustrated by Erbil Tuşalp, a political commentator. He asked:

> Will they really exterminate those unbelievers; will they force women to wear the veil? Will they flog and lash those who are not fasting, praying, and will they amputate the hands of those

> who are stealing? Will they kill those who committed adultery by stoning? If the answers to those questions are 'no', what then has life in Iran, Pakistan, Libya, and Saudi Arabia shown us? (Tuşalp, 1994, p. 16).

Clearly, Tuşalp and many other commentators believed that the fundamentalist threat was an imminent one and that the answer to all of these questions was 'yes'. The examples of many Muslim countries suggest they will not tolerate anything other than Islamic Sharia law.

Islamic Fundamentalism against Modernity

This approach views political Islam as an atavism, a rejection of modernity and the Western way of life (Seyyed Vali, 1995, pp. 121–39). It is widely believed that Islamic fundamentalism is an ideology and movement based on the fundamental principles of Islam extracted from the 'secret text' of the Koran. In other words, it is seen as an ideology shaped around AD 700 that cannot be compatible with the needs of contemporary society. Islamists are often viewed as 'fossilised relics, insulated from and oblivious to their surroundings, living perpetually in a bygone age' (Caplan, 1987, p. 5). Abrahamian (1991, p. 102) argues that 'for radicals, [Islamic fundamentalism] conjures up the image of theological obscurantism, political atavism, and the rejection of science, history, modernity, the Enlightenment, and the Industrial Revolution'. It is in fact a mistake to see these movements as anti-modernist, backward-looking or reactionary, because they are far more modern than the image presented by liberals and radical commentators would suggest. There are some ideological elements that conflict with a modernist, rational outlook, but this does not mean that they are not as modern as any other contemporary social or political movement. As Larry Ray (1999, p. 205) points out, 'rather than being implacable enemies of modernity, Islamic revolutionary movements share important aspects of rhetoric and organizational style with the modernist, Jacobin, social imagination'.

Turkish anti-modernist discourse has a similar approach to political Islam. According to Emre Kongar (2000, pp. 240–1), political Islam developed as a counter-movement to the modernisation project of the early days of the Kemalist revolution. The republic banned religion in politics in a Muslim society, thereby, he says, striking a direct blow against political Islam. As the antithesis of republican ideology, political Islam has been the main opposition to the Kemalist regime. For Islamists, the sultan under the Ottoman Empire represented the divine order transmitted through the caliphate, but the nationalist movement lacked such legitimacy. Tekeli (1997, p. 423), on the other hand, analyses the rise of political Islam in a dialectical relation with a modernisation project that started long before the Kemalist revolution. For him, the 1980s and after have been the era of the decline of the project of modernisation and the rise of political Islam.

Ahmet Yücekök (1997, p. 41), another student of Islam, also took an evolutionary approach. From the time of the Patrona riots in the eighteenth century (1730) to 1950, all opposition movements had religious characteristics and were against Western influence. However, he argued, from the early 1950s the social characteristics of the religious groups changed. They became petit bourgeois and entered into a confrontation with Istanbul's grande bourgeoisie.

Server Tanilli views these movements as resistance to modernity and progress, saying they aimed to turn the clock backward (1996, p. 173). The real agenda of Islamic fundamentalism is not freedom of belief or religious practices that should be kept in the private sphere, but rather to destroy the democratic and secular republic and modern legal system, and to abolish women's rights and all of the gains of the 150 years of the Enlightenment movement in Turkey (ibid., p. 181). The majority of modernist, secularist writers, commentators and academics view political Islam as opposed to modernity, secularisation and the contemporary way of life.

However, as mentioned previously, it is a great mistake to classify these Islamist movements as anti-modernist. On the contrary, they are modern movements using traditional or classical themes for contemporary causes and borrowing from modern secular ideologies as well (see Halliday, 1995a, p. 49; Ray, 1999, p. 205). They are modernist in terms of ideology, political strategy and tactics, and organisational structure. For example, according to Özbudun (2000, p. 80) the WP is the only modern mass political party in Turkey.

In fact, rather than being anti-modernist, these movements react against the failures of the modernising, secular states in many Muslim countries. There are many reasons for this. Although many of these countries have been independent for more than half a century, so far none of them have managed to solve the economic and social problems they face (Halliday, 1995a, p. 48). Very visible foreign domination since the Gulf War and a lack of democracy have also legitimatised Islamic movements; faced with foreign domination, Islam turns into a nationalist ideology.

Contrary to the common modernist view, the WP/VP in Turkey pursued modern, worldly objectives. As Olivier Roy (1994, p. 4) points out, its political cadre were mostly graduates of modern universities, and its grassroots members were educated in modern state schools too.[16] As we shall see in chapters 5, 6 and 7, the grassroots activists of the VP were modern in every sense. They were educated in modern Turkish schools, were highly skilled, high-earning and middle-aged. They were no different from the rest of society in appearance and were not mullahs (clerics) or hocas (priests). The VP itself was not based, as some may think, within mosques or religious brotherhoods, but rather on a modern political party structure. Similarly, the Turkish Islamist movement as in many other countries borrowed socialist and Marxist rhetoric and slogans, reinterpreting them successfully, as did the WP's *Adil Düzen* (Just Order) (see chapter 3).

The Postmodernist Approach

Writers such as Ahmed Akbar (1992) and Haldun Gülalp (1995) have argued that the rise of Islamic fundamentalism is a direct consequence of the failure of the modernist project in the postcolonial arena. Some have said that it was the modernist vision of future societies that attracted the revolutionary elite in many Muslim countries (Ray, 1999, p. 198), but with the failure of the modernist development strategy, modernity lost its credibility.

In his article 'Islamism and Postmodernism', Gülalp argues that there is a similarity between the criticism of modernity by Turkish Islamist writers and the postmodernist critique of modernity. He examines the most representative writings of two prominent Islamic scholars, Ali Bulaç and İsmet Özel. Both of them accuse modernism and secular philosophy, which promise 'paradise on earth', of failing to deliver (cited in Gülalp, 1995, pp. 58–73). However, even though these Islamist writers criticise modernity, materialist values and secularisation, they do not share the postmodernist outlook.

Contingent Approaches

A further interpretation of political Islam is non-religious but is based on a causal explanation, or what Halliday (1995a, p. 48) calls a 'contingent' approach. This approach emphasises modernity and contingency in these fundamentalist movements. Halliday argues that the rise of 'fundamentalisms' in Muslim countries originates as a reaction against the failures of the modernising, secular state, which is perceived as corrupt, unable to solve economic and social problems, and mostly undemocratic. Fundamentalist movements are responses to underlying problems facing these countries, most importantly mass urbanisation, unemployment and foreign domination (ibid.).

Halliday uses the term 'contingent' in an article entitled 'Fundamentalism and the Contemporary World' (Halliday, 1995a). He specifies two alternative explanations: 'scriptural' and 'contingent'. In contrast to the 'scriptural' approach, the 'contingent' approach emphasises the modernity and contingency in fundamentalist movements. It begins by drawing attention to the contemporary causes of these movements (ibid., p. 48). There are several scholars whose interpretations of fundamentalist movements focus on the relationship between the rise of Islamic movements and the socioeconomic, demographic and political conditions in which these movements emerged.

Contrary to the previously mentioned approaches, there are several commentators and academics who agree that fundamentalist movements are not simply engaging with re-Islamisation or restoring religious fundamentalism. Rather, they are rising as a response to the economic and social crisis: unemployment, income dispersion among the lower and lower-middle classes, the growing gap between poor and rich, rapid urbanisation and inadequate government services. In addition, these countries are infamous for their oppressive, corrupt, anti-democratic nature and bad human rights records.[17] Since the 1970s, especially following the oil crisis, the socioeconomic problems of many developing Muslim countries have deepened.

The majority of these countries experienced rapid population growth and urbanisation due to 'push factors' in rural areas. For example, Tehran's population tripled from 3 to 9 million between 1970 and 1990, as was the case for many other great Muslim metropolises in a similar time period (Roy, 1994, pp. 53–4). Perhaps one of the best examples is that of Turkey. Rapid urbanisation, accelerated by the restructuring policies of the IMF, was one of the most important factors behind the unprecedented rise of the WP in elections in the mid-1990s. The major Turkish cities were encircled by *gecekondu*s (shanty towns), from which the WP/VP took most of its electoral support.[18]

The *gecekondu* population is more or less homogeneous and unique (Gökçe, 1994, p. 286). The majority of *gecekondu* dwellers are on low incomes. The material conditions of living space (housing) and standards as well as social mobility and education are usually very poor. Residents spend most of their income on food, which is a sign of poverty. Another distinct social characteristic of life in the *gecekondu* is that it is a close-knit community, where family ties are strong and solidarity is high (ibid., pp. 286–7). The issue of social justice has always been important in these communities. Islamist movements continuously exploit the demand for social justice and equality and the feeling of being let down by the system among the masses across the Muslim world. The decline in prestige of progressive ideologies and the failure of the 'Arab Socialist' model in particular have left the arena open to new forms of protest ideologies (Roy, 1994, pp. 51–2). Thanks to the decline of the left across the world, Islamist movements emerged as the only vibrant major opposition to the New World Order and its neoliberal economic policies of the 1990s.

Throughout the 1990s and 2000s, Islamist movements were the most significant opponents of injustice in most parts of the Muslim world. It is no surprise that the WP in Turkey adopted social democratic rhetoric to express the grievances of the millions in the cities. Its social policies, summed up by the slogan *Adil Duzen* (Just Order), did indeed attract many urban poor votes from the *gecekondu*s. Turkey had experienced mass migration, a very high level of inflation (over 70 per cent per year) from the 1970s to the end of the 1990s, high unemployment, a very sharp fall in the income of the working classes, deteriorating living standards and rampant corruption since the 1990s.

The economic problems of the 1980s and 1990s were followed by the political problems of increased party fragmentation, high electoral volatility and organisational decline (see Özbudun, 2000, pp. 75–9). The WP and subsequently the VP were the most vociferous critics of growing inequalities, widespread corruption, unemployment, poverty and lack of basic services in the *gecekondu*s. Unsurprisingly, Halliday (1995a) and Keddie (1981, p. 243) observed very similar symptoms prevalent in Iranian society just before the Islamic Revolution in 1979:

> The growth of an explosive situation in the cities, with mass migration, rampant corruption, and inflation; the failure of the regime to allow for legitimate forms of political discontent, and prior suppression of the mass secular forces, nationalists and communists, the success of Khomeini in leading and organising a mass political movement, focused on a set of simple, and wide goals – the ousting of the Shah and the ending of western, particularly American, influence in the country (Halliday, 1995a, p. 52).

There is no doubt that rising foreign influence over the Middle East, especially following the Gulf War, the process of globalisation, the increased interference of the IMF and the World Bank, and internal socioeconomic and political conditions in developing countries provoked growing anti-imperialist feeling in many Muslim societies. In Turkey and elsewhere, Islamist movements have been equated with fundamentalism. This is a problematic approach for several reasons, as argued above.

How Can the Rise of Political Islam Be Explained?

Unlike mainstream students of political Islam, I examine the *causes* of the rise of these movements rather than dealing with appearances. My approach is different because the main aim of this book is to grasp the dynamics of the rise of political Islam in Turkey, and in particular to find out the effects that grassroots activism has had on the rise of the WP in the mid-1990s. It is not my goal to judge, condemn or defend the Islamists' worldview.

The central research questions can be formulated as follows:

1) What were the reasons behind the unprecedented rise of political Islam in Turkey in the late 1990s and early 2000s?
2) What was the role of grassroots organisations and grassroots activism in this unprecedented electoral success?

The Main Objectives of this Book

The rise of political Islam cannot be explained on the basis of its anti-Western, anti-modernist attitude or as a postmodern condition or a simple religious/Islamic revivalism. There is a series of socioeconomic and political preconditions, 'worldly reasons', for its emergence and sudden rise. I argue that besides the fundamental changes in socio-economic and political conditions (e.g. the neoliberal restructuring programme that took effect from the early 1980s, rapid urbanisation and the expansion of political participation), it was the WP/VP's very well-organised, militant grassroots activists who played the crucial role in increasing its share of the vote and public support, leading to the unprecedented rise of political Islam in Turkey.

The main objectives of this book are to:

- identify the underlying shifts in the socioeconomic and political spheres that caused the ascendancy of political Islam in Turkey
- examine political party organisations and party activism in Turkey – especially the WP/VP – in perspective, including the party effort and its impact on voting

- examine the socioeconomic and political background, such as the demography, education, occupation, income, age, marital status and residential status of the WP/VP's grassroots activists
- study the activists' motives, aspirations, ideological and political attitudes and the major incentives to become a political activists
- determine the main activities of grassroots activists and how they influenced the WP/VP's electoral outcomes
- look into the relationship between the WP/VP's activists and its supporters/voters
- examine the types of grassroots organisation and their structure, including how they were operated in a particular local party branch
- further develop the existing theoretical framework as a method for a sociological investigation of the pro-Islamic political parties in Turkey.

The Turkish Contingent Approach

The Turkish contingent approach recognises the contingency and modern characteristics of political Islam in Turkey. There is a handful of scholars and political scientists who give priority to the socio-economic and political conditions in which the Islamic movements emerged and grew. They have been seeking answers to questions such as why and how the pro-Islamic WP/VP gained popularity in Turkey in the 1990s. One of the early studies was carried out by Şaylan (1992), who found that disaffection had been growing, especially among unemployed university graduates who favoured the WP more than other age groups (1992, pp. 127–9). Şaylan and other researchers examine the socioeconomic conditions and increasingly emphasise the class dimension of this Islamist trend. For them the pro-Islamic WP was supported mainly by the urban poor from *gecekondu* areas, which constitute more than half of the population in the major cities. This is, primarily, due to the second phase of rapid urbanisation that the country faced from the early 1980s. Rapid urbanisation in Turkey is a phenomenon that started much earlier, in the 1950s, but due to the restructuring policies of the 1980s, migration from rural to urban centres rose to a level unseen before the 1980s.[19] As a result, millions migrated to the cities with no regular employment, no secure income and no housing or basic services. The lower-middle and lower classes saw their salaries and incomes fall more than 50 per cent by the mid-1990s. Craftsmen, artisans, small merchants and shopkeepers, whose existence was undermined by the neoliberal policies and by globalisation, also supported the WP. Traditional religious circles and the Kurdish population, disillusioned with current mainstream political parties, were also drawn to the WP (Ayata, 1993; Kalaycıoğlu, 1996; Öğütcü, 1994; Öniş, 1997; Sarıbay, 1985). For instance, Toprak (1987, p. 227) observed that it was not a question of purely religious concerns. She says:

> what has been depicted as the 'resurgence' of Islam in contemporary Turkey is, at one level, the reassertion of a historic/cultural consciousness by individuals who are unassimilated into the modernist centre, and for whom the new 'palace culture' is an anomaly. ... At a second level, the apparent revival of Islam in contemporary Turkey is a reflection of social structural differences. Here again it is less a question of purely religious concerns than the expression of economic discontent through religion.

For Toprak the revival of political Islam should be analysed on two levels. On the first level what we see is an attempt to reassert a historical/cultural consciousness by some 'unassimilated' individuals. This point is similar to those Western and Turkish 'modernist approaches'. However, at the second level Toprak adopts a contingent approach where she points to social structural differences and socioeconomic reasons rather than purely religious concerns. The rise of political Islam, therefore, has been by and large a direct consequence of the neoliberal restructuring policies implemented since the early 1980s. These policies led to a huge income gap between rich and poor in the country.

Although Turkey is classified as an 'emerging market' with a dynamic, fast-growing market economy, it has one of the worst Gini coefficients – for 1994 it was estimated as 0.50 in terms of income distribution (Öniş, 1997, p. 751).[20] While neoliberal restructuring policies led to a process of intensified income disparities, their political implications caused party convergence. As a result, the policy differences between centre-left parties and centre-right parties dissipated. In this process, as in many other countries, the leftist party moved to the centre-right, adopting the political rhetoric and economic policies of neoliberalism to such an extent that they became a bad copy of the conservative or centre-right parties, thus leaving a vacuum in the political spectrum. In many ways, the WP/VP filled the vacuum left by the decline of social democratic politics. According to Öniş (1997, p. 748), the party:

> emerges as a political movement expressing the grievances of the poor and the disadvantaged in both rural and urban areas in a social democratic guise. The appeal of political Islam as a viable alternative to secular social democracy arises not only from the strength of its moral argument in favour of equity but also from specific and concrete anti-poverty projects designed to improve the material conditions of the disadvantaged, albeit on a highly target-oriented, selective and visible basis.

These movements were supported by a variety of social groups and classes for a variety of reasons: economic deprivation, cultural alienation and political disillusionment with the mainstream political parties. To clarify the point, I have examined some election surveys. For example, according to one of these surveys, only one-third of those who voted for the party did so primarily because it was an Islamic party (Heper, 1997, p. 35). This clearly indicates that the majority of people associated with political Islam were not religiously orientated *jihad* fighters as they are often portrayed, but in many cases were merely disaffected with current party policies. The weekly *Nokta* magazine made a similar point:

> In the December 1995 elections, not all who voted for the Islamist Welfare Party did so because they wanted to replace Turkey's secular democracy with a theocracy based on Sharia.

> The 'hard core' of Islamists who voted for the WP in 1995 has been estimated at around seven percent of the total electorate.[21]

Another survey by Necdet Erder challenges *Nokta*'s findings and puts the figure at around 10 per cent of all voters in Turkey.[22] Contrary to common belief, political Islam does not have a monolithic or homogeneous social basis but rather forms a coalition of different groups and strata that one way or another are disaffected with the centre-right and centre-left parties. This coalition itself was not permanent but rather was loosely connected and changed over time.

In conclusion, among the various approaches, the 'contingent approach' offers a sociologically coherent and analytical explanation for the emergence and rise of political Islam. This approach emphasises the modern characteristics and above all the contemporary causes of the rise of political Islam. However, it does not address all of the essential problems. First, there are problems with the definition of the concept of 'political Islam' itself. Second, the diversity of Islamic movements has not been addressed. Third, and most importantly, the peculiar role of grassroots activism within these movements has not been properly acknowledged. The effects of grassroots activism on the electoral process are the focal point of this book.

Why Grassroots Activism?

As the current literature indicates, party membership and local party organisations have been one of the least studied aspects of political parties. In recent years, however, there has been a renewed interest in the role of party organisation and grassroots activism and their influence on the electoral fortunes of the political parties.[23] The significance of local party organisation and grassroots activism is closely connected to the functions of political parties in general. Political parties with their large memberships were one of the most successful forms of political organisations in the twentieth century in Western democracies (Scarrow, 1996, p. 1). To this day, despite all the anti-party rhetoric, political parties are the key components of democratic governance.

Neumann (1963, p. 352) described political parties as the articulate organisations of an active group of people who jointly seek access to governmental power. The control of governmental power involves electoral processes; therefore access requires popular support. A political party links social forces and ideologies to governmental institutions. If the main purpose of political parties is to contest elections in order to gain control of public offices and organise the governments (Huckshorn, 1984, p. 21), then winning elections becomes the first and most important condition that every aspiring party must achieve. To do this, the party must elect candidates to compete and organise election campaigning to mobilise the voters around the candidates.

In this case, a well-organised party organisation must be the first condition for any kind of electoral achievement. Political parties have a variety of functions such as informing the electorate about the party's policies and goals, creating an identity and unity, strengthening party attachment and commitment among grassroots activists and, finally, campaigning to influence the electoral outcome (see Pattie et al., 1995, p. 969).

Elections are about obtaining sufficient electoral support. This is where the vitality of the election campaigns and the crucial role of party activism comes in. Parties need to go out to mobilise their constituencies. Local party organisations and their activism have proven to be significantly influential in the electoral process.

In general, there has been an apparent lack of attention to party membership and local party organisations in Turkish political literature. Nonetheless, with the unprecedented rise of the pro-Islamic WP in local elections (1994) and general elections (1995) the influence of grassroots activism and local party organisations began to appear in the writings of Turkish commentators. The WP was the only modern mass party with local party organisations operating nationwide and supporters engaging in militant grassroots activism. Before it was closed down by the high court it had over 4 million registered members and was Turkey's largest political party in terms of membership.[24] This section briefly examines a sample of Turkish commentators' views about the rapid rise of the WP throughout the

1990s and the role of party organisations and grassroots activism in this process.

According to Sayarı (1996, p. 36) the WP's dedicated grassroots activists were one of the most important elements in its growing popularity. He pointed out that:

> Refah owes its increasing electoral support to an efficient, disciplined, highly motivated, and well-financed organisation. The Islamists have the largest number of party workers among all Turkish political parties. Refah's grassroots organisations are staffed with dedicated cadres, male and female, who work with a missionary zeal and benefit from advanced technology, such as computers with voter registration data. Tightly organized in cell-like units in each neighbourhood, Refah relies less on the media for disseminating its views and more on face-to-face contacts with the voters.

Sayarı highlights the key connection between the unprecedented rise of the Welfare Party, efficient, highly motivated, well-financed party organisations and highly dedicated, missionary-like grassroots activists utilising advanced technology in their daily activities in the neighbourhood.

Sencer Ayata (1997, p. 52) also notes the positive correlation between the rise of the pro-Islamic WP in the 1990s and highly motivated, well-disciplined and dedicated grassroots organisations and their distinctive activities.

> As a matter of fact, the party owes its strength to its responsive and well-organized grass roots membership. The highly motivated, well disciplined, and strongly committed activists believe in their political cause as a mission ordained by God. They function at the community level, visiting every single quarter, street, and family separately, evaluating the data, and finding solutions for each problem. To penetrate small communities, the young activists, including an army of women who can arrange home visits at any time of the day, have emerged as the party's major assets.

Similarly, Kalaycıoğlu (1997, p. 36) gives some examples of what the Welfare Party's activists were doing during the election campaign in 1995 when the WP became the largest party in the parliament. He notes that:

> On the eve of the 1995 elections, numerous party activists, at the grass roots level, kept track of every voter deemed critical to the party's victory. They visited each voter before the elections, and, on election day, provided transportation to and from the polling stations for those who needed it.

More than any other mainstream political party, the WP always maintained face-to-face relations as its communication model at the grassroots level. The WP's grassroots activists organised charity work, set up community help centres in the neighbourhood, and made regular door-to-door visits to transmit party messages and policies. They also listened to the comments of their potential voters rather then relying only upon mass communication as the mainstream parties do (Şen, 1995, p. 83). It was this approach that gave the Welfare Party the upper hand.

The main strategy of the WP's grassroots organisation was focused on the elections. The party aimed to mobilise all of its members for election campaigning and to recruit as many new members as the party had received votes at the last elections. The WP's model of organisation was unique; it was called *tesbih* (rosary) and it appointed a representative to every single neighbourhood. These representatives appointed representatives to every street, quarter and apartment block. Right after an election, the WP's highly motivated grassroots organisations started to campaign for the next election as if it were going to be held the following day (Çakır, 1994, pp. 51–9).

The way that a party organises itself is very important for effective and successful election campaigning. Besides the youth and neighbourhood committees, the VP's Hanım Komisyonları (ladies' committees) turned out to be very effective campaigners. They went street-to-street in their respective neighbourhoods, canvassing building-to-building, door-to-door, and met people, mostly women, in their private living spaces in a friendly manner. They organised house meetings where a *hatip* – a good speaker or agitator – would speak to 30 to 50 people at once.

Özbudun (2000, p. 84) looks at the changing nature of campaign strategies and argues that while door-to-door canvassing by Turkish parties through local branches traditionally played an important role in securing votes, this has changed in recent years. Labour-intensive campaigning techniques are increasingly being abandoned in favour of media-led 'capital intensive' election campaigns ultimately requiring large financial resources. He argues, however, that because of changes in the way the Turkish economy is run, it is very difficult for political parties to generate enough spoils to distribute to their followers, 'which in the absence of strong ideological motivations is important in sapping their organizational strength' (ibid., p. 84). From the early 1980s Turkish political parties increasingly abandoned traditional campaigns run by local party organisations and adopted 'capital intensive' campaigns. But the problem with this new style was that it required considerable resources, which were lacking. In short, the old system had been abandoned without a viable alternative to replace it.

Western commentators such as Barkey (1996, p. 45), Darnton (1995) and Zubaida (1996, p. 11) also emphasise the outstanding role of grassroots activists in facilitating the rise of political Islam in Turkey. Henri Barkey (1996), in his article 'Turkey, Islamic Politics, and the Kurdish Question', points out that the success of the Welfare Party in the 1995 elections was due to the party's efficient utilisation of the activists' capabilities and a complete failure of the mainstream parties to maintain consistent messages. For Barkey, the WP was the only mass-based political organisation: 'The local cadres throughout the country worked street-by-street, building-by-building, offering their services, sometimes even money or fuel or other necessities, to the urban poor who have been largely ignored by the mainstream parties' (Barkey, 1996, p. 45).

Zubaida (1996, p. 11) highlights the WP/VP activists' very effective tactic of combining community work with year-round election campaigning in their respective neighbourhoods. John Darnton

(1995) also notes that 'no political machine can beat the Welfare Party when it comes to grass-roots organisation. Women wearing headscarves go door to door in the slums proselytising and meet intercity buses to take new arrivals in hand'.

These comments suggest that the WP/VP emerged as a distinct political party. It was its very well-organised, highly active and committed grassroots activism that distinguished the WP/VP from other parties. As noted earlier, however, the literature on this subject has so far been speculative, lacking empirical evidence. One of the major aims of this study therefore is to test these hypotheses.

The Debate on Grassroots Activism

It seems that no matter how advanced expertise on communication technologies or sophisticated election campaigning has become, political parties need active party members ready to spend their time, energy and resources on achieving the party's goals within a well-organised, motivated, committed, missionary-like grassroots organisation.

Seyd and Whiteley (1992, pp. 219–20) note that political parties still need and will continue to need members for the traditional electioneering functions of canvassing and leafleting voters and persuading supporters to go out and vote. Grassroots activists are the elected representatives of the party in the neighbourhoods and they carry out electioneering. Furthermore, they have a key role in their constituencies as opinion-formers. They are often the bridges between the political party and wider society. In this sense, they are also the voice of the community and set the local agenda.

Many scholars believe that the impact of local party organisations and grassroots activism has been significantly diminished. The most common reason put forward for this is developments in communication technologies and campaigning techniques, with party organisations losing their importance as the primary means of campaigning. New technologies such as computers and mass-mailing systems have increasingly enabled leaders to get their message across to voters without the assistance of party members and grassroots organisations. In other words, the development of new and faster communication technologies provided the tool party leaders needed for direct contact with the voters (Scarrow, 1996, p. 6).[25]

However, there is a growing body of literature contradicting this view, and there is convincing evidence from various case studies that grassroots activism is an effective force in determining the parties' electoral fortunes.[26] Crotty (1971, p. 447) observes that 'a well-organised party that extends itself to campaigning for its candidates can have a decided impact on increasing its proportionate share of the vote'. Party activity made a difference, and often a substantial difference, in terms of increasing votes. In a similar vein Pattie et al. (1995) point out that 'the local campaign, while not as widely publicised or as glamorous as its national counterpart, still plays an important function in shaping the outcomes of British general elections'.

A case study from Britain showed that local party activism before the general election in 1997 made a significant contribution to Labour's unprecedented victory. Whiteley and Seyd, 1998, p. 4 emphasised three important factors, combined with local party activism. These were the declining partisan attachments among the electorate, increased electoral swings due to party dealignments in the 1990s and the transformation of the Labour Party to 'New Labour', which included 40 per cent of the grassroots party from 1994 to 1997 (ibid., pp. 4–8). Declining partisan attachment and electoral swings played the role of a catalyst, making it easier to influence voters in campaigns at both national and local levels. It is obvious that when partisan attachments have weakened in this way electoral canvassing becomes relatively easier for party activists. The increased level of party dealignment allows party activists to persuade people to vote for and support the party, and even to recruit new members more easily.

Returning to the case of Turkey, we have already heard how 'Turkish parties and the party system have been facing a long-term process of institutional decline, growing fragmentation, ideological polarisation, and electoral volatility in the party system' (Özbudun, 2000, p. 73). Individual parties had also been experiencing also a decline 'in the organisational capacity, party identification and declined public support for the parties among the citizens since the 1970s'. In general, Turkish politics is seen to be experiencing an impasse, and the state of Turkish political parties is extremely important in explaining this situation.

Throughout the 1990s, with the exception of the WP/VP, Turkish parties suffered a decline in their party organisations and a weakening of party identification. Generally speaking, the decline of party identification has been a problem that affects developed countries and new democracies (see Crotty, 1973; Özbudun, 2000, p. 79; TESEV, 2000). Nonetheless, the Turkish case is significantly different in many ways to the general global trend. It has been distinct because electoral volatility has been very high. As large sections of the electorate have grown disillusioned with their parties, more than one in five have voted for a different party from one election to the next. Consequently, a different party won in each of the last four elections. Yet the situation has been deteriorating. Recent surveys show that on the whole no party seems to appeal to more than 10 per cent of voters in the country.

Organisational decline is another characteristic of Turkish political parties. Apart from the WP/VP, none have been mass-membership parties and have mostly been 'cadre' or 'catchall' parties with widespread clientelistic characteristics. Therefore they have failed to establish and maintain local party organisations throughout the country. Instead of developing well-organised horizontal party networks, their organisational networks have been based on vertical, clientelistic ties. Consequently, they are undergoing a period of political impasse in which political parties create more problems than they solve.

The WP/VP appears to be the one exception among Turkish political parties. Despite the general downward trend in party support, the WP/VP increased its share of votes and became the largest party in parliament in the general election of 1995. The WP/VP escaped the trend of increasing fragmentation, electoral volatility, party realignment, and declining party identification, party loyalty and local party organisations. In fact, it emerged as a beneficiary of this process. How did the WP/VP buck the trend, and why did it become the largest party while other political parties disintegrated and lost electoral support? What are the underlying causes of the collapse of the Turkish party system? I set about the task of answering these questions with an open mind, and endeavoured to gather as much information and speak with as many grassroots activists, party members and ordinary citizens in the field as possible. The main aim of this book is to answer these questions particularly in light of a more detailed analysis of grassroots activism (in chapters 2, 3 and 7).

The Location of the Research

Since the early 1950s there have been a number of studies concerned primarily with the relationship between socioeconomic conditions and voting tendencies in Western Europe and North America. These studies focused particularly on the relationship between social and economic neighbourhood factors and social and political participation. For example, one of the earliest empirical studies of American voting behaviour concentrates on the 'social bases of American partisanship'. This study found that 'an *Index of Political Predispositions* based on social classes, religion, and rural/urban residence was a strong determinant of voting choice' (Dalton, 1988, p. 152). Bell and Boat's (1956) study, in San Francisco, showed that family and socioeconomic neighbourhood characteristics influence the development of informal group relations between friends, relatives, neighbours and co-workers. A series of similar studies carried out in Britain discovered a strong correlation between socioeconomic class characteristics in a neighbourhood and voting behaviour.[27]

With the transition to the multiparty system in 1946, similar voting patterns were noted in Turkey. During my fieldwork in Ankara I observed that the social bases of party support in certain areas were determined by socioeconomic characteristics (e.g. income level, type of occupation, sector of employment and level of education) in a community in the studied areas. In other words, class cleavages, which had not been sufficiently credited by some observers, played a decisive role in voting choice in Turkey. We will not discuss this issue at length here but it seems that class cleavages and party support in Turkey were neglected in favour of alternative approaches like 'new political cleavages and new politics'.[28]

Ankara

Since the 1950s rapid urbanisation has been one of the most common characteristics of developing countries. In Latin America and the Middle East the peasant societies of the 1940s and 1950s became urban societies in the 1970s (see Roberts, 1995, pp. 1–27). Political Islam has been the product of this rapid urbanisation process in many Muslim countries.

Contrary to the mainstream Western approaches considered above, the Islamist movements are urban-based and modern in many respects. From pre-1979 Iran to the FLN in Algeria or the Congress Party in India, in many developing countries 'the rise of fundamentalism originates as a reaction against the failures of the modernising, secular state,

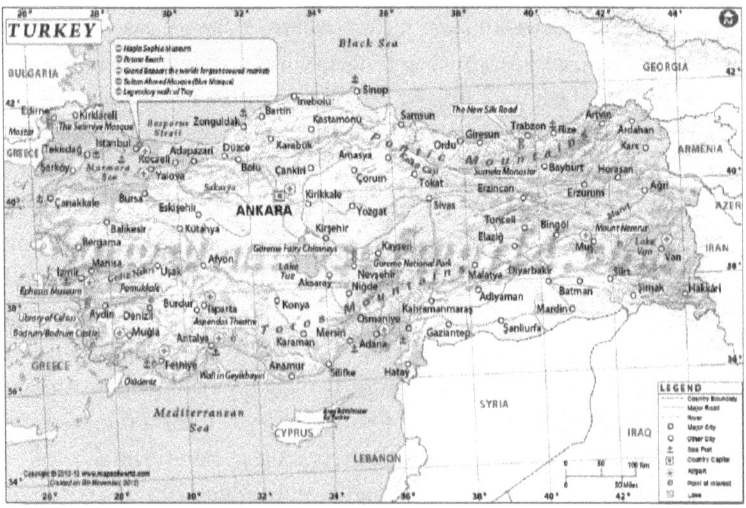

Figure 1.1 Map of Turkey showing Ankara

which has been perceived as corrupted, unable to solve economic and social problems, and, often, dictatorial'. In addition, fundamentalist movements are responses to the very deep problems of these countries, such as mass urbanisation, unemployment and former or current foreign domination (Halliday, 1995a, p. 48).

It has been argued by several scholars that these movements are the product of the modern world. Young militants educated in modern schools and raised in recently urbanised families often come from an impoverished middle class, and, despite common belief, they are rarely mullahs. They have borrowed Marxist terminology and tactics from socialists. Nor are the masses who support and follow these Islamic movements 'traditional' or 'traditionalist'. By and large, they live with the values of the modern city, adopting the current trend of consumerism (see for example Roy, 1994, pp. 3–4).

The Islamist movement in Turkey has many characteristics in common with Islamic movements elsewhere, as highlighted by scholars such as Halliday (1995) and Roy (1994). It can be argued that, with the exception of Afghanistan, Islamist movements in most countries are a product of rapid urbanisation and the consequent social problems. For this reason the best location for the study of political Islam in Turkey has to be an urban area.

Of the Turkish metropolitan cities, Ankara had several advantages as a candidate for this study. First of all, it is geographically central. The main cities are located in the Marmara region (Istanbul, Kocaeli), the Aegean region (İzmir), or the Mediterranean region (Adana). They are all either on the fringes or Western coast of Turkey, relatively far from the Anatolian heartland, whereas Ankara is right in the centre. This makes Ankara geographically easier to reach from around the country and therefore the city has a much more diverse migrant population than other metropolitan cities. The empirical evidence from my fieldwork shows that: (a) the vast majority (76.20 per cent) of the WP/VP's grassroots activists were born outside Ankara, and, (b) they came from every part of the country.[29]

Second, Ankara is a modern city. It was a small town when chosen as the capital city of the Turkish Republic. It has no significant traditional, cultural or historical past to influence the political preferences of its inhabitants. It is a city where the vast majority of inhabitants are migrants from around the country. This diversity makes it highly representative of the general population in Turkey.

Third, as the capital city of the staunchly secular Turkish Republic, Ankara was one of two metropolitan cities (the other was Istanbul) where the WP won the municipality in the 1994 local elections (see Shmuelevitz, 1996, p. 175). The election results testified to the effective, well-organised and highly committed grassroots activism of the WP/VP in Ankara.

For this study I chose two local party organisations in two different administrative *ilçes* (sub-districts) of Ankara: those of Keçiören and Mamak. They have many similarities and differences. Although both have a substantial *gecekondu* population, Keçiören has a large population of traditional middle classes (artisans, merchants, shopkeepers, tradesmen). In terms of housing, both districts contain a large proportion of *gecekondu* settlements. This means both districts are home to thousands of poor, lower-and lower-middle-class residents. Mamak, however, has a proportionally higher *gecekondu* population than Keçiören.

Keçiören and Mamak Sub-Districts

Keçiören is one of the five main administrative districts of Ankara. According to the 1997 census, its population was then 615,021 people. It is located in the northern part of the city and covers 199 square km of land.[30] According to Özdemir (1999, p. 138) in the mid-1990s half of its population (55 per cent) lived in the *gecekondu*s. This ratio was slightly lower than the average for Ankara as a whole (58.4 per cent) in 1993. This means that Keçiören had a large lower-middle- and middle-class population.

Mamak is one of the poorest administrative districts of Ankara. The social and economic gap between Çankaya, a prosperous district, and Mamak is like the divide between the rich north and the poor south. Çankaya, with its luxurious apartments, villas, shopping and leisure centres, green areas and parks, and, above all, its wealthy upper-middle-class residents, is indistinguishable from the prosperous urban suburbs of a Western European city. Unlike Çankaya, Mamak

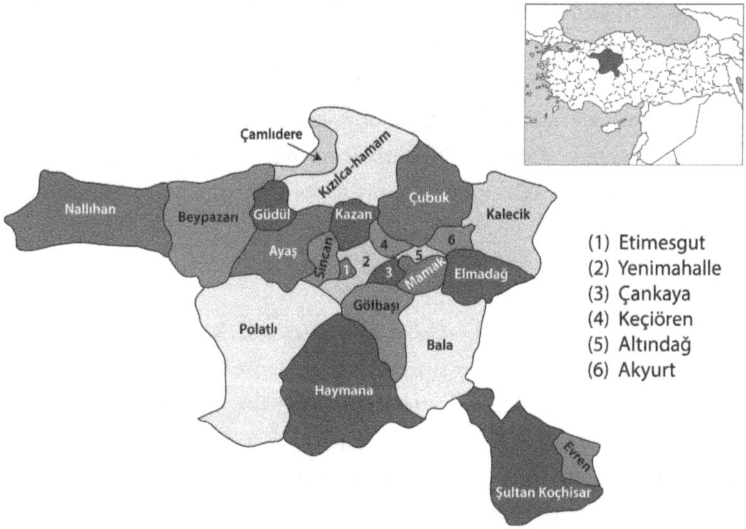

Figure 1.2 Map of Ankara showing sub-districts of Keçiören and Mamak

is poverty-stricken. Some of its neighbourhoods are very poor with inadequate housing conditions, income per family is very low and unemployment is higher than the national average.

Mamak is located in the east of Ankara, near to Elmadağ alongside the Samsun Highway and the Nato Highway, and covers a large area (254 square km) compared to the other four administrative districts of Ankara. According to the 1997 census Mamak had a population of 405,066 people within its territory, and its population density in 1990 was 1,616 people per square km. The majority of Mamak's neighbourhoods are *gecekondu* areas and are occupied by urban poor. There are a very few neighbourhoods that are occupied by traditional middle classes or new middle-class professionals like doctors, lawyers, etc. In 1999 Mamak had 95,000 houses in total, of which 75,000, or more than 79 per cent, were squatter dwellings.[31]

The choice of these two sub-districts provides an opportunity to examine the diversity in party electoral support. The WP/VP enjoyed electoral support from the traditional middle classes, some sections of the new middle classes, the urban poor and much of the largely Kurdish South-east region. Each of these social groups has different issues to represent, different expectations and attitudes, yet they all supported the WP/VP. The diversity of its electoral base makes an interesting case for examining why and how the party attracted support. Nonetheless, we should remember that the vast bulk of its electoral support came from the urban poor of the *gecekondu*s of the big cities.

Varoşlar (Shanty Towns) Seize the City

Despite the differences between Keçiören and Mamak, the similarities are great, as they both have large *gecekondu* populations. As is evident from socioeconomic indicators, for the vast majority of new migrants cities did not provide better living conditions at all, and for them the vicious circle of the poverty trap, inequality, uncertainty and unemployment has continued. The socioeconomic conditions of the *gecekondu* areas are central to this study, as people from these areas made up more than one-third (8,750,000 people, 33.9 per cent of the urban population) of the urban population in 1990 and the WP/VP had broad support in these areas.

It is essential to pay particular attention to the *gecekondus*, or *varoşlar*.[32] Their importance was recognised in the early 1990s, when the WP's unprecedented success in local elections (1994) led to close scrutiny of the political reality of the *gecekondu* areas (see Shmuelevitz, 1996, p. 175).

Methodology, Scope and Sampling

In this study, I used the qualitative approach as my main research method because it has played a major role in political and social sciences. Qualitative methods have been used extensively in the study of individuals and groups inside the formal political arena. For example, party officials and members of parliament have been interviewed for their views on the internal politics of political parties, political attitudes and people's behaviour. Qualitative methodology has also been used in the study of local politics in Britain (Devine, 1995, pp. 137–9).

Among qualitative methods, priority was given to ethnography, a form of qualitative research that combines several methods.[33] Ethnographic research was carried out in Ankara from January to May 1999 and two follow-up visits and additional interviews were done in April–May 2000. In one of the follow-up visits, there were opportunities to participate in the First General Congress of the Virtue Party on 18 May 2000. The bulk of the interviews were carried out on my first visit to Turkey before and after the local and general elections of 18 April 1999.[34] As part of the ethnographic study, different methods and techniques were employed. An important aspect of this ethnographic study involved participatory observations of various occasions among the VP's party activists.

The election campaigns started two months after my ethnographic research commenced. Consequently I had a great opportunity to observe the local party organisations in action and the activities of the grassroots activists, and was also able to compare the grassroots activism in both situations: during the election campaign and in 'normal' daily or weekly activities. I participated in all sorts of party activism, from house and coffee house meetings, to visiting individual shops and households, street meetings, leafleting, hanging party flags and posters in the neighbourhoods, distributing campaign materials to the election bureaus in the neighbourhoods, organising charity work for those in need in the neighbourhoods, as well as attending saloon meetings, street rallies and car convoys. I combined participatory observations with interviews with neighbourhood representatives or members of the neighbourhood committee, ordinary party activists, party supporters, local party administrators and party candidates. I also analysed party documents, election manifestos and candidates' speeches, and recorded and later decoded various forums, discussions and conferences attended by the VP's leaders or candidates together with opposing party leaders. I gathered a considerable amount of printed material, news articles and commentary on election campaigning and the VP in particular. I had regular daily contact and meetings with all sorts of VP people from the upper echelons of the party to the ordinary party supporters in the mainly *gecekondu* neighbourhoods. I used an in-depth, open-ended, semi-structured interviewing technique. In social sciences, interviewing is one of the most common research methods (Fielding, 1994, p. 135). My main research method was a census of party leaders in each neighbourhood. There were a total of 105 neighbourhoods in two districts (63 in Mamak and 42 in Keçiören) and each of the neighbourhoods had its neighbourhood executive committees and their leaders. In total, 42 out of the 105 in-depth interviews were conducted with the local party leaders in the relevant neighbourhoods. In order to ensure accurate representation, a systematic sampling[35] method was used (see Arber, 1994, pp. 65–80).

Scope of the Research

This book is about the long march of the Islamist movement in Turkey. This extraordinary development in Turkish politics caused a series of very serious consequences that lasted a long time and have probably shaped internal politics for coming decades. They range from a 'postmodern coup' by Turkey's strong military forces in 1997, to the ousting of the Islamist-led government, to the closure of the WP, the main actor in this political turmoil. Having reopened in 1997 under a different name, the Virtue Party was quick to adopt all the strategies and tactics of the WP. It inherited from the WP the same grassroots organisations and grassroots activism and was the only modern and mass political party in the country. By 1998 the VP itself was closed down, and all this tension created a schism in the party. As a result the AKP came to power in November 2002, and since then it has been ruling the country.

Since the late 1980s, the Turkish political party system has experienced high levels of fragmentation, electoral volatility and ideological polarisation. Also, following *ad hoc* changes in the law, traditional political parties' organisational capacity, identity and public support have declined. In the 2002 general elections the majority of Turkey's mainstream parties were voted out of parliament. The newly established pro-Islamist AKP captured 34 per cent of the vote but, thanks to the electoral system, secured 65 per cent of the seats and formed a single majority government. Arguing that these events intensified 'the crisis of legitimacy' (Delibaş, 2011) addresses the empirical ramifications of the erosion of trust in political institutions and agencies and the complex ways in which this process affects citizens' political participation and the perceived legitimacy of the democratic process and of governance at the local level.

There have undoubtedly been a number of factors that played an important role in the rise of political Islam in Turkey but, like every other study, this study had its limitations and I had to draw clear boundaries. The scope of the study was bound by the main hypothesis, which was that the grassroots organisations and grassroots activists of the WP/VP were crucial to the electoral successes of the party. Therefore it is a study of the grassroots activists. While applying a historical and empirical approach, it aims also to offer a sociological account for the unprecedented rise of the pro-Islamist parties throughout the 1990s and early 2000s.

Structure of the Book

The rest of this book is organised as follows.

In chapter 2 the background information on Turkish politics in the 1990s and 2000s is considered in some detail. The chapter examines the main concepts and develops a theoretical framework to explain how political Islam emerged and came to power with unprecedented speed. Also, a brief summary is given of the major approaches to political Islam in general and the Turkish case in particular, and offers critiques of such approaches.

Chapter 3 provides a literature review of the grassroots activism and organisation, as well as the effects of grassroots activism on the political process. The chapter also examines the socioeconomic and political preconditions of political Islam in Turkey. I explore the Islamic movement's process of the transition to a successful political party. The surprising ascendancy of the pro-Islamic parties from the mid-1990s is traced, along with the factors that made the WP/VP so successful.

Finally, in this chapter the functions of the political parties in general and the origins of Turkish political cleavages are briefly explored.

Chapter 4 moves on to examine the urban roots of political Islam in Turkey. It argues that, contrary to common belief, Islamic movements in many Muslim countries are urban movements. They are not, as many believed, confined to the pre-modern conditions of backward, illiterate, traditional and conservative communities in rural areas, but rather flourished in towns and cities areas where rapid urbanisation created tremendous socioeconomic problems.

Chapter 5 investigates the patterns of participation among pro-Islamist WP/VP's grassroots activists. In other words, it asks how and why the members joined the party in the first place. Since this process is one of the less studied aspects of political participation, examining the dynamics of how people join a political party will be essential to understanding why people join pro-Islamist parties in the first place.

Chapter 6 considers conceptual definitions such as the mass party, party membership and grassroots activism, and the emergence and development of the mass political parties. The subsequent section is devoted to the grassroots activists, considering the socioeconomic and demographic characteristics of the WP/VP's activists.

Chapter 7 examines the effects of grassroots activism on the electoral process. The chapter is divided into two sections. In the first section the question of whether or not party organisations matter is discussed. The counterargument contests that local party organisations have any impact on electoral performance. In the second section the 'pro-argument', as I call it, challenges this view. It will be argued that despite their declining image in recent years, our findings show that mass-membership parties are still able to influence electoral outcomes. In the second half of the chapter I analyse the empirical data collected from fieldwork. This section aims to describe all aspects (e.g. how often activists meet potential voters, how much time they spend on activism, where they meet) of grassroots activism in Ankara.

Chapter 8 presents the general conclusions and analysis of all empirical findings. Here, the original hypothesis will be re-evaluated in light of empirical findings and the foregoing analysis. Finally, the theoretical implications and possible contributions of this study to social sciences in general and to the study of political parties and political Islam in particular will be assessed.

CHAPTER 2

THE DECLINE OF THE TURKISH POLITICAL PARTY SYSTEM, 1980–2002

The Failure of the Mainstream Parties and Rise of Political Islam

From the late 1980s to 2002, when the AKP came to power, Turkish politics witnessed a period of political impasse. The reason for this was the country's long-term economic deterioration: a high rate of inflation, huge foreign and domestic public debt, a growing gap between rich and poor, abandonment of most social policies, and widespread political corruption created deep pessimism and disillusionment among voters. As a result, political parties experienced increased fragmentation, electoral volatility and organisational weakening as well as a sharp decline in party identification ties. However, there was one exception to this downward trend. The WP/VP emerged as the major winner of this process.

This chapter attempts to answer the following questions: why did the party system collapse? How did it happen? What were the underlying causes of party decline in Turkey? And how did the WP/VP thrive while the other parties were losing popularity? However, before delving into these questions, a short summary of the roots of the crisis would be helpful.

The Roots of the Political Impasse (from 1980 to 2002)

It could be claimed that Turkey never fully recovered from the oil crisis of the mid-1970s. The economic crisis of the 1970s, coincided with a political crisis deepened by the provocations of extreme right-wing groups. Gradually this economic and political crisis led the country to an impasse.

In this extremely polarised and politicised atmosphere came the military coup of 12 September 1980, which caused another interregnum in multiparty politics. All of the political parties were banned from politics and a 10 per cent nationwide threshold was introduced into the electoral system (Kalaycıoğlu, 1998). This meant that parties needed at least 10 per cent support nationwide before they were allowed to take up any seats in the parliament. The military coup of 1980 had an enormous impact on Turkish political life and parties (Ergüder, 1991, p. 51).

The implementation of military rule between 1980 and 1983 had a long-lasting effect on the Turkish political party system. It led not only to further polarisation in party politics, but also to the depoliticisation of society. From the political perspective, one of the unintended consequences of the intervention may have been the increased fragmentation of political parties. Due to this further polarisation, none of the political parties were able to secure a majority in the parliament until 2002, when the pro-Islamist Development and Justice Party (AKP) emerged as the largest party with 34.2 per cent of the votes. The AKP emerged when the likewise pro-Islamist Virtue Party closed down in 2001, and the historic Milli Görüş (National Vision) movement split in two; young cadres led by Recep Tayyip Erdoğan formed the AKP.

So the post-1980 political party system was ostensibly the product of an extremely undemocratic, oppressive and restrictive regime. In one sense, the coup of September 1980 was staged to suppress the awakening of the masses. The military elite believed that the country's social awakening was too far ahead of its economic development. Evidently, this development was seen as a threat to the social and political order so it was believed that this situation needed to be 'corrected'.

When the military intervened, the existing political parties and their leaders, alongside university students and trade union members, were blamed for the social unrest. On this basis, the military elite wanted to prevent the pre-1980 party leaders from engaging in politics by closing down all the parties. After the coup all the leaders – Süleyman Demirel (Justice Party), Bülent Ecevit (Republican People's Party), Necmettin Erbakan (National Salvation Party), Alparslan Türkeş (Nationalist Action Party) – and high-ranking cadres, MPs and district leaders were interrogated and imprisoned. After release from prison the leaders were banned from politics until 1987. They were even prevented from engaging in journalism (Tekeli, 1990, p. 261).

The military regime had three major aims in reorganising the political party system: (1) to establish a two-party system, (2) to impose a programme of depoliticisation which included civil society associations, and (3) to close down all existing political parties and ban all of their leaders and high-ranking cadres from politics.[1] These policies clearly aimed to redefine the boundaries of Turkish politics.

The policy of depoliticisation was very successful indeed. It worked by limiting political activity to a very small section of the population. The 1982 constitution and the regulation of political parties restricted the political participation of public sector workers, civil servants, trade union members, students, teachers, soldiers, and others. The third leg of the policy achieved a complete departure from the pre-1980 political system. By allowing new political parties and new agents, the military elite wanted to create a new political style.

The Crisis of 2001

From 1999 to 2001 Turkey was hit by one of the worst economic and political crises of its modern history. Economically as well as politically the country was on the verge of total bankruptcy. According to media reports, the treasury was no longer able to make interest repayments, which amounted to billions of dollars of foreign and domestic debt. It was estimated that total debt reached a staggering level of around 80 to 90 per cent of the country's GDP.

The treasury announced in a briefing in July 2001 that most of the income (TL 16.561 trillion) generated from tax during the first six months of 2001 had gone towards interest repayments (TL 15.741

trillion) and left a budget deficit of TL 8.104 trillion.[2] Many commentators and economists agreed that the situation was no longer sustainable. Things were so bad that the government considered declaring a moratorium on debt payment.[3]

Throughout the 1980s and 1990s the Turkish economy had been crippled by a very high rate of inflation. This long-term trend of high inflation caused extreme poverty and a huge income gap between the richest and poorest in society.[4] Various surveys indicated that in terms of income inequalities Turkey had one of the worst records.[5] However, 'the real roots of the country's problems', according to *The Economist* (16 May 2001), lay in politics rather than economics.

The political side of the crisis revealed itself in a much cruder, more expressive way than the economic side. The economic and political crisis reached the stage where the country was no longer governed by the elected government but by the International Monetary Fund (IMF) via Kemal Derviş, who was vice-president at the World Bank until March 2001.[6] The government, which was a three-party coalition, was left with no alternative, no power and no initiative to make any economic or political decisions. All it could do was to assist Derviş, who was appointed as minister of the economy, in implementing the IMF's structural adjustment policies.[7]

It seemed that the beginning of the twenty-first century brought a new phase in relations between the IMF and recipient countries. The IMF pushed aside the national governments in countries such as Turkey and Argentina by appointing someone from either the IMF or the World Bank as a 'governor' who was able to override the government's capacities and implement further restructuring policies: this led to a sharp drop in the value of the national currency against the dollar.[8]

The socioeconomic consequences of the crisis in Turkey were brutal. The Turkish lira was devalued by over 100 per cent, falling from TL 680,000 to the dollar in February 2001 to TL 1.5 million to the dollar on 17 July 2001.[9] Unemployment soared: around 580,000 workers lost their jobs in just six months.

On the face of it, it seemed as if the government had totally surrendered to the demands of international institutions such as the IMF, the

World Bank and international markets (see Kumcu, 2001). No other government in Turkey's history had experienced such humiliation in having to surrender its powers to foreign institutions and their local collaborators to this extent.[10]

The once proud, dignified and self-confident Anatolian nation, 'the lords of the horizons', was brought to its knees by international institutions and the country's own ruling elites, who were corrupt, dishonest and unimaginably incompetent.[11] As public support for the mainstream parties and political elite disappeared, they increasingly sought external support. This process inevitably heralded the end of party politics.

Although the situation appeared to be mainly an economic crisis, it was closely connected with the impasse that the Turkish political party system had been experiencing. For a long time Turkish political parties were not able to produce policies to overcome this political impasse. All of them, with the exception of the WP/VP, were declining rapidly under the hegemony of sultan-like leaders. Polls at the time showed that no party had scored more than 10 per cent of the votes. The majority of voters were disillusioned with the existing parties and were searching for an alternative (Hasan, 2001).

Parties and Representative Democracy

Political parties are the key components of representative democracy. They help to run the election machinery and serve as the vehicles for political campaigns. They stimulate public discussion on important issues, and most importantly they serve as a bridge between the people and their governments (Huckshorn, 1984, p. 7). They also function as agents of elite recruitment and agents of interest aggregation, serve as a point of reference for voters and offer direction to government (Hague et al., 1998, p. 131). There is no doubt that political parties are one of the most distinctive and most successful forms of political organisation (Scarrow, 1996, p. 1); they are the major facilitators of representative democracy. For Neumann (1963, p. 352), the political party is

> the articulate organisation of society's active political agents, those who are concerned with the control of governmental power

> and who compete for popular support with another group or groups holding divergent views. As such it is the great intermediary which links social forces and ideologies to official governmental institutions and relates them to political action with the large political community.

Obviously, the control of governmental power involves an electoral process in which parties need popular support, thereby forming a link social forces and ideologies to governmental institutions. However, in Turkey this link went missing between 1980 and 1983. Due to the collapse of this 'bridge', the Turkish party system has suffered representation problems. Parties have become organisations that serve their self-interest more than they do wider public interests.

The Causes of Party Decline: Party Fragmentation, Organisational Decline and Volatility

The post-1983 era began when the new political party law came into effect on 24 April 1983 and the following day the NSC lifted the ban on politics. Within a week or so 17 parties had been formed (Ahmad, 1993, p. 188). Since all of the pre-1980 parties had been closed down by the coup, these parties were established by the new political elite. The majority of them were new to politics or were the lower-ranking elites from pre-1980 parties. Not all parties were new, however; for example, the Great Turkey Party, was Demirel's Justice Party in disguise and the Social Democratic People's Party was the continuation of the Republican People's Party. The generals closed down the Great Turkey Party immediately; the Social Democratic People's Party was not banned but was not allowed to take part in the first elections in 1983 (ibid., pp. 188–9). In the end three parties were allowed to take part in elections. They were the People's Party (later merged with the Social Democratic People's Party), which represented the left, the Nationalist Democracy Party established by a retired general and supported by the military rule, representing the centre-right, and the Motherland Party, founded by Turgut Özal. Due to Turkey's relatively high levels of electoral volatility and fragmentation compared to the rest of Europe, the Turkish party system has historically been unstable.

Table 2.1 Volatility and fragmentation in the Turkish party system, 1961–1995

Elections	Volatility[a]	Fragmentation of votes[b]	Fragmentation of seats[b]	Disproportionality index[c]	Effective number of parties[d]
1961	–	0.71	0.70	1.0	3.3
1965	24.5	0.63	0.63	0.75	2.6
1969	11.4	0.70	0.59	7.4	2.3
1973	28.4	0.77	0.70	5.6	3.3
1977	18.3	0.68	0.60	5.5	2.5
1983	–	0.66	0.61	4.5	2.5
1987	–	0.75	0.51	15.7	2.0
1991	16.6	0.79	0.71	7.1	3.5
1995	23.0	0.83	0.77	5.8	4.3

Notes: [a] Total volatility is the sum of the absolute value of all changes in the percentages of votes cast for each party since the previous election divided by two. The 1961 elections are omitted because the Democratic Party was dissolved by the ruling military council (NUC), and two entirely new parties (the Justice Party and the New Turkey Party) competed for its votes. Likewise, the 1983 elections are omitted because the military government (NSC) closed down all existing parties; thus, the three parties that competed in this election were new. The 1987 elections are omitted because two of the three parties authorised by the NSC (the People's Party and Nationalist Democratic Party) were relatively artificial parties that soon disappeared after the return to competitive politics. Had these three elections been included, the average volatility score would have been much higher. In calculating the volatility scores, only parties that gained representation in parliament in at least one of the two consecutive elections were taken into account. For the 1991 elections, which the WP contested in an alliance with the Nationalist Action Party and the small Reformist Democracy Party, percentages of votes in the 1998 local elections were taken as a close approximation. Compiled by the author.

[b] Based on Douglas W. Rae's (1967, p. 56) index of fractionalisation, New Haven.

[c] Based on Arend Lijphart's index of disproportionality, which is 'the average vote-seat deviation of the two largest parties in each election'; *Democracies: Patterns of Majoritarian and Consensus Government in Twenty-One Countries*, Yale University Press, New Haven, 1984, p. 163.

[d] Based on Markku Laakso and Rein Taagepera's formula: $Pe = \frac{1}{\sum_{i=1}^{n} Pi^2}$

Source: Özbudun, 2000, p. 77.

According to the TESEV's study (2000, p. 12), Turkey's average volatility score between 1954 and 1999 was 21 per cent.[12] This means that one in every five electors changed their vote from one party at one election to another at the next. In the post-1980 period, the first important signs of this fragmentation came with the elections of 1989.

Although the military elite wanted to create a two-party system, the post-1983 era turned out to be much more fragmented than before. The reason for this was the duplication of political parties on the centre-right as well as the centre-left.

The military government left office with the elections of 1983. But only three parties out of 17 were permitted to take part in the 1983 elections. In reality this plan soon backfired, because despite being closed down by the coup, almost all the pre-1980 parties were re-established either by *emanetcies* (leader's puppets) or some low-ranking party officials.

By the time the pre-1980 leaders' ban was lifted (in 1987), these parties were already established under these new leaders, some of whom did not want to leave the post or the party. So the pre-1980 leaders had to establish their own parties or reopen their old parties if the court allowed. This situation not only caused extra parties to set up in an already crowded political arena, but also led to an inflation of the political elite – a new class of politicians on all sides of the political spectrum.

In the first elections after the military coup, in 1983, the Motherland Party won an unprecedented election victory with 45 per cent of the votes and 52.7 per cent of seats in the parliament. The People's Party received 29.2 per cent and the Nationalist Democracy Party achieved 17.7 per cent of the votes. The fragmentation index was measured as 0.61 in 1983 for the Assembly seats (see Table 2.1).

It would not be an exaggeration to say that the most important event affecting party system fragmentation and ideological polarisation in the post-1983 era was the return of the pre-1980 leaders (Demirel, Ecevit, Erbakan and Türkeş) to politics. After four years of transitioning to democracy, a referendum was finally called to decide the political fate of these banned leaders. The result of the referendum, held on 6 September 1987, was a narrow yes (50.3 per cent) in favour of lifting the ban.

The local elections of 1989 gave an especially strong indication of the fragmentation and polarisation on both sides of the political spectrum. This time the Motherland Party received only 21.8 per cent of the vote while its rival, Demirel's True Path Party, received 25.1 per cent, the Social Democratic People's Party took 28.7 per cent, Ecevit's Democratic Left Party 9 per cent, and the Welfare Party got 9.8 per cent (see Table 2.2).

In the 1991 elections the trend continued, with the index of fragmentation going up to 0.71 (see Table 2.1). The Motherland Party received 24 per cent and the True Path Party managed 27.0 per cent of the votes. This time the electoral centre moved further towards the extreme right. The reason for this was the pre-election alliance between the WP and the Nationalist Action Party to get into parliament, which both did by winning 16.9 per cent of the votes. In fact, when compared with the 1987 general elections, both centre-right (4.4 per cent) and centre-left (1.9 per cent) parties lost votes to this alliance.

These election results showed that the centre-right was so profoundly fragmented that its fortunes could not be reversed in the foreseeable future. The subsequent elections in 1995 and 1999 confirmed this tendency (see Table 2.1) and the situation was largely the same for the centre-left parties too. From the early 1990s the Turkish party system returned to the high fragmentation and electoral volatility experienced in the 1970s.

As Kalaycıoğlu (1998, p. 12) pointed out, 'Turkey has moved from a two-party format that functioned more like a predominant party system in the 1950s to moderate pluralism of the 1960–1980 era, and eventually towards extreme pluralism in the 1990s'. By the 1970s new elements had contributed to fragmentation. The Islamic movement transformed into a political party named the National Order Party in 1970. It later became the National Salvation Party, which was one of the key players in the endless bargaining of the coalition governments in the 1970s. The establishment of the ultra-nationalist Nationalist Action Party (NAP) marked the height of this era of polarisation of the party system in Turkey (Özbudun, 2000, p. 75). The 1970s also saw a steep rise in trade union activism and student movements all over the country.

Table 2.2 Turkish election results, 1983–1999

Percentages of votes in Turkish parliamentary and local elections (1983–99)									
	Elections								
Party	1983 (Parlmt)	1984 (Local)	1987 (Parlmt)	1989 (Local)	1991 (Parlmt)	1994 (Local)	1995 (Parlmt)	1999 (Local)	1999 (Parlmt)
MP	45.2	41.5	36.3	21.8	24.0	21.0	19.7	13.0	13.3
PP	30.5	8.8	–	–	–	–	–	–	–
NDP	23.3	7.1	–	–	–	–	–	–	–
SDPP	–	23.4	24.7	28.7	20.8	13.6	–	–	–
TPP	–	13.3	19.1	25.1	27.0	21.4	19.2	7.0	12.1
WP/VP	–	4.4	7.2	9.8	16.9	19.1	21.4	17.0	15.5
DLP	–	–	8.5	9.0	10.8	8.8	14.6	10.0	22.3
NAP	–	–	2.9	4.1	–	8.0	8.2	20.0	18.1
RPP	–	–	–	–	–	4.6	10.7	–	8.9

Source: Election results years 1983 to 1995 taken from Özbudun, 1996, p. 128. The 1999 election results are taken from *Milliyet* (20 April 1999). State Institute of Statistics.

By the mid-1990s the fragmentation in the Turkish party system was worse than ever before. The WP became the largest party in the parliament but it received just 21.4 per cent of the vote (ibid., p. 76; Kalaycıoğlu, 1998, p. 12). Signs of further fragmentation came with the local elections in 1994 and a year later in the general election of 1995.

From the early 1990s, the political centre entered a process of rapid decline. In the 1995 election the WP become the largest party, winning 21 per cent of the votes and 158 seats out of 550. This result indicated the degree of the fragmentation index which was at a record level of 0.77. As the trend continued, the Motherland Party lost more votes – from 24 per cent in 1991 to 19.7 per cent in 1995. The True Path Party also lost votes – from 27 per cent in 1991 to 19.2 per cent in 1995.

Yet the 1999 general elections proved to be the worst result for the mainstream centre-right and centre-left parties. As Figure 2.1 shows, the fragmentation index was at 0.88, the highest ever in Turkish

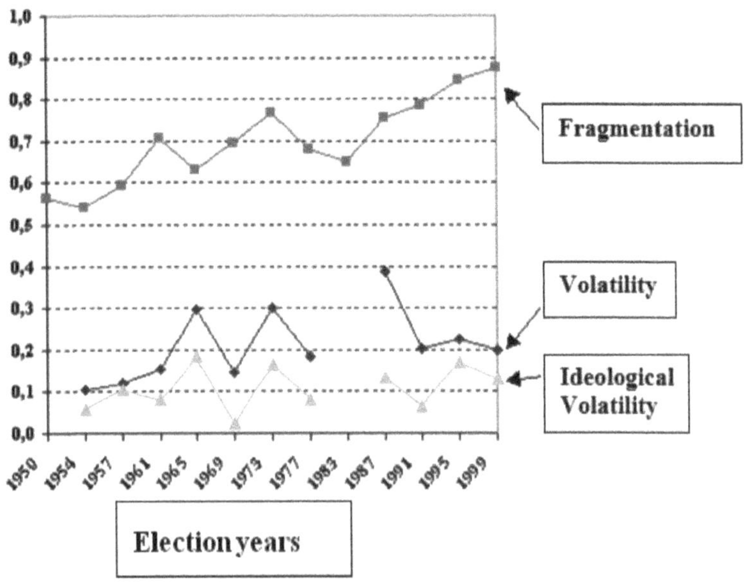

Figure 2.1 Fragmentation and volatility in the general elections, 1950–1999
Source: Erdem et al., 2000, p. 5.

political history. Both parties of the centre-right lost a considerable number of votes. The Motherland Party only received 13.3 per cent and the True Path Party polled 12.1 per cent, while the Nationalist Action Party doubled its share of the vote to 18.1 per cent. However, the fourth party on the right of the political spectrum, the Virtue Party, lost some of its previous share of the vote (from 21.4 to 15.5 per cent). This loss was largely caused by the disruption that came with the closure of the WP just a year previously. This had not left enough time for the VP to reorganise. Although many of its local branches had simply changed their name from Welfare to Virtue, the closure still caused organisational disruption. An additional explanation is that the intervention that came on 28 February[13] sent a clear message to the WP/VP's supporters and potential voters that the party would not be allowed to come to power, regardless of its electoral strength. This theory was in fact confirmed by the results of the local elections held at the same time as the general elections on 18 April 1999.

In the local elections the VP did not lose as much support as it did in the general elections of 1999, dropping only 2.7 percentage points from 19.1 per cent in 1994 to 16.4 per cent in 1999. This indicates that voters supported the VP in the local elections but not in the general election because they feared confrontation with the military and wanted to avoid further escalation of the tension.

On the left of the political spectrum there were two surprises: the first was the Democratic Left Party's unexpected success in gaining 22.3 per cent, the highest total of any party. The second surprise was that the Republican People's Party failed to enter parliament because with 8.9 per cent of the vote it scored lower then the 10 per cent national threshold. So the oldest party of all, the founding party of the republic, was ejected from parliament by the voters. This illustrates the extent of fragmentation and electoral volatility in the Turkish party system, which was to be followed by increased ideological polarisation. It is estimated that throughout the 1990s approximately 10 per cent of the electorate switched from one ideological group to another from one election to the next (see Figure 2.1).

There were two reasons for this. First, military interventions (see TESEV, 2000, p. 11; Özbudun, 2000, p. 76) and party closures destroyed the sociopolitical bases of the parties, and prevented the subsequent development of strong party identification, party organisations and party loyalties. Second, the political parties in Turkey are not deeply rooted in civil society (Özbudun, 2000, p. 78). Unless parties are firmly embedded in society they will not have much electoral stability.

Organisational weakness was another malaise of the Turkish party system. Throughout the 1990s parties faced a real problem with the erosion of public confidence. According to surveys carried out in the 1990s and 2000s, political parties were the least trusted institutions in Turkey (see Strateji MORI, 1998, p. 35, cited in TESEV, 2000, p. 16). From the late 1980s to the early 2000s most of the parties suffered a decline in their party organisations and a weakening of party identification (Özbudun, 2000, p. 79; TESEV, 2000). In contrast to the mainstream parties, the WP/VP gave first priority to strengthening its local party organisations. It was the only party that actively engaged in increasing its membership. With its active engagement strategy, the party gave a role and voice to every one of its members in the local party branches. These branches engaged in year-round campaigning which was geared to electoral purposes but also had a charitable function: distributing fuel in the winter, food, overcoats, shoes and grants for school children. They established and maintained a very intimate relationship with the local residents. All of these activities were only possible because of the existence of a strong, well-organised and efficient party organisation that was unique to the WP/VP.

Organisational Characteristics of Turkish Political Parties

As far as organisational characteristics are concerned, all Turkish parties share similar features because political party laws impose a standard organisational model, which consists of party congresses and elected executive committees at the national and local level (Özbudun, 2000). This obligation prevents political elites from developing a structure that is more suitable to their own needs, or that reflects the local realities and conditions.

In general terms, the majority of them can be described as cadre or 'catch-all' parties with strong clientelistic characteristics. The WP is the only exception to this generalisation. The WP had mass-party features (ibid., p. 80). The Virtue Party (VP), the heir of the WP, was also founded on the same principles.

In the contemporary literature, party models are widely classified as (1) Cadre/Elite Party; (2) Mass-based Branch Party; (3) Catch-all Party and (4) Cartel Party (Maor, 1997, pp. 96–113). The cadre/elite parties, catch-all parties and cartel parties are all characterised by marginalised party membership. In most cases membership is maintained but not cultivated (Özbudun, 2000, p. 101).

There is agreement among students of politics that local party organisations and activists do make a significant contribution in terms of increasing parties' share of votes in the elections.[14] From this point it can be claimed that those parties that have large memberships and nationwide party organisations do get better electoral results. However, as mostly cadre or catch-all parties with strong leadership tendencies, the majority of Turkish political parties are clearly missing out on these benefits. Although party membership is increasingly seen as a burden or as costly for the party leaders to maintain, it still has many benefits for political parties (see Scarrow, 1996). If parties are defined as the bridge between the people and government, then members are the bridge between parties and people.

For Scarrow, party members provide several benefits for their parties such as legitimacy, outreach, financial support, labour, networking, innovation and personnel (1994, pp. 42–6). Some commentators argue that due to technological and social developments (e.g. the emergence of specialist PR experts, campaign managers, fundraisers, etc.) party leaders have increasingly become independent of party members and organisations. They argue that while large grassroots organisations were once necessary and constituted the only way of electioneering, this is no longer the case. Now, they say, the leaders have the means to be in direct contact with the electorate. This claim is true up to a point, but party organisations remain an asset for leaders. In many Western European countries party organisations and membership are still valued for their role.[15]

In the post-1980 party system, except for the WP/VP and later the AKP, none of the Turkish political parties have had active membership organisations, or widespread membership activities. A 1996 survey showed that 12.1 per cent of voters were party members; however, due to the nature of party registers and the loose link between parties and members, it suggested that in Turkey a great many more people were party supporters than were party members (Özbudun, 2000, p. 80).[16] In 1993 the WP was the fourth largest party with over 1.1 million members, but in 1994 the WP started the local election campaign with a massive membership registration campaign and reached 4.5 million members before its closure in 1998 (Çakır, 1994, pp. 51–2).

With the exception of the WP/VP, mainstream parties have lacked a crucial bridge, an important organic connection between the party and the people on the ground. This is not only important for expounding the party's policies, ideas, key issues and strategies, and for strengthening the party identity, but parties with large memberships also tend to have greater stability and continuity in difficult times.

It can be said that membership is especially important in a political atmosphere where the ideological differences between political parties are disappearing, or ideological commitments are declining. In such an atmosphere membership provides an anchor for stability and continuity.[17]

Due to the lack of grassroots organisations and mass membership, the majority of Turkish parties have become overly dependent on state resources – financial and otherwise. This problem has been made worse by the under-institutionalisation of the post-1983 political parties. For a variety of reasons, many of them have not been institutionalised. This lack of institutionalisation has been aggravated by the lack of membership support, in terms of financing, labour for day-to-day tasks in the organisations, election campaigning, etc., hence the need to use capital-intensive media-led campaigning methods which are very expensive. To do this, the parties must rely on state resources. Although they are entitled to receive some state aid according to their representation in parliament, it is often not enough to run expensive election campaigns. Therefore they have to find other ways to subsidise their election expenses. This need forces them to become overly dependent on governmental power to create resources while in office.

The Genesis of the Turkish Party System and Patronage

The first quarter of the twentieth century was marked by the disintegration of the Ottoman Empire and the foundation of the Turkish Republic. Following this period, the revolution of 1923 shaped the direction and characteristics of the modern Turkish political system (Feroz, 1977, p. 2). However, the genesis of Turkish political parties goes back to the nineteenth century. Rustow (1991, p. 10) argues that since then Turkish political parties have reflected both the profound changes and the underlying continuity in the country's political history. Among the major developing countries, Turkey's party system was the earliest to develop. Fredrick Frey argues that in the 1950s:

> Turkish politics [were] party politics. ... With the power structure of Turkish society, the political party is the main unofficial link between the government and the larger, extra governmental groups of people ... [Turkey was characterised by] extensive, powerful, highly organised, grass roots parties ... (Frey, 1965, pp. 301–3, cited in Özbudun, 2000, p. 73)

Similarly, Heper points out that:

> As compared with the situation in many Third World contexts, with their fairly well developed and distinct party platforms, relatively complex organisations highly differentiated from traditional social structures as well as from the military and Church, and with their active role in government, the Turkish political parties have had a significant impact on politics (Heper and Landau, 1991, p. 3).

Dodd (1969, p. 162) also describes the general characteristics of Turkish political parties in a similar vein. For him they were far more than the tools of an elite group. He notes that they entered into real competition for nomination and election to the party electoral list: 'in brief, Turkish society is deeply permeated by political organisation'.

As the above literature review indicates, parties have always been prominent in Turkish politics. For example, the establishment of the Republican People's Party even before the advent of the republic shows that parties were given a significant role in politics. In this respect the RPP was a true grassroots party made up of small resistance groups in Anatolia.

In many ways, Turkish political parties are comparable to Western European parties. In some respects, the Turkish party system and representative parliamentary democracy is older than those of certain EU members, such as Spain and Greece.

From 1946 to 1960, the Turkey was dominated by a typical two-party system. The Republican People's Party (RPP) represented the centre, and the Democratic Party represented the periphery. The military coup on 27 May 1960 put an end not only to the Democratic government but the two-party system as well.[18]

It was the establishment of the Democratic Party on 7 January 1946 that turned Turkish politics into a two-party system.[19] This development inevitably introduced political activity and competition into Turkish politics. The change of power via the electoral process not only strengthened the chance for democracy in the 1950s in Turkey but also improved the public perception of political parties and party organisations enormously.

Towards the end of the 1960s the Republican People's Party began to recover from its continual bad electoral performance and showed signs of becoming a serious challenger to the Democrat government (Tachau, 1991, p. 99). After 1955 the party started to renew its cadres. The young cadres brought new blood and dynamism to the party organisations. In time they became effective in the party management and after 1965 this young generation started to determine the direction of the party (Kabasakal, 1991, p. 211).

Following the 1960 coup, the Justice Party formed in 1961. It was the party of the new commercial and industrial middle classes, traditional landowners and the religious sector (Dodd, 1969, pp. 140–1). For some students of Turkish politics, the Justice Party was the only real grassroots party in the Middle East.[20] For instance, Levi (1991, pp. 146–7) argued that the party's organisation was the strongest of all Turkish parties' in the 1960s and 1970s. Its local branches were stronger, and its chairman was well respected by the district's branches. Unlike in most other parties, the Justice Party's parliamentarians were natives of the districts they were representing in the Assembly. Compared to the Republican People's Party, more women and workers entered parliament through the Justice Party at that time. It was more inclusive than any other party and through its organisations many of the new rural-to-urban migrants integrated into the social life of the urban centres (ibid., p. 148).

It is true that the Justice Party had well-organised, strong grassroots organisations across the country, but they were based on the what Özbudun (2000) calls 'vertical loyalties' rather than 'horizontal loyalties'. Also, the patron–client relationship was one of the defining characteristics of the Republican People's Party until its closure in 1980 (Ayata-Güneş, 1990, pp. 159–85). The historic alliance between the military-bureaucratic elite and local prominent figures was a prime reason for this clientelistic aspect of the party (Sayarı, 1977, p. 125). These patrons secured electoral support for the party through their client relations, and in return they benefited handsomely from the state's facilities.

The Emergence of the Working Class and its Political Impact

The emergence of the working class was helped by the rapid urbanisation that started in the early 1950s, and as this new social group grew in size its political influence expanded too. This expansion brought class politics into Turkish politics. The Republican People's Party moved its position to the centre-left by abandoning some of its traditional allies. As a result, throughout the 1960s and early 1970s electoral support for the Justice Party and the RPP fell off dramatically.[21]

The modernisation of the 1960s and 1970s brought change to the party system. A degree of socioeconomic modernisation after the elections of 1969 marked the beginning of realignment in the Turkish party system (Özbudun, 1976, p. 151; Tachau, 1991, pp. 108–9). The Justice Party lost its traditional support as a result of the shift in *gecekondus*' voting patterns.

From 1965 to 1972 the RPP adopted a new ideology – the rising ideology of social democracy – and organisational structure (see Ayata-Güneş, 1990, p. 16). Bülent Ecevit, the new leader of the RPP, had the strong support of the provincial party organisations and tried to give a new role and initiative to the local party branches.

However, despite all of these efforts at reform, the defining characteristic of the RPP, political patronage, was not eliminated. Its membership support was not reliable. There were very few card-carrying members. But the provincial delegates had a great deal of power and they were appointed rather than elected (ibid., 1990, p. 163). It appeared that, despite all the organisational and ideological changes, clientelism continued to exist within the RPP.

Since the early 1980s, Turkish political parties have been moving away from organisation-centred politics to candidate-centred politics. In the process they have dispersed their organisations and neglected the party membership. Historically, argues Özbudun (2000, p. 84) Turkish parties played an important role in electoral mobilisation via local party branches, door-to-door canvassing by party activists, and various grassroots activities to influence voter turnout and party preferences. However, this has reversed, with parties now heavily reliant on media-led, high-tech campaigning methods (ibid.). It seems this shift from organisational to candidate/leader-centred politics did work for a brief period in the 1980s. Nonetheless, due to the state's decreased role in the economy and the privatisation of many public companies, the state revenues that government parties receive have fallen sharply, and along with it their high-tech, media-led election campaigning ability.

Widespread clientelism among Turkish parties is another problem that causes fragmentation, volatility and organisational decline.[22] Since the beginning of multiparty democracy in 1945, the Turkish political elite's approach to socioeconomic problems has been dominated by questions of political patronage (Heper and Keyman, 1998, p. 258). Over the decades very few governments have made any efforts to develop coherent socioeconomic policies to solve the country's problems but have, instead, responded oversensitively to the demands of particular groups and particular socioeconomic issues.[23]

> What passed as 'policies' on such matters were, on the whole, no more than slipshod decisions essentially motivated by a desire to garner votes ... Thus politics have not revolved essentially around the pros and cons of socioeconomic policies; political patronage has become the basic strategy of obtaining votes ... (Heper and Keyman, 1998, p. 258)

The workings of the Turkish party system reflect the relationship between the people and the state in a patron–client relationship (TESEV, 2000, p. 2). Party organisations work on the basis of creation and distribution of patronage. Instead of allowing internal democracy, a small elite group or individual leader plays a significant role in every stage of party activity (see Kalaycıoğlu, 1998; Özbudun, 2000).

In this regard, the post-1980 political parties also adopted patron–client relationships throughout the country. Even new parties such as the Motherland Party failed to develop vertical grassroots organisations. As Güneş-Ayata (1994, p. 57) points out:

> The Motherland Party (MP)... refrained from establishing an elaborate organisational network. Even while in power, it did not attempt big campaigns for membership and developed a style of clientelism that was radically different from that of its predecessors. The MP applied pork-barrel distribution of spoils as party-directed patronage in the rural areas. However, it avoided creating vertical networks based on party cadres, preferring to concentrate on a few leaders in the big cities who later became financiers and vigorous supporters.

Perhaps the reason for this was the party leader himself, Turgut Özal. He was an engineer and believed in the infinite power of technology. He was a staunch supporter of the new age religion, 'neoliberalism'. The 'social' did not matter for him. Like Britain's Margaret Thatcher, he did not believe in 'society' at all: he was the chief proponent of liberal capitalism and individualism in Turkey. With this perspective, plainly, he did not value party membership or the local party organisations.

Özal adopted American-style expensive high-tech, media-led election campaigns and brought some expertise from the United States to help him campaign for a second term in office. As the Motherland Party had never set up an elaborate party network, and did not have deep roots in society, it had to offer a kind of clientelism that would secure sufficient electoral support. However, the support generated through this kind of clientelism disappears very quickly when clients are no longer satisfied. This may explain why the Motherland Party's share of the vote plummeted from 45.2 per cent in 1983 to 13.3 per cent in 1999.

In the case of the True Path and Social Democratic People's Parties, as descendants of pre-1980 parties they both inherited elaborate party organisation networks (Güneş-Ayata, 1994, p. 58). From the moment of its establishment the True Path Party was able to set up its local organisations very quickly because it could make use of former Justice Party organisations and their former staff. In 1988 True Path officials declared that around 70 per cent of their local party heads were former Justice Party members. The True Path Party inherited clientelistic relations and party patronage from its predecessor the Democratic Party, and from the Justice Party (Acar, 1991, p. 190).

Patronage politics increased noticeably in the post-1991 period and reached its peak in 1996–97 (Heper and Keyman, 1998, p. 268). However, it is not always easy to satisfy large client groups, especially in times of slow economic growth with a reduced state role in the economy. With the exception of the WP, the majority of Turkish parties experienced a decline in their organisational strength (Özbudun, 2000, p. 84). This was a result of the slowing of economic growth and restructuring policies, which caused a decline in the state's role in the economy. Özbudun (ibid.) notes:

> These changes mean that there is a limit to spoils parties can distribute to their followers, which in the absence of strong ideological motivations is important in sapping their organisational strength. ... The WP is the only party that has avoided this decline.

In time, clientelism became the overriding characteristic of the Turkish party system. In general, political parties have emerged as a product of social conflicts and cleavages and always reflected the interests of certain groups or classes. But in Turkey since the 1980s in particular, political parties seem to have functioned mainly to acquire and distribute the spoils of public resources in order to maintain public support. If they are out of power, they promise to do so when they get back into power. As a result, they have lost the perspective of long-term planning and investment, of approaching problems with strategic, long-term, broad, visionary plans rather than narrow, short-term palliative solutions. This in turn further destabilises the whole economic and political system.

Since the patron–client relationship is based on the provision of some kind of benefit, good or service by a patron to a client in return for loyalty or political support, either side can easily change this relationship. If a client is not happy with what he gets, he can look to other patrons to maximise his benefit. This is what has happened to many of the major Turkish parties, which are based on clientelistic relations. Those relations can be very unstable in times of major economic upheaval, of the sort Turkey has witnessed several times since 1983. The clientelistic nature of the Turkish party system has fed the widespread corruption in Turkey as well.

As a result of restructuring policies, the creation of new resources (or spoils) that parties can distribute to their followers has been limited to the extent where parties could not sustain their clientelist networks. This situation caused an eventual decline in their electoral support and high levels of electoral volatility.

As a consequence, the majority of Turkish parties have lost touch with the people. They have no means of establishing and maintaining direct contact with their potential voters. The only exception to this is the WP/VP, which has robust local organisations to carry out year-round party activity. Most other mainstream parties have not been organised as mass parties; they lack staff, have very little active membership, and above all lack ideological conviction and enthusiasm, which is very important in maintaining party support. Because they are not ideological parties, members lack any meaningful reason to join in the first place or later become party activists. The empirical evidence shows, however, that by contrast there was a high level of religious and ideological reasoning among the WP/VP's grassroots activists (see chapter 5).

As the party of the periphery the pro-Islamist WP/VP had to rely on grassroots organisations and party membership for election campaigning and carrying out day-to-day duties at the local organisations. It has set an example to other parties to look and learn from its successful experience with the grassroots organisations.[24]

Despite the fact that the WP lacked intra-party democracy, until its closure in 1998 it was the only mass party in Turkey (Özbudun, 2000). Consequently it did not need to develop an extensive network of patron–client relations. It could easily mobilise millions of supporters without relying on clientelistic relations. Further evidence for this is the high level of religious and ideological involvement among its members. The majority (61 per cent) joined the party for religious and ideological reasons rather than expectations of any sort of material benefit that patron–client relations provide (see Table 5.7).

Having large membership organisations is valuable not only when it comes to election campaigning but also for many other vital functions that benefit the party (Scarrow, 1996, pp. 42–5). For example, in a political atmosphere with high electoral volatility and persistent political party fragmentation, large membership organisations provide strength, stability and continuity for political parties. This is where the WP/VP had superiority over its rivals.

The Political Economy of Party Decline

In the 1990s the Turkish party system witnessed a high level of fragmentation, electoral volatility and weakening of party organisations (see Table 2.1 and Figure 2.1). However, the ultimate questions of why this happened, what were the underlying causes of this process, and what caused the rise of the WP/VP and the simultaneous decline of other parties all remain to be answered.

Grievances, either individual or social, are one of the first and most important conditions and social bases of political action. This action can take place in either conventional politics or protest politics. It has been suggested that people protest because they are fed up or because they experience a subjective sense of dissatisfaction (Marsh, 1990, p. 109). The concept of dissatisfaction could be experienced at a personal or political level (see Barnes et al., 1979; Farah et al., 1979). According to Dalton (1988, p. 50), policy dissatisfaction is one of the six main factors that influence a citizen's decision to participate in politics. Political action can take various forms and might take place at the individual or collective level. In terms of electoral politics, policy dissatisfaction is evaluated in relation to the party's performance while they are in government. In fact, one of the best ways of testing a political party is to look at its performance while in power. As has been discussed widely in political literature, there is a positive correlation between political action and dissatisfaction at the personal as well as political level (Barnes et al., 1979, pp. 381–3).

Politics can be described as 'interest aggregation' through political parties. The interests, either individually or collectively, are reflected as issues by the political parties in return for public support. In a functioning democracy, citizens control and evaluate the government's policy performance by legitimate means, such as elections. The outcome of such evaluations determines the stability of politics in general and specifically the continuation of public support for governments. As Farah et al. (1979, p. 409) pointed out:

> It is the responsibility of the elected officials to translate these demands into public policy; their performance is subsequently evaluated by the constituency and if rated positively, ceteris paribus, they continue to be supported. On the other hand, when performance is viewed negatively, either the electoral option of 'voting the rascals out' or other methods are used to express dissatisfaction.

Therefore, it is the job of elected politicians to put into practice the issues raised or demanded by citizens, as they are constantly watched and evaluated on the basis of their performance. In this process government performance is the key for political stability and continuity. If governmental outcomes are viewed negatively by a majority of citizens, they will make use of legitimate control mechanisms such as the electoral process.

In Turkey, from 1983 to 2002 the performance of the majority of the governments was viewed negatively. Governments changed frequently, which led to instability and a worsening political impasse.

As the number of political parties and the possible permutations of coalition governments were limited, this constant dissatisfaction with consecutive governments' performances led to a political stalemate. It seemed all options had been tried and had failed.

The 1980s: The Özal Governments

The Motherland Party could be described as a free-market-oriented party. Its economic orientation was not very different from many Western right-of-centre parties of the 1980s (Ergüder, 1991, p. 154). Perhaps the most important aspect of the Motherland Party was its adoption of a clientelism that was radically different from its predecessors' (Güneş-Ayata, 1994, pp. 49–65).

Turgut Özal's economic policies were predominantly inspired by the thriving ideology of the 1980s, the new-right, Thatcherite or Reaganite policies. New-right neoliberal policies were implemented in the Turkish context even though industrial capitalism in Turkey was not as developed as it was in the countries where neoliberal capitalism had emerged. Therefore the restructuring programme, combined with the Motherland Party's clientelistic attitude, soon became a means for small sections of the bourgeoisie close to the government to get rich in a very short time. They used public resources while millions experienced significant reductions in their income and living standards. Özal's legacy can be summarised under four headings:

1) The economic inheritance: In this era the inequalities and income gap worsened at the expense of the majority of the people. A huge gulf emerged between rich and poor.
2) The political inheritance: The attitude of the secular, democratic and social state was undermined. Instead political Islam was allowed to flourish.
3) The social inheritance: The public sphere was closed to civil society organisations. Working-class organisations were weakened.
4) The cultural inheritance. Positive feudal values such as loyalty and trustworthiness were rejected in favour of negative feudal values such as authoritarianism and exploitation. (Kongar, 2000, pp. 331–2)

While the Motherland Party was in government, getting rich by any means and at any price was a widespread ethos that undermined the social fabric. Social and moral values were deeply shaken. The party destroyed all the values previously held sacred. As Ahmad (1993, p. 209) observes:

> Ten years ago we as a nation used to consider swindling, theft, bribery and corruption as dishonourable. Now they are normal things. The Banker Yalçın affair reflects this; Yalçın, whom we would have criticised a few years ago, has become everyone's darling today.[25]

There have been very few governments or political leaders that have had such a far-reaching impact on so many aspects of social life. Although the Motherland Party came to power with a great majority, its clientelistic attitude meant that only a small minority benefited from its years in government.

Under Motherland Party governance, the share of wages and salaries within GDP fell from 28 per cent to 14 per cent; the agricultural sector also lost half of its share of income within the GDP (see chapter 4). As income disparity increased so did the grievances of the lower classes and lower-middle classes, shopkeepers, artisans, merchants and the peasantry. By the end of the 1980s the Turkish working class was on the march to reclaim its rights lost under the 12 September military regime. Nevertheless, the biggest challenge to Özal came from the pre-1980 political leaders and their new parties, the True Path Party and the Social Democratic People's Party.

The local elections of 1989 gave the strongest indication of the decline of the Motherland Party's popularity. There were many reasons for this; most important were the continuing high rate of inflation (around 70 per cent a year), unemployment, increased inequalities, a widened income gap, Özal's dictatorial attitude, growing allegations of widespread corruption in politics involving the Özal family and the Motherland Party's upper echelons, the unresolved Kurdish problem and political violence.

In contrast, this election was a turning point for the centre-left Social Democratic People's Party. The SDPP increased its share of the vote by 4 per cent, to 28 per cent, and captured 40 out of 67 provincial centres including many metropolitan municipalities like

Istanbul, Ankara and İzmir (Mango, 1991, p. 180). It was a success for the SDPP and could have been a historic opportunity if the party had implemented sound social democratic policies, transparent, accountable management and responsive local governance. It would have won the general elections in 1991 on its own. But the SDPP made fatal mistakes, especially in Istanbul and Ankara, and lost its chance for the general election (see Kongar, 2000, p. 223). The SDPP was not only unsuccessful in governing the municipalities and providing services, but many of its mayors and senior officials in the municipalities were involved in corruption scandals. Scandals that involved several billion Turkish lira, such as that concerning the İSKİ utility company in Istanbul and ASKİ in Ankara, tarnished the SDPP's image as the party of the centre-left and caused a sharp decline in its popularity. The growing influence of Ecevit and his Democratic Left Party was another factor that led to the decline of the SDPP.

The 1990s: The Era of Great Expectations and Disappointments

Prime Minister Mesut Yılmaz called for early elections to be held on 20 October 1991, and the results were hardly surprising. Demirel's True Path Party became the largest party, capturing 27 per cent of the vote and 177 seats in parliament; the Motherland Party gained 24 per cent of the vote and 114 seats, the Social Democratic People's Party 20.8 per cent and 89 seats, the Welfare Party 16.9 per cent and 62 seats, and the Democratic Left Party 10.8 per cent of the vote and 7 seats (Gökçe, 1996, p. 43; Özbudun, 2000, p. 76). This election highlighted the increasing fragmentation of the party system to a degree where the largest party, the TPP, received only around a quarter (27 per cent) of the votes. This situation forced a coalition government of the TPP and the SDPP. It is now clear, after more than a decade, that the TPP and SDPP government was only the beginning of a long and unstable era of coalition governments in Turkey.

The Demirel/İnönü government was announced on 20 November 1991, and despite initial fears the coalition turned out to be stable and effective. This situation of course raised expectations that the government should solve the chronic problems of inflation and unemployment and find democratic solutions for the Kurdish problem. The TPP/

SDPP government delivered very little. Instead Turkey faced a worsened economic crisis and an intensified war in the south-east.

The April 1994 economic crisis, which was one of the worst in Turkish history, fuelled growing public disenchantment with the government. The government took drastic measures, known as the economic decisions of 5 April: an austere programme to control inflation, strengthen the Turkish lira and increase exports and economic growth. Instead of solving these problems, inflation jumped from 74 per cent in March 1994 to 144.3 per cent in March 1995. In terms of income inequalities, Turkey became the fifth worst nation for unequal wealth distribution behind Brazil, Colombia, Mexico and Chile (Tosun, 1999, pp. 178–9). The Turkish currency was devalued by over 50 per cent, thousands of workers were laid off, and wages and salaries were eroded by more than half in real terms. The agricultural sector also suffered huge losses under the TPP/SDPP coalition government.

As mentioned above, the TPP was popular in small towns and villages while the SDPP's policies and ideology appealed to the working class and the new migrants of the *gecekondus*.[26] But with the economic programme of 5 April the government sabotaged itself. This austerity programme hurt the working class, wage and salary earners, lower and lower-middle classes, shopkeepers, merchants and artisans who voted for the SDPP.

Conclusion

What do the experiences of these post-1983 governments tell us? It appears that they all had one thing in common: failure. They all failed to solve the country's long-term socioeconomic and political problems – high inflation, unemployment, income inequalities, over-urbanisation, housing shortages, deprivation in the *gecekondus* budget deficits, huge external and internal public debt, the Kurdish question, substandard education and health services and so on. Undoubtedly this situation caused growing public disillusionment with all centre-left and centre-right parties.

As a result of the neoliberal restructuring programmes, especially privatisation of public companies, millions lost their jobs, wage and salary earners experienced a loss of over 50 per cent in their real incomes; the agricultural sector, which employs 43 per cent of the workforce, saw its share of GDP fall from 28 per cent to 14 per cent. This meant that millions of families with small and medium-sized farms lost half their earnings. The total external debt rose to around USD 119 billion, while internal debt soared dramatically to around USD 90 billion. The level of debt reached a point where the country was desperate to find new loans to keep up the interest repayments. All the austerity programmes of the previous two decades had produced nothing but increased burdens for ordinary people.[27] Without exception, all post-1983 governments have failed to live up to their election promises and without exception each new government turned out to be worse than the previous one.

Political parties are evaluated on the basis of their policy performance in government. If citizens evaluate their performance positively they will be returned to office, but if they are evaluated negatively the public support behind them disappears. This is exactly what has happened in Turkish politics. The centre-right parties – the Motherland Party and the True Path Party – and the centre-left parties – the Social Democratic People's Party and the Republican People's Party – were elected in different elections with considerable electoral support, but none of these governments satisfied voters.

The Turkish party system jumped from cadre party to a catch-all or cartel party by bypassing the mass-party phase. Perhaps this is where most of the problems with the Turkish party system lie (Özbudun, 2000, p. 99). Due to the constant upheavals of military interventions, party closures and political system disruption since 1960, Turkish politics had become 'unrepresentative and unresponsive' (*The Economist*, 2001). In a country where party fragmentation, electoral volatility and party dealignment is common, the role of party organisations and their campaigns becomes crucial in influencing voters' electoral preferences.

It appears that Turkish parties have lost touch with the people. They have no means of establishing and maintaining direct contact with potential voters. Except for the WP, none of the Turkish parties have had robust local organisations able to carry out year-round party activities: going door-to-door to spread the party's message, ideology and policies and above all listening to people to gain feedback. Their organisations have simply not been structured as the local branches of a mass party. They have lacked staff and have had very low membership, ideological conviction or enthusiasm. Since they are not ideological parties, members have lacked any meaningful reason to join the party and become party activists. In contrast with the WP's grassroots activists, the majority of party members have appeared to act with the motives of maximising their interests, receiving some sort of benefit either material or otherwise, such as finding a job, or receiving services or favour from the party.

This chapter has shown that mainstream political parties on the centre-right and centre-left have lost their appeal. They have weakened in terms of organisational strength and electoral support. Also, there has been widespread disillusionment and decline in party identification and party attachment. But one party, the WP/VP, with its vast and very well-organised grassroots organisations, emerged as the major winner of this process. The WP/VP, by advocating social policies like *Adil Düzen* (Just Order), came to represent the majority and the most vulnerable sections of society: the lower-middle classes and lower classes. Its clean, uncorrupted image also helped enormously in increasing the party's popularity among a different section of society.

It is important to underline again that in an atmosphere of considerable volatility, fragmentation and decline in party attachment, party organisations and their campaigning assume a critical influence on the electoral outcome. When partisan attachments have weakened, it becomes easier to influence voters through campaigns at the local and national levels.

CHAPTER 3

FROM MOVEMENT TO POLITICAL PARTY: THE CHANGING CONTOURS OF POLITICAL ISLAM IN TURKEY

Introduction

The previous chapter examined developments in the Turkish party system from the early 1980s to the 2000s in line with global changes in the socioeconomic and political spheres. It examined the causes of the decline of the Turkish political party system, identified the organisational characteristics of the major parties and party policies, and discussed governmental performance. Apart from the WP/VP, Turkish parties declined during this period for various reasons. This chapter concentrates specifically on the WP/VP.

I examine the circumstances surrounding the emergence of the Islamist movement and then the process of the transformation of Islamist movements into a political party in 1970.[1] In the section that follows, I examine electoral performance, party structures and the major policies of all of the Islamist parties from the National Order Party to the WP, VP and AKP. The latest of these – the AKP – has ruled the country since 2002. The final objective of this chapter is to identify the continuities and discontinuities throughout the last three decades and articulate the rationale behind the party changes in Turkey.

The ideology of Islamism emerged in the mid-nineteenth century, and various internal and external factors paved the way for its emergence. Islamism as an ideology first appeared at the periphery of the Ottoman Empire (in India) in the mid-nineteenth century but moved to the centre from the 1870s. There were at least two axes for this movement. One consisted of the intellectuals and elite who advocated Islamism as a worldview. The second axis was the ordinary masses who – although they could not formulate an ideology – were in search of an 'Islamic Order' (Mardin, 1995, pp. 11–12). It should be remembered that besides Islamist ideology there were two other ideological groups: Westernism and Turkish Nationalism. These three groups engaged in fierce competition with one another.[2] According to the Islamists, the weakness and decline of the Ottoman Empire came about because of the abandonment of Islam. For them, the un-Islamic way of life and the absence of an Islamic mentality was the real reason for the Empire's decline. If this backwardness was the result of un-Islamic governance, the cure must be Islamisation itself. If the Ottoman Empire wanted to be developed, civilised, prosperous and glamorous it must return to Islam in its true sense (Sarıbay, 1985, p. 60). It should be noted, however, that the majority of Islamists were moderate men educated in the modern schools. They believed the goal of modernisation could be achieved without losing the religious and cultural heritage of Islam. They thought that the backwardness of Islamic societies was caused not by the religion of Islam but by deviations from it (Geyikdağı, 1984, p. 33).

Especially during the second *Meşrutiyet* (1908),[3] Islamism became one of the most widespread political ideologies (Mardin, 1995, pp. 15–16; Sarıbay, 1985, p. 61), due to Sultan Abdulhamid II's pragmatic Islamisation policies. In fact, Abdulhamid II was the first sultan to actually turn Islam into a political ideology to fight against the separatist and nationalist movements of the non-Muslim elements that engulfed the Empire from the 1870s onwards. One of the most important external factors for the politicisation of Islam was Germany's imperialist ambition in the Middle East (Sarıbay, 1985, p. 62). However,

Islamism was then a limited movement intended to save the Empire from further disintegration. Neither Abdulhamid II's Islamism nor the German pan-Islamist aspirations were sufficient to mobilise society as a whole around the Sultan and the Palace.

According to Rustow (1991, p. 10) throughout the nineteenth century Turkish political parties underwent significant changes. Not surprisingly, the major modern parties have their origins in the events that took place in the last quarter of the nineteenth century. Although the roots of the Islamic movement go back to this era, it was only in the last quarter of the twentieth century that it was transformed into a political party.

First-Generation Islamist Parties

The National Order Party

The Islamist movement was transformed into a modern political party at the beginning of the 1970s and the first Islamist party, the Milli Nizam Partisi (National Order Party; NOP), was established on 26 January 1970 (Sarıbay, 1985, p. 99). It was an organised reaction by various sections of society which, for a number of reasons, were not able to integrate fully into the new social structure shaped by advancing industrial capitalism. These groups were increasingly threatened by the advancement of Istanbul's large bourgeoisie.

By the 1960s the Turkish economy had achieved a degree of capital accumulation and sufficient integration into the world economy to facilitate the transformation from commercial to industrial capitalism. No doubt this transformation was helped by the arrival of an entrepreneurial bourgeoisie, which was created, by and large, by the state. In other words, the state acted as a 'surrogate mother' (Keyder, 1987). By the 1960s this new breed of bourgeoisie began to worry the Anatolian petit-bourgeoisie town merchants, artisans, small shopkeepers and tradesmen in the hinterland of Anatolia. In this sense the 1960s marked a new era. As Ahmad (1993, p. 376) argued:

> The Sixties marked the beginning of a process of transformation from commercial to industrial capitalism. This process required

> major reforms such as reform of agriculture and taxation, which the landowner and the privileged classes naturally resisted. It also jeopardized the livelihood of the Anatolian artisans and merchants who could not compete with large-scale industry and enterprises.

Islamist reaction to the secular establishment came as a consequence of economic modernisation and the increased division of labour. As industrial production intensified in the cities of Turkey, it began to disturb the livelihood of the traditional artisans and merchants who had been producing and trading locally in a manner unchanged for centuries. However, goods had become cheaper and available in vast quantities. Production in far-away factories, sometimes abroad, had become possible. So traditional production was unable to compete and many local producers went out of business.

Yücekök (1971, pp. 175–8) points out that Islamism emerged as the ideology of resistance, a tool of rebellion against the modernising secular establishment. Due to the rapid social change that resulted from industrialisation, mass migration and urbanisation, religious ideology emerged as an anchor for the displaced and distressed migrant masses. In circumstances where rapid social change occurs, religious values and networks offer a sense of continuity and a communal identity that had been lost, as well as a sanctuary from uncertainties, risks, threats and anxieties brought about by modernisation.

Unsurprisingly, the reaction to this assertive industrial capitalism was strongest in the less developed regions. Election results in the 1970s had confirmed that the National Order Party was very popular in the poorest regions and districts.[4] It was a decisive moment in Turkish electoral history.

The National Salvation Party (1970–80)

The emergence of the Milli Selamet Partise (National Salvation Party; NSP) can be viewed as the fragmentation and polarisation of the Turkish bourgeoisie according to economic interests (Sarıbay, 1985, p. 99). By the 1960s, capitalist development had brought two sections of the bourgeoisie to a head-to-head collision. The Anatolian 'petit bourgeoisie' was united under the banner of Islam against the advancing 'grande bourgeoisie'. In addition to the clash of interests, the process of modernisation sparked a popular reaction, which turned into a fully fledged Islamist movement in the 1960s.

With the advancement of capitalism, large Turkish businesses developed ties with the Western world, often becoming the local subsidiaries of Western companies. This development simultaneously squeezed out the small merchants, traditional artisans, small tradesmen and shopkeepers. Necmettin Erbakan, the founder of the National Order Party, expressed the grievances of the small Anatolian entrepreneurs thus:

> The economic mechanism has been working to the advantage of the big city traders. The Anatolian tradesmen feel like orphans. Three to four large city traders have taken the lion's share of the import quotas ... It is the people of Anatolia who put the money into the bank accounts but this money is being given to big city traders as credit ... The chambers of commerce have become the vehicle of a small *comprador* [grand-mason] group [my translation]. (Quoted in Sarıbay, 1985, pp. 98–9)[5]

Erbakan was complaining about the unequal relations brought about by an economic mechanism that was dominated by big city traders. The Anatolian petit bourgeoisie became increasingly vulnerable to modern industrial production, industrial capitalism and increased capital accumulation from the early 1960s. Threatened by the big industrial capitalists, the Anatolian bourgeoisie needed to organise around a political party to protect its very existence, and the National Order Party was the product of this process.

However, the social base of both the NOP and the NSP was not limited to the petit bourgeoisie. It also included support from some traditionally religious sections of society, the old *ulema* (scholars), small farmers, and migrant workers who had not integrated into the urban life of the big cities.[6]

The establishment of the NOP cannot be attributed only to capitalist development. Historical, cultural and external factors were also very significant. It is well known that Islam played a major role in Ottoman times and in this context religion, in particular, 'has a unifying appeal for mass political mobilisation' (Toprak, 1987, p. 219). In many developing countries, religion is the often only source of collective identity.[7] Traditionally the Turkish Islamic movement developed parallel to *tarikat* (brotherhoods) organisations (Şaylan, 1992, p. 154). For instance, M. Zahid Kotku, the leader of the very influential İskender Paşa Dergahı – one of the leading brotherhoods in Turkey – actively encouraged and supported the establishment of the NOP. Most members of the Nurcu brotherhood joined the NOP in the early days of its foundation.[8, 9]

Foreign governments also used Islam for their own strategic interests. The 'Green Belt' strategy was developed by strategists like Brzezinski in the US to stop the expansion of the USSR in the Middle East and South Asia in the 1950s and 1960s. The project was based on the encirclement of the Soviet Union with a 'Green Belt' of Islam in the form of countries such as Iran, Iraq, Pakistan, Afghanistan and Turkey.[10] There was a parallel development to this project. The governments of various parties openly or discreetly encouraged, supported or directly organised religious organisations such as the Association to Combat Communism as early as 1962 and presented Islam as the antidote to communism.

The Saudi Arabian connection was crucial in providing resources for religious organisations to finance their various activities throughout the country (Şaylan, 1992, p. 237). Ironically this connection was strengthened after the military intervention in 1980. It developed to such an extent that the Saudis were allowed to pay the salaries of the Turkish *İmam*s (priests) in Western European countries.[11] Nevertheless, it was internal conditions that led to the emergence and rise of political Islam in Turkey. One of these internal factors was the use of religion as a counter-force against an imagined communist threat in the political arena until the late 1980s. This process started in 1947 with the Republican People's Party's seventh congress, through Democratic Party governments from 1950 to 1960, and continued with the 1972 military ultimatum and military coup of 12 September 1980. In fact, the last military government had employed the most enduring policy, with the help of right-wing intellectuals and specifically the Aydınlar Ocağı (Club of Intellectuals). They developed a new official ideology called *Türk İslam Sentezi* (Turkish–Islamic synthesis) based on Islam and Turkish nationalism.[12]

Ideology and Party Policies of the NOP/NSP

Ideology as an institution of superstructure reflects the socioeconomic conditions in a society at a given time. The NOP was undoubtedly in favour of the re-Islamisation of Turkish social life (Mardin, 1991, p. 136). In its foundation manifesto, the decline of the Ottoman Empire was blamed for the abandonment of religious and national values, local traditions, customs and Islamic ethics that once made the Empire a great civilisation. To reverse this decline and make Turkey once more a proud, world-class nation, what was needed was the protection of Islamic identity and ethics: loyalty to Islamic and national values and material and spiritual development supported by the law and democratic order (Sarıbay, 1985, p. 101).

Shortly after the closure of the NOP in 1972 the party's cadres established the National Salvation Party. The ideology of the NSP was a continuation of a debate over Islam and the West which was at least a century old (Toprak, 1987, p. 227). Like the NOP, the NSP stressed that the decline of the Ottoman Empire had been caused by the abandonment of Islamic civilisation in favour of Western civilisation. It was argued that:

> Our nation that once was one of the greatest in history that founded a model civilization, enlightened humanity and governed the world was also ahead of the West in terms of material conditions. It was far ahead in the areas of science, technology, natural sciences, teaching and training. Especially our ethical-moral superiority, which was the keystone of the basis of all of our success ... They who wanted to divert our nation from its own consciousness and erode its ethical and moral practices to destroy our nation have been successfully doing it from within for a few centuries. [author's translation][13]

The NSP adopted an exclusive *Milli Görüş* (National View) ideology, a reaction by the small Anatolian bourgeoisie against capitalist developments in the 1960s. This ideology was also a reaction to the process of Turkish modernisation and its implications in social and political life. The NSP, like its predecessor, incorporated the two important ideological components of industrialisation and Islamisation, which are the dimensions of the National View that have changed least since the 1970s. The first chairman of the NSP, Süleyman Arif Emre, said of the movement:

> Our constitution gives the responsibility to the state to prepare the conditions in which every individual would develop himself or herself materially and spiritually. Our party puts this principle at the centre, and aims to plan the material and spiritual developments evenly. The leftist and liberal ideologies that give first priority to material development by neglecting the spiritual side are far from fulfilling the nation's needs. [author's translation][14]

It seems the National View expressed a yearning for a balance between the material and spiritual worlds. What constituted this balance was controversial, however. The advocates of the National View argued that since the 1920s the ruling elite had abandoned national and sacred values in favour of Western values. Material and economic development and modernisation became the only goals. What they were opposing was the abandonment or neglect of spiritual development, believing that if someone is overly concerned with the materialistic aspects of life he will neglect his duties towards God. This view can be interpreted from another perspective as well. The process of modernisation, especially in the rapidly expanding cities, brings confusion and stress.[15]

Main Policies of the Islamist Parties

In its definition of secularisation, the National View used the official definition, which was misunderstood in the first place. So secularism is defined as 'the dictatorship of unbelievers over believers' (Sarıbay, 1985, p. 118). Islamists have always condemned the West for its imperialist attitudes towards the Ottoman Empire. Inescapably, the NSP's foreign policies also reflected its view on past relations between the Empire and Western Europe. In its programme, the NSP also blamed the West for causing the collapse of the Ottoman Empire and equally opposed Turkey's close relations with Europe since the establishment of the republic in 1923.

The European Economic Community (EEC) was seen as an extension of the Western imperialism that caused the collapse of the Ottoman Empire. As far as the NSP was concerned, the EEC was formed by Zionist circles with large amounts of capital with the goal of profiting from the community. The NSP declared:

> [The EEC] has aims and activities that are beyond economic goals. For example it requires that all member states must allow foreigners to purchase land. It will allow those Zionists all over the world to buy much land from Turkey for their malign plan. It will end up making Turkey a sub-state of Israel. Zionists and the West want Turkey to join the EEC for their imperialist aims.[16]

In terms of party membership the NOP and NSP had a very restrictive attitude. According to the NOP's constitution, there were a set of requirements for membership. Aspiring members must be Turkish citizens, should not be excluded from politics, must be over 18 years old and must not be Masons. Applicants for membership should indicate that they genuinely accepted party principles, were respectful of spiritual values and had a good reputation.

The party charter allowed those who did not regularly pray (*namaz*) or fast, but they could not fill any administrative positions (Yalçın, 1999, p. 51). There was another restriction that was not written in the party's charter: the anti-communist stand. The NOP's main aim was the Islamisation of cultural and political life in Turkey.

When the NSP closed down because of its 'anti-secular' activities, the WP was founded shortly afterwards in 1972. The same trend continued with the establishment of Refah, the WP, when the NSP was closed, and later after Refah's closure in 1998 the Fazilet Party, the VP.

The Welfare Party, 1983–98

When the military government allowed the establishment of new political parties, the old cadres of the NSP founded the Refah Partisi

(Welfare Party) under the leadership of Ali Turkmen, a lawyer who had served as advocate, Erbakan, and 33 founding members in 1983. Due to Erbakan's prison sentence and ten-year prohibition from politics, Ali Turkmen a close aide of Erbakan, became its first leader. The WP had to find survival strategies under the military's scrutiny. It could not say it was a totally new party, but if it openly admitted it was a continuation of the NSP this could have jeopardised its survival. So the WP highlighted slogans such as *Milli Görüş* (National View) and *Milli Şuur* (National Consciousness). These terms sent a message that it was continuing in the tradition of the NOP and NSP (Çakır, 1994, p. 24).

The Turkish constitution (article 163) bans any political party from 'exploiting' religion for political purposes and prohibits any defunct party from reopening either with the same name or under a different name. In reality it is almost impossible to decide whether or not a new political party is a continuation of a former party that has been wound up. The choice of the name 'Refah' for the new party – meaning 'welfare' or 'prosperity' – signalled the continuity of the NOP and NSP in this new party. The words 'welfare', and later on 'virtue', were taken from the *Milli Görüş* (National View) manifesto. By choosing these words the cadres wanted to show that traditional virtues and the traditional values of the old party were being carried on by the new party.

The WP transformed the traditional norms and institutions with its modernist and secular characteristics. This major change was perhaps due to the development of capitalism and the expansion of modern and secular schooling across the country, contributing to the emergence of a new generation of Islamist elites.

In terms of organisational characteristics, ideology, specific party policies and the social bases of its support, the WP was different from its predecessors as the only modern mass political party. It had a nationwide, effective party organisation with a large, highly committed and active party membership.[17]

The Programme and Basic Principles of the WP

At the beginning of its programme the WP explicitly declared its loyalty to the republic, democracy, constitution and Atatürk's principles.[18] The main goal of the party was to elevate the nation above the level of contemporary civilisations. According to the party's 1985 manifesto:

> In order to do so: i) we will make sure that every corner of our country is developed and fully built. ii) cultural and spiritual development will be encouraged. iii) all our national characters and features will be in perspective while these developments take place.[19]

Among its main goals the WP made connections, though implicit, with its past – especially with the ideology of the National View. There were, however, some efforts made to distance themselves from the traditional National View such as putting democratisation and freedom of thought and expression high on the programme:

> Our party will strive to establish democracy in its true sense and create a full national representation. We oppose any idea and action that obstructs the normal function of the governance of the republic. Our party believes in the freedom of thought, expression and conscience. We consider any attempt to repress these rights as primitive and against secularism.[20]

Despite the fact that the WP tried to distance itself from its past, at the core of its ideology was the traditional ideology of the National View. The reason for this was that the party elite 'inner circle', both the traditionalist so-called *Aksaçlılar* (elders) and *Yenilikçiler* (progressives), came from the Milli Görüş Teskilati (National View Organisation) which many call the party academy. It was the only ideology to which they were strongly attached. The National View and the Just Order were indispensable concepts for the WP, and their centrality as its core ideology was admitted openly in a 1991 election manifesto.[21] Nevertheless, the rhetoric of the traditional National View did not prevent the WP from grasping social and economic changes and developing its strategy and tactics to win the sympathy of the wider electorate.

At its fourth congress on 10 October 1994, Erbakan, the leader of the WP, announced the agenda of the WP government: (1) clean government; (2) a return to the *Milli Görüş* (3) spiritual development; (4) establishment of the Just Order, which included a 'just economic order' and real pluralist democracy; (5) decentralisation and strengthening of local government; (6) an end to the state's economic interventions and activities; (7) reforms in security; (8) reforms in the judiciary and legal system; and (9) preventing the deterioration of the natural environmental balance (Çakır, 1994, p. 195).

The Unstoppable Rise of the WP

The increasing public support manifested itself in the local elections on 26 March 1989 in which the WP received 9.8 per cent of the votes (Soner, 1999, p. 193). The following general election on 20 October 1991 was a turning point for the WP. This time its support rose from 9 to 16.2 per cent and, for the first time since the military coup of 1980, the party won 62 seats in parliament.[22]

One of the reasons for the WP's election success was the change of the traditional propaganda style adopted during election campaigning. The WP had one of the best organised grassroots organisations.[23] From the early 1990s the WP added two new dynamic forces into this grassroots army. The active participation of women and youth in election campaigning made an extraordinary contribution to the electoral success of the WP (see Ayata, 1997, p. 52). The WP's grassroots organisations were very adept at recruiting new members and convincing potential voters. With this new era women members were organised under the so-called Hanım Komisyonları (Ladies' Committees). They persistently and skilfully toured neighbourhoods and did building-by-building, door-by-door vote canvassing. This method proved very successful for several reasons.

Before the 1991 general elections, the WP had changed its traditional election campaign style. For example, they placed unveiled women on propaganda posters. The candidates couched their messages in modern terms. In this election, the WP used issues and slogans for the first time that the left had been using for a long time. In their election posters, in addition to the modern-looking women, portraits of workers struggling for rights, sex workers, intellectuals opposed to oppression and torture, and environmental activists frequently appeared. It was as if the traditional religious party had gone and in its place a modern party had emerged.

The Social Bases of the WP: Changes and Continuities

There have been continuities in terms of the regional bases of the pro-Islamic parties the NOP, NSP, WP and VP. According to statistical data collected since the early 1970s, the Islamist parties had been very popular in the less developed regions of Central Anatolia, East, South East and Northern Black Sea regions.[24] The WP, especially in its early years, continued to have electoral support from these less developed regions.

The election results showed that traditional artisans, merchants, tradesmen and shopkeepers, plus traditionally religious sections of society, reminiscent of the Ottoman clerical class, the mosque community, some religious brotherhoods and Sufi orders, supported the NOP and NSP. However, during the 1990s, due to rapid urbanisation and migration, its support base changed. The urban poor from the growing *gecekondu*s also started to support the WP.

It would not be wrong to argue that among the Turkish political parties it was the WP's cadres who correctly read the swiftly changing needs of Turkish society in the early 1990s. As a result of the economic restructuring programmes, rural migration accelerated and the population balance shifted from rural to urban. This rapid mass migration soon exhausted industry and formal sector capacity. This unabsorbed population contributed to the growth of *gecekondu*s encircling all of the big cities where, in effect, more than half of the urban population live.

It was the WP who saw the problem and developed policies and a political rhetoric that addressed the social, cultural and economic problems of the *gecekondu* masses. It gave the new migrants an identity, and an avenue through which they could participate in politics; they could air their opinions and express their grievances against the establishment. In the meantime the left responded too slowly to the changes and needs of the masses. In this respect the WP's economic programme, the so-called Just Order, appealed to the urban poor, especially the *gecekondu* population.

The WP's support has shifted from traditional, rural bases to more modern, dynamic forces in the cities. Çakır observed that before the 1991 general elections the WP's meetings were thronged with thousands of young people wearing rubber boots and dirty jeans, long haired, looking like spectators at a local football match with plastic ribbons around their necks and arms. The Islamist writer Mehmet Metiner described the WP's election strategy in Istanbul as the 'siege of Istanbul' by the rural poor (1994, p. 80). The WP was no longer a party that limited itself to traditional, humble sections of society.

The WP's electoral appeal for support was wide-ranging. It included retired military officers, ex-models and unveiled, successful women dressed in modern clothes, such as the dentist Filiz Ergün, as well as members of the minority Alevi sect (see Çalışlar, 1995, pp. 58–60). The WP was targeting the non-religious, secular sections of society in a bid to increase its share of the vote.

The Moment of Change: From Cadre Party to Mass Party

Katz and Mair (1995, pp. 2–28) identify four models of party: elite (cadre), mass, catch-all and cartel parties. What category do most of the Turkish political parties fall into? How can we classify them by using this format? According to Özbudun (2000, p. 86), 'Most Turkish parties combine some characteristics of cadre and catchall parties, with some elements of cartel parties'. With the exception of the WP, Turkish parties have never gone through a mass-party phase. 'Organizationally, the WP is the only Turkish party that comes close to the model of a mass party, or a party of social integration.' Nevertheless, according to Özbudun the WP lacked intra-party democracy (ibid., p. 92). After the mid-1990s, the WP attained political legitimacy and, in turn, adopted the procedural rules of democracy – that is, those designating the constitutional means of competing for and holding political office. The party also adopted an increasingly secular platform and political strategies aimed at expanding its political base of support (Heper, 1997, p. 37). But the party still did not develop intra-party democracy.

Compared to its predecessors, the WP made great efforts to transform itself from an ideological cadre party, as it was in the 1970s and 1980s, to a mass party from the early 1990s until its closure. The leadership of the WP had to make a historical but pragmatic decision, knowing very well there was no chance of acquiring power with electoral support of between 8 and 12 per cent, which came from brotherhoods. For this reason the leadership preferred to direct a mass party with a religious flavour (Kışlalı, 1995, p. 186).

The struggle for change within the WP entered a new phase with its fourth congress. The WP completed its restoration and decided whether it was going to continue to be an extension of the NSP or become a party in its own right – a party for the 1990s. It was entering a new period where its theory and practices were distinct from the NSP's (Şen, 1995, p. 115). The fourth congress was a sign of its growing confidence. The leadership felt that the WP had proven itself with the local election victory in 1994. They decided to extend this tactic to the general elections in a bid for national power. For that reason Erbakan said: 'From now until the day that the WP come to power we call this "the period of taking power"' (quoted in Şen, 1995, p. 115). To do that, the WP's leadership needed to broaden its appeal.

The Major Policies

One of the best indicators of a party's characteristics is its membership policy. As Cord et al. (1974, p. 305) point out, political parties are either 'open' or 'closed' in their membership requirements. With the WP, the old NSP's perception of membership had changed from a truly 'closed' elitist organisation to an 'open' party. The stringent membership policies had changed. Members were not expected to be devoted Muslims with an Islamic lifestyle who prayed five times a day, non-smokers and abstainers from alcohol with a reference from a religious brotherhood or Sufi order. As one of my informants put it, 'the party used to be like a small community, a family business, but with the Refah it became like a company opened up to the market, to everyone'.[25] They were primarily expected not to be good Muslims but to develop a party *identity* (Welfare). This identity was a secularist one with an Islamic make-up (Çakır, 1994, p. 59).

In the policy sphere *Adil Düzen* was the crowning glory of the WP. Many mistakenly interpreted this Just Order as merely economic policies but it was part of an important social project that included social and political dimensions. Although the *Adil Düzen* has been much discussed and written about, it has never been clear what it really was. According to the Islamist writer Akgül (1997a, p. 38) the Just Order was a project prepared by an elite group of Turkish and foreign experts. Its aim was to achieve a 'social balance' in the image of the 'natural balance' and unite Islam with humanity.

> Under the Just Order all people from different religions, ethnic groups and social classes will live in peace and harmony. Every fundamental right and freedom will be granted and protected for all. The Just Order is an original Islamic, scientific and humanistic project. (ibid., p. 42)

Akgül went on to say that there would be four different but coherent and interconnected orders within the state. These were: (1) Just Economic Order; (2) Just Political Order; (3) Just Scientific Order; and (4) Just Moral Order (ibid., pp. 43–4).

Erbakan described the global economic system as a 'system of slavery'. This system, he claimed,

> has been oppressing millions of people under economic hardship, poverty, unemployment and underdevelopment. This system has been robbing the rights and incomes of these millions of people and transferring them to a small minority group of Imperialists, world Zionists and their collaborators. As a result, the majority gets poorer while a small minority becomes richer and richer. This situation has been causing social unrest in those countries and threatens security and peace in the world.[26]

Erbakan defined five *microbes* (germs) in this slavery system as responsible for the present situation. These were interest, unjust tax, the mint, exchange and credit (Erbakan, 1991, pp. 11–12, quoted in Çakır 1994, pp. 133–4). For him the Just Order was a 'complete and eclectic' system. He said that it contained useful elements of communism and capitalism but had no place for negative aspects of either system (ibid., p. 17). But the meaning and content of the Just Order has never been fully explained.

According to the WP, the Turkish economy was dependent on the US and those institutions controlled by the US, such as the IMF and World Bank. The profit acquired from Turkey through these institutions was allegedly transferred to the World Zionists (Çakır, 1994, p. 161).[27]

Erbakan (ibid.) argued the following in a pamphlet in 1993 called 'Turkey's Problems and Solutions':

> In this changing world all humanity is searching for an order that will bring peace and happiness all over the world. The order that has been sought is the Just Order, which the WP and the *Milli Görüş* (National View) have been insisting on. Therefore now Turkey's responsibility is to establish the Just Order as a good example.

In the same pamphlet Erbakan, after criticising Turkey's close ties with the West, outlined a five-step plan to improve relations with Islamic countries. These were the establishment of:

1) a Muslim Countries' United Nations (or Islamic UN)
2) a joint Muslim Military Force (Islamic NATO)
3) a Union and Organisation of the Muslim Countries Common Economic Market (Islamic EEC)
4) a common currency of the Muslim Countries (Islamic euro)
5) an Organisation of the Muslim Countries Cultural Relations (Islamic UNESCO/ ERASMUS). (ibid., pp. 161–2)

One can see that Erbakan was planning a series of counter-measures against what he perceived as Western domination. Those counter-measures were to create a community of united Muslim countries. I will not discuss the nature and relevance of these plans, but they elucidate the WP's ideal foreign policy. Although the party softened its rhetoric against Zionism and Western imperialism, it did oppose Turkey's NATO membership and its application for full membership of the EU. It fiercely criticised the Customs Union and declared that it would renegotiate its terms and conditions.

Perhaps the most important change in the WP's programme was the definition of secularism. It was defined for the first time as follows: 'Secularism is not the enemy of religion; on the contrary it is a principle developed to safeguard the freedom of religion and conscience against any fraudulent attempts' (Çakır, 1994, p. 37; see also Soner, 1999, p. 187).

However, reality is often different from theory. It has been widely discussed whether the WP was a secularist or an Islamist fundamentalist party. Opinions are divided, with some saying the WP was a secular organisation, putting the party before Islam. They argue that the WP actually brought its less secular followers into the modern and secular world. Çakır argues that although the WP looked like a religious organisation externally, its organisational attitude can be classified as a secular one. The WP aimed to make its members identify first and foremost as *Refahli* ('people of the WP'). In effect, the identity of the WP was that every member acquired a secular identity with an Islamic veneer (Çakır, 1994, pp. 51–9).

There are, of course, opposing opinions on this matter. Opponents argue that whatever the WP said about their loyalty to the principle of secularism, they were lying. Once the WP came to power, they believed it would abandon secularism and make Turkey a theocracy like Iran, ruled by Sharia law.

The Virtue Party, 1997–2001

The social origins of the Turkish political parties go back to the late years of the Ottoman Empire, and it seems that since then socio-cultural cleavages have played a very important role in terms of party preference and electoral behaviour (Kalaycıoğlu, 1998, p. 4). The relations between different social classes are not as clear-cut as one might expect; they overlap, and this complicates the analysis of political life. Until the late 1960s Turkish politics revolved by and large around the axis of statist-elitist versus traditional-religious and liberals. The divide between these two cultural camps did not disappear with the collapse of the Ottoman Empire but continued for more than 70 years to dominate the Turkish polity (Sarıbay, 1991, p. 122). The Turkish political system is 'composed of a coherent and organised "state" elite that constitutes the centre, and pitted against it persists a culturally heterogeneous, complex, and even hostile periphery' (Kalaycıoğlu, 1994, p. 403).[28] Even today the cleavage of secularist (laicist) vs religious-traditionalist continues to be one of the most influential variables that determines party preferences and electoral outcomes in Turkish politics.

However, from the late 1960s onwards some new political issues, such as the emergence of class politics, ethnicity and gender, were added to the political equation that determines party preferences and electoral behaviour (see Kalaycıoğlu, 1998, pp. 3–7).

The Virtue Party was founded as the successor of the WP in 1997 by a group of Erbakan's close aides. It had continuities and discontinuities with its predecessor. Where did the VP stand on the political spectrum? To answer this question I asked my informants: how would you place the VP on the left–right scale?

Table 3.1 Respondents' answers to the question 'How would you place the VP on the left–right scale?'

	No. of people	%
Centre-right party	14	33.33
Islamic party/Party of believers	13	30.95
A mass party which is neither on the left nor on the right	10	23.80
Right-wing party	3	7.14
Conservative-right party	2	4.76
Total	42	100

Source: Fieldwork data from Ankara.

As mentioned above, the VP was the continuation of its predecessor pro-Islamic parties. Yet the changes that came with the VP are apparent and do not leave much space for speculation.

Table 3.1 shows that the VP moved from the religious-extremist right to a centre-right position. My empirical findings seem to confirm this observation. According to one-third (33.33 per cent) of my informants, the VP was a centre-right party. The party leadership took this line and made every effort to move the party towards the centre-right. However, as my finding suggest, this policy of moving to the centre was not accepted by all of the party activists, because a substantial proportion of them viewed the VP as an Islamic party. Around one-third (30.95 per cent) of my informants placed the VP towards the far-right end of the left–right scale; as an Islamic party or, as some of them put it, 'the party of believers'. The third-largest bloc, which consists of around one-quarter (23.80 per cent), viewed the VP as a mass party that was neither on the left nor on the right, while 7.14 per cent saw it as a right-wing party and 4.76 per cent as a conservative right party.

This result is surprising in one sense, because it seems the party had split into three large blocs: one representing the centre-right, the second the religious fundamentalist or Islamist right and the third a mass party neither on the left or the right. But in another sense it confirms the fault line that existed between the moderates or so-called 'progressives' or 'youngsters' led by Recep Tayyip Erdoğan (ex-mayor of Istanbul) and the 'elders' or 'grey-haired' traditionalists led by Erbakan. The third bloc, however, seems difficult to place in context: for some of the respondents in this group the VP was neither on the left nor on the right. For some others the VP was a true mass party that was beyond the old left–right divide. The majority in this group were members who joined the VP for non-religious and non-ideological reasons. However, at the ideological level this third group did not seem to be unified or homogeneous.

In fact, the VP's first congress on 15 May 2000 confirmed this when two groups of centre-right delegates and Islamists clashed fiercely over the control of the party organisations and positions. The third group did not have a significant presence at the congress.

The full impact and consequences of this transition process, which started with the closure of the WP and the founding of the VP in its place, will be discussed later, but as one would expect the closure of the WP had a negative effect on the election results of the new VP. The WP enjoyed 21.4 per cent of the total vote and 158 seats in parliament. It had become the largest party in parliament. However, the VP suffered a 6 per cent loss of support in the 18 April 1999 general elections; it received 15.0 per cent of the vote and 105 seats in parliament.[29] Nevertheless, it did rather well in the simultaneous local elections.[30]

The final split emerged when the VP closed down in 2001. The party divided in the middle and became two different parties: the AKP under the leadership of Recep Tayyip Erdoğan representing the centre-right ideology, and the Saadet Partisi (Felicity Party) representing the traditionalist line of Erbakan's Islamic ideology.

The Aims of the Party

In its constitution the main principles and goals of the Virtue Party were declared as being to 'bring peace, freedom, justice, and respect for the nation. To this end, we act with respect to the charter of universal human rights and basic human rights.'[31] In his opening speech of the meeting, the so-called First Step, the VP's leader, Recai Kutan (1998a, p. 3),[32] explained his party's five main views and aims:

1) democracy
2) human rights
3) freedom
4) rule of law
5) development and contemporariness

> When we have acquired these five conditions, there will be peace and safety, freedom, justice welfare, prosperity and respectability.

The party was founded in an atmosphere of political turmoil. During the 28 February 1997 process, the military had been determined to punish the WP. Under these conditions the VP had to be extremely careful not to attract the attention of the military or the courts. In its programme the VP gave priority to politics and the state. It criticised the present condition of Turkish politics, arguing that politicians had lost their credibility, causing people to shy away from politics (Kutan, 1998b, p. 6). In this rapidly changing world, Turkey increasingly faced both internal and external changes in the economic, social, political, scientific and cultural spheres (ibid., p. 7).

The party stated that, in its view, politics and government were not there to oppress people or ignore the demands for change, but to act on these demands and criticisms by bringing about peace and development. It claimed that its central aim was to elevate these demands to the level of political representation to transform them into the most important ingredient of democratic government and economic development.

It is obvious that the VP presented very liberal policies, compromising to a far greater extent than the WP.[33] Following the postmodern coup of 28 February 1997, political Islam had been seeking new means and avenues to survive.[34] Perhaps the clearest sign of the change in strategy was the defection to the VP of some MPs from nationalist-conservative parties, and in some cases liberal politicians such as Nevzat Yalçıntaş, Ali Coşkun, Abdülkadir Aksu, Cemil Çiçek and Nazlı Ilıcak. All of them are well-known, prominent political figures in Turkey. Their joining the VP was a clear sign that the VP had no interest in reviving the WP, but rather had departed from the traditional NOP/NSP/WP line altogether.[35] As one would expect, there were reactions against all these changes in strategy. Some traditionalist, conservative elements tried to limit the changes but the newcomers knew what was waiting for them, and after negotiating with Erbakan they secured their places. What Özbudun (2000) called the WP/VP's 'pragmatist tradition' always helped in its survival.

The Major Policies: Change and Continuity

In the VP's election manifesto, secularisation was described as:

> one's freedom to choose whatever belief one wants. It means the state is a referee not a player. It cannot be seen as a means of

> pushing aside any sort of religious expression in society and it cannot deny religious and moral freedoms. Otherwise this institution of solution will itself become a problem. Religion is not something that you could remove from inside the people and throw away. (Günışığında Türkiye, 1999, pp. 38–9)

This statement makes it clear that the party's attitude towards secularisation had become more positive. The NOP and NSP saw secularism as the oppression of religion and of believers by atheists. The VP no longer held the traditional National View. The VP was, however, acknowledging that there were complaints and grievances over this issue. The VP's leadership rightly complained that the concept of secularisation had been politicised and needed to be redefined according to its original meaning. Kutan argued that: 'We have to define secularisation according to the democratic characters of these societies from where the concept came' (1998a, p. 23). The traditional National View attitude to secularisation was negative and unsophisticated. It was not so much debated as a concept but rather rejected outright.

The way in which the VP brought the topic of secularisation into the public debate indicates a new approach, presumably the result of their new programme focused on democracy, human rights, freedom, rule of law and development.

The VP made an even more dramatic change when it came to the traditional National View's so-called Just Economic Order (JEO). The JEO confused many people, for good reason. It offered policies that attracted the lower-middle and lower classes but it was, in reality, the free-market economy with a few added slogans. The VP rightly abandoned the previous watered-down version of the free-market economy and became wholehearted supporters of it, declaring themselves in favour of fast-track privatisation, maintaining all ties with foreign banking and financial institutions, and so on. The party's basic economic policies are summarised as follows:

- The economy must be in accordance with the free-market economy, private ownership and private entrepreneurship.

- An economic strategy that is open, highly competitive and sustainable must be developed (Kutan, 1998b, p. 56).
- The state must be withdrawn from the economy to undertake its primary duties.
- Healthy relationships must be established with the IMF and the World Bank (ibid., pp. 36–7).

With this new era the VP dropped its opposition to Turkey's integration into the world economy. Thus the VP needed to distance itself from the *Adil Düzen* project. Ali Coşkun, the VP's deputy chairman responsible for economic issues, pointed out that the programme of Just Order was an empty concept unsuitable for addressing Turkey's problems. For that reason, there was no trace of it in the VP's programme (Çakır, 1998a).

As will be discussed in chapter 4, since the 1980s Turkey's economy has been through several major economic crises, including long-term high inflation, a high unemployment rate, high rates of internal and external debt and extensive budget deficits. Neoliberal economic policies had led a major restructuring process that had not yielded any benefit for millions of people across the country. On the contrary, it had caused a significant drop in the real earnings of salary and wage earners. The impact of the neoliberal policies on the agricultural sector was even worse, triggering what I call 'the second phase of rapid urbanisation', starting from the early 1980s.

The WP's Just Order and its importance can only be appreciated against this background. First of all, the Just Order offered an alternative to the neoliberal restructuring policies that had been hitting the working classes so hard. It offered a kind of 'third way' solution to the problems and ills of neoliberalism. In fact, it was not limited to the economic policies of the WP, but promised a just social, political, legal and moral order too. It promised something akin to a regime change based on a sort of religiously inspired quasi-egalitarianism. Throughout the 1990s the party's main slogan was *Adil Düzen Gelecek Zulüm Bitecek!* ('Just order will prevail, oppression/injustice will perish!'). Although the project of Just Order was neither coherently developed nor well articulated to avert potential criticism, it did attract massive attention from the lower-middle and lower classes across the country.

Studies have shown that Just Order did indeed contribute to the electoral success of the WP in the local (1994) and general (1995) elections. A 1996 survey found that around 13.4 per cent of those who voted for the WP did so because of the WP's promise of Just Order (see Özbudun, 2000, p. 90). Thus the VP's abandonment of the Just Order policy risked alienating these voters, particularly as the VP did not come up with an alternative economic policy and instead fully endorsed the neoliberal policies of the market economy, as explained above. As things stood then, the VP might not have been able to appeal to the urban poor as the WP had in the 1990s. However, the economic issues were not the only questions of importance for voters.

In terms of membership, the VP worked very hard to acquire new members. The WP had over four million members and the VP aimed to reach at least that figure. But according to Kutan (1998a, p. 2) the VP had just 310,000 members in May 1998.

Based on information provided by administrators of the Welfare Party which subsequently became the Virtue Party prior to the elections of 18 April 1999, I estimate that membership stood at around one and half million at that time.

When I asked when members had joined the VP, I found that the majority (85 per cent) had been members almost from the start (the VP was founded in 1997). As Table 3.2 shows, more than a quarter (27 per cent) declared they had been members of one of the pro-Islamist parties for at least 19 years – indicating the NSP period – while 59 per cent had been members for between three and 17 years – indicating the WP period – and only 15 per cent had joined the VP since 1997.

The most striking departure from the party's traditional line came with its policies on external relations. The VP dropped almost every objection that the National View had maintained since the early 1970s. After assessing the New World Order and the process of globalisation, the VP laid down its basic principles on foreign policies as follows:

Table 3.2 Respondents' answers to the question 'When did you become a member of the VP?'

Years' membership at time of survey	Years of joining	Parties name during period	No. of people	%	Cumulative
0–2	1999–97	The Virtue Party	6	14.63	14.63
3–7	1996–92	The Welfare Party	7	17.07	
8–12	1991–87		10	24.39	
13–17	1986–83		7	17.07	58.53
19–23	1980–77	The NOP / NSP	0	0	
24+	1976–70		11	26.82	26.82
Total			41		100

Source: Fieldwork data from Ankara.

- Our first priority is to develop good relations in our region with our neighbours. Without having good relationships no country can prosper.
- Among our priorities is to increase the economic, cultural and political relations with our neighbours, and develop regional integration.
- Due to its history and geographic position Turkey cannot stay away from Europe. In this respect the Customs Union needs to be rearranged in line with our political interests.
- We believe Turkey's role within NATO should continue.
- We support the full membership of Turkey into the EU.
- Our long-term friendship with the USA will continue. In addition to its Atlantic and European dimension, Turkey should develop its relations in North Africa, South Asia, East Asia, the Balkans and the Caucasus. To this end any kind of relationship with the Central Asian republics will be developed. (Kutan, 1998b, pp. 43–7).

Table 3.3 Comparing Turkish Islamist parties, 1970–2001

	The NOP/NSP	The Welfare Party	The Virtue Party
Party characteristics	Cadre party. Anti-system.	From cadre to mass party Anti-system rhetoric dominant.	Mass party.
Membership	Restricted. Members must be good Muslims. Prayers practised regularly. No alcohol, no smoking.	Open, not so stringent. Being good Muslims preferred but not essential. Gave the identity of WP to members.	Open to everyone. No specific requirements. Religious aspects trimmed off. Smoking is allowed in party buildings.
Support base	From traditional, religious segments. Small towns and rural areas.	Much broader support bases. Shift from rural to urban. Lower-middle and lower classes. *Gecekondu* poor.	Same as the WP's support base.
Attitudes towards secularisation	Dictatorship of unbelievers over believers. It is damaging social structure.	Not enemy of religion but the concept will be changed. Obstacle to democracy.	Freedom of belief but Anglo-Saxon version preferred.

Economic policies	State run. Usury prohibited. High priority given to economic modernisation and industrialisation.	*Adil Düzen* (Just Order). Social democratic rhetoric. Decreased state role. Islamic banking.	No more *Adil Düzen* (Just Order). Free-market economy.
Foreign policies	West is condemned. EEC imperialism and Zionist plot. Turkish identity will be eroded. EEC is Catholic unity.	Anti-Zionist, anti-Western and anti-USA. Islamic UN, Islamic NATO, Islamic EEC and Islamic UNESCO.	A total shift. Good relations with the West essential. Membership of EU is the goal. NATO is essential.
Style of propaganda	*Teblig* (religious invitation), traditional religious ties used.	Grassroots activism. Well organised. Party organisation, militant membership. Active membership recruitment. Door-to-door canvassing	Nationwide party organisation and effective grassroots activism.
Involvement of women	None exists.	From 1990 active female involvement through ladies' committee. But no candidates.	First women MPs (3). Very active ladies' committee.

Conclusions

Although the Islamist party was not a newcomer to Turkish politics, the electoral successes of the WP triggered a flood of suspicion and paranoia among Turkey's secularist elites. Its narrow general election victory with 21.3 per cent of the vote and 158 seats out of 550 in parliament created shock waves not just at home but also abroad (Sayarı, 1996, p. 35). *Irtica fobisi* (Islamophobia) dominated the daily news reports. Some newspapers urged immediate action against the *şeriaatcı yükseliş* (rise of fundamentalism); others urged the military to intervene to restore the principles of secularism.

On the other hand, it is hardly surprising that the WP made big election gains from 1991 onwards. The bulk of its supporters and votes come from the lower- and lower-middle-class urbanites – new migrants in the shanty towns who had escaped from rural poverty but found themselves trapped in urban poverty, wage and salary earners who had lost half of their real wages, the petit bourgeoisie, shopkeepers, artisans and small merchants – who were all increasingly threatened by the advance of big business.

The religious dimension of the WP/VP was the focal point of Turkish political discourse. Were they fundamentalists? Was there a threat of Islamic revolution in Turkey, and was there a plan for bringing Sharia to Turkey? Were they democrats or fundamentalists? Were they doing *takkiye* (deceiving us)? When faced with a similar question, the leader of the VP, Recai Kutan, replied: 'I swear we are not cheating; we genuinely believe in a secularist republic, peace, the coexistence of all citizens, democracy and human rights.'[36] However, my empirical findings show that at the grassroots level three in five joined the VP for Islamic or ideological reasons. This means they were more radical than ordinary members and voters. For this group, Mawdudi's 'theo-democracy'[37] could have been more desirable. They wanted the republic to take an Islamic tone rather than an authoritarian, secular one; but even this issue would not be discussed explicitly in public.

The role these party members saw for religion is, however, not easily understood. Although they did not want to see a sharp separation of state and religion, they did understand that in contemporary Turkey it was impossible to introduce Islamic laws. Some of them totally opposed this separation and insisted that without religion the state and society would diminish, but the majority stated clearly that they wanted the principle of secularism redefined as it is in Western democracies. This meant having religion and the state totally independent from each other. What most of them was a situation where religion was not free from the interference of the state. On this point, as with so many others, the Islamist movement is not static, despite general perceptions of it. As with the rest of society, it changes with the times.

Most media commentators, as well as many writers and academics, have made a major mistake in their approach to Islamist movements. They see them as static relics of the past rather than as a product of present times. Many see religious or Islamic fundamentalist movements as never-changing, as if they existed in an ivory tower. But this is not the case. As Table 3.3 shows, since the 1970s the Turkish Islamist movement has changed beyond recognition. Between then and the end of the twentieth century, the pro-Islamic parties changed from anti-system cadre parties (NOP/NSP) to a mass party (VP/AKP). This change affected its membership policies, its support base, and its attitudes to secularism, to economic policy, foreign policy and gender policy, among others.

CHAPTER 4

THE URBAN ROOTS OF POLITICAL ISLAM

> The destiny of Turkey's political system is determined by three metropolitan cities – Istanbul, Ankara and İzmir – because the majority of MPs are elected by those three. Yet, the power balance in terms of voting is determined by the urban poor of the *gecekondus*. (*Milliyet*, 1999)

Introduction

Many observers believe that Islamic movements are rural, traditionalist and anti-modern phenomena. On the contrary, I argue that these movements are modern in their understanding of the world and in their organisational structure. In many majority-Muslim countries, including Turkey, they emerged as a result of modernisation and rapid urbanisation.

This chapter examines the relationship between the process of rapid urbanisation, political participation and the rise of political Islam in Turkey. It describes the nature of Islamic movements, their urban characteristics, and the effects of urbanisation on political participation. The focus is on the political implications of rapid urbanisation. The chapter seeks to answer the question of whether the process of urbanisation in Turkey facilitated a greater degree of political participation or not, and describes how the WP/VP responded to this process. Local politics are also affected by rapid urbanisation, and the chapter also highlights the ways in which urban local politics has changed and the impact of this change on the rise of political Islam.

Rapid urbanisation has become one of the most common characteristics of developing countries, and today they almost all have large urban populations. However, the pattern of urbanisation has been very different from to that of developed countries. Examine the causes and the implications of over-urbanisation, and I examine the reasons why urbanisation broadens the social bases of political participation. Specifically, in the Turkish context I focus on the characteristics of urbanisation and its implications for the political process.

One of the prime objectives of this chapter is to investigate whether the rapid migration from rural to urban centres has any impact on voting patterns. More precisely, the aim is to see whether the second phase of rapid urbanisation in Turkey, which started in the early 1980s, strengthened the religious right in the middle of the 1990s – that is, that massive migration in the 1980s, fuelled by the neoliberal restructuring programmes of that decade, had a strong effect on the rise of political Islam.

Urban Politics

Cities as the Social Bases of Political Islam

The last quarter of the twentieth century witnessed a rapid and unprecedented revival of religious movements of every faith around the world. Among these movements, political Islam has been the most frequently discussed due to the potential implications of political Islam for many regimes in the Middle East, and other Muslim countries such as the newly emerged Turkic-Muslim countries of the former Soviet Union, Indonesia, Pakistan and Turkey, as well as the external consequences of political Islam. Islamic parties and movements have been given a great deal of attention, but very often they are viewed as fundamentalist, anti-Western or anti-modern. According to Olivier Roy, writing in 1994:

> Many in the West seem to view the end of our century as the era of the 'Islamic threat.' The eruption of Islam into the political landscape is often perceived as an anachronism; how is it possible, late in the twentieth century, to return to the Middle Ages? We envision bearded mullahs everywhere, surging forth from mosques and villages to attack the modern-day Babylons, seeking to create a reactionary, irrational, and violent world. (Roy, 1994, p. 1)

As Roy points out, many commentators in the Western media as well as academics of various disciplines tend to equate these movements with 'extremism', and 'terrorism'. They are often perceived as 'irrational', 'intolerant' 'fanatics' who 'want to turn the clock back to 700 AD'. For some they are the 'Green Menace', echoing the 'Red Menace' of the former Soviet threat.[1] It seems from the analysis and comments of these influential writers that the vision of Islamic movements or militant Islam as a threat to the West has gripped the imagination of Western governments and the media (Esposito, 1995, p. 3).

The majority of approaches are narrow in their focus on the ideology of the Islamic movements as a simple, 'literal reading' of the 'secret text' – the Koran – and their desire to turn to the past, and are a distorted image of these movements. Such approaches mostly fail to read the realities of Islamic movements altogether.

As argued in chapter 1, in many Muslim countries, from pre-1979 Iran to Algeria, political Islam emerged as a reaction to modernising, secular, oppressive states that failed to solve socioeconomic problems and corruption. Contemporary problems such as mass urbanisation, unemployment, and former or existing foreign domination have been the primary cause of their growth, not just purely religious reasons (see Halliday, 1995a, p. 48). Contrary to the dominant view, Islamic movements and parties have successfully adapted their ideologies and organisational structures to the contemporary world.

The emergence and subsequent rise of Islamic movements has been closely connected with the major socioeconomic changes that have occurred in Muslim countries. As Esposito (1995) points out, the modernisation and Westernisation process that many Muslim countries undertook after their independence was primarily understood as a substantial degree of urbanisation. As the modern governments, private companies and foreign investors focused on urban areas, a process of rapid urbanisation began, triggering massive migration from rural to urban centres. However, due to the realities of poverty in urban slums and shanty towns, the new migrants' hopes for a better life did not often materialise (Esposito, 1995, p. 16).

In addition to these unrealised expectations, and the loss of small community ties and traditional values, the newcomers to the cities were shocked by modern urban life and its Westernised culture and mores. Therefore many of them felt alienated and marginalised, and they found an anchor in religion. Islam offered the urban poor a sense of identity, fraternity and cultural values that helped them to overcome their fear of their new environment. Evidently, in many Muslim countries the urban poor and the lower-middle class found a welcome sense of meaning and security in religious revivalism (Esposito, 1995, p. 16). There are individual case studies that support this observation. In many Muslim countries, notably Algeria, Egypt, Iran, Lebanon, Pakistan, Syria, Sudan and Turkey, where Islamic movements have a strong presence, socioeconomic problems such as rapid urbanisation, rampant poverty, unemployment, housing shortages and lack of basic services have been prevalent. For example, Iran, prior to the revolution, had undergone a massive socioeconomic transformation accompanied by rapid urbanisation and uneven economic development. In fact, this was the real cause of the collapse of the Iranian monarchy.

In his analysis of the Iranian revolution, Halliday outlines a process of rapid and uneven economic development throughout the 1960s and 1970s, which caused great inequality and social tension in cities. The advancement of modern capitalism created widespread injustice and social tension which unified and mobilised the bazaar merchants, the Iranian clergy and the urban poor to overthrow the Shah's regime in 1979 (Halliday, 1995a, pp. 48–53).[2] Similarly Walton and Seddon (1994, p. 174) observed the heavy involvement of Islamic movements in many urban popular protests during the 1980s:

> From 1979 onwards, after the Iranian revolution the relationship between popular urban protest and the dramatic rise of Islamism, with its explicit objective of overthrowing 'illegitimate' regimes, became a matter of major concern to many governments, while commentators persistently drew attention to the revolutionary appeal of Islamism and to the increasing strength of the Islamic movements, particularly among the urban and disadvantaged in a period of rapid and traumatic economic and social change.

Halliday suggested that 'although the Iranian revolution seemed to be a reaction against the modernisation process' it had a 'unique combination of modern and traditional in its institutional and ideological features [...] Its modernity is the product of rapid urbanization, industrialization, and the demographic and social tensions created by the social transformation of the 1960s and 1970s' (1995a, p. 72). For him the Iranian revolution was only partially a religious revolution, being more of a great modern urban movement that was created by the process of social transformation (ibid.). In a similar vein, Roy (1994) argued that these movements were the product of the modern world. They involved young militants educated in modern schools and raised in recently urbanised families; some were from the impoverished middle class and, contrary to common belief, few were mullahs. They borrowed Marxist terminology and tactics. The masses who supported and followed these Islamic movements were not 'traditional' or 'traditionalist' either. By and large, they lived with the values of the modern city where they had adopted its consumerist attitudes (Roy, 1994, pp. 3–4). For a long time, many commentators mistakenly believed that Islamist movements would only flourish in societies where modernity and urbanisation had failed to materialise. In assuming that Islamist movements are anti-modernist, irrational and archaic phenomena, these commentators mostly failed to see their true characteristics. It is extremely important to emphasise that

Islamist movements are not traditionalist, rural, small-town organisations or an archaic phenomenon.

Political Islam followed a similar route in Turkey to that of Iran. Throughout the 1960s and 1970s, Turkey also underwent a massive socioeconomic transformation that led to further polarisation of society. The 1960s were the beginning of a process of transformation from commercial to industrial capitalism (Ahmad, 1993, p. 376). This transformation heightened the tension between the Anatolian petit bourgeoisie (the artisans, town merchants, tradesmen and shopkeepers) and the upper classes of Istanbul.[3]

The Anatolian petit bourgeoisie organised and rather cunningly utilised Islam's political potential to mobilise some sections of the electorate in rural and urban areas. When the NOP was founded in 1970, it was rather popular in the poorest regions and districts (see Sarıbay, 1985, p. 144). But later in the 1970s, as a result of rapid urbanisation, a new political cleavage emerged in the cities. The NSP became popular in the big cities as well as the less developed regions.[4]

In the 1970s the social bases of the NOP/NSP consisted mainly of the self-employed – artisans, town merchants, shopkeepers and tradesmen – those religious entrepreneurs who had graduated from the modern secular schools of the republic, and the urban poor who had been displaced and disappointed with their urban experiences in the cities (Çakır, 1994, p. 21). In the rural areas, however, its social bases were different, with support from traditional, religious strata in the less developed semi-feudal regions.

As a direct consequence of the neoliberal restructuring policies of the 1980s, very rapid urbanisation took place, and by the early 1990s the population balance had shifted from rural to urban centres. As of 1997, 65 per cent of the population lived in cities (see Table 4.1).[5] In the 1990s the WP became a predominantly urban-based mass party.[6]

It was mainly the *gecekondu* areas that encircle the main metropolitan cities that supported the WP/VP. Their supporters were the migrant workers who were disillusioned by the unwelcoming environment of the cities with their harsh living and working conditions, unemployment, poverty, lack of housing and basic services. They were wage and salary earners whose income dropped 50 per cent between 1980 and 1990; the lower-middle classes, including artisans, traditional merchants, small shopkeepers and tradesmen whose existence was further threatened by the neoliberal restructuring policies; and finally the Kurds, who were in search of their own identity and cultural rights. The WP/VP's non-nationalistic, Islamic approach towards ethnic groups appealed to some sections of the Kurdish population.[7] The appeal of the WP/VP lay in its inclusive, broad-ranging religious yet non-religious approach. It emphasised religious values, respected national and moral values, and emphasised industrialisation, social justice and honest government (Özbudun, 2000, p. 91).

Analysis of election results indicates that after the early 1990s the support base of the pro-Islamic WP/VP shifted (Çakır, 1994, p. 223). The party had its support in rural villages and provincial towns in the 1970s and 1980s. In general, developing countries have faced multiple problems of underdevelopment: poverty, unemployment, rapid population growth, low life expectancy, rapid urbanisation, lack of housing and basic services, minimal education and health services, and above all political instability and undemocratic government. The majority of the Muslim countries share many of these problems as well (Kepel, 1994, pp. 13–46). Therefore any attempt to understand the emergence and development of Islamic movements must take these conditions into consideration.

A Dramatic Population Shift and the Causes of Rapid Migration

The speed and scale of urbanisation that took place between 1950 and 1980 puts Turkey in the ranks of the fastest-urbanising countries in the world.[8] By 1950 only 25 per cent of the population lived in the cities compared to the 75 per cent living in the rural areas. However, at the end of the twentieth century 65 per cent of the population (40 million people) lived in urban centres.

When Mustafa Kemal took power in 1923 his prime task was the creation of a modern and secular nation-state. In order to achieve this goal Kemal must have come to the same conclusion as Lucian

Table 4.1 Urban and rural population of Turkey, 1927–1997

Census years	Total population	Urban population	% Urban	Rural population	% Rural
1927	13,648,000	3,305,876	24.2	10,342,391	75.78
1935	16,158,018	3,802,642	23.53	12,355,376	76.47
1940	17,820,950	4,346,249	24.39	13,474,701	75.61
1950	20,947,188	5,244,337	25.04	15,702,851	74.96
1960	27,754,820	8,859,731	31.92	18,895,089	68.08
1970	35,605,176	13,691,101	38.45	21,914,075	61.55
1980	44,736,957	19,645,007	43.91	25,091,950	56.09
1990	56,473,035	33,326,351	59.01	23,146,684	40.99
1997*	62,865,574	40,882,357	65.03	22,179,676	34.97

Source: 1990 Census of Population, State Institute of Statistics, Printing Division, Ankara, October 1993, pp. 8–9.

* Data for 1997 taken from the State Statistical Institute's web pages: http://www.die.gov.tr/TURKIS/SONIST/NUFUS/ankara.gif.

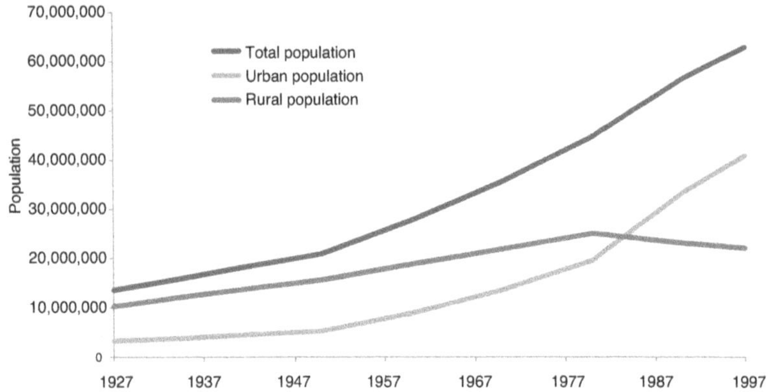

Figure 4.1 Change in the urban and rural population, 1927–1997
Source: Data drawn from Table 4.1.

Pye (1963). Pye (quoted in Danielson and Keleş, 1985, p. 3) argued: 'Any systematic effort to transform traditional societies into modern societies must envisage the development of cities and modern urban societies.' Since then the policy of rapid urbanisation has been put forward as a primary means of transforming a backward, 'uncivilised' traditional society. Despite Kemal's enthusiasm for rapid urbanisation, the growth of city centres between 1927 and 1950 was modest. Apart from Ankara's impressive transformation from a small, dusty Anatolian town into a city with over 300,000 inhabitants by 1950, urbanisation in general was slow.

In the 1950s, only one-quarter (25.04 per cent) of the population lived in the cities. The majority (74.96 per cent) lived in the rural areas (see Table 4.1). Between 1950 and 1990 the annual rate of population growth was 24.45 per thousand. At 43.94 per thousand the urban growth rate was almost twice this figure for the same period. Reflecting this increase in urban population, the growth rate has been declining in rural areas since the 1950s. In 1960 Turkey's population stood at 27.7 million, of which approximately one-third (32 per cent) lived in the cities and two-thirds (68 per cent) in the rural areas. In 1970 the population reached 35.6 million, of whom 38 per cent lived in the urban areas and 62 per cent in the rural areas. In

1980 the population was 44.7 million (44 per cent in the urban areas and 56 per cent in the rural areas). By the 1990s the population had increased to 56.4 million with 59 per cent living in urban areas and 41 per cent in the rural areas. In 1997 the population had risen to 62.8 million and two-thirds (65 per cent) was urban and one-third (35 per cent) rural. According to the latest (2011) census the population has reached 74.7 million and by now nearly three-quarters (76.9 per cent) of Turkey's people live in the cities and one-quarter (23.2 per cent) live in rural areas.[9]

Between 1985 and 1990 Turkey's population rose at a rate of 21.71 per thousand per year.[10] Furthermore, between 1980 and 1990 the rural population suffered a negative growth of – 7.91 per thousand per annum. This negative growth of population in the rural areas was not due to falling birth rates but indicates significantly accelerated rural to urban migration from the early 1980s.

Table 4.1 also illustrates a dramatic fall in the rural population; by contrast, between 1980 and 1990 the urban population jumped by 52.85 per thousand a year. It appears that the 1980s marked a new phase of rapid urbanisation in Turkey. Furthermore, there was a positive correlation between the restructuring policies of the 1980s and dramatic population movement from rural to urban areas.

Not only have the salary and wage earners in the cities lost out since the 1980s, but the agricultural sector has also been badly affected by neoliberal economy policies. One of the objectives of the neoliberal restructuring programme was the termination of low interest rates for agricultural loans and credits provided by the state-owned Ziraat Bankası (Agricultural Bank) and, more importantly, the abolition of agricultural subsidies crucial to maintaining small- and medium-scale farmers.

The 1980s in Turkey started with a military coup on 12 September 1980. This was the third time since 1960 that the country's military had seized power and dismantled the entire political structure; all political parties were closed down, parliament and the government were dismissed, trade unions, civil society organisations and all kinds of associations were outlawed, and thousands of people were detained and interrogated. All kinds of politics were banned, politicians were imprisoned and even after serving their sentences they were banned from politics. However, the most lasting legacy of the coup was the introduction of neoliberal restructuring policies. These had already been negotiated between the IMF and the Demirel government (on 24 January 1980) but their implementation was postponed until the military's intervention.

At the beginning of the 1980s the agricultural sector employed over 43 per cent of the total population compared to 34 per cent in the late 1990s. Therefore, it is plausible to argue that any policy change in this sector was bound to affect millions of lives. By the end of the 1990s agriculture was on the verge of collapse: it had lost nearly 50 per cent of its share of GDP, falling from 24 per cent in 1984 to 14 per cent in the 1990s. This decline was reflected in a sharp drop in income among the rural population. The decline of income in the agricultural sector continued in the 2000s and by 2008 it had dropped to 10 per cent of GDP.

Research by the Turkish Statistical Board indicated that

> Inequality in income distribution of Turkey still remains: The income inequality between the top 20 percent of income earners and the bottom 20 percent did not change in 2008, with the top quintile making 8.1 times more than the bottom quintile. According to the research, 45.5 percent of population cannot buy new clothes and 88.8 percent of population cannot afford one week holiday away from home. The results reveal that the top 20 percent of income earners make 46.7 percent of all income in Turkey, while the bottom 20 percent earn only 5.8 percent.[11]

As income steadily shrank, more and more people sought employment in big cities, causing the problem of over-urbanisation in the major cities.

The Problem of Over-Urbanisation

There has been a great transformation in developing countries in recent decades. Unlike the peasant societies of the 1940s and 1950s,

Table 4.2 The growth of Turkey's five largest cities, 1950–1990 (000s of inhabitants)

	1950	1960	1970	1980	1990	Growth index (1950=100)
Istanbul	983	1,467	2,132	4,433	7,309	744
Ankara	289	650	1,236	1,878	3,236	1,120
İzmir	228	361	521	1,096	2,694	1,119
Adana	118	232	347	575	1,934	1,640
Bursa	104	154	276	445	1,603	1,540

Source: Danielson and Keleş, 1985, p. 50, and 1990 Census of Population, State Institute of Statistic, Printing Division, October 1993.

they now consist of large urban populations. From the 1950s onwards, underdeveloped countries urbanised rapidly, such that their urban population doubled in the 30 years to 1975. The rate of urbanisation increased even faster from 1975 to 1990. In 15 years it doubled again, reaching 40 per cent of the population of all developing countries by the beginning of the 1990s (Roberts, 1995, pp. 1–27).

What makes the urbanisation process much more problematic in the Turkish context is that half of this urban population has been concentrated in Turkey's five megacities – Istanbul, Ankara, İzmir, Adana and Bursa – and has fuelled a rapid growth in the *gecekondu* population (see Table 4.2).

As mentioned earlier, from the early 1930s onwards urbanisation was seen as a means of modernisation and economic development in Turkey.[12] However, the way in which underdeveloped countries urbanised was very different from the urbanisation process in developed industrialised nations. For many reasons the underdeveloped countries could not repeat the same process of urban growth.

Many developing countries witnessed rapid urbanisation from the 1950s onwards so that by the 1970s their urban population had doubled, but the rate of industrial growth did not match the rate of urban growth in many of these countries. The gap that appeared in this process created a different kind of phenomenon known as 'over-urbanisation'. For Castells (1977, p. 41):

> The phenomenon [...] known as over-urbanisation [...] connotes the idea of a level of urbanisation higher then that which can 'normally' be attained, given the level of industrialisation. Over-urbanisation appears as an obstacle to development, in so far as it immobilises resources in the form of non-productive investments, necessary to the creation and organisation of services indispensable to great concentrations of population, whereas these countries do not justify themselves as centres of production.

Over-urbanisation is not only an imbalance between the growth rate of the urban population and the level of industrialisation but also an obstacle to economic development because of the resources transferred to non-productive investments such as services for the urban population. If the urban population growth is not led by the demand for labour, what then is the driving force for over-urbanisation? Castells points out that there are two factors in the acceleration of the growth of urbanisation: (a) an increase in the natural growth of population in the rural and urban areas, and (b) rural–urban migration (Castells, 1977, p. 46).

The increase in the rate of natural population growth is due to advances in medical knowledge. The question of the driving force of the rural–urban migration is rather complex. In Turkey the flood of migration from villages to cities has since the 1950s been caused more by the rural *push* than the urban *pull*, but due to the major shifts in socioeconomic conditions the *push* factors became intolerable from the early 1980s.

In relation to the social and political implications of over-urbanisation Castells argues that the combination of a high rate of unemployment and low standard of living can create a fertile ground for political extremism (Castells, 1977, p. 41). By concentrating vast numbers of people in a certain space over a given period, urbanisation facilitates social mobility and increases human contact with others. It also increases the opportunities for economic, social and political participation.

Urbanisation and Political Participation

There are a number of studies pointing to a strong link between socio-economic conditions and voting tendencies in Western Europe and North America. An early empirical study of American voting behaviour concentrates on the 'social bases of American partisanship'. This study established an '*Index of Political Predispositions* based on social classes, religion, and rural/urban residency', and observed a strong correlation between voting behaviour and social class, religion and type of residency (Dalton, 1988, p. 152). Similarly Bell and Boat's (1956–57) study, in San Francisco, showed that family and socioeconomic neighbourhood characteristics influence the development of informal group relations between friends, relatives, neighbours and co-workers. A similar study carried out in Britain found a strong correlation between socioeconomic class characteristics in a neighbourhood and voting behaviour (Berry, 1970, p. 34).

All of these studies had one thing in common: they found that urbanisation is one of the key determinants of political involvement. In general, the processes of modernisation and urbanisation have played a very important role in creating the social bases and networks of political participation for the larger sections of societies. Deutsch (1963) argued that urbanisation combined with other features of social mobilisation would increase the interaction and political communication of citizen to citizen and citizens to state. He also envisaged that this could lead to greater awareness among citizens of the 'instrumental stakes of politics'. Similarly Lerner (1958, p. 46) noted that historically urbanisation has been the first stage of modernisation, and that the most important aspect of urbanisation is the increase in political participation.

Almost 20 years later Roberts (1995), in his study of *Latin American Urbanisation*, pointed out that with the introduction of new political issues like age, gender and ethnicity, alongside those of living and working conditions, urbanisation has, in many ways, extended political participation among citizens. This expansion in citizens' political participation is led by what Inglehart (1977, p. 168) called 'cognitive mobilization'. He argued that:

> The coming of advanced industrial society leads to a syndrome of intergenerational changes that bring significant further increases in citizen intervention in politics. A long-term rise in educational levels and in mass political skills has characterized all industrial societies. An extension of social mobilization beyond the transformations brought by urbanization and early industrialization, this process has been termed 'cognitive mobilization'. [...] Cognitive mobilization is based on invisible changes that upgrade individual skills.

For Inglehart (1997, p. 169), mass political participation developed in two major stages, the first of which was based on an older model of elite-led political participation. In this stage citizen mobilisation was led by institutions such as political parties, trade unions, churches, etc.; it was a low level of participation mostly limited to voting. The second stage of political participation is known as the 'elite-challenging model' and, because it requires relatively high skill levels, it is facilitated by the development of cognitive mobilisation.

In addition, in the urban context the networks of participation were now denser than they had been in the past and less family-oriented. There had been an increase in the flow and quality of information because citizens now enjoyed better and easy access to the mass media. Also thanks to the mass media, the wrongdoings and failures of the rulers could be transmitted across the nation immediately (Roberts, 1995, p. 211). Roberts' analysis of political participation in the Latin American experience indicated that the process of urbanisation in developing countries followed a different path and created social problems, yet urbanisation broadened the social bases of political participation. The emergence of new political issues such as gender and ethnicity indicated the emergence of a new kind of citizen who was better educated, more worldly-wise, self-conscious and demanding. Nevertheless, Roberts points out a fundamental characteristic of developing countries: 'The fear of poverty is as much a preoccupation of the majority of the population as it was in early periods of urbanisation' (1995, pp. 19–20).

Perhaps not surprisingly, following Roberts' (1995) findings one can detect several parallels between the urban centres and living conditions of the urban poor in Latin America and in Turkey.

The unprecedented rise of the WP in the 1994 and 1995 elections was strongly related to the process of rapid urbanisation that took place between 1980 and 1990. The WP gained the largest share of the municipalities across the country, securing 19 per cent of the votes and 26 municipalities out of 72 provincial capitals including Istanbul and Ankara (Margulies and Yıldızoğlu, 1997, p. 144). According to Shmuelevitz (1996, p. 175) there is a direct relationship between migration and rise of the WP/VP.[13]

The Implications of Rapid Urbanisation

Economic Consequences and the Growth of Shanty Towns

The social base of party support in certain areas is determined by the socioeconomic characteristics (income level, type of occupation and level of education) in the areas studied. Although many observers are mistrustful of the concept of class cleavages, they play an important role in voting behaviour in Turkey.[14]

The sub-districts of both Keçiören and Mamak have a large proportion of *gecekondu* settlements. This means both districts are home to thousands of poor lower- and lower-middle-class residents. Mamak has a larger number of *gecekondu* houses.[15] Historically, *gecekondu*s first emerged on the outskirts of rapidly expanding cities from the 1950s onwards.[16] From the sociological point of view, *gecekondulaşma* (squatterisation) was due to a growth of population that was not matched by industrial growth (Danielson and Keles, 1985, p. 38). When we focus on the historical development of the phenomenon of *gecekondulaşma* we notice its dual dimensions: quantitative and qualitative. The quantitative dimension refers to the numbers of *gecekondu*s and their populations and the proportion of *gecekondu* dwellers within the general population. From 1950 onwards the number of *gecekondu*s and their populations have been increasing.

As with many other rapidly urbanising countries, newcomers responded to the lack of regular housing by occupying state-owned land illegally and building *gecekondu* houses. *Gecekondu* settlements soon become the main source of housing (Danielson and Keleş, 1985, p. 41). There appears to have been a wide gap between the growth of population and the growth of industrial investment in the major Turkish cities.

In Turkey rapid urbanisation was a response to the major socio-economic shifts that occurred from the early 1950s onwards. However, as mentioned earlier, since the 1980s there has been another major restructuring of the Turkish economy that has led to the second phase of rapid migration from rural to urban centres. It was this second phase of rapid migration that changed the population balance from rural to urban. In under 20 years the urban population increased from 19.6 million (1980) to 40.8 million (1997) (see Table 4.1).

As Table 4.2 illustrates, migration was concentrated around the five largest cities: Istanbul, Ankara, İzmir, Adana and Bursa. From 1945 to 1990 Turkey's population multiplied 3.04 times. While the urban population multiplied 9.67 times, this rate was just 1.45 among the rural population. Istanbul's population grew by 7.44 while Ankara's population multiplied by 11.20, and İzmir's population multiplied 11.19 times.

The second phase of rapid urbanisation took place between 1985 and 1990. During this period Turkey's population increased by 21.71 per thousand per year. In Istanbul, however, this rate was more than twice the national average (44.78 per thousand per year). Ankara's population grew (21.28 per thousand per year) more slowly than Istanbul's but was still higher than the national average; in İzmir it was 30.14, in Adana 22.86, and in Bursa 38.26 per thousand per year. Some cities such as Antalya grew by as much as 47.88 per thousand per year, making the difference in population increase between rural and urban areas more visible.[17]

Although in the 1950s urbanisation was led by industrial growth and economic vitality in the cities, the massive population flowing from the countryside to the cities soon exhausted the jobs and housing facilities created by the industrial growth. The reason for this rapid urbanisation was the 'push' factor of rural Anatolia.[18]

Keyder (1987, p. 136) argued that under the impact of rapid urbanisation as experienced in most developing countries, the shanty town became a tangible correlative of substantial demographic movements reflecting the dramatic flow of population into urban areas. It created serious implications and upheavals in social balance. Following the massive migration there appeared a belt of *gecekondu*s that grew rapidly and soon encircled all of these expanding cities.

Between 1980 and 1985 2.9 million people migrated and the vast majority (two-thirds) of them ended up working irregularly in the low-income marginal sectors (Peker, 1996, p. 19). By 1995 over one-third (35 per cent) of Turkey's entire urban population lived in the *gecekondu* areas. The vast majority of *gecekondu*s concentrated around the country's five largest cities. In 1955 *gecekondu*s accounted for just 4.7 per cent of the urban population. The ratio increased almost four times (16.4 per cent in 1960 alone) in five years; by 1970 this trend slowed down slightly, to 23.6 per cent, and the figure was 26.1 per cent in 1980. By 1990 *gecekondu*s were home to 33.9 per cent of the urban population, indicating a relatively high increase since the 1980s. In 1995 there were two million *gecekondu* dwellings and 10 million *gecekondu* dwellers, making up more than one-third (35 per cent) of the entire urban population in Turkey (see Table 4.3).

Table 4.3 Ratio of *gecekondu* population within the urban population, 1955–1995

Years	Number of units	Number of individuals	Ratio of *gecekondu* population within the urban population
1955	50,000	250,000	4.7
1960	240,000	1,200,000	16.4
1965	430,000	2,150,000	22.9
1970	600,000	3,000,000	23.6
1980	1,150,000	5,750,000	26.1
1990	1,750,000	8,750,000	33.9
1995	2,000,000	10,000,000	35.0*

Source: Keleş, 1993, p. 383.
* Kongar, 2000, p. 566.

Table 4.4 Squatter housing in Ankara, 1950–1990

Years	Number of squatter houses	Number of people living in squatter housing	Percentage of population living in squatter housing
1950	12,000	62,400	21.8
1960	70,000	364,000	56.0
1970	144,000	748,000	60.6
1980	275,000	1,450,000	72.4
1990*	350,000	1,750,000	58.4**

Source: Figures 1950–80 taken from Danielson and Keleş, 1985, p. 166.
* Figures for 1990 taken from Keleş, 1993, p. 384.
** The fall in the ratio of *gecekondu* housing from 72.4% in 1980 to 58.4% in 1990 in Ankara is unlikely to indicate a slowdown in the rate of urbanisation/squatterisation in 1990 in general, but it might be an indication of the rapid transformation of old *gecekondu* areas into authorised apartments whilst new *gecekondu* areas grow in other parts of Ankara (see Özdemir, 1999).

However, some researchers have observed that most of the urban population growth was concentrated around those big cities with a population of one million or more (see Kongar, 2000, pp. 556–7). Thus, the ratio of *gecekondu* population to overall population is far greater in those large cities.

For instance, in 1980 the *gecekondu* population comprised 70 per cent of Ankara's total population. Comparable figures were 55 per cent in Istanbul and 50 per cent in İzmir (see Gökce, 1996, p. 92). These figures clearly indicate that between half and two-thirds of the entire populations of Istanbul, Ankara and İzmir were made up of *gecekondu* dwellers at the time. A close examination of Ankara's demographic is helpful in gaining a better understanding of the political significance of *gecekondu* areas in general and the electoral success of the WP/VP in particular.

Mustafa Kemal chose Ankara as the capital city of the modern and secular republic in the early 1920s, and it has been one of the fastest-growing cities in Turkey. In the 1920s Ankara was a small, dusty Anatolian town with a population of about 20,000 (Keleş, 1971, pp. 1–2). By 1950 its population was 289,000. This rose to 650,000 by 1960, 1,236,000 by 1970, 1,878,000 by 1980 and 3,236, 000 in 1990. By 2000 the population of the city was 4,007,860. Between 1990 and 2000 alone Ankara's population increased by 21.37 per cent (see Table 4.2).[19]

Parallel to the rise in Ankara's overall population we see an increase in the proportion of the *gecekondu* population. In 1950 there were 12,000 *gecekondu* dwellings and 62,400 *gecekondu* dwellers consisting of only 21.8 per cent of the population; in the following decade we saw a fivefold increase in the numbers of *gecekondu* dwellings (70,000) accommodating 364,000 *gecekondu* dwellers making up 56 per cent of Ankara's population. By 1970 there were 144,000 *gecekondu* dwellings with 748,000 inhabitants, making up 60.6 per cent of the population. In the following decade the number of *gecekondu* dwellings went up to 275,000 and the *gecekondu* population doubled to 1,450,000, making up almost three-quarters (72.4 per cent) of Ankara's population. According to one estimate, by 1990 there were 350,000 *gecekondu* dwellings with 1,750,000 inhabitants (see Gökce, 1996, p. 92).[20]

Restructuring Policies and the Urban Poor

The 1980s were in many respects a turning point that brought major shifts in the direction of the economy and politics in Turkey. The structural adjustment programme, which was backed if not imposed by the IMF and the World Bank and aimed to replace the closed, interventionist economic model with a neoliberal market economy, had a profound impact on Turkish society. The socioeconomic and political implications of these restructuring programmes have been enormous.[21]

By the late 1970s Turkey's economic crisis had deepened. Coupled with widespread social unrest, increased violence and political killings in the streets, this led to the military seizure of power on 12 September 1980.[22] The military government was widely seen as an opportunity for the big bourgeoisie to implement the IMF's well-known '24 January' (1979) decisions, which had been adopted by the conservative Demirel government but not yet implemented.

Just a few hours after the 1980 military coup, the Chief of the General Staff made a speech in which he plainly and explicitly expressed his support for the neoliberal restructuring programmes.[23] Big business interest groups, such as the Turkish Industrialists and Businessmen's Organisation (TÜSİAD), had accused successive governments of applying 'populist policies' that made the workforce uncontrollable and led to the failure of the economic model. Such groups believed that the labour market must be reorganised under an authoritarian regime (Tosun, 1999, p. 146). As Vehbi Koç, one of the most prominent representatives of big business, explained:

> Before the 12 September action we had to do everything under the democratic system. It was necessary to spend months to pass an amendment or a law. [...] The difference under the military government is that because you do not need to pass the decisions and laws from parliament everything is so fast, even when they make a mistake they correct it quickly without any political approach. It is because they have no fear of losing a seat in parliament or losing the voters' support.[24]

Obviously, Koç was not just justifying the military coup but also expressing how desperately the business sector needed the radical economic reforms made possible by the coup. The main objectives of the restructuring programme were as follows:

1) The economy was to be exposed to free-market forces and international competition.
2) The private sector was to be supported and public investment was to be restricted.
3) A rapid and extensive privatisation programme would lead to the privatisation of the State Economic Enterprises.
4) Exports and foreign capital would be encouraged by all available means, for which various incentive measures would be taken.
5) The Turkish Lira would be devalued.
6) Wages and salaries would be kept at low levels. In order to achieve this goal the trade union and collective bargaining legislation would be changed.

7) Finally, but very importantly, agricultural subsidies would be abolished altogether. (Dodd, 1990, p. 101; Ramazanoglu, 1985, pp. 220–42)

This so-called structural adjustment programme consisted of extensive privatisation, closure of many state-owned enterprises, mass redundancies in the public sector, rolling back the state from economic areas in favour of private investment, flexibility of the labour market, increasing subcontracting, and restrictions on unionisation. Turkey was introduced to the neoliberal economic model by Turgut Özal, founder of the Motherland Party.

By the mid-1980s there was a sharp rise in the urban population and an equally sharp decline in the rural population. Between 1980 and 1997 around ten million people migrated to the cities' poorest *gecekondu* areas. No doubt this high rate of migration automatically added many new social and economic problems to the ever-expanding squatter areas. This population was particularly badly affected by the countless austerity programmes imposed by successive governments.

The structural adjustment policies in Turkey had a particularly destructive effect on the urban poor. Privatisation is one of the main pillars of neoliberalism and can have devastating consequences in a country where the state acts as the locomotive force of economic development. In Turkey, for example, until the 1980s, for historical reasons such as the lack of an industrial bourgeois class, the state was very active in the economic sphere. Since the 1930s the state had been the main entrepreneur for infrastructure investments: from roads, bridges, electricity and irrigation to industrial production in areas such as coal, mining, steel, cement and sugar. It had also dominated the financial, services and agricultural sectors, and there was even a state monopoly in the production of cigarettes, alcoholic drinks and salt. In fact, the public share of capital in the state-owned enterprises amounted to nearly 50 per cent of the total capital. In the late 1990s the government employed 3 million out of 8 million regularly employed workers (Çam, 1999, p. 697). Thus, it is plausible to argue that the implementation of neoliberal restructuring programmes, such as the privatisation of public enterprises, deregulation of the labour market, restrictions on unionisation or collective bargaining, increased subcontracting, and temporary or part-time employment (see Peker, 1996), had a profound impact on the wage and salary earners; the low and lower-middle classes, the poor, the landless, the small peasantry, shopkeepers and artisans.

Consequently, as is evident from Table 4.5, the share of wages in the GNP declined sharply: from 26.7 per cent in 1980 to 24.6 per cent in 1981 and 1982; 24.8 per cent in 1983; 21.6 per cent in 1984; 18.8 per cent in 1985; 17.5 per cent in 1986; 17.0 per cent in 1987; 14.0 per cent in 1988; and finally to 11.0 per cent in 2008. The decline of the share of wages within the GNP meant a loss of more than one-half of real wages for most ordinary wage earners. As a result of neoliberal economic policies, particularly the low wage and income transfer policies, the gap between the richest 20 per cent and the poorest 20 per cent of households widened further. For example, the share of total disposable income for the poorest quintile of households within the total GNP was 5.24 per cent in 1987 and 4.86 per cent in 1994. On the contrary, the share that the richest quintile household received from total GNP rose from 49.94 per cent in 1987 to 54.88 per cent in 1994.

Consequently Turkey became one of the five worst countries – alongside Brazil, Chile, Colombia and Mexico – in terms of unequal income distribution (Tosun, 1999, pp. 179–80). A parallel process involving the index of real wages shows a substantial decline in wages between 1976 and 1986. Real wages fell more than 50 per cent in ten years. The index of 100 in 1976 fell to 49 in 1985 (Boratav, 1990, pp. 206–7). This means that wage and salary earners and their dependents lost 50.9 per cent of their income in less than ten years. Undoubtedly, under the restructuring programme the lower classes in the cities were the most affected.

The IMF-designed restructuring programmes did not solve the major shortcomings of the Turkish economy, as had been promised. Many economic austerity programmes were supposedly designed to bring about economic recovery, but, without exception, all of them failed to achieve that goal. As Theo Nichols (1996, p. 2) argued, 'continuing IMF and World Bank policy interventions have made

Table 4.5 GDP shares of the different types of incomes, 1980–1988

Income types %	1980	1981	1982	1983	1984	1985	1986	1987	1988
Agricultural incomes	23.9	23.0	21.8	20.5	20.4	19.1	18.1	17.6	15.8
Non-agricultural incomes	76.1	76.9	78.2	79.5	79.6	80.9	81.7	82.4	84.2
Wages	26.7	24.6	24.6	24.8	21.6	18.8	17.5	17.0	14.0
Income other than wages	49.5	52.4	53.5	54.7	58.0	62.1	64.2	65.4	70.2
GNP growth rates	–1.1	4.1	4.5	3.3	5.9	5.1	8.0	7.4	3.4

Source: Özmucur, 1989, quoted by Baharoglu, 1993, p. 74.

the distribution of income in Turkey among the most polarized in the world'. Those who lived on agricultural incomes also witnessed a dramatic (44 per cent) drop in income. The share of agricultural incomes within GNP was 23.9 per cent in 1980, 20.4 per cent in 1984 and 15.8 per cent by 1988.

There are two important points to make here. The first one is that the neoliberal economic policies, by causing income disparities, destroyed rural life so that millions of peasants had to seek employment in the cities. The second point is that the low wages and salary policies deepened the poverty of the millions of urban dwellers in the cities. The low wage policy of the 1980s had the worst effect on the *gecekondu* areas, inhabited by millions of recent migrants to the rapidly growing cities.

The Political Implications of Rapid Urbanisation

The first political implication of the expansion of *gecekondu*s was in the growth of local politics. Between 1945 and 1990 the numbers of municipalities increased nearly four times (352 per cent), from 583 municipalities in 1945 to 2,053 in 1990. In line with the massive growth of *gecekondu* areas there was increasing need and political pressure on the central government for the provision of infrastructure and services. Therefore the political significance of *gecekondu*s increased.

The second implication was the shift of the electoral preferences of *gecekondu* dwellers. Studies show that there have been important electoral swings from time to time in *gecekondu* areas.[25] Throughout the 1950s and 1960s a culture of optimism was prevalent among *gecekondu* dwellers. But this economic growth and culture of optimism was undermined by the economic stagnation deepened by the lack of foreign currency and the unforeseen petrol crisis in the mid-1970s. The optimism of the first generation of migrants gradually faded away. In this crisis atmosphere, as Özbudun (1976, p. 106) points out, the Republican People's Party moved to the left, stressing the need for greater equity and attention to the problems of the poor.

Table 4.6 Party support by city and type of housing in the national elections, 1965–1973

City	Election years (national elections)								
	1965			1969			1973		
	JP	**RPP**	**Oth.**	**JP**	**RPP**	**Oth.**	**JP**	**RPP**	**Oth.**
Istanbul*	52.0	30.4	17.6	47.8	33.8	18.4	28.5	48.9	22.6
Istanbul *gecekondus*	62.4	19.1	18.5	53.8	21.8	24.4	26.7	47.5	25.8
Ankara*	46.5	30.2	23.3	42.4	36.0	21.0	29.2	44.8	26.0
Ankara *gecekondus*	52.5	25.8	21.7	43.4	30.1	26.5	27.7	45.9	26.4
İzmir*	62.1	29.8	8.0	53.2	35.1	11.7	40.9	44.6	14.5
İzmir *gecekondus*	72.1	17.0	10.9	60.7	22.6	16.7	36.5	44.2	19.3

Note: JP: Justice Party (conservative), RPP: Republican People's Party (left of centre), Oth. = other parties, including the NSP (National Salvation Party), TLP (Turkish Labour Party) and some other small parties.

*Rows of data for cities do not include *gecekondus*. These were estimated separately.

Source: Danielson and Keleş, 1985, pp. 107–109.

As shown in Table 4.6, voting preferences changed drastically. Throughout the 1970s, the slide of lower-income voters towards the left accelerated. Two decades later, a very similar swing took place in the voting behaviour of *gecekondu* dwellers. As the neoliberal restructuring programmes went ahead, they created enormous inequalities, unemployment, income losses, growing uncertainty, abandonment of social security policies, mass migration to the cities, and so on.

As mentioned above, the effects of the neoliberal policies were most brutal on the *gecekondu* population, so there has been a significant swing in their voting behaviour. In the 1990s, *gecekondu*s chose to support the Welfare Party for precisely the same reasons they had supported the Republican People's Party in the 1970s. The WP/VP was the only party that seemed to care about the problems of the urban poor and to pay attention to the demand for social justice and equality.[26]

The 1990s was undoubtedly a decade of great expectations in many respects, but it turned into rather a disappointment for large sections of society in Turkey. The lower-middle and lower classes, the urban poor, and the Kurdish minority in particular were increasingly disaffected with the mainstream centre-left and centre-right parties and turned to the WP/VP in their millions.

The 1990s witnessed two other important developments as well. First was the emergence of the *gecekondu* areas as a key electoral force. The second was the process of party convergence, leading to the collapse of centre-left politics. In this atmosphere the WP/VP emerged as the 'one guardian' of the exploited, poverty-stricken urban masses. With its promise of *Adil Düzen* (Just Order), greater equality, restoration of the state's role in the economy, and clean, uncorrupted government, and with its very well-organised, very active and committed grassroots activists, the WP/VP appealed to the *gecekondu* dwellers more strongly than any other party.

Conclusion

This chapter illuminates the modern faces of political Islam. It argues that, contrary to common belief, Islamist movements are the product of the process of modernisation and rapid urbanisation. They emerged and flourished in rapidly urbanising societies rather than rural towns or traditional communities. As is evident from my own empirical data on grassroots activists of the pro-Islamic Virtue Party, the cadres of these Islamic movements are educated in Western-style modern schools. They tend to be better educated than the majority, with a higher level of occupation and income. The activists and leading figures of these movements may have anti-imperialist attitudes, but to view the movements as a threat to the West would be misleading.

I have argued that the peasant societies of developing countries in the 1940s and 1950s underwent a great transformation and within 30 years became the urbanised societies of the 1980s and 1990s. Likewise, many underdeveloped Muslim countries, such as Iran and Egypt, also experienced rapid rural to urban migration and faced the social, economic, cultural and political consequences of such mass migration. It has been highlighted that there is a positive correlation between urbanisation and political participation. Urbanisation, in various ways, expands the social basis of political participation. As participation gains a more rational and less family/traditional orientation, the number of networks of participation also increases. With urbanisation the rate of literacy and newspaper readership grows. Due to developments in new information technologies, communication and information transformation becomes ever easier. Today an ordinary citizen has an extraordinary amount of information within reach.

Since the 1950s Turkey has witnessed a rapid urbanisation process. However, the pattern of urbanisation has been very different from that of developed Western countries. Urbanisation of the developing countries was not led by significant industrialisation or economic development, but was created merely by the factors of rural push. Because the over-urbanisation in Turkey was led by *rural push* rather than *urban pull* it was prone to cause social problems. One of the most noticeable phenomena following the rapid urbanisation was the *gecekondu* settlements that enveloped the metropolitan areas. Due to the lack of resources for housing, the newcomers took the initiative and built their own houses. In fact, they created their own cities in many cases.

It is now time to consider the relationship between neoliberal restructuring programmes implemented since the 1980s, which are a significant part of the globalisation process, and the unprecedented rise of the WP/VP throughout the 1990s. Is there any sign of an alternative to this process? Could the rise of the WP/VP be interpreted as an alternative movement against neoliberal policies?

Global capitalism has significantly eroded the functions and the borders of nation-states. As a result, national governance has become ineffective (Hirst and Thompson, 1996, pp. 175–95). This development has also undermined the ability of governments and political parties to govern. International corporations have increasingly taken over the nation-states' space by pushing them out of both economics and politics. In this process they have acquired increasing power to dictate policies of taxation, privatisation, flexible labour markets and other issues to suit their interests. This influence often takes the form of IMF-led economic 'restoration' or 'stability' programmes that are usually tied to new credit.

As Guehennon (1995, cited by Hague et al., 1998, pp. 36–7) argues, 'the demand of the global economy has transformed politics into management'. He claims that 'governments no longer make choices, they simply manage their country's engagement with global markets'. The expansion of economics in the form of neoliberalism has left very limited room for politics. The very essence of politics has been negated. It is left without any purpose or function. Inevitably, extremely weakened politics has caused widespread apathy among citizens. Because politics is reduced to management, voters lose interest and simply turn away from it. The best example of this can be found among Western democracies. For example in Britain, the turnout in the general elections declined from 77 per cent in 1992 to 71.4 per cent in 1997, to 59.4 per cent in 2001.[27] As neoliberalism takes over the world on the back of globalisation, it creates inequality, injustice, poverty and misery for millions, as well as dissent and dissatisfaction. As a result, the majority of the urban poor lose hope and turn away from politics.

This is not so in the Turkish case. As the neoliberal restructuring policies obliterated everything in their way, the urban poor of the *gecekondu* areas became increasingly politicised and raised their voice against this process. By voting, supporting the WP/VP or becoming party activists, the urban poor actually make a strong statement. They declare that they will not give in or surrender to global capitalism but instead will fight against it. The poor urban communities indicated their dissatisfaction with the whole process and showed their intention to create an alternative by throwing their own leaders into the arena and uniting around the WP/VP, which was opposed to this process. The WP/VP offered a kind of third way between capitalism and socialism – *Adil Düzen*.[28]

As a result of neoliberal economic policies, millions migrated from villages to the periphery of the major urban centres. There they were further disappointed and disillusioned with the mainstream political establishment. This dissatisfaction of the urban masses due to the economic crisis and political instability changed voting patterns. At times of crisis, especially among those newcomers, there is a tendency to turn to extremes, both on the right and the left (Shmuelevitz, 1996, p. 168). The urban lower-middle and lower classes and the underclasses of the *gecekondu* sought an alternative to incompetent, corrupt, elite mainstream politics.

In the 1990s the *gecekondu* areas, *varoşlar*, became the main battleground for political power. Today the three major cities of Istanbul, Ankara and İzmir, where the majority of MPs are elected, and the *gecekondu*s with their large populations hold the electoral balance. It was pointed out that at the 1995 general elections the majority of those urban poor who earned US$654–$1,000 a year voted for the WP.[29] The WP emerged as the party of social justice and prosperity, as its name implies. Many scholars note that the WP, with its *Adil Düzen*, filled the gap left by the decline of the centre-left RPP due to its privatisation programme while in power (1991–95). By using this historic opportunity, the WP strengthened its position among the urban poor and disadvantaged masses by giving voice to their grievances, concerns and identity problems.

The WP/VP had a massive and very active grassroots organisation in action not only at election time but all year around. As one of my grassroots activist informants told me, 'We are not "seasonal workers" like the other parties' activists.[30] We are permanent workers in our neighbourhood.' They performed a lot of social work in the *gecekondu* neighbourhoods, so that they were active not just for a few months before the elections but throughout the year.

The 1999 general and local elections – held at the same time – took place against a background of torrid corruption scandals that rocked nearly all political parties and politicians, and under the shadow of the 'Susurluk scandal'[31] which revealed the deep, unlawful connections between hundreds of bureaucrats, upper echelons of political parties and politicians, especially both the centre-right parties (the True Path Party and Motherland Party) TPP and the Mafia. (Ecevit's Democratic Left Party and to some extent the Nationalist Action Party were left untouched by the corruption scandals.)

In the meantime, the social democrat Republic People's Party, like many social democrat parties in Western Europe, lost belief in its core ideology of freedom, equality and social justice and failed to put forward an alternative ideology against the rising new right. Instead, the party became a bad imitation of the new right. Consequently, it lost its traditional working-class support. By contrast, the VP continued to enjoy the support of the urban poor.

CHAPTER 5

EXPLAINING THE MEANING OF PARTY MEMBERSHIP: ROUTES TO AND REASONS FOR PARTY MEMBERSHIP

> A certain number of recent sociological studies (Ferry and Renaut, 1987; Piotte, 1987; Melucci, 1989; Ion, 1990) have focused on a phenomenon previously overlooked by researchers: namely, what individuals gain from their involvement in collective action, what motivates them, their need for self-assertion and a recognition of their difference. In other words, these recent studies emphasise that in order to grasp the scope or meaning of social movements, researchers must take into account the ways in which individuals become involved, the concerns that motivate their involvement, and what they as individuals derive from their participation in a collective project. (Hamel, 1995, p. 236)

Introduction

Party members, argues Whiteley (1995, pp. 211–33), are a distinct group of people who by joining a party participate in politics far more than ordinary citizens. Consequently, these members are an ideal group to use for examining high-cost types of political participation.

The literature concerning political participation shows that most of the research in this area is devoted to the basic type of political participation – that is, voting – and such studies examine voters and their attitudes. Interestingly, party members, especially party activists, have not been studied at all. Some scholars have noticed this lack of attention and suggested an urgent need for more comprehensive research on party activists. The question of why some party members choose to become political activists while others do very little remains unanswered.[1]

There are different theories to explain citizens' involvement in politics. These theories run from rational self-interested individuals to class action; from resource mobilisation theory to opportunity structure theories; from psychological, individual needs to a function of an individual's social position. However, in my study I prefer to use the standard model developed by Verba and Nie (1972) and used by many students of politics. They argue that:

> The individual's decision to participate and how to participate depends on his social circumstances – the set of social characteristics that defines his 'life space,' where he lives, what he does for a living, his education, his race, and so forth. These social circumstances generate sets of attitudes conducive to or inhibitory of political participation. How and how much he participates will also be affected by the institutional structures within which he finds himself. All of these forces lead him to a decision to participate or not. (Verba and Nie, 1972, p. 19)

An important aspect of understanding why people join a political party is to examine the actual mechanics of how they join in the first place (Whiteley et al., 1994, p. 77). The way in which an individual joins a party, association or an interest group reveals a lot about that individual: their intention, level of commitment, expertise, social environment, motives, aspirations and the resources that he or she might possess. The same is true for the organisation itself.

This involvement process reveals the structure and the working principles of an organisation; for example, whether the organisation is open to everyone or if there are any restrictions or conditions, and whether it actively recruits new members or takes a passive attitude. This process demonstrates whether the party is resourceful and outgoing, whether it reaches out to ordinary people at the grassroots level, and whether it is actively engaged in recruiting or not. To uncover the workings of this involvement process, it is necessary to ask: what are the patterns of membership and why did members join the VP in the first place? By doing this I intend to reveal more about the driving forces behind joining the party and then becoming a political activist.

In chapter 2, I concentrated on the decline of the political party system in Turkey. It was observed that apart from the WP/VP, mainstream political parties have experienced widespread fragmentation, electoral volatility and organisational decline. Due to its nationwide, well-organised grassroots organisations and highly committed party activists, the WP/VP escaped this trend. As observed, grassroots organisations played a key role in the WP's rise to power. This chapter aims to reveal how and why the WP/VP's members joined the party in the first place and then to further analyse the socioeconomic circumstances of the party members. To do this I examine data collected in the field in Ankara from January to May 1999 and two follow-up visits and additional interviews from April to May 2000 to discern patterns such as activists' perception of their activities, how they describe themselves and their current position within the local grassroots organisations.

The Current Position of Members

When asked, the majority (79 per cent) of my informants described their role within the Virtue Party as grassroots activist or active member in the first instance. As Table 5.1 shows, the majority of them were leaders and representatives of neighbourhood executive committees.[2] One-third of them (9 of these 33 activists) said that in addition to their duties in the neighbourhood executive committee, they had either membership or office in the VP's sub-district (*ilçe*) organisation as well.

The second group (14 per cent) of my informants consisted of those who put their membership in the VP's *ilçe* committees before their

Table 5.1 Informants' answers to the question 'How would you describe your relationship with the VP?'

Type of participation	No. of people	%
A sympathiser/supporter of the VP	–	–
A VP voter	–	–
An active member of the VP (grassroots activist)	33	79
An activist who also holds an office membership in sub-district committee	6	14
Other (activists, party workers, branch administrators, etc.)	3	7
Total	42	100

Note: The fourth and fifth rows overlap each other. Some of these grassroots activists also hold an office or membership in the ilçe's excutive committee.
Source: Fieldwork in Mamak and Keçiören, Ankara.

position in their neighbourhoods. Those who put their role in the *ilçe* as office-holder or member of *ilçe* executive committee before their duty and role in the neighbourhood organisations showed a strong desire for upward mobility and high expectation of climbing up the career ladder in politics. There are studies indicating that career expectations are one of the motives for political participation and becoming a political activist. This point is analysed in detail later in this chapter, but for now it is enough to bear it in mind as a possible explanation among various others.

Only 7 per cent of respondents said they were activists without any office or membership of any committee. Some of them were also party workers – for example branch administrators or data processors. This group were also active not only in their local areas but, as full members of the VP, in other areas as well.

Activists were asked what their current positions were, in order to determine whether they held any elected office, position or membership in a particular committee, or whether they were just party activists with no elected office or membership (see Table 5.2). It appears

Table 5.2 Activists' answers to the question 'What is your current position within the VP's local organisation?'

Position	No. of people	%
Neighbourhood representative (leader of the neighbourhood committee)	17	40
Member of neighbourhood executive committee	6	14
Member of sub-district executive committee	4	10
Active member with no office or committee membership	4	10
Member of youth committee	5	12
Other (party inspector, worker, etc.)	6	14
Total	42	100

Source: Fieldwork in Mamak and Keçiören, Ankara.

that the majority (55 per cent) of the informants were members of either neighbourhood or *ilçe* executive committees. Four out of ten (41 per cent) of them were representatives of neighbourhood executive committees. They were the chairmen of the party organisation in that particular neighbourhood and they were directly accountable to the party's *ilçe* branch. They normally chaired the weekly meetings with the members of the executive committee if there was no one from the *ilçe* party organisation present. Some 14 per cent of them were members of executive committees in their neighbourhoods. The neighbourhood executive committees consisted of 14 members and they had a clear-cut division of labour among them. Some of the specific tasks done by the members included public relations, or serving as chairmen of the electoral affairs, education and propaganda, financial and other arms of the party. These members were responsible for carrying out their daily tasks in cooperation with the rest of the executive committee.

There was a systematic and efficient division of labour in the VP's local neighbourhood organisations. In terms of organisational structure, the neighbourhood organisations were too highly developed and specialised to function as a mass political party. Another aspect of this organisation was the sense of accountability within the party hierarchy. In a sense, all VP organisations were accountable, from the smallest neighbourhood organisation to the sub-district, and from district to the national centre of the party. One-fifth of my informants were current members of the executive committee in *ilçe*. This is a clear sign of upward mobility within the party organisation and very important for those activists. All of the members of the *ilçe* executive committees were also members of neighbourhood executive committees. In most cases they were natural chairmen of these neighbourhood organisations, but they wanted to be seen as members of an upper-level organisation in the first place. There was a vibrant, organic relationship between the neighbourhoods and the *ilçe* party organisations.

A further one-fifth of the activists held neither elected office nor any membership, but this does not mean that these members were less active or committed. They were very active and dedicated to their party. In fact, as they were free from all administrative duties and the paperwork required in the local branches, these activists could spend more time on canvassing, leaflet distribution, fundraising or meeting the people in the neighbourhood. Twelve per cent of my informants stated their current position as being a member of the youth committee. Several commentators on Turkish politics have noticed that the youth and ladies' committees were real assets of the Welfare Party (Ayata, 1997, p. 52; Çakır, 1994). In terms of political mobilisation, the WP/VP was the only political party in Turkey to have successfully integrated women into its party organisation. Often in poor *gecekondu* neighbourhoods, veiled women of every age group went door-to-door canvassing votes while the men were working. They used interesting and clever tactics and strategies: a mixture of religion – for example reading verses from the Koran or reciting poetry by Islamist poets – and conveying political propaganda in an often indirect, implicit way during their house meetings.

The youth committee, however, had a much more direct approach. The division of labour adopted by this committee was a mirror image of the neighbourhood executive committee. Their tasks were more diverse and more demanding in some ways. They varied from organising sporting activities and support facilities for young, often unemployed, people, to fundraising and organising charity events, to collecting money, food, clothes, shoes, coal and wood for heating, medicine and the like to give to the poor, elderly, disabled, orphans or widows in their neighbourhoods. The youth committee held seminars to educate those who felt drawn to the VP. These seminars were designed to indoctrinate newcomers and win over those who had not formally joined. The majority of the youth group were educated; most of them were at least high school graduates, many went to the religious İmam-Hatip Lises (prayer-leaders' and preachers' high schools) and some had university degrees.

During the election campaigns they usually carried out activities that required more muscle than brain. They put flags, posters and leaflets all around the *ilçe*. They worked late into the night. While I was in Ankara for my fieldwork, I witnessed them putting posters on all available walls in their neighbourhoods, hanging hundreds of plastic party flags between the electricity pylons and high buildings, and between balconies. Even the mosque minarets could not escape being decked with flags.

The Gençlik Komisyonu (youth committee) was an independent group with its own division of labour, but during the election campaign seemed to subordinate themselves, their youthful energy and its members their enthusiasm to the neighbourhood executive committee. During this time their physical strength and dynamism became crucial for the party's local election campaign.

The last category in my informant group was classified as the 'others', consisting of 14 per cent of my sample. These activists were not office holders or members of any committees, but they had important duties within the local party organisations. Some of them were working as full-time professionals for the party, but should not be confused with the professionals who organised the party campaigning or professional party workers in other, larger parties. Despite their professional status, they were no less active or less committed to the VP. Usually they were from the traditionally religious, conservative regions and were raised from an early age within Islamist groups such as Milli

Gençlik Vakfı (MGV; Foundation of the National Youth), which had been known as the school of the party since the early 1970s. This group included the party inspectors whose duties were to inspect all sorts of party activities on the ground and report to the *ilçe*. They were party activists with the special task of making sure that every unit and every individual did their bit in the service of the party. There were *müşahit* (teachers) and *başmüşahit* (head teachers) who educated the party members on various issues, from how to watch the ballot box on election days, to how to talk to or approach people in their neighbourhoods. There were administrators, secretaries and other clerical staff whose work was crucial for the party as well.

Path to Membership

Regional Disparity and Party Preferences

There are several dynamics involved in the process of party membership. It may be a rational choice for an individual seeking material benefit from his or her engagement with the party. It may be altruistic, emotional or expressive attachments that drive a person to join a particular party, or the person may be drawn by the social norms or collective incentives (see Whiteley et al., 1994, pp. 77–89). There are many theories concerned with the reasons for political involvement: resource mobilisation theory, collective action theory, Standard Socioeconomic Status Model, general incentive model, and others. The majority of my informants were born outside Ankara and in this context it is worthwhile considering whether there is any regional pattern or any significant relationship between regions and party membership.

The first pattern that emerge is that the majority of my informants came from less developed regions. More than three-quarters (76 per cent) of my informants were born elsewhere and migrated to Ankara at an early age. Most were born in the poorest Black Sea and Eastern Anatolia regions, historically strongholds of the pro-Islamic National Salvation Party and later the WP/VP. There is a close correlation between the index of regional development and party preferences. Therefore I suggest that people from the poorest regions in Turkey not only tended to vote for the WP/VP but also were (and are still) more inclined to become party activists compared to people from other provinces.

From an electoral perspective, regional divisions have been one of the important aspects of political life in Turkey. The studies of electoral support for political parties have indicated a direct and clear connection between the level of regional socioeconomic development and party support. Turkish scholars from the 1960s also noticed a connection between regional diversity and party support (see, for example, Özbudun, 1976, p. 104). There is a long-established pattern of regional differences in voting behaviour.

For example, in the elections of 1973 the National Salvation Party gained much of its electoral support from under developed and partially developed district (see Table 5.3). Its share of the vote in the developed regions was below the national average. This trend seems to have continued during the 1980s and 1990s.

It appears that regional diversity is also influential in terms of party membership. The results of my field survey showed that the majority of the VP's activists came from the poorest regions in the country. Turkey is geographically divided into seven regions. Not all the regions have a clear or consistent electoral trend, but the region of central Anatolia has been known for its traditional, conservative attitudes since the 1940s (see Mardin, 1991, p. 90). Especially in Sunni communities in the Eastern districts between the Kızılırmak

Table 5.3 The distribution of votes (%) in the 1973 election according to rate of regional socioeconomic development

Category of district	RPP	JP	NSP	DP	RRP	Others
Developed	38.6	32.3	8.4	10.3	3.8	6.6
Semi-developed	30.5	32.1	13.7	13.6	5.5	4.6
Under-developed	27.5	23.4	15.4	12.8	7.4	13.5

Note: RPP: Republican People's Party, JP: Justice Party, NSP: National Salvation Party, DP: Democratic Party, RRP: Republican Reliance Party; Others: other smaller parties such as the Worker's Party of Turkey (TIP).
Source: Şen, 1995, p. 20.

River and Erzurum, people were traditionally indoctrinated and set against the Alevis by the Sunni religious leaders (ibid.). In addition, this region has also experienced one of the highest rates of migration to urban centres.

It seems that throughout the 1980s and 1990s the Islamic movement made considerable political gains in central Anatolian towns such as Yozgat, Çankırı and Çorum. Parallel to this process the WP became the most popular party of the *gecekondu*. The increasing popularity of the WP/VP in poverty-stricken *gecekondu* areas relates to the same dynamics that apply in the less developed regions.[3]

It is not surprising, therefore, that three-quarters (76 per cent) of my informants came from four provinces: Yozgat, Çankırı, Çorum and Ankara. Three of these towns were among the 20 provinces where the WP had the highest share of the total votes in 1991 (see Çakır, 1994, p. 218). In the general elections of 1991 the WP received 39.5 per cent of the votes in Yozgat, 29.2 per cent in Çankırı and 27.9 per cent in Çorum (Çakır, 1994, pp. 216–26). From my survey data it appears that more than a quarter (26.19 per cent) of my informants were born in Yozgat. They later migrated to Ankara. Twelve per cent of my informants came from Çankırı. A similar number came from Çorum, another town that was at the centre of sectarian divide between Sunnis and Alevis. At the regional level this sectarian division determines the political cleavages. The second largest informant group (24 per cent) was born either in central Ankara or in Ankara's sub-districts. The rest of my informants, with the exception of two activists who were born in western towns, were mainly born in two eastern regions. These are Eastern Anatolia and the Eastern Black Sea region. One-fifth of my informants were born in Erzurum, Malatya and Gümüşhane in the Eastern Anatolia Region.

It has been pointed out by many students of politics that one of the most important variables in terms of political participation, voting behaviour and party preferences is socioeconomic condition. The socioeconomic status model was fully developed by Sidney and Nie (1972). They argue that those citizens who occupy higher social and economic status participate more than the average citizen with lower social status. Similar arguments are made by Barnes and Kaase,

1979; Milbarth, 1977; Parry, Moyeser and Day, 1992; Dalton, 1988; and Dowse and Hughes, 1986. As citizens identified themselves as belonging to a certain group or social class, they voted for parties that explicitly stood for their interests (Hague et al., 1998, p. 106).

What can we make of all this? It is evident that there has been a clear connection between the index of socioeconomic development and support for political parties at the regional level. As observed, the majority of VP activists migrated to Ankara from the less developed Central, Eastern Anatolia and Black Sea regions. From the early 1970s the Islamist parties have been the parties of the petit bourgeoisie, traditional small merchants, tradesmen, artisans, shopkeepers and the poor peasantry in these less developed regions (Yücekök, 1997, pp. 40–51). From the mid-1980s the WP expanded its social bases among the urban poor (see chapter 4).

The core of the WP/VP's support has been the mass of wage and salary earners, traditional small artisans, merchants, tradesman and shopkeepers as well as the lower and middle classes who had lost out under the neoliberal economic policies implemented since the 1980s.[4] The WP made considerable election gains from mainly *gecekondu* areas of the big urban centres.[5] As argued in chapter 4, from the late 1980s the WP/VP assumed the role of the social democrat parties in these rundown areas, where it ran support networks for newcomer *gecekondu* dwellers. Its grassroots organisations mobilised the *gecekondu* population very effectively.

How Did People Become Party Members?

I asked party members questions about the recruitment procedure: whether the party recruited them or whether they decided by themselves and approached the party. The question was: 'If you go back to the date that you joined the party, did you approach the party or did the party approach you?'

The process of membership is one of the less studied but more important aspects of political participation. The way an individual joins a party, association or interest group indicates a lot about the individual's intentions, level of commitment, expertise and the resources

Table 5.4 How activists became members of the party

Reason	No. of people	%
I thought and decided by myself	16	39
Party approached via a friend of mine	11	26
Someone from my family/relatives asked me to join	9	21
Loyalty to/admiration for the party leader	6	14
Total	42	100

Source: Şen, 1995, p. 20.

that he or she might possess. The same is relevant for the organisation itself. This process would indicate if the party was resourceful and outgoing – actively engaging in recruitment or not.

As shown in Table 5.4, two-fifths (39 per cent) of my informants can be classified as 'self-starters', which means they themselves thought carefully and decided to join the party. To become a member as a 'self-starter' is a significant indicator of the emotional and ideological commitment of the specific individual. According to the 'general incentive model' that is used in this study, 'self-starters' can be classified as activists who have a high degree of expressive motive to participate (Whiteley, 1995, p. 223). Self-starters may well be the cream of the party activists because of their high level of ideological conviction and passion for the party. The second most numerous group (26 per cent) comprised those who were recruited by the party to join, which shows the party's considerable effectiveness in recruiting new members, especially in the case of party activists.

The WP/VP used various strategies and tactics both for recruiting new members and for vote canvassing. They were always keen to approach people in an informal, friendly way – usually by using friends, traditional family networks, kin relations or *hemşehri* associations.[6] More than one-quarter (26 per cent) of activists reported that they were approached by the party via a friend. This indicates at least two different dynamics at the local level. One of them was a very well–organised, militant, hard-working and active local party organisation that was able to recruit new members.

It must be acknowledged that the WP/VP skilfully tapped into the existing traditional, religious and cultural resources. From the early days pro-Islamist parties had always creatively made use of traditional religious networks, relationships, associations, groups and cultural resources. They also utilised the traditional solidarity organisations that have been around for centuries. Additionally, they innovatively reconfigured the old, traditional political culture especially in relation to religious issues, social justice and equality, for example the rhetoric of *Adil Düzen*, with a greater emphasis on Islamic brotherhood and the like. Also, the WP/VP, in its political campaigning, used a certain type of language and phrasing with which most people identify. The glorification of the Ottoman era as the 'golden past' has been one of the strongest aspects of Islamist activists on the ground. The third group, making up 21 per cent of the activists, said someone from their family had played a leading role in their involvement with the party. Like many things in our lives, politics and political attitudes are learned from an early age. This process is called political socialisation. According to Cord et al. (1974, p. 184) political socialisation is:

> the process by which the individuals in a given social system learn their values, norms, concepts and attitudes about both the political and the individual's relationship to the political system [...] In the broadest sense, political socialisation is the way in which a society perpetuates its political culture. It is a continuous, lifelong process, which is part of each individual's conditioning and education as much as of the culture he is born into.

In this process the individual learns from family – father, mother, brother, sister and other relatives – about all aspects of politics. In later life he or she may retain these ideas, as most people do. Studies have shown that even long after we have left home the influence of our parents continues to affect many aspects of our behaviour. For example, most people vote as their parents did. The family is the most influential factor in a person's political behaviour because it controls the early years crucial to the development of the personality of an individual, between three and 13 (Cord et al., 1974, p. 185; see also

Dawson and Prewitt, 1969, pp. 5–6). Literature indicates that those who are raised in politically active families are very likely to inherit the family norms of participation and their political persuasion will be affected by 'family tradition' (Seyd and Whiteley, 1992, p. 65; see also Butler and Stokes, 1974). Table 5.4 shows that for 21 per cent of my informants, membership happened through the family. Table 5.5 also clearly shows the influence of family on a person's political choices.

Also crucial is a person's emotional attachment and loyalty to other primary groups, or what Whiteley (1995, p. 223) referred to as 'significant others'. He argued that 'party activists are motivated by the perception of social norms, the opinion of "significant others" or people whose opinions they respect and value'. People develop very deep emotional ties and long-lasting loyalties and a sense of belonging towards primary groups such as family, peer groups and small, close communities. The last group of members is those who joined the party because of their loyalty and admiration for the party leader. Some 14 per cent of them joined the party for this reason. This was confirmed by my observations too.

Family and Party Membership

> Among all of the influences acting on partisan identification, the family is the strongest. (Crotty and Jacobson; 1980, p. 26)

The vast majority (79 per cent) of the VP's activists had another member of family who was, one way or another, involved: either a member or even a party activist in some cases, or otherwise a VP supporter or voter (see Table 5.5).

What is most interesting and significant in terms of the role of family and political participation is that within this group 26 per cent said their whole family were members of, supporters of or at least voted for the VP. In this context the term 'whole family' includes extended nuclear family: parents, brother and sisters, children if they are over 18, uncles, aunts and cousins. Sometimes it can be interpreted as a clan-like family, who especially in less developed rural regions tend to live together under an elder leader. These traditional large families support political patronage – the traditional form of

Table 5.5 VP activists' answers to the question 'Apart from you, is there anyone in your family or close kin who is also a member, supporter or voter of the WP/VP?'

Answers	No. of people	(%)
Yes, there is someone	33	79
Who are they?		
Parents	8	19
Wife	8	19
Children	6	14
Brother/sister	3	7
Uncle/aunt	2	5
Part of family	4	10
Whole family	11	26
No, there is no one	9	21
Total	42	100

Source: Fieldwork in Mamak and Keçiören, Ankara.

political participation. In the next section I discuss how my informants assess their own role as grassroots activists in relation to the electoral outcomes.

Political Efficacy and Party Membership

Seyd and Whiteley (1992, pp. 219–20) point out that if the individual believes that his or her participation will be for the collective good then there is a greater chance that he or she will participate. During my field research I observed that grassroots activists were influential on both sides: within the local community as well as rallying for local needs, problems and demands at the sub-district level. I asked: 'If you were asked to rate the significance of grassroots activism upon the party's performance on a scale, how would you rate it?'

As Table 5.6 indicates three-quarters of VP grassroots activists believed their political activism was 'very important for the party's election results', and one in five of them believed it was 'important'.

Table 5.6 VP activists' opinions on the importance of grassroots activism

Degree of importance	No. of people	%
Very important	33	74
Important	8	19
Not so important	1	2
Insignificant	–	–
Other	2	05
Total	42	100

Source: Fieldwork in Mamak and Keçiören, Ankara.

This means that the vast majority of activists valued their participation highly and strongly believed it would make a difference. Following Seyd and Whiteley's (1992) logic it can be argued that my informants joined the party and chose to become political activists because they strongly believed that their grassroots activities were 'very important' to the electoral performance of the VP.[7]

Most Important Reasons for Membership

When asked the most important reason for becoming members, informants' answers varied from religious grounds to ideological reasons, from national and sacred values to the WP/VP's specific economic policy of a 'just order', or as a reaction to other parties. The literature review confirms that the discourse of political participation is a contentious issue among students of politics.

Since my research focused on the grassroots activism of the WP/VP I had to grasp the initial motivation of the members for joining the party. As such, I designed an open-ended question in my questionnaire to gauge the motives for membership. The choice of an open-ended question was a deliberate attempt not to restrict or lead informants to pre-coded categories. Hence the informant felt free to express the most important reasons for joining the party. I asked 'Can you tell me what was the most important reason for you to become a member of the VP?'

Without delving into theoretical debates, I describe what my informants said about the process of becoming a member and getting involved

Table 5.7 WP/VP members' answers to the question 'Can you tell me what was the most important reason for you to become a member of the VP?'

Reason for joining the WP/VP	No. of people	%
Religious reasons, because it is an Islamist party.	17	40
Ideological closeness/The WP/VP respects and protects the national and sacred values.	9	21
Only the WP/VP can best solve the socioeconomic problems for the country.	6	14
Other reasons: trustworthiness, cleanness, loyalty to leadership, protecting the poor, etc.	7	17
As a reaction to other parties.	3	7
Total	42	100

Source: Fieldwork in Mamak and Keçiören, Ankara.

with the WP/VP. The stated reasons varied but they could be collected under the following headings: religious, ideological, the party's ability to solve the socioeconomic problems, reaction to other political parties, and other reasons including trustworthiness, loyalty to the leadership, and protecting the rights of weak and poor people.

Religious Reasons

It is an established fact that the WP and its predecessor the VP have been described as the religiously oriented or pro-Islamist party, and this fact, it seems, played a very significant role in the process of membership (see Kalaycıoğlu, 1998, p. 15). More than 40 per cent of grassroots activists joined the WP/VP for religious reasons (see Table 5.7). In other words, they were drawn to the WP/VP as an Islamist party. For this reason, I used the interviews to determine in greater detail the reasoning behind the religious motives for party membership.

Through the interviews, I examined the issues, priorities, problems and reasons that respondents expressed for joining the WP/VP. Throughout my fieldwork I talked to many political activists about why they joined the party. Süha Çelik was one of them: he was a member of the administrative committee of the VP Keçiören subdistrict. He owned a furniture shop in Siteler, a large industrial estate where the major furniture production and trade is based. I asked him the most important reason why he joined the VP.

> Because of my beliefs and my attachment to the Refah (Welfare) party in the past I have chosen this party [the VP]. Also, the VP is the closest party to my beliefs, worldviews and my race and I believe only the VP would back me in this manner [...] I joined the VP because we (my friends and I are mostly tradesmen, shopkeepers and artisans) are criticising things constantly among us. Later I thought if we are criticising things and if they are bad and you are good then you have got to do something to change this. Then I thought, I must come forward and work towards this end. If you go then you would deter one bad person. If a man is good then he must do the same thing. So, I thought, by doing this we would clean up politics.

It is well known that grievances are the first conditions of any political action, but they usually do not mean much unless an individual, one way or another, decides to take action. In Süha Çelik's case he and his associates were criticising aspects of their lives and these discussions led him to take action. He explained this as a desire to deter one 'bad politician' from office by involving a 'good' man in politics. Alongside religious reasons, he firmly believed that if the 'good people' like himself and friends got into active politics rather than just passively criticising things, they could serve a cause: to provide some sort of public good.

The second case was Nizami Demir, one of the oldest informants at 68. He had been actively engaged in politics since the late 1960s. He joined the Islamic movement with the foundation of the National Order Party – the first party born out of the Islamic movement in 1969. He explained why he joined the Islamic movement and became a political activist:

> I have been in this movement since the National Order Party (1969) and the reason for my membership was that I wanted

> to serve the rise of Islam, for the sake of Allah and in order to establish a state that is based on Allah's laws, the Sharia. When I joined the party no one asked or guided me there. I myself searched and decided to join. I have passionately devoted myself to this cause; it is for the sake of Allah. I hoped and wanted to live a true Islam with its real meaning and so joined the party.

A similar statement was made by another activist:

> For me the most important reason was to support our Islamic cause. Also, supporting the VP to rescue Tayyip Erdoğan and Hoca from imprisonment, as well as defending the İmam-Hatips [religious schools]. (Halis, VP Aktepe neighbourhood representative)

Mütalip Özbay explained his membership as follows: 'It is an attempt to make the religion of Islam prosper. I believed that I can find a better opportunity under the WP/ VP government, and live my life as my religion orders me.'

A great many people joined the VP because it was an Islamist party. For example, Fazlı Dalkıran of Yeşiltepe neighbourhood said 'it is an Islamist party and inclined towards Islam. Where there is Islam, there we are.' In the case of religious beliefs and party preferences, the party's attitudes towards religious beliefs were also a determining factor for membership. Dalkıran said: 'I have joined the VP because it is a party which most suits my religious beliefs'.

The fact that the VP had an Islamist outlook attracts like-minded people from all walks of life. Naci Tunalı, representative of Ekin Başak neighbourhood, also joined for a similar reason. He said:

> Because it is close and warm to Islam. We are raised in this way; there would not be any other party. It was only the WP who provided a life that Islam orders us. It proposes *Adil Düzen* as well.

Mustafa Şahin, a member of the municipality parliament of Mamak, said: '[I joined the party] because of its Islamist worldview, and its

Islamist policies'. To serve or to support the Islamic cause, 'to establish an Islamic regime', as they put it, was one of the most frequently cited reasons among this group. It can be argued that those activists who joined the party for the cause of Islam were ideologically more radical than the other VP activists. It has been observed by students of political science that ideological radicalism is one of the most important causes of the political participation (Ashford, 1972; Barnes and Kaase, 1979; Marsh, 1990; and Milbrath and Goel, 1977). This is true of some of the WP/VP's activists who joined the party to serve the Islamic cause, to establish a regime based on the Koran's principles. They would argue that all Muslim communities, unless an unbeliever's army occupies them, must live by God's book and orders, not by man-made laws and rules. From the perspective of this group, Turkey – as a staunchly secular state – is not a place where they can live by the Koran. This perspective made them get involved in politics in a more active way. As Kitschelt (1989, p. 407) suggested, those party militants who are more radical and calling for rapid, comprehensive and profound changes in society and politics, are more likely to be recruited by the political parties, to make converts among party activists and to gain office.[8]

Perhaps, then, it is not surprising that large numbers of people joined the VP for religious reasons; religion has always been a social variable that influences political preferences, and this is true in the Turkish case too. As Jennings et al. (1979, p. 463) argued:

> Although advanced industrial societies are becoming increasingly secularised, the vestiges of religious cleavages are impressive indeed. One of the most successful predictors of party allegiance and voting in most Western European countries remains religious preference, however nominal that preference may be. Many European parties are divided into the secular versus confessional based, and sometimes within the later between Catholic and non-Catholic [...] Moreover, religious institutions continue to be strongly evident in all countries.

In another major study, religion was placed among the seven variables that influenced political participation: education, income, sex, age, race, religion and location (see Verba and Nie, 1972, pp. 97–101). Despite changing value systems, 'most of the political parties are still organised around Old Political cleavages of class and religion' (Dalton, 1998, p. 148). The interaction of religion and politics is a historical fact. Religion had dominated almost every aspect of social life for centuries. When the political parties emerged it was there and ready to provide social bases for political parties, with the class cleavage entering the arena later.

Other studies also show that the influence of religion on voting behaviour continues (see Kalaycıoğlu, 1998, p. 10). In Turkey there exists a historical sociocultural cleavage that runs along the secular/religious divide.

If we go back to the empirical data there are a variety of statements that describe what respondents really meant by religious reasons. Some of them joined the party to support the *İslami dava* (Islamic cause), or so that the religion of Islam could prosper, as well as to support the establishment of a Sharia regime on the basis of the Koran. For some it was the VP's warm and intimate approach to Islam, while others said 'because it is compatible with my Islamic identity'.

In many societies, including Turkey, religion is one of the bases of political ideology (Turan, 1994, p. 42). As a primary element of culture, religion has acted as a constant source of political ideology. Especially in times of rapid change, religion provides certainty, stability and continuity.

As one would expect, there appears to be a close correlation between Islamic identity and party membership. For example, Remzi Özcan, a representative of the neighbourhood of Misket, said that:

> We all have an Islamic identity. For me the most important reason was the VP's Islamic character, which is compatible with my religious beliefs. When I decided to join a political party I went to different political parties and listened to different discussions; in the end I saw that I had a deep-rooted passion for this party. I said, so this is the party where I am going to work, and God let me do so.

Similarly, other activists argued that the VP represented an Islamic identity. This is important for people who are very loyal to their religion. Now I shall look at the second most cited reason for party membership.

Ideological Motives: Loyalty to the National and Sacred Values

On the second rank of Table 5.7 come the ideological reasons. The VP's loyalty to the *milli ve manevi değerler* (national and sacred values) seemed to play an important role when activists decided to join. More then one in five (21 per cent) of VP activists joined the party because they believed that like its predecessors, it was the only party loyal to those values. In general terms, respect for the national and religious values and traditions, desire for the preservation of the traditional lifestyle, old customs, and above all a glamorisation of the past were important ideological values shared by VP members. Also, in this context, it is important to recall that the *milli ve manavi değerler* have always been at the centre of the ideology of the Islamic movement in Turkey (see Sarıbay, 1985, p. 99; Yücekök, 1971, pp. 175–78; Yücekök, 1997).

Muhlis Karaağaç, from the neighbourhood of Kutlu in Mamak, grew up in Sungurlu, a sub-district in the district of Çorum. He was born in 1949, and his father was a *kapici* (doorkeeper) in Sungurlu. He moved to Ankara when he was 13 years old and studied in a vocational training college. He got involved in a right-wing student union at an early age and later joined the ultra-nationalist Nationalist Action Party. Karaağaç noted:

> We are, from birth, inclined towards right-wing parties. I finished Elementary School in Sungurlu and when I was going to start high school I came to Ankara. Through a friend of mine I got involved in Milli Turk Talebe Birligi (the National Turkish Student Union) in 1975. After my graduation from high school the left–right clash started and my father was shot by Dev Sol [Revolutionary Left] people. Then I shot one of them and got imprisoned.
>
> I was originally a member of the Nationalist Action Party and at that time the National Salvation Party seemed pacifist to us

> or so we thought. After the military coup in 1980 I was not involved in any political party until 1987. In 1987 we (my five brothers and me) set up the NAP's first *Bizimocak* branch in Dereboyu Street where no leftists were allowed to enter. I was a member of the NAP at that time but came from the same social background as the majority of the WP/VP people. For example, we pray five times a day, we are true believers, and we always defend these people in our workplace. I mean, no matter what your outlook, because I was praying regularly they would call me *Refahlı* – Refah's people. To tell the truth I was defending the ideas of the WP but I was not a member or anything like that. Finally I joined the WP. The most important reason for my membership was its loyalty and respect for national and religious values.

This short summary of Karaağaç's schooling and migration from Çorum to Ankara and the process of joining the WP/VP tells us a lot about his political orientation. Starting from an early age, he always identified himself with right-wing politics. He was raised in a poor working-class family; his father was a doorman and was probably not able to maintain his large family in Sungurlu, so migration was essential for the family's survival. In Ankara he got involved in an ultra-nationalist student movement, became an activist, and was caught up with the street violence that characterised the 1970s. He shot someone from a leftist group and was imprisoned for a while. But as he grew older he started to move towards the WP and finally became a member and activist in 1994.

Twenty-one per cent of my informants joined the party for similar ideological reasons. In the case of Remzi Özcan from the neighbourhood of Misket, he too was formerly close to the ultra right-wing Nationalist Action Party and like many others he migrated to Ankara to find a job in his early teens. He explains:

> I was close to the (NAP); I mean in my childhood I was with the NAP as were 90 per cent of the people from the district of Yozgat. Before the military coup of 1980, approximately

> 90 per cent of Yozgat supported the NAP. At that time I was a student. After school I went away to find a job. There I started to join political gatherings, meetings and so on. By then because of my Islamic identity I liked Hoca's [Erbakan's] speeches so started to listen to him [...] As I said, the most important reason for my membership was the ideological closeness. It is also close to my religious beliefs, because I have got an Islamic identity and I saw that there are big similarities between my beliefs and the WP's ideology. Before joining the WP/VP I thought and enquired about some of the other political parties, I listened to their speeches and I attended their meetings. I saw that none of them were for me, so I said well this is it, it is the WP where you are going to serve people. And Allah helped me to get to work for this party. I am here because it follows Allah's path.

He continued:

> I have no material expectations from my service of this cause. For ten years I have been working personally for this party without any expectations or any material gain. I have never asked for any favour or put forward any demand to the party. So far I have been managing things by my own resources, self sufficiently. I do whatever I can do and up to the point I can carry on.

There are great similarities between the last two cases. Both identified themselves with the ultra-nationalist NAP in their youth and both approached political Islam for ideological reasons and national and religious values. In this interview Özcan highlighted a very interesting aspect of political activism; that is, the expectations of the party membership. As I argue in chapter 6, membership has certain responsibilities and benefits. Although the rights and responsibilities of party membership vary according to the party type, in most cases resources, material benefits or influence are also gained from membership. Özcan says, 'I have never asked for any favour or put forward any demand', but at the same time he actually indicates that there are activists within the VP who benefit either materially or otherwise from their membership, which is usually seen as the by-product of party activism. Of course, this matter is rather sensitive and hard to talk about but Özcan's interview provides some insight. There are many more activists who joined the VP for ideological reasons rather than for what they could gain from party membership.

It is rather remarkable to see that since the beginning of the 1970s the pro-Islamic party's core ideological aspect – its religious and national values – had not been dented at all. In other words, they were still the highest-ranking values. In the field this fact was mentioned by many party activists. For example, a retired worker from the Turkish Railway told me that:

> The reason I am in this party is that the VP gives greater priority to religious values. Also they are trustworthy, would not steal or deny anyone's rights. The leadership is uncorrupted. I used to be a supporter of the NAP but later they got corrupted and started to turn into criminal gangs in every corner.

The fact that the majority of VP activists appeared to be more radical than the VP leadership and the ordinary VP voter seemed to be a paradox, and a contradiction of my original hypothesis. In chapter 1, I hypothesise that the rise of political Islam was not necessarily a result of a re-Islamisation of society, widespread Islamic revivalism or an expansion of Islamic fundamentalism. Rather, it was partly a reaction against the major socioeconomic shifts and partly due to the WP/VP's very well-organised, militant grassroots organisations. How can this paradox be explained?

It is observed that rank-and-file activists in a political party are more radical than the party leadership on the one hand, and the party voters on the other (Seyd and Whiteley, 1992, p. 100). This point is confirmed by my findings as well. The empirical findings suggest that there is curvilinearity between the VP's activists on the one hand, and the leader and party voters on the other hand. At first glance it seems that an ideological gulf between a group of individuals within the same party is unthinkable, but their positions within the party led them to different ideological positions.

Is there any evidence of an ideological gulf between the voters and party activists within the VP? It seems that such an ideological gap existed (see Table 5.7). For example, research showed that only one-third of WP voters voted for the party because it was an Islamic party (see Heper, 1997, p. 35). The law of curvilinear disparity is visibly illustrated when comparing Heper's (1997) findings with Table 5.7. The comparison of the data (Table 5.7) with data from Heper (ibid.) suggests that there was a disparity between the grassroots activists and the WP/VP's voters. Three in five (62 per cent) of my respondents joined the party because of religious and ideological incentives, whereas according to a survey (ibid.), 'only one-third of the WP's voters voted for the party primarily because it was an Islamic party'.

Finally, the fact that 62 per cent of my informants expressed either religious or ideological incentives as the most important reason for their membership of the WP/VP indicates a strong ideological and radical presence among VP grassroots activists. And it seems at this point we can answer one of our initial questions: 'what draws members to join the party in the first place?' The answer has to be ideological radicalism, because it seems that on average the VP's members were twice as radical as ordinary VP voters.

Ideology, Identity and Political Participation

One of the most acknowledged predictors of political participation is ideology, and for this reason ideology is the most studied factor of the political process.[9] Everything other than ideology is part of culture, especially the political culture.[10] But ideology can be distinguished from political culture by its clarity, coherence and greater internal consistency. Because of its consistency it can influence political action more than political culture. Ideology also 'contains a set of political values, states to be desired and, if possible, striven for, attained and maintained' (Dowse and Hughes, 1986, p. 236). Therefore, it can be said that to understand a particular political ideology is to understand that political culture. I will briefly introduce the development of the Islamic ideology in Turkey but first it is important to emphasise a few crucial points regarding the importance of ideology in the political process, especially its role in party support and membership.

Empirical evidence suggests that the rate of conventional political participation is positively influenced by the degree of political sophistication (Klingemann, 1979, p. 281). The first function of ideology is to help the individual to order, retain and understand political information. It provides a framework into which new information can be placed, coded and given wider meaning. It becomes possible to process new information once a framework has been established. The level of ideological thinking, in other words 'ideological conceptualisation', is seen as the first and most important precondition for making and acting upon political judgements, but according to Marsh (1990, p. 58) it is not always a sufficient condition. For Marsh, 'it is when the holder of an organised body of political knowledge identifies with one set of ideological values, within the Left, Right, or whatever, that strong political judgements are made'.

According to Daniel Bell (cited in Daves and Hughes, 1986, p.238), ideology can be described as 'the conversion of ideas into social levers'. For Bell, ideology has the capacity to make people take action. Again, he suggests that 'the most important, latent, function of ideology is to tap emotion', so that those who share this ideology will act to achieve the ends indicated by the ideology. As far as Sorel (ibid.) is concerned, ideology creates a sense of mission and nobility. It creates solidarity among believers.

In terms of ideology and value consciousness, on average my informants had a high level of ideological conceptualisation and a strong adherence to national and sacred values. A Europe-wide study found that the level of ideological thought and political action are very closely connected and those who acquire a high level of political thought tend to participate in high-level political activity, for example becoming political activists (see chapter 3; Klingemann, 1979, Marsh, 1990, p. 279). It seems this generalisation also applies to VP activists in Turkey. I observed that the majority of VP members had a high level of ideological conceptualisation and recognition; party activists especially seemed to have a very advanced knowledge of Turkish politics, and a knowledge of current socioeconomic and political issues.

Although I have processed the religious and ideological reasons separately, they can be seen as a different way of expressing the same thing. Religious reasons (40.42 per cent) and ideological reasons (21.42 per cent) such as ideological closeness and loyalty to national and sacred or religious values can in fact be classified under the *principle of Islamism*, which includes the principles of Islam and the desire for greater Islamisation in society.[11] In this case, those who chose to become members and activists of the VP comprised almost two-thirds (62 per cent) of all VP activists.

'The VP is the Best for the Country'

The main incentive to this group's involvement with the VP was 'the collective positive incentive' resulting from the implementation of a party programme or the value of collective goods. Whiteley, Seyd and Richardson developed the collective benefit incentive (1994; see also Seyd and Whiteley, 1992, chapters 4 and 5). It is assumed that those party activists who most agree with the general party views should have the greatest incentive to seek the implementation of those policies and therefore to work hard in their constituencies (Whiteley et al., 1994, p. 114).

As already noted, two in five of my informants joined the VP for reasons other than religious or ideological. Nearly half of this group (14 per cent of all VP grassroots activists) joined the VP because they thought it was the best available option among political parties to solve the country's problems (see Table 5.7). This category will be examined under two sections. The first group, which consists of 14 per cent of all informants, expressed their trust in the VP to serve the country better. What incentives drew them to join the VP? It was apparent from some of the interviews that there were individuals who joined the party thinking of the welfare and well-being of the people.

> I thought about how I can contribute to the welfare and the well-being of the people of Turkey. In this process the VP appeared as the party in which I could do these things if I joined, and so I became a member of it. Otherwise there wasn't any personal expectation or anything like that. (representative of Aşağı Ayrancı neighbourhood)

The Aşağı Ayrancı representative clearly indicates the elements of the solidaristic views among the grassroots activists. It is a desire to contribute to the welfare and happiness of others with whom activists associate. In this context it can be argued that unlike the first two categories of participants this third group joined the VP for non-ideological and religious reasons. This means they are not concerned with Islamic principles but with worldly, everyday problems such as how to help others in society, and how to solve long-term socioeconomic problems.

As mentioned earlier the WP/VP developed a new political rhetoric from the early 1980s onwards: 'serving the people'. In a historical context this had never been the case in Turkey. It had always been the other way around: only the state deserves its citizens' service and obedience. From the start of one-party rule, this view was the mainstream approach among political parties. Contrary to this, one of the VP's leaders said that politics is a competition for the 'best servant of the people'. In a similar vein, another informant said:

> I wanted to be a member of the VP because they could serve our country much better. They are trustworthy, they treat everyone equally, they like their fellow citizens and they are the best people.

The second element is that the party is seen as honest, trustworthy, morally superior and uncorrupted. Widespread corruption and corrupt politicians have been a matter of concern for some time in Turkey. Since the 1980s the issues of political corruption, bribery, nepotism and favouritism, combined with organised criminal gangs, some business circles and mafia connections have been common elements of the political scenery. For example, Hasan Tüzün from the Ayvalı neighbourhood highlighted the lack of any interest among mainstream political parties in protecting the rights of disadvantaged sections of society; instead the parties are seen as corrupt and involved in organised crime. For him, the opposite is true for the VP: 'I found the VP closer to me because they defend the rights of the poor and the weak people. They are never involved with the mafia or organised criminal gangs.'

For representatives of the Hürel neighbourhood, the most important issues were similar to those mentioned by previous informants: 'the political situation, widespread injustice, the plight of the nation and socioeconomic conditions' were the main reasons why the respondent from this district joined the party. Here again the driving forces behind his participation were a sense of dissatisfaction with the current social and economic conditions, social inequalities and mistrust of other political parties.[12] One of my informants noted that the pro-Islamic parties advocated alternative development strategies, which combined material (economic) development with spiritual (religious) development:

> Now, Hoca used to use a phrase '*maddi ve manevi kalkinma*' [material/economic and spiritual/religious development]. He was saying that we would take these two issues together. So I liked the idea. I think it is our most natural right as Muslims. We need economic development as well as spiritual in this world. Every Muslim should be rich so that he can live in good faith. On the other hand, good faith is necessary when we go to the other World. Yes we are believers. Believing in all His commands, all His Verses that are sent us, is *sunet* and *sebiyets* therefore we joined the party. (İrfan Erdoğan)

When we look at how and why İrfan Erdoğan joined the party it appears that he considered the issues addressed by the leader of the WP/VP: economic development, modernisation and industrialisation, not only in material terms but also in the context of spiritual development and well-being. It seems that for him the spiritual and religious aspects of life played a key role in his involvement in the Islamic movement, as did his the hope for economic development and higher living standards. The issue of economic development on the basis of greater industrialisation has always been given great importance by the leadership of the Islamic movement.

It must be said that this close interaction, cooperation and coordination was highly significant for the success of the party. As the only mass membership party the WP/VP developed a close relationship and cooperation between the party and the potential voter.[13] Thus it made a real difference in terms of voter turnout and public support for the VP. The closer relationship between the party and the people gave the VP a very positive image. This positive image could then be translated into voter support at the elections. This aspect was also a frequently expressed reason given by many grassroots activists for their close involvement with the party.

Other Reasons for Joining the Party

The fourth group shown in Table 5.7 was classified as 'others'. This group gave other reasons than religious or ideological ones. They made up 17 per cent of the total informant group. They saw the VP as trustworthy, which means politically clean, uncorrupted and the party of the poor. Some said they trusted the VP because it would not steal people's money, and it was open and not corrupt, unlike other parties. Some of them expressed loyalty to the leadership. There were people who supported the VP as an act of solidarity because of what they saw as its unfair treatment by the media, security forces and other parties. In first place came the issue of corruption, and the party's record on this matter.

In a country where public resources and power are distributed, by and large, through clientelist networks, there is inevitably widespread corruption and injustice. I stated earlier that in the 1990s corruption, favouritism and clienteles had reached a degree that undermined citizens' trust in governmental agencies and the legitimacy of the whole system. The widespread corruption and nepotism not only created an atmosphere of contempt, resentment and alienation of large sections of society, but it also allowed a small group of multi-millionaires to mushroom while the problems of unemployment and poverty get steadily worse. This had also dangerously eroded the most fundamental ethical and moral values in society.

Ordinary people in Turkey believe that all politicians and parties are involved in corruption to some degree, but the question is which party is least corrupt. In this case, because of its religious orientation and supposed moral superiority, the WP/VP had the upper hand in elections.

It seems that moralist politics developed as a reaction against institutionalised and widespread corruption scandals, patron–client relations and non-transparent governance. The more politics was dominated by moral issues, the more support the WP/VP enjoyed, and the more members it gained.

Here are some of my informants' views on the WP/VP. Ahmet Çavuşoğlu, a member of the Mamak *ilçe* executive committee, explained what he thought about the VP when he joined:

> I have found the WP/VP truthful and genuine. Their words and promises match with their actions. You could not see this in other parties. This party comes from within the people so it deals with the people's problems. It acts with the people.

Similarly the representative of Bahçeleriçi neighbourhood argued that:

> [The VP] are trustworthy, uncorrupted, genuine, truthful and would not promise anything that they could not deliver. What they say is that they work for the sake of Allah [...] There are people who have been discriminated against because of their beliefs. It is something that is widespread. All citizens feel that way. For example, my wife is veiled and she won't lower it even if you offered her an apartment in the Çankaya district. But my daughters do not wear a headscarf and they won't wear it for an apartment in Çankaya either.

He points out the moral and ethical characteristics that were important for his involvement with the party. The characteristics that he highlights, such as trustworthiness, are those that every political party should normally have, but this is often not the case. He also raises the issue of discrimination and repression on the basis of religious and ideological beliefs. Such issues are obviously very important and are discussed below. For now I return to the issue of corruption and its implication for politics from the early 1980s to the 2000s.

The Issue of Corruption

Corruption has infected all institutions and many layers of Turkish society since the early 1980s. The reason for this widespread and persistent corruption has been the involvement of three important circles: *derin devlet* (deeper state or the inner circle), the mafia and the politicians. One of the prime reasons for the scale of this corruption is the low-intensity war against the Kurdish rebel group the PKK in the south-east of the country. Many unlawful acts have been carried out in the name of national unity and defence of the country against the separatist movement. During the 1990s Turkey witnessed rampant corruption, gigantic scandals and abuse of public funds, which inevitably eroded the already low public confidence in political parties and parliament. No wonder that for more than a decade politicians have been the least trusted and respected people in Turkey.[14] Loss of confidence in the political elite badly affected the political parties, to the extent that for more then a decade no party was able to obtain a majority, or even 25 per cent of the vote, to form a single-party majority government. Consequently, unstable and patchy coalition governments ruled Turkey until the 2002 general elections, and since then the pro-Islamic AKP has been in government.

Although the relationship between the *derin devlet*, the mafia, business people, politicians and bureaucrats had been speculated on for a long time, a traffic accident involving a lorry and a Mercedes near the town of Susurluk opened a Pandora's box.[15] It revealed the multiple dimensions of the corruption and the close triangular relationship between politicians, the mafia and the police.[16] It is believed that despite the many revelations that followed the Susurluk accident, reports by the state-appointed inspector, the senior legal figure Kutlu Savaş, media reports, and accounts by many independent reporters, only the tip of an enormous iceberg was uncovered.[17] As political corruption became more visible in everyday practices, the long-forgotten ethical and moral dimensions of politics made a comeback into political discourse. Ethical and moral issues and religious values came to be seen as serious election issues. The WP/VP, as the pro-Islamic party, rightly criticised its opponents for being unethical and immoral and claimed superiority.

In this context the WP was helped by two factors. The first was that it had not been in government since the 1980s, so had no record of corruption, scandal or any wrongdoing. Second, and more importantly, because the WP was a religious Islamic party it was able to claim moral superiority over its rivals. Indeed, it did not require much effort by grassroots activists to turn this moral superiority and clean image into electoral success by the mid-1990s. By offering ethical policies and clean politics and promising to clean up the corrupt state mechanism, the WP became the largest party in parliament by 1995.

Freedom of Religious Beliefs and Expression

It is important to remember that the origins of the problem with freedom of religious belief and expression lie with the modernisation project, which started in the late nineteenth century and entered a new phase with the Kemalist revolution. Some of the activists and many of those with whom I had regular contact mentioned a genuine grievance and unease about their freedom of religious belief and expression. Some of the themes that my informants brought up during interviews were part of an age-old problem of the role and place of religion in the Turkish Republic. The republic was built in the image of the West, especially the French Republic, and religion was brought under state control as a direct consequence of the principle of secularism. The term *laicity* was borrowed from French and of course implied the French approach, which is tolerant of religion.

As a modernist and secularist movement, the republican elite had never been sure of what to do with one of the most influential and historically fundamental social institutions: religion. Religious freedom is part of the current political debate. It is an old one but can take different forms as well. From the mid-1980s onwards the *türban* (headscarf) issue led to confrontation between the secular authorities and religious movements. Since then it has been transformed into a major symbol of freedom of belief and expression. The issue was dormant when the Özal government from 1983 to 1993 permitted students attending school to wear headscarves in the interests of freedom of religious belief and expression, but later headscarf wearing was banned. The process of 28 February (1997) once more made the *türban* issue one of the key battlegrounds in schools and universities. For VP grassroots activists the *türban* is a religious obligation and every Muslim woman should wear it. Not only is it seen as a religious condition, it has also been elevated to the level of human rights. They argue that it is a matter of freedom of expression and an individual's right to wear whatever he or she wants. However, the authorities see it as an ideological uniform, an extension and expression of Islamic fundamentalist ideology and a threat to democracy.

The events of 28 February had many victims, and the subsequent closure of the WP, which had received 6 million votes in the 1995 general elections, created an atmosphere of resentment, injustice and denial of basic rights. Those who identified with the party also felt victimised by the system. For example, one of my informants, Şerif from Peyami Sefa neighbourhood, explained why he had joined the WP:

> I came to identify myself with the WP/VP because of the unfair treatment of the party by all other parties, the media, the judiciary and the military. All this ill treatment made me side with the weak victim.

Victimhood is a powerful social unifier. Many ethnic or religious minority groups, such as the Jews, share this experience of victimisation and it bonds these groups very strongly. I observed a similar attitude among the WP/VP members and grassroots activists. Ordinary WP voters also felt that state surveillance of the Islamic movement and the closure of the WP was a direct attack on their freedom and democratic right to choose.

Contrary to the popular image – which portrayed the WP as no more than an Islamic fundamentalist party – surveys showed that the WP combined religious and class appeal (see Özbudun, 2000, p. 89). Between one-third and one-half of its voters' support was associated with religion and ideological reasons. When the voters were asked why they voted for the WP, half of them gave ideological reasons, such as the WP's defence of religious values (20.6 per cent), its promise of a

Just Order (13.4 per cent), and its respect for 'national and moral values' (12.5 per cent). Fewer than one-third of them (29.6 per cent) said they supported the party because they viewed the WP as an honest and reliable party. One-third (33.1 per cent) of all the WP's voters viewed their party as the party of the 'poor and oppressed' (Özbudun, 2000, pp. 90–1). From the 1994 local elections onwards, the WP had strong roots in the *gecekondu* areas. By winning most of the municipalities, it diminished the left parties' leading role in the low-income *gecekondu* areas (Özbudun, 2000, p. 91).

Reaction to Other Parties

Some 7 per cent of all grassroots activists joined the VP because of political dissatisfaction with existing mainstream political parties. The political literature on dissatisfaction is rich. Due to constraints on space and a desire for clarity, I do not review this literature in detail here. The relationship between dissatisfaction and political behaviour is at least as old as the serious study of politics. It is widely believed that those who are dissatisfied are the source of public unrest, and that political violence is too often caused by individual frustration (Barnes et al., 1979, p. 381). The theory of personal dissatisfaction and political action has been greatly influenced by the concept of relative deprivation (ibid., p. 384).[18] Marsh (1990, p. 110) argued that:

> As soon as people realise in sufficient numbers that they are not getting the things they want and feel they ought to have, they become frustrated. Frustration leads to dissatisfaction that leads to demands, which, if unmet, will lead to anger and aggression and thence to protest action.

As Marsh puts it, frustration and dissatisfaction feed each other unless this circle is broken by adequate policy implementations. In conventional politics the personal dissatisfaction can be expressed via voting behaviour, supporting a party or possibly becoming a party activist. It is argued that policy dissatisfaction increases support for the political process and thereby political participation. (Dalton, 1988, p.50)

There were grassroots activists who joined the WP/VP as a reaction to mainstream centre-right and centre-left parties. However, the number of people who voted for the WP/VP because of their dissatisfaction or disillusionment was far greater than the number of political activists, and it had far-reaching consequences for Turkish politics. There has been a significant climate of partisan realignment and electoral volatility since the mid-1980s (see Kalaycıoğlu, 1998, pp. 4–5; also Özbudun, 2000; Tosun, 1999). In fact, for some political commentators, electoral volatility and partisan realignments were partially responsible for the WP's sudden rise in the local (1994) and general (1995) elections.[20] As Sayarı (1996, p. 36) explains:

> The declining strength of the mainstream parties, especially those on the centre-right, is the best indicator of the electorate's dissatisfaction with the parties' perceived failure to resolve the country's pressing social and economic problems. In increasing numbers, Turkish voters have deserted them and turned to the Islamists.

For Sayari there are three factors behind the growing support of the WP. First is the widespread public disenchantment with the mainstream parties on the right as well as on the left; second is the militant grassroots activism; and third is the increased role and visibility of religion in Turkey.

There is no doubt that if the failure of the mainstream secular parties left voters disillusioned due to continuing social, economic and political problems, the same process alienated those who felt policy dissatisfaction to a greater extent than ordinary citizens for personal reasons (e.g. those individuals with a high social status will not just switch their party support from A to B but may decide to get involved in and participate in politics at a higher degree by becoming a member of B).

The Left and the Urban Poor

The WP and later the VP exploited the vacuum created by the evaporation of social democratic parties and policies in Turkey. The left end of the spectrum of Turkish politics had been rapidly shrinking since the 1980s and this created a vacuum, which the WP successfully filled. I had a conversation in Ankara in 1999 with Ahmet Albayrak, one of the campaign managers and a close aide to the newly elected Mayor of Mamak sub-district. He was a university graduate holding an MA in political science. In answer to my question about his views on the WP's rise, especially in *varoşlar*, he said:

> The left lost its support in the *varoşlar* while the WP/VP got stronger. It was the left who used to welcome those newly migrated people from rural areas to the big cities. They used to build some of their houses to show solidarity and find them jobs. But later the leftist parties stopped doing this. Instead of the left, now, the VP's cadres have been doing these things.

In reply to the question 'What do you think is the reason for the loss of support for the left in Turkey?, Albayrak said:

> The left was weakened because during Demirel's government they were in the government as a junior partner of the coalition,[21] and controlled many municipalities. During this time they were involved in lots of corruption scandals and faced many sleaze allegations. So they lost their credibility and public confidence. They were unsuccessful too. The left betrayed the people's hopes and dreams. The people saw them as a way forward, as a hope for a better future, but they turned their backs on the people. They did not respect people's values and beliefs. [...] Turkey has been changing very rapidly and this situation has created the problem of a cultural identity crisis. Our traditional elite still have this mentality of 'I can educate the nation, I can teach the people' but the people say 'no I will be how I want to be, not how you want'. In fact the situation has transformed into a class war.

Albayrak raised serious issues, which help explain the fall of the left and the unstoppable rise of political Islam in Turkey. Albayrak first pointed out a very major shift in the attitude of left-wing parties towards their social base. The Turkish left, represented by the Republican People's Party, lost touch with its historical social base – the lower-middle and lower classes, salary and wage earners, the poor and landless peasantry and unemployed underclasses – in the post-1983 period. It was no longer interested in social policies, unemployment, poverty, low wages and salaries or the widening gap between the poor and the rich. As well as shirking solidarity with *gecekondu*s, the RPP dumped 'social democratic policies' in favour of the free-market economy, privatisation of large public companies, privatisation of traditionally free public services, and large budget cuts from social programmes. Second on Albayanak's list of grievences came the left's corruption and unsuccessful government years as a junior partner of a coalition government with the centre-right True Path Party and municipalities.[22] Third, he bemoans the uncompromising elitism that runs deep in the leftist parties, manifesting itself as looking down on the people, disregarding and disrespecting local culture and traditional or religious values that are accepted and respected by the majority of the population.

Conclusion

In this chapter I have examined the roots of and reasons for party membership. I began by identifying the participation of my informants within VP local branches. I wanted to see how they described their position with particular branches and found that the vast majority (79 per cent) of them viewed themselves as party activists. There were other substantial groups who saw themselves as activists but also held elected office or membership at the sub-district executive committee. The rest consisted of party workers, branch administrators and so forth.

Next I described my informants' present position within their particular local party branch. Two-fifths (40 per cent) of them were leaders of their neighbourhood committees. Some 14 per cent were representatives of their neighbourhood executive committee. One-fifth were members of the *ilçe,* executive committees, which were prestigious and influential at the local level, with membership of one signifying a desire for upward mobilisation. Another 10 per cent described their position as 'activist members' without any elected office or membership of any kind of committee. Twelve per cent of my informants were members of the youth committees – very vibrant, creative, energetic and enthusiastic units within the local branches. This figure confirms the overall ratio of youth involvement in the VP.

After clarifying the relationship and the position of my informants within the VP, I moved to the process of participation and becoming a member of the VP. It is important that we grasp the process of participation including the decision-making process, and that we consider which factors play a role before an individual joins the VP. Table 5.4 shows that 38 per cent of my informants joined the VP as 'self starters', which means they were highly motivated (see Whiteley, 1995, p. 223). Also it is very possible that the 'self starters' may well be the cream of party activists since they possess a high level of initiative. More than one-quarter (26 per cent) of activists reported that they were approached by the party via a friend.

Some 21 per cent of my informants said that someone from their family played a leading role in their involvement with the party. It was observed that political attitudes are learned from childhood, which is a sign of the persistent consequences of the political socialisation to which every individual is subjected from a very early age.[23] The family continued to be one of the key components of the political process and it played an important role in my informants' decisions to become party members.

The last group (14 per cent) in this section are those who joined the party out of loyalty to or personal admiration for their party leaders. They became members because they were motivated by social norms. In this group it seems that 'party activists motivated by social norms are responding to the perceived opinions of "significant others" e.g. leaders, or people whose opinions they respect and value' (Whiteley, 1995, p. 223). As expected, a very high degree of devotion, admiration and emotional attachment was observed among all of the VP's people, from ordinary rank-and-file members to the members of parliament.

Another aim of this chapter has been to identify the major incentives of party membership. It was observed that the paths to membership were influenced by four different variables: religion, ideology, collective positive incentives including moral integrity, and finally political dissatisfaction. The literature review has shown that all of these variables have been widely recognised and extensively studied as predictors of political participation. These variables have been treated as the main predictors of political action regardless of whether it is conventional or unconventional political action.

Thrity-eight per cent of my informant group joined the VP for reasons other than religion or ideology. For some 14 per cent of them, the VP was the best option for the country. In other words, they joined the party because of 'collective positive incentives'. Another 16 per cent joined the VP for 'other reasons': the party's trustworthiness or clean image, or their own loyalty to its leadership. They saw the VP as being the party free from corruption and the party of the poor. Some said they trusted the VP because they would not steal people's money. The last group, some 7 per cent of my informants, said they joined the VP as a reaction against other parties. For this group, political dissatisfaction with established parties was the driving force for membership.

CHAPTER 6

THE GRASSROOTS ACTIVISTS: THE MAKING OF ISLAMIST ACTIVISM

> The people who may not think of themselves as heroes, but in many ways are the biggest heroes of all, are the party members who stuck with us through the hard times as well as the good. [...] It is you, after all, who saw us through the period of deepest despair, stuck with the party and helped see it back to power. Even when we were written off we bounced back and that was down to members and trade unions in every community continuing to fight for us. (Blair, 2000)

Introduction

This chapter consists of two parts. The first is devoted to conceptual definitions and a brief history of mass membership parties. Despite the decline of mass membership parties, membership is still critical for political parties. In this context the benefits and costs of membership for the parties are discussed. For operational purposes I focus on the differing concepts of membership, remembering that the concept differs from party to party. Later, in order to define the grassroots activists, I explore the literature on membership.

In the second part of this chapter I investigate the socioeconomic and demographic characteristics of the Virtue Party's grassroots activists.

My first goal is to see whether there is a consistent and coherent pattern among active members of the VP. Then I identify members' social class, educational background, occupational characteristics, employment sector, social status, and length of time spent in the city/urban area. Different variables will be tested and compared with data from other studies to see whether there are peculiar socioeconomic or demographic characteristics prevalent among VP activists that may have led to political participation or party activism. To this end I use statistical data and the analysis of some Turkish studies on socioeconomic and demographic backgrounds, political attitudes, voting behaviour and membership attitudes.[1]

The Conceptual Framework

The Emergence and Development of Mass Membership Parties

Political parties are the key components of representative democracy. They are the bridges between politics in general and society. Parties are the most permanent agencies of political participation and have played their role with great success (see Scarrow, 1996).

Historically the concept of membership, as Duverger (1964, p. 63) points out, is the product of an evolutionary process, which led from the cadre party to the mass party. The establishment of political parties in general, and particularly mass parties, was the outcome of a series of major revolutions and transformations that occurred throughout the nineteenth century. In Europe, modernisation, the industrial revolution and urbanisation coupled with nationalism contributed to the awakening of the masses. Although the mass party was created through nationalism and religious institutions, the real and functioning mass party emerged with the rise of the communist and the socialist movements between the 1840s and 1870s. By the end of the nineteenth century there was a sizeable working class with institutionalised working-class parties (ibid).[2]

Membership of political parties developed through an evolutionary process. When working-class movements around Europe were transformed into political parties, notably in Germany where the SPD was founded in 1875, and in Britain where the Labour Party was established in 1900 (see Berger, 1994, p. 1), membership emerged as the pillar of these political parties. In France the Socialist Party was also born as a vehicle for the political participation of the working class.

It can be seen that mass membership was the only way for these socialist or working-class parties to sustain their financial needs and undertake routine tasks such as the organisation of local party branches, registration of new members, organisation of ward meetings, distribution of party outlets, vote canvassing, and the like.[3]

Working-class parties also made a breakthrough by creating and utilising membership effectively for election purposes, registering new members and collecting membership fees. Thus, by a quarter of the way through the twentieth century working-class parties were more powerful than any other parties in Europe.

Why Membership Is Valued

The concept of membership was an invention of the mass parties and it represented a higher step on the ladder of party evolution. There have been some changes in the party systems, and inevitably these shifts led to changes in the functions, scope and perception of party members. Nevertheless, as mentioned above, members remain highly valued by their parties and party leaders. For example, in his speech at the celebrations of the centenary of the Labour Party, Labour leader and Prime Minister Tony Blair praised local activists as the 'biggest heroes' throughout the party's 100-year history. While he reminded his audience that there could be no going back to the party values of the 1980s, he used the occasion to reach out to party activists (Blair, 2000). By praising the grassroots activists as the 'biggest heroes' in the Labour Party's 100-year history, in effect Blair acknowledged the key position of party activists for the party's future and sought to reassure those activists who increasingly felt alienated from Downing Street.

According to Scarrow (1996, pp. 42–6) party members have the following benefits for the party:

Legitimacy benefits: Legitimacy is measured here not in the legal sense but in social terms such as acceptability and popularity.

Direct electoral benefits: Members are valued by their parties for their electoral benefits as voters.

Outreach benefits: As Scarrow (ibid., p. 43) puts it, even low-level members can function as ambassadors in their community.

Financial benefits: Members' financial contributions are still valuable and appreciated as such.

Labour benefits: Especially at pre-election times, for an active election campaign members can be invaluable.

Linkage benefits: Party members are also essential in order to maintain the connections between the party and the 'grassroots'.

Innovation benefits: Parties value their members for new ideas and improve party policies accordingly.

Personnel benefits: Through membership party leaders get the opportunity to know their supporters better.

The driving force for mass membership varies from party to party and through time and place, yet there are some universal factors in place.

The Concept of Party Membership

In order to define the membership or the 'grassroots', first we need to answer the question of who and what a member is. How can we define a member of a political party? One of the immediate problems in coming up with a definition of a member is that party membership can take a different meaning from one type of party to another (see Duverger, 1964, pp. 142–7). Being a member of a fascist party can be very different from being a member of a liberal democratic party. The totalitarian or absolutist party would require total submission and adherence from its members, whereas the liberal party would be much more flexible with its membership. For example, strict obligations, numerous responsibilities and few privileges are typical of American parties. The opposite is true for Italy's Lombard League (Scarrow, 1996, p. 17). Across different countries members may all pay dues and be enrolled on membership lists but their relationship with the party, their position and their gains from membership may be very different.

Leiserson (1958) argued that the extent and the nature of the party's demands on its membership give a good clue to the character of the party. He defines three types of political party and party membership. The first is what he calls the totalitarian party, which includes communist and national socialist parties. Totalitarian parties are defined as demanding of their members an 'exact, unquestioning obedience and loyalty to its tenets, its program, and its orders over and above the claims of government and law, family, church, employer, or trade union' (ibid., p. 137). The criteria for membership of communist parties are rigid and severe, including recommendation by full members and a period of provisional membership varying from six months to two years, and above all approval by a party committee (ibid., p. 142).

The second type of party that he defines is the absolutist party. These parties expect their members to observe secretly 'some religious or ethical doctrine, the solidarity of some racial or national group, or the higher ethical quality of a socioeconomic policy' (ibid., p. 137). He points out that although absolutist parties require application forms for membership, they are far less exclusive, militant and rigidly disciplinary than communist parties. As they have a broad cross section of ideological applicants such as the working class, religious brotherhoods and racial or national groups, these parties are inclined to see party organisation as a 'mass educational and social movement' and their members as party workers. Members 'attend meetings, participate in organisation programs, speak publicly and act as a faithful carrier of the word to the rest of the potential membership group'.

The third type is the liberal party. For Leiserson the majority of European and American parties fall into this category. A liberal party, he argues, 'arises in a situation in which the party places the Constitution or the welfare of the Commonwealth as the highest political value, and frankly admits its instrumental, pragmatic role of providing the personnel and policies most conducive to those ends' (ibid., pp. 137–8). It must be said that Leiserson's description of liberal parties is rather uncritical. Nevertheless, his assessment of liberal parties' conception of membership is quite valid. As Leiserson (ibid.,

p. 144) states, 'the liberal ideological conception of party membership is relatively loose and informal'. Most liberal parties require their members to be formally enrolled in the party, but the requirements are far less exclusive, specific and demanding. It is also true that today most of the political parties in Europe and America have a similar understanding of membership.

Leiserson differentiates the type of membership according to the type of party ideology. However, there will be different types of members within a single party. The best-known example of this is the British Labour Party. Since 1918 it has made a distinction between its affiliated members and individual members (Duverger, 1964, p. 61). It may appear contradictory to have more than one kind of membership within a single party, but this is how the relationship between parties and their members works. Some members have greater aspirations than others to devote themselves to party activities. Some have less time but greater financial resources to contribute. Others, like grassroots activists, have ambition, and a sufficient degree of political education to advocate the party's views and indoctrinate other members.

This is not a simple division of labour among party members, but constitutes different degrees of participation and therefore different kinds of membership too. Moreover, there are some criteria that help us to define the concept of 'member':

> In everyday language the concept of 'member' of a party coincides with that of adherent – in Europe at least. The latter is distinguished from [a] 'supporter', who declares his agreement with the doctrines of the party and sometimes lends it his support but who remains outside its organisation and the community it forms; the supporter is not, properly speaking, a member of a party. (ibid., p. 62)

Duverger emphasises the difference between members and grassroots activists and 'supporters'. A supporter is not within the created organisation, the so-called party, but he or she stays on the periphery, agreeing with the party's fundamental principles but not enrolled or attending any kind of regular meeting or activity. According to David Berry (1970, pp. 31–2): 'party members are those who individually subscribe to a political party, hold a membership card, and presumably have their names recorded on membership lists'. In his account, a subscription to the party's membership list and holding a membership card are the most important elements of membership. Scarrow (1996, p. 16) points out that:

> Two of the most common obligations imposed by parties on their members are the injunction to refrain from joining rival parties, and the requirement to contribute to party funds. Common privileges include the right to participate in candidate selection, and the right to influence programmatic decisions. In some countries, parties also (or alternatively) offer their members special access to goods and services.

Scarrow's definition of membership also draws a line between the supporter and the member of a party. For her we can only distinguish a member from the rest of the 'party supporters' if they have both obligations and privileges within the party organisation. The most common obligations are that no party tolerates involvement of their members with rival parties, and the party expects a financial contribution from the grassroots level. Scarrow also points out some privileges members may have, for example the right to take part in candidate selections and the right to influence various levels of decision making.

Members

A pattern emerges from the above attempts to define members of a party. A member is a person who: (1) is formally enrolled in a political party; (2) shares and acts upon the ideology, programme or policies defined by the party; (3) is constrained from joining or being involved with another, especially a rival, party; (4) makes financial contributions to the party and; in return, (5) enjoys privileges within and outside the party. These privileges vary from country to country and from party to party but they can include good opportunities for a political career as well as, according to Scarrow, special access to goods and services, which are mostly drawn from public resources.

This describes the pattern of party membership in general, but it is also important to define the *activist member/grassroots activist*, which is the focal point of this research. In coming up with this definition, it is useful to consider the concept of *militant* as proposed and used by Duverger (1964, pp. 109–116) and Micaud (1975, p. 125) in the context of the French Communist Party. Finally, Karl W. Deutsch's (1970, p. 48) definition of *political activists* will be explored.

The Militant

There are strong similarities between the 'militants' that Duverger (1964, p. 109–116) describes in his classification of party membership and the 'grassroots activists' that are the subject of this study. Duverger (ibid., p. 110) argues that:

> The militant is an active member: the militants form the nucleus of each of the party's basic groups, on which its fundamental activities depend. Within the branch, for example, there is always to be found a small circle of members, markedly different from the mass, who regularly attend meetings, share in the spreading of the party's slogans, help to organise its propaganda, and prepare its electoral campaigns. These militants constitute a kind of caucus within the branch. They are not to be confused with the leaders: they are not directors but executives; without them it would not even be possible to carry out any activities.

The question raised by Duverger's definition of 'militant' is whether there are differences between the ordinary members – or, as he calls them, the 'masses' – and the active members, which he calls 'militants'. Clearly, the militants are fewer in number and have more influence and activity within the branch. They regularly attend meetings and spread the party's ideology and slogans. They are vital for preparing and executing the election campaigns. Although Duverger uses the term 'militant' instead of 'active member', at the beginning of his definition he admits that the militant is an active member.

Micaud's definition of militant is different from Duverger's. Duverger's concept of militant does not imply a strong ideological devotion, but Micaud's militants – defined in the context of the French Communist Party – are strongly bound with the Communist Party's ideology and organisational structure. Micaud wrote that 'The real strength of the party resides in its large number of devoted militants [...] and well trained and efficient local leaders' (1975, p. 125). As his term, 'militant', is so closely associated with communist parties and our subject, the WP/VP, is far from being communist, we should seek out some other definitions. Deutsch's definition of 'political activist' seems more in line with the WP/VP's activists. He proposes six tests for identifying the political activist:

> An activist is a person (1) who is member of a political organisation; (2) who gives money to a political organisation or candidate; (3) who frequently attends political meetings, whether of committees or of large groups; (4) who takes part in electoral campaigns; (5) who writes letters on political topics to legislators, political officeholders, and/or the press; or (6) who talks about politics to people outside his immediate circle of family or friends. (Deutsch, 1970, p. 48)

Deutsch considers a political activist to be anyone who fulfils at least three of these six conditions. On the basis of his not particularly stringent tests, 3 per cent of the population in most countries can be classified as political activists. The first two conditions, being a member of a party and paying regular dues, are the same criteria as for membership of a party. But the rest of the conditions – frequent attendance of political meetings, taking part in electoral campaigns, writing letters on political issues to government officials or the press, and talking about politics in public or outside their circle of family or friends – are the conditions that constitute an activist.

If we compare the two concepts – Duverger's 'militant' and Deutsch's 'political activist' – we see that there are some parallels and differences between the two. The parallels are regular attendance at meetings; taking part in election campaigns; spreading the party's views, goals and slogans; writing letters; and preparing electoral campaigns and the like. However, the differences are equally important, especially when applied to our case study: the grassroots activists of the VP in Turkey. Duverger's definition of 'militant' is much more exclusive and implies some clear-cut lines between member and active member. For example, he places emphasis on the small number of people whose activities are fundamentally important for the party. In Deutsch's definition of active member there is no such fundamental role for a small number of people who are considered to be activists.

The Grassroots Activist

To solve the problem of conceptual definitions I adopt an eclectic approach. It seems that both definitions – militant and political activist could be converged into one, although Duverger's description of 'militant' seems much closer to the VP's grassroots activists that I study. But, because the term 'militant' has unfavourable associations with the communist parties of the 1950s and is particularly negative in the context of Turkish politics, I instead use terms such as 'party activist', 'active party member' or 'grassroots activist'. I define the grassroots activist as a person who: (1) is an active member of a party; (2) is in many respects different from the rest of the members; (3) regularly attends political or informative party meetings; (4) actively shares and actively advocates the party's ideology, policies and goals; (5) actively engages all aspects of the electoral campaigns; (6) has some sort of financial, political, ideological or cultural resources, if not free time for party activities; (7) has a strong ideological conviction, extensive political knowledge, and devotion to the party leadership.

It is evident that grassroots activists are the core of party organisations. They are the real fighters of the parties on the ground. They are the ordinary people struggling to increase the party's dominance and the scope of its influence over non-members as well as to re-educate members and carry the party into power. This is in order to realise their own political agenda, which is generally more radical than that of the ordinary members.

The Case of the WP/VP and Its Grassroots Activists

Political rights and duties in general are drawn up by section 4 of the Turkish constitution (1982). The rules concerning party formation, membership and withdrawal from membership are outlined by articles 68 and 69 of the constitution and by the law on political parties panel code 2820 (see Dodd, 1990, pp. 172–3). Paragraph 11 of panel code 2820 specifies the conditions of becoming a member of a political party. There are certain restrictions on who can be members and who cannot. Civil servants in the public sector and corporations, judges, prosecutors, members of higher judicial organs, member of the armed forces and students are restricted from joining political parties or organisations.

From my observation and interviews with the grassroots activists in Keçiören and Mamak, it can be said that the VP worked very hard in Ankara to acquire new members. Its predecessor, the WP, had over four million members before it was closed down. The VP aimed to reach at least that number. Unfortunately the VP did not declare its membership figures and my request from its head office was also fruitless, but I can form an estimate on the basis of information provided by the administrators of both party branches. Before the elections on 18 April 1999, the individual branches registered one-third of the members that they had in the VP, so a rough estimate puts the membership at the time at around 1.5 million.

Becoming a Member of the VP

To become a member, the candidate initially had to fill in the membership form. This form contained three parts. First the candidate declared that he fulfilled the conditions set by the law of political parties, and that he or she would observe the party's programme, rules and code of conduct and would pay the membership dues for a year. Second they were required to provide demographic information: neighbourhood, his or her name, surname, parents' names, birthplace and date, education, skills and occupation, residential address and telephone numbers. The third part consisted of the referees' names and signatures. Referees were required to make a declaration to say 'I know him/her and support his/her membership'.

It took about ten minutes to complete the form. The reference system did not always work precisely as stated in the form but in these cases the administrative secretary would know who the referees were and usually they could find someone who knew both applicant and referee. Applicants were issued with membership cards showing their photographs. Members were very keen to obtain their membership cards from the administrator and display them proudly. Some still treasure and retain old cards issued by the party before it was closed down. Membership fees were not always paid. In Turkey political parties can, according to their share of the vote, get generous state funding, and therefore parties do not have to rely on membership dues for their financing.

As discussed in chapter 2, from the beginning of the 1990s until 2002 the Turkish party system experienced a major impasse. The country faced increased party fragmentation, electoral volatility and organisational decay. This process went hand in hand with increased party detachment, reduced organisational capacity and declining party identification among citizens (Özbudun, 2000, p. 73). There was also a process of policy convergence between the centre-left and the centre-right parties caused by the process of globalisation and neoliberal restructuring policies.[4] Hence parties were in desperate need of something different that separated them from other parties. In this context, well-organised grassroots organisation and committed grassroots activists equipped with modern technology made a real difference. During the fieldwork it was observed that compared to other centre-right and centre-left parties (which I visited several times in their local party branches), the VP had far better grassroots organisation and far better election campaign strategies. The strategies, tactics and campaign methods used by the WP during the first half of the 1990s became the 'new standard' of election campaigning. In contrast, throughout the 1980s and 1990s, particularly with Özal's Motherland Party (MP) and many others, election campaigns were organised and executed in the American style: media-led election campaigns using mass communication technology, increased use of opinion polling, PR expertise and the like.[5] In the general elections of 1987 and 1991 the MP subcontracted its election campaign to a famous American PR company, which carried out George Bush's presidential campaign. Other parties such as the True Path Party invited expensive consultants from abroad.

Throughout the fieldwork, I noticed that grassroots activists were putting together a vibrant campaign. Many of them were generous with their time, working long hours in the neighbourhoods. Some activists owned shops, groceries, warehouses, petrol stations, etc., and in order to join the campaign they would either find someone to run the shop or close the shop altogether. Even some of those usually employed in the public sector would use their annual holiday or obtain bogus sick notes from the doctor through networking just to be able to join the campaign. These examples show how committed the VP's grassroots activists were to their party activities.

The Socioeconomic Profile of Party Members

People who talk together vote together. (Miller, 1977, p. 65, quoted in MacAllister et al., 2001, p. 42)

The Social Environment: The Sub-Districts of Mamak and Keçiören

Before it became the capital city of the modern and secular Turkish Republic in 1923, Ankara was a small, dusty Anatolian town. Ankara started to grow as the only planned town reflecting the ambition of the new Kemalist elites to create a modern capital city with its wide streets, long boulevards, picturesque monuments, modern theatre and art buildings. Until it became exhausted by the influx of migrants from rural Anatolia, Ankara continued to grow as a planned city.

Ankara witnessed a rapid urbanisation process from the 1940s onwards. As all the governmental offices were concentrated there, its development was driven predominantly by public sector employment, mainly in office jobs and the public and private service sectors. Although there has been growth in the industrial sector, its rate is relatively modest compared to Istanbul and the rest of the Marmara region. Keçiören and Mamak are both administrative districts of Ankara.

Keçiören Sub-District

The type of housing (e.g. whether it consists of mainly *gecekondu* housing, apartment blocks, luxury apartments or villas) in a neighbourhood is one of the main indicators of its socioeconomic conditions. In general terms, the location of a neighbourhood in a town or city is also an important indicator of its inhabitants' social and economic backgrounds. It is of the most significant variables influencing the political process.[6]

From the early 1950s onwards there have been a number of studies primarily concerned with the relationship between socioeconomic conditions and voting tendencies in Western Europe and North America.[7] These studies focus particularly on the relationship between social environment, for example neighbourhood factors, and social and political participation. For example, one of the earliest empirical studies of American voting behaviour concentrates on the social bases of American partisanship. This study found that 'an *Index of Political Predisposition* based on social classes, religion, and rural/urban residence was a strong determinant of voting choice' (Dalton, 1988, p. 152). Similarly Bell and Boat's (1956–7) study, in San Francisco, shows that 'family and socioeconomic neighbourhood characteristics influence the development of informal group relations between friends, relatives, neighbours and co-workers'. Another similar study carried out by Berry (1970, p. 34) in Britain found that there was a strong correlation between socioeconomic class characteristics in a neighbourhood and voting behaviour.

The concept of neighbourhood effect has been employed in electoral studies for a long time (MacAllister et al., 2001). In my research I am particularly interested in the neighbourhood's effects on political participation and voting choices. The reason for this is that since the 1970s many scholars have rejected the effects of the class and socioeconomic status of neighbourhoods on the electoral process. However, MacAllister et al. (2001, p. 59) point out that as recently as the 1997 general elections in Britain there was evidence of such influence:

> We have provided strong evidence of very significant differences in voting behaviour within each of the country's three main social classes at the 1997 general election according to the socio-economic status of the area in which they lived. The lower the area's status – at a range of spatial scales including not only the constituency and ward but also bespoke neighbourhood varying from populations of 10,000 to less than 500 – the greater the ratio of Labour: Conservative voting within each class. Geography clearly does matter.

It was observed during my fieldwork in Ankara that party support was predominantly affected by the socioeconomic characteristics (income level, type of occupation, type of employment and level of formal education, etc.) of the neighbourhoods. In other words, class cleavages which had not been credited much by some observers, still played a decisive role in voting preferences. This will not be discussed in detail here, but it seems that class cleavages and party support in Turkey were being neglected in favour of alternative approaches such as 'the new political cleavage and new politics'.[8] We shall return to this point in later chapters and will focus on the socioeconomic parameters in Keçiören and Mamak.

In terms of type of housing, both sub-districts have a high proportion of *gecekondu* settlements. This means both districts are home to thousands of poor, lower- and lower-middle-class residents. Mamak has a larger proportion of *gecekondu* dwellers than Keçiören.

As mentioned in the first chapter, more than half (55 per cent) of Keçiören's population currently lives in the *gecekondu*. However, there has been a steady change in the composition of Keçiören's population. There has been continuing growth in its middle and upper-middle classes, the traditional bourgeoisie including artisans, merchants, tradesmen, shop owners, contractors and so on. There has also been growth in the number of professionals, such as doctors, chemists,

Figure 6.1 A typical middle-class settlement in Keçiören sub-district

Figure 6.2 A typical *gecekondu* settlement in Keçiören sub-district

solicitors, public and private managers, etc., who have moved to Keçiören's more prestigious, richer neighbourhoods.

The proportion of *gecekondu* in Keçiören housing in comparison to the general population is below the average (58.4 per cent) for Ankara (Table 4.4). This is partly due to the growth of middle-class areas and also to the rapid transformation of the *gecekondus* into authorised apartment blocks and the expansion of new settlement areas by the cooperatives in the Keçiören district.

Mamak Sub-District

The second district I chose to study is Mamak, where I had lived for around two years between 1989 and 1992. Just after graduating from university I moved to Ankara to do a Master's degree in the department of Sociology at the Middle Eastern Technical University in Ankara. I settled in the Mamak neighbourhood of Misket, where my parents have a home. The majority of people in the neighbourhood were poor, and the housing and services were of low quality. The way people lived, the things they were concerned with and the values they shared were also very different from Ankara proper. I was not surprised when returning to the neighbourhood for my field research that very little had changed since I left. Apart from a few roads that had been widened and improved, the rest had stayed as it was ten years previously. Nor had things improved for the inhabitants. They still had the same concerns and worries about the next day's bread.

Compared to the wealthier districts (e.g. Çankaya), Mamak has all of the socioeconomic characteristics of cities in the developing world. Some of its neighbourhoods are very poor, the housing conditions are inadequate, family income is very low and unemployment is higher than the national average.

Although *gecekondu* housing is found by many students of urban studies to be relatively prosperous compared to its equivalents in many Asian and Latin American cities, most *gecekondu* dwellings have considerable deficiencies. Lack of space and overcrowding is a common problem. *Gecekondu* dwellings average 2.6 people per room,

Figure 6.3 A typical *gecekondu* settlement in Mamak sub-district

Figure 6.4 A typical *gecekondu* in Mamak sub-district

compared with 2.1 for all urban housing (Danielson and Keleş, 1985, p. 167).

Only a few of Mamak's 63 neighbourhoods are non-*gecekondu* urban areas and occupied by traditional middle and new middle classes. These non-*gecekondu* urban areas are mainly in central Mamak and have developed alongside the main road, Tip Fakultesi Caddesi. Some of these non-*gecekondu* urban neighbourhoods are as follows: A. Pasa, Cebeci, Demirlibahçe, some parts of Türközü, and inner Tuzluçayır. The rest of Mamak sub-district mainly consists of *gecekondu* settlements. In Mamak at the time of the research there were 95,000 houses in total and 75,000 of them were classified as *gecekondu*.[9]

Profile of WP/VP members

> All other parties have got members, but we have got believers in our party. (Erbakan, leader of the WP).

I have highlighted that the WP/VP owed its unprecedented rise to very well-organised, effective party organisations established across the country and to its highly committed, hard-working, very active militant grassroots activists.[10] Now is the time to examine who these activists actually were. Were they educated or uneducated, employed or unemployed, young or old? What did they do for a living, where did they live, where were they born, what was their social status, etc.? All those questions will be dealt with in this section.

First, however, it is important to draw attention to the gender issue in my research. All 42 informants that I interviewed were male. Although I have made some observations and had occasional contact with members of the VP's Hanim Komisyonları (ladies' committees) I conducted formal interviews with male party activists only. There are a number of reasons for this. First of all, despite the fact that the ladies' committees within the WP/VP were often acknowledged for their important contribution in vote canvassing, they usually became inactive once elections were held. While they deserved this acknowledgement for their impressive role in terms of door-to-door vote canvassing, grassroots activism needs consistency and long-term commitment. Second, whatever their contribution may have been, female members tended to not take the full initiative but relied on directives and advice from district branches via neighbourhood organisations, which were totally dominated by the male activists. The third reason was based entirely on concerns with the logistical problems of fieldwork. Given the boundaries of gender relations in this particular group and especially as an outsider, at least in the beginning, I anticipated some problems regarding accessibility for observation and undertaking interviews. I decided therefore to concentrate on the mainstream grassroots activists, because women party members constituted only 4 per cent of the total party membership in Turkey (TESEV, 2000, p. 23). Therefore I decided to concentrate on the dominant mainstream grassroots activists of the VP.[11]

In the following section I aim to profile the socioeconomic and demographic characteristics of the VP's grassroots activists. The reason for this is first of all to find out who the activists are, including what sort of social background they come from, social status, age, income level, education, occupational background and marital status. Finally I intend to uncover the dominant socioeconomic characteristics of the VP's activists and compare these social variables with the socioeconomic status model developed by Verba and Nie (1972, chapter 8) and Verba et al. (1978), and used by many others such as Dalton (1988); Marsh (1990) and Milbrath and Goel (1977). It has been argued (Verba et al., 1978, p. 6) that there is a strong relationship between socioeconomic status and political participation: 'Individuals with higher levels of education and higher levels of income will be more active in politics'. Dalton (1988, p. 49) stresses the role of social status as the main stimulant to participation. Social characteristics strongly correlated to political participation are: age, education, gender, socioeconomic status, type of residency, strength of party identification, sense of political efficacy and policy dissatisfaction (Dalton, 1988, pp. 49–50; Dowse and Hughes, 1986, pp. 272–3; Marsh, 1990).

Place of Birth and Type of Residency

First of all I asked where my informants were born. Table 6.1 shows that fewer than a quarter (24 per cent) were born in Ankara, the vast majority (76 per cent) being migrants from rural Anatolia.

Although I did not have any questions about family history, it is most probable that informants born in Ankara were the sons of

Table 6.1 Place of birth of VP activists

Place of birth	No. of people	%
Ankara	10	24
Elsewhere	32	76
Total	42	**100**

Source: Field survey in Mamak and Keçiören districts, Ankara.

Table 6.2 Amount of time that VP activists had been living in Ankara

Period	No. of people	%
(Years)		
0–5	0	0
6–10	1	3
11–15	3	9
16–20	7	22
21–30	10	31
31+	11	34
Total	32	**100**

Source: Field survey in Mamak and Keçiören districts, Ankara.

first- or second-generation immigrants who migrated to Ankara when it was thriving in the 1950s. The majority of our informants (76 per cent) themselves migrated at a relatively early age for a better life in Turkey's fast-growing urban centres

Table 6.2 shows the amount of time the respondents had been living in Ankara. Some 87 per cent of grassroots activists had been living in Ankara for more than 16 years. My data revealed a similar pattern between the time that our informants migrated to Ankara and the pattern of rapid urbanisation that took place since the 1950s. More than one-third (34 per cent) of the VP's grassroots activists had been living in Ankara for more than 31 years and must have migrated to Ankara with the first wave of rapid migration. Another 31 per cent migrated between 21 and 30 years previously, while fewer than a quarter (22 per cent) settled in Ankara between 16 and 20 years prior to the research. Around 9 per cent migrated between 11 and 15 years previously and only 3 per cent had come to Ankara between 6 and 10 years earlier.

How can we interpret this data relating to length of domicile in the city and becoming a political activist? It looks as if there is a pattern. The data suggests that the longer a person has spent in the city, the more likely it is that he or she will participate in politics and become a political activist. More than two-thirds (66 per cent) of our informants said that they had been living in Ankara for at least 21 years. As discussed in chapter 4, there are strong correlations between political participation and urbanisation in general, and between participation urban residence and time spent in urban areas in particular. Berry (1970, p. 34), Danielson and Keleş (1985, pp. 100–102), Deutsch (1963) and Lerner (1958, p. 46) all agree that urbanisation combined with other features of social mobilisation increase interaction and political communication from citizen to citizen and citizen to state.

Marital Status

Marital status is another social variable that plays a significant role as a predictor of political participation and voting behaviour. Like age and political participation, marital status is a variable classified within the category of 'Life Cycle and Participation' (Verba and Nie, 1972, p. 139). As Yücekök (1997, p. 69) suggests, there is a relation between the ethnicity and marital status of an individual. Those sub-ethnic or religious groups who describe themselves as 'Muslims' and 'Kurds' have a much higher ratio of marriage than those who described themselves as 'Turks' and 'Turk-Kurds'. As shown in Table 6.3, the majority (81 per cent) of my informants are married. Fewer than 20 per cent (19 per cent) are single or widowed. Only a small minority (11 per cent) are unmarried or single, the other 7 per cent being widowed.

Different ethnic and religious groups have different priorities in their lives. For example, in Istanbul among other sub-groups those

Table 6.3 Marital status of VP activists

Marital status	No. of people	%
Single	5	12
Married	34	81
Widowed	3	7
Divorced	0	0
Other/cohabiting	0	0
Total	42	100

Source: Field survey in Mamak and Keçiören districts, Ankara.

who defined themselves as Muslim and Kurdish have a high marriage rate. At present 80 per cent of 'Kurds' and 76 per cent of 'Muslims' are married, while the rate is 72 per cent for the 'Turkish' group and 73 per cent within the population as a whole. In his study Yücekök (1997) found that 13 per cent of the population was single and 11 per cent was widowed or divorced.

The Family

At this stage we have no clear indication of the relationship between marital status and involvement in politics. Over 80 per cent of our informants (active members of the VP) were married but there were many factors at play. Being married with a family can be highly valued for a candidate of an important seat, but people do not get married just because they are in politics. There are traditional and cultural norms and religious factors as well. It has been suggested that those who are married are more likely to take political action than single people.

The family size and the number of children of our informant group was another social variable closely related to political participation. The average household size of our informant group was 5.07. As parents comprise 2 per household, the average number of children is 3.07 for this group. In 1990 the size of the average household in Turkey was 4.97 overall, 4.33 in district centres and 5.75 in the sub-districts and villages.

Table 6.4 Number of children of VP activists

Number of children	No. of people	%
1	2	5
2	9	24
3	6	16
4	5	13.5
5+	5	13.5
Unanswered	10	27
Total	**37**	**100**

Source: Field survey in Mamak and Keçiören Districts, Ankara.

In Ankara the size of the average household was 4.23 in total, 4.08 in the province centre, 4.51 in districts and 5.22 in the sub-district and villages. It was observed that a quarter (24 per cent) of our informants had 2 children per household, which is below the national average of 2.97 children in 1990 (Census of Population, 1990, p. 179). Less than one-fifth (16 per cent) had 3 children. Thirteen per cent had 4 children and 13 per cent had 5 or more children. Only 5 per cent of our informants had only 1 child (see Table 6.4). In terms of the average number of children, our informants had 3.07 children per household, 0.99 more children per household compared to the average of 2.08 children per household in Ankara at the time. This tendency to have more children may have been affected by their religiosity as members of the VP.

Education

I will analyse my informants' pattern of educational qualifications and the possible implications for their party preferences. The informant group was highly educated. More than one-third (38 per cent) had attained a high-school education, a rate three times higher than in Ankara as a whole (11.59 per cent) and four times that of Turkey as a whole. There were no illiterates among them and only a very small percentage (2.38 per cent) had no diploma. More than one-fifth (21.24 per cent) had a primary education, 19 per cent had an elementary/junior high education and almost one in ten (9.25 per cent) had a university degree or equivalent. The rate of university graduates among them is twice the overall rate in Turkey (see Table 6.5).

The rate of illiteracy or literacy without a diploma (3.38 per cent) among the respondents was very low compared to 18 per cent in Ankara and 21 per cent of the national population. Those with only primary education made up 21 per cent of respondents compared to 44 per cent in Ankara and 52 per cent of the male population as a whole. In contrast, 19 per cent had attended junior high school or elementary schools compared to 12 per cent in Ankara and 11 per cent of the male population in Turkey as a whole.

If we break down the data about the type of school attended, we will see a very important aspect of the schooling among our informants. Half of those who had attended junior high or elementary school, and 25 per cent of high school diploma holders, had graduated from religious İmam Hatip (İH) schools, originally intended for training prayer leaders and preachers. This is very significant in terms of formal education and political preferences.

The positive relationship between education and political participation has been observed in many studies since the 1950s (see Dalton, 1988; Dowse and Hughes, 1986; Lerner, 1964). The type and the duration of formal education are influential upon the political process. In his study of 'Elections and Party Preferences in Turkey', Kalaycıoğlu (1994, pp. 402–25) examined the critical role of formal education in determining party preferences. He argued that education is important in determining one's political allegiance to the values of the centre or the periphery: 'Those who attended secular schools for longer tend to support the parties of the centre (or the SDPP or DLP); those who do not attend secular schools do not tend to support the parties of the centre' (ibid., pp. 419–20).

In fact, he argues, secular education is negatively correlated with religiosity. Further evidence shows that at the end of the 1990s 'centre–periphery value orientation, formal education and ethnicity emerged as the most important independent variables with

Table 6.5 Distribution of educational level in the survey districts, compared with Ankara, and with Turkey as a whole

Highest educational qualification	Keçiören and Mamak		Ankara*	Turkey**
	N	%	%	%
Illiterate	0	0	5.29	11.18
Literate without a diploma	1	2.38	12.83	10.27
Primary school	9	21.24	44.15	52.26
Elementary/secondary (in total)	8	19.04	12.42	10.84
(a) İmam Hatip (Religious/prayer leaders and preachers)	4	(50.00)	–	–
High school (in total)	16	38.09	11.59	10.74
(a) Modern/ non-vocational	8	50.00	–	–
(b) Technical/vocational	4	25.00	4.34	–
(c) *İH* (Religious/prayer leaders and preachers)	4	(25.00)	–	–
University	4	9.25	9.25	4.75
Total	42	100.00	100.00	100.00

Source: Data collected during the fieldwork in Ankara.

* Drawn from 1990 Census of population, p. 89.

** See 1990 Census of population, pp. 12–13.

As our informant group consisted of male grassroots activists we have chosen the male side of the column.

the highest predictive capability in determining party preferences in Turkey' (Kalaycıoğlu, 1998, p. 10). In Turkey İH schools have been at the centre of a long-running controversial debate on the role and the possible impacts of such schools on the rising Islamic movement.

Since the 1980s there has been an explosion of religious İH schools[12] and Koran courses. Although the schools were opened with a limited purpose to produce religious functionaries – *İmams* (prayer-leaders) and *Hatips* (preachers) – for community needs, since the 1960s they have transformed into an alternative mainstream education system (Akşit, 1991, p. 147). The number of İH schools and students went on rising during the 1990s, and by 1995–1996 there were 561 such schools with a total of 492,809 pupils (Gökçe, 1996, p. 130). Thousands of these graduates, instead of taking employment as prayer-leaders and preachers, went on to study at universities to become engineers, public administrators, doctors, teachers, lawyers, etc.

The question arises whether or not these schools can be regarded as anti-secular. There has been a great deal of conflicting argument and confusion over this issue. Some people argue that since these schools are run and maintained by the Ministry of Education and, most importantly, their curriculum is prepared by the ministry, they cannot become institutions where anti-secular, anti-establishment ideas are harboured. For them, the İH schools are places where students learn their religion alongside modern science and literature, as well as the principles of Atatürk. Others would condemn them for brainwashing students as young as 12 years old, producing an anti-secular, anti-republic, fundamentalist populace to provide potential voters for the right-wing parties. For many, since the 1950s, these schools have been the domain of the conservative right-wing parties (see Erbil Tuşalp, 1994, pp. 54–5). Those claims have focused especially on the supposedly organic connection between the pro-Islamist WP and the İmam-Hatip schools. Many media reports have claimed a strong association between the İH schools and successive pro-Islamist parties: the National Salvation Party (in the 1970s), the WP (from 1983 to 1998) and the VP (from the late 1990s), and the AKP (from 2001 to date). However, these claims are no more than media allegations and need to be sociologically investigated.

There is little empirical evidence to support either of these opinions, apart from a few existing studies. For instance, Akşit found that the 'fathers of İmam-Hatip school students are overwhelmingly rural farmers, farm workers, urban small traders, craftsmen and civil servants. Most of them articulate conservative and traditional attitudes towards gender roles and relationships.' A quarter of them accepted that 'women should be educated' and 'must work', but only 8 per cent accepted that 'women can travel alone'. More than half (60 per cent) did not believe that modern science could solve all the problems we face but, interestingly, the other 40 per cent professed greater faith in science. Yet only one in ten agreed that people could be good without religious faith (Akşit, 1991, pp. 150–1). These students came from the class of traditional, rural small traders and craftsmen – the petit bourgeoisie from which the pro-Islamist National Salvation Party, the predecessor of the WP, derived its electoral support. Although the social basis of the WP/VP had changed since the 1980s, these strata still supported them.

My data show that nearly one-fifth of my informants (19 per cent) attended İmam-Hatip schools. This finding can be interpreted to mean that İmam-Hatip schooling was an important independent variable that had a considerable influence on my informants' political preferences and their decisions to become political activists. Among many influence, education is one of the most important determinants of political participation (see Dalton 1988, p. 50).

Age and Political Participation

It has long been suggested that there is a close relationship between a person's age and their degree of political participation. Many studies have found a distinctive curve of participation related to age or what Verba and Nie (1972, pp. 138–9) call 'position in the life cycle'. They argue that political participation is low in both the early life and the later years of the citizen. It starts to rise slowly from the age of 20, reaches a peak in the mid-forties then declines in the fifties.

One of the most important findings here is that the average age of my informants was 42.83 years, a figure that echoes Verba and Nie's findings.

Over three-quarters (76 per cent) of my informants were aged between 26 and 55 years old. Fewer than 10 per cent were 25 and under, while one-quarter (24 per cent) were between 26 and 35. More than one in five (21.42 per cent) were between 36 and 45. The largest single group, constituting one-third (31 per cent) of the informants,

Table 6.6 Age of the VP activists

Age group	No. of people	%
25 and under	4	10
26–35	10	24
36–45	9	21
46–55	13	31
56–65	2	5
66 and over	4	10
Total	42	**100**

Source: Fieldwork.

were between 46 and 55 years old. The congruence between these figures and those of Verba and Nie shows that, despite arguments to the contrary, there are many similarities between political activists in the West and Islamist political activists in Turkey.

Occupational Characteristics

Occupation as a person's regular work or profession is one of the main pillars of the social status of an individual (see Collins, 1992, p. 1037). And social status is a primary factor that influences a citizen's decision to participate (Dalton, 1988, p. 50). The relationship between social status and political participation is among the most commonly studied aspects of politics (see Barnes and Kaase, 1979; Marsh, 1990; Milbrath and Goel, 1977; Verba and Nie, 1972). In their famous study Verba and Nie (1972, p. 130) developed a model called the socioeconomic standard model (SES).

More than one-third (31 per cent) of our informants were blue-collar workers, while 12 per cent were classified as routine white-collar workers including office clerical workers as well as low-ranking civil servants, teachers, etc. The second largest bloc (16.66 per cent) was made up of shopkeepers and artisans. It is not surprising that this group comprised the second largest among the VP's grassroots activists because shopkeepers and artisans – the petit bourgeoisie – due to their class position had supported the religious right in Turkey since the days of the

Table 6.7 A comparison of the occupational distribution of activists with the Turkish population nationally

					Turkey as a whole**	
Occupation[a]*	**Activists in district of Mamak**	**Activists in district of Keçiören**	**No. of people**	**%**	**Total (N=819)**	**%**
Blue-collar worker	7	6	13	30.95	313	17.4
Routine white-collar worker	5	0	5	11.90	97	5.4
Shopkeeper or artisan	3	4	7	16.66	314	17.4
Employer (public or private sector manager)	1	2	3	7.14	13	0.7
Self-employed (professional; doctor, advocate)	2	4	6	14.28	23	1.3
Retired (from public or private sector)	5	1	6	14.28	na	na
Other (unemployed, student)	1	1	2	4.76	59	3.3
Total	24	18	42	100	819	***

Source: Fieldwork and TÜSES, 1999.

[a] 1) Blue-collar worker; 2) Routine white-collar worker (office job, teacher, nurse); 3) Shopkeeper or artisan (self-employed); 4) Employer (non-agricultural private managers); 5) Self-employed (self-employed professional, solicitor, doctor, chemist, financial consultant, etc.); 6) Retired (from public and private sectors); 7) Other (unemployed, student, unspecified, etc.).

* I am using, with some modification, the occupational classification used by TÜSES, 1999, pp. 47, 170–1.

** TÜSES, 1999, p. 47. This nationwide study represents the entire electorate.

*** Two groups – small-hold farmers (n = 498; % = 27.7) and housewives (n = 483; % = 26.8) – are excluded from the table. So the total percentage is less than 100.

National Salvation Party in the 1970s. A 1999 study confirmed that shopkeepers and artisans share first rank with small farmers in terms of supporting the WP/VP. Among both groups 16 per cent voted for the WP/VP (see TÜSES, 1999, p. 115). The self-employed (professionals, advocates, doctors, financial consultants and the like) and retired workers' groups constituted the next largest groups of party activists (both with 14.28 per cent). Routine white-collar workers constituted 12 per cent of our informants while employers constituted 7 per cent. The only small category (4.76 per cent) was that classified as 'others', including students, the unemployed and unspecified groups.

The only way of making sense of the statistical data is to compare them with other available information. To gain a wider picture, or to be able to 'see the wood for the trees', I compared my findings with the statistics concerning the male population in Ankara (1990)[13] and a nationwide study by TÜSES (1999) that examined voters, political party affiliation and social structure in Turkey. When comparing to the occupational pattern of my informant group with the TÜSES (1999, p. 47) findings, it appears that the rate of blue-collar workers (31 per cent) among my informants was almost twice the national average of 17.4 per cent. This was also true for routine white-collar workers (11.90 per cent among my informants and 5.4 per cent as the national average). The ratio of shopkeepers and artisans was in line with the national average (17.4 per cent), though it was a little lower among my informants (16.66 per cent). The rate of employers and public and private managers was 7 per cent among my informants while it was less than 1 per cent within the general population.

However, when the occupational pattern of our group is compared with the population by gender and occupation in Ankara it appears that, in general, my findings are much more in line with the occupational pattern in Ankara (see Table 6.8). For example, the rate of blue-collar workers (31 per cent) was 2 percentage points lower among our informants than for Ankara as a whole (33 per cent). The proportion of routine white-collar workers (12 per cent) was lower than for Ankara as a whole (15 per cent). One of the biggest differences between the two sets of data was that for shop ownership. An average of 17 per cent of my informants were shopkeepers and artisans compared to only

Table 6.8 A comparison of the occupational distribution of activists within Ankara and the Turkish population nationally

Occupation	Activists in districts of Keçiören & Mamak		Turkey as a whole*		Ankara as a whole**
	Total (N)	Per cent (%)	Total (N)	Per cent (%)	Per cent (%)
Blue-collar workers	13	30.95	313	17.4	33.32
Routine white-collar workers	5	11.90	97	5.4	15.01
Shopkeepers & artisans	7	16.66	314	17.4	6.02
Employers (public & private sector managers)	3	7.14	13	0.7	1.22
Self-employed (self-employed professionals, doctors, advocates)	6	14.28	23	1.3	11.53
Retired (from public & private sector)	6	14.28	na	na	na
Others (unemployed, students)	2	4.76	59	3.3	22.82
Total	42	100	819	100	90***

Source: Fieldwork.

* The occupational percentage in Turkey as a whole (TÜSES, 1999).

** Occupational percentage in Ankara (male population). Data drawn from 'population by gender and occupation in Ankara (in 1990)', available at www.die.gov.tr/TURKISH/ISTATIS/ESG1/06 ANKARA/nufus4.html

*** The occupational group of agriculture, fishing, hunting and forestry, comprising 10 per cent of occupations in Ankara, is excluded.

6 per cent in Ankara as a whole. As the difference is big (11 per cent) there seems to be a positive correlation between grassroots activism and shopkeeping in Ankara.

As mentioned earlier, shopkeepers and artisans were among those groups that strongly supported the WP/VP. Another similar study found that 29 per cent of the 'party workers' – including all major Turkish parties – across Turkey were artisans and shopkeepers. This percentage is over 50 per cent when tradesmen are included in this group (TESEV, 2000, p. 22). Again, there are more self-employed individuals (14.28 per cent) among our group than in Ankara as a whole (11.53 per cent).

Table 6.8 shows that our informant group has a higher than average ratio in Ankara in two groups: the shopkeepers and artisans, and self-employed professionals. One-third of our informants (31 per cent) are shopkeepers, artisans or self-employed individuals compared to 17.55 per cent in Ankara as a whole. Undoubtedly these two types of occupation are very different from blue-collar or routine white-collar occupations in terms of available time, income and social status and therefore social influence. We must emphasise that because one-third of our informant group had a relatively higher earner status occupation, they were probably resource-rich activists.

Income

One of the most common explanations for political activism focuses on the importance of social status as a stimulus to political participation. By its nature politics requires a certain level of activity in order to stay informed and to understand the complexity of the political process. So the first consideration for participation is whether one's social status matches these requirements. It is assumed that higher-status citizens are more likely to have the necessary resources such as more money, time, easy access to political information, and the knowledge and ability to become politically involved (see Dalton, 1988, p. 49; Di Palma, 1970, p. 3; Verba and Nie, 1972, pp. 125–37).

High social status, a high income level and a higher level of education play a vital role in political participation. In terms of income distribution there is a big gulf between rich and poor in Turkey. The distribution of household income by quintile clearly shows how unequal income distribution is in the urban population (see Table 6.9). The richest 20 per cent (in 1994) earned as much as ten times the income of the poorest 20 per cent of households in Turkey. While the richest 20 per cent received half of all income, the poorest 20 per cent got just 5.43 per cent of total income. The second quintile did not do much better, receiving less than 10 per cent of total income. The third quintile earned only 14 per cent of total income, whereas the top two quintiles accounted for 70 per cent of income. If we return to our case, the occupational pattern and income figures from our fieldwork data will inevitably reflect the general picture.

As Table 6.8 shows, my informant group seemed to have higher social status in terms of their occupation. Compared to Turkey in general and to Ankara in particular, my informants held more prestigious occupations. Of course it was much more difficult to outline a comprehensive income index for Turkey at the time, particularly because of the high rate of inflation Turkey witnessed from the mid-1970s to the mid-2000s. However, following the crisis of 2001 the Turkish economy started recovering. It was a deep crisis and recovery was

Table 6.9 Distribution of household income by quintiles (annual), 1994

Groups	Total average income		Urban average income		Rural average income	
	(%)	TL (000)	(%)	TL (000)	(%)	TL (000)
First 20%	5.24	964	5.43	1,126	5.21	824
Second 20%	9.61	1,768	9.33	1,934	10.03	1,586
Third 20%	14.06	2,588	13.60	2,819	14.98	2,370
Fourth 20%	21.15	3,892	20.71	4,294	21.97	7,565
Fifth 20%	49.94	9,189	50.93	10,559	47.82	7,565

Source: 1994 Statistical Yearbook of Turkey, p. 284.

rather painful. As explained previously, due to Kemal Derviş's tight economic policies,[14] thousands were left jobless. The banking sector in particular went through severe restructuring: around 70 to 80 banks and similar financial operations were dissolved and around 20 were rescued by the treasury, costing another USD 17 to 20 billion. The bill to the taxpayer of the whole rescue packet came to between USD 80 and USD 120 billion. But thanks to Derviş's policies the economy started recovering fast, and by the time the AKP came to power in 2002 it was already growing. In fact, the current government actually benefited from the crisis and the heavy burden it brought.

In the first years of the AKP government, the economy continued growing and inflation was brought under 10 per cent. This development helped to cut six digits from the Turkish currency. With a law introduced on 1 January 2005, 1,000,000 TL was revalued to 1 new Turkish lira (YTL).[15]

One of the main problems with studies on Turkey is the complexity of extracting economic data, made more difficult by major differences between regions, cities and above all neighbourhoods. Ten per cent of my informants earned 70 million Turkish lira or less in a month, which works out at USD 184 or GBP 115 per month at the exchange rate of the time. This amount was equivalent to the national minimum wage (68 million TL) for an adult (over 16 years old) in 1999, which increased to 109 million TL from January 2000. We should bear in mind that the minimum wage is determined by a committee of employers and employees and the Ministry of Employment and Social Security and is applied in the formal private sector. It also reflects the wage rate in the public sector and a large proportion of state employees fall in a similar wage band.

The next poorest fifth (21 per cent) of my informants earned between 71 and 100 million TL (USD 185.5–262) a month.[16] The largest group, comprising more than one-third (38 per cent) of our informants, earned 101 to 150 million TL (USD 265–525) a month. The third largest group (17 per cent) earned between 151 and 200 million TL, equivalent to USD 396–521. The top earners in our table are the small number of people (5 per cent) who earned

300 million (USD 787) or more in a month. If we compare within our group, the gap between the poorest earners and the richest is narrower (4.28 times), compared to 10 times the distribution of the national household income by quintiles in 1994 (see Table 6.10). The median monthly income of my informant group was 140.7 million TL per month, which was very close to the average earnings of 137.8 million TL. However, there was a clear difference in terms of average monthly income between those who lived in Keçiören and Mamak sub-districts. The average earnings of the Keçiören group among my informants were 140.7 million TL per month while the Mamak group earned 131.1 million TL per month. The median income (140 million TL) of the Keçiören group was very close to the average earnings (140.7 million TL) of this group.

According to the State Statistics Institute in Turkey, the GDP per capita at the time was USD 3,200 per annum. In Ankara this rate was USD 3,521 (as reported in *Milliyet*, 16 April 1999). The arithmetic mean of the income (the average earnings) of my informants was 137.8 million TL per month. If we transform this into dollars it works out at USD 4,377 per year – higher than the GDP per capita in Ankara. It seems that there are parallels between my findings and the TESEV's (2000). They studied a sample of local party

Table 6.10 Monthly earnings of VP activists (000,000 TL)

Earnings per month (TL million)	Sub-district		No. of people	%
	Keçiören	Mamak		
Less than 70	1	3	4	10
71–100	4	5	9	21
101–150	7	9	16	38
151–200	3	4	7	17
201–250	1	3	4	10
300+	2	0	2	5
Total	18	24	42	100

Source: Fieldwork.

leaders and workers from five mainstream parties in 16 selected provincial capitals across Turkey. The average earnings in this group were 160 million TL (ibid., p. 23). This figure is higher than what my informants earned on average, but this is to be expected since the TESEV's research was carried out with the party organisations in the district capitals among party workers – leaders and higher representatives – whereas my informants were from neighbourhood committees. Nevertheless, it shows that both groups earned more on average than ordinary people in Ankara. This confirms previous findings that suggest a positive correlation between higher socioeconomic status – high income level – and a high level of political participation. It appears that my informants had relatively high-status occupations and high income. Therefore, I can conclude as predicted that this factor must have played an important role in their becoming political activists within the VP.

Conclusion

In this chapter I asked the question: 'why do parties need membership?' Despite the trend for mass-party organisation, membership still holds a key role within parties.

The second part of the chapter examined the socioeconomic and demographic characteristics of the WP/VP's grassroots activists. The first goal was to see whether there was a consistent and coherent pattern among the active members. We have looked at the socioeconomic and demographic characteristics of our informants. For this we have examined social class, age, marital status, the length of time spent in the city/urban area, educational background, and occupational classification and income levels. All these variables are compared against relevant groups with data from the State Statistic Institute's figures, other studies and sources. In so doing, I have uncovered important and consistent patterns among our informants. Now we have a portrait of the pro-Islamist VP grassroots activists. For example, 76 per cent of them migrated to Ankara at an early age. More than 65 per cent of them had been living in Ankara for at least 21 years at the time of the research. This is evidence to support the existence of a relationship between urbanisation and the degree of political participation (see Di Palma, 1970; Özbudun, 1976). I found that the vast majority (81 per cent) of our informants were married, with an average of 3.07 children. Both of these figures show a clear similarity with Yücekök's (1997) findings. In his study he classifies a group of people with Muslim identity among Istanbul residents. The similarities mostly occur in areas such as marital status and family size. In terms of educational qualifications, our informant group is well above average for Turkey and Ankara. There are no illiterates among them compared to 5.29 per cent illiteracy in Ankara and 11 per cent in Turkey as a whole. Sixty-five per cent of them had received at least an elementary/secondary and higher education. Another important point about our group is that 19 per cent of them attended religious İH schools at the higher junior and high school level.

The analysis of the educational characteristics of the VP's activists can be interpreted as follows. First, the findings have supported the idea that 'participation is greater among the better educated', and second, formal education plays a role in terms of party preference. Those who attended religious İH schools tend to vote for and support pro-Islamic parties such as the VP. In fact, the rate of religious education was significantly high among my informants. Nearly one-fifth (19 per cent) of the WP/VP activists were graduates of İHs – half from high school and the other half from İH's junior sections (see Table 6.5). Having a religious educational background has a significant influence on an individual's decision, to participate in politics, as well as being very influential on his or her decision to become a political activist as well.

I have looked at age and political participation and found that the pattern of age for our grassroots activist group was identical to Verba and Nie's (1972) findings. The average age of our group was 42.83 years. My data display a very similar pattern to Verba and Nie's findings on 'life cycle and participation'.

As regards occupational characteristics, we found a distinct pattern in our group. For example, compared to the average in Turkey, the rate of prestigious occupations such as employers (7 per cent) and self-employed professionals (14 per cent) was very high. One-third of our informants (31 per cent) were shopkeepers, artisans or self-employed individuals compared to 18 per cent of Ankara's general population at the time. Undoubtedly, such relatively high-status occupations will provide a higher income level.

The final finding of this chapter was the higher rate of average income among our informant group. For our group the average income was 139 million TL per month. In Ankara at the time the average GDP per capita was USD 3,521 a year. In dollar terms, the average income of 139 million TL amounts to USD 4,377 per annum per grassroots activist. On the basis of these figures, it is plausible to argue that our group was slightly better off as they appeared to earn more in relation to their local community. As a result, they had more resources in terms of money, free time, easy access to information about complex political issues and the knowledge to participate in the political process.

Finally, to summarise the portrait of a grassroots activist, we could say that he is a migrant from rural Anatolia, arriving about 21 years prior to my study, who settled in a *gecekondu* neighbourhood, most probably among his fellow former villagers. He is 42.83 years old and is married with 3.07 children. He attended at least elementary/secondary school. His occupation is of a relatively high status compared to his neighbours and his earnings are higher than the neighbourhood average. He was most probably an active member of the WP, joined the VP as soon as the WP closed down and is politically active. He regularly attends party meetings, actively engages, and spreads the VP's ideology and slogans in his workplace, tea houses, mosques and weddings, and during regular visits to the neighbourhood's sick, elderly or bereaved (see Table 7.3). He speaks sometimes implicitly but more often explicitly about political issues. He practises his theological knowledge and relates reported incidents from the Prophet Mohammed's times, if possible, to support the ideas that he is raising. He reads the *Milli Gazete*, the official daily of the VP, while having a strong ideological conviction for better political knowledge and a devotion to the party leadership.

CHAPTER 7

NOT LIKE ANY OTHER PARTY: THE EFFECTS OF GRASSROOTS ACTIVISM ON THE ELECTORAL OUTCOME

> As the [British] general election approaches . . . local parties are gearing themselves up to do their bit – and the evidence is that they do make an important contribution to turnout and party support. A key to Labour's landslide in 1997 was the revival of the grassroots party set in train by Tony Blair. From 1994 when he became leader until the 1997 general election, the grassroots party increased in size by about 40%. Many of these new recruits helped to turn the Labour vote out on polling day (Whiteley and Seyd, 2001).

Introduction

'Do grassroots party organisations make a difference in terms of increasing parties electoral fortunes?' In this chapter I will try to answer this question. Regarding the effects of grassroots organisations on the electoral turnout, there are two competing approaches. The first approach is called, for the purpose of this chapter, the 'counter argument', which argues that the influence of party organisations has been diminished. Led by Butler and Kavanagh (1992), Crotty and Jacobson

(1980), Herrnson (1986) and Huckshorn (1984), scholars in favour of this argument asserted that due to technological developments such as television, computers and mass-communication technologies, and the rise of new expertise groups – PR experts, campaign managers, pollsters, fundraisers, etc. – the local party organisations have lost their role as the means of election campaigning. However, this approach is fiercely opposed by another group of political scholars. Their approach is called the 'pro-argument', and it defends the impact that party organisations have on the electoral process (see Crotty, 1971; Frendreis et al., 1990; Huckfeldt and Sprague, 1992; Seyd and Whiteley, 1992; Whiteley and Seyd and Richardson, 1994, 1999). They say that despite developments in party structures and in campaigning techniques, party campaigning makes a considerable contribution to the parties' election results. For example, Whiteley and Seyd (1998) explain the British Labour Party's landslide victory in 1997 on the basis of Labour's hard-working grassroots activism. There is evidence to show that in many Western countries an active membership organisation is an asset for the party, and, as the 1997 British general election demonstrated, grassroots activism can make a very positive difference. After discussing both approaches I will move on to the case of the Virtue Party in Turkey.

At the start of this book I hypothesised that the rise of political Islam cannot be described simply as religious revivalism or Islamic fundamentalism. Instead, there are, one could say, 'worldly reasons' for its popularity. As well as socioeconomic and political reasons, the Virtue Party's well-organised, militant-like grassroots activism was very influential in its increase popularity.

To test this hypothesis I will be consulting in empirical data collected during my fieldwork (in 1999 and 2000) in Ankara. In the second half of this chapter I will explore the methods and techniques used by the VP's grassroots activists. How often did they meet with potential voters? Where did they usually meet with potential voters? What were their strengths and weaknesses? What was distinct about them? What was distinct about their activities?

In short, in this chapter I aim to uncover the role and effects of grassroots activism in connection with the unprecedented rise of political Islam in the mid-1990s. If it turns out that local party campaigning had a positive effect and played a significant role, then I will be asking how local party organisations contributed to the success of the WP.

The Turkish Discourse on Grassroots Activism

There has been little research into grassroots activism in Turkey. For example, we do not know much about activists' socioeconomic, demographic and political backgrounds or their ideological beliefs. We also know little about why they are drawn to this ideology and why they have become political activists. And, more importantly, we do not know what the specific characteristics of grassroots activists are. I will investigate whether they are in any way distinct from other party activists or not.

With regard to grassroots activism or local party campaigning in Turkey, it is evident that it has been utilised more often by the pro-Islamic WP than by other political parties (see Özbudun, 2000; Kalaycıoğlu, 1998). There is no doubt that other parties have membership organisations and do organise local election campaigns during election periods, but none of them match the scale of the WP's grassroots organisation. For example, Ersin Kalaycıoğlu (1997, p. 36) points out that:

> On the eve of the 1995 elections, numerous party activists, at the grassroots level, kept track of every voter deemed critical to the party's victory. They visited each voter before the elections, and, on election day, provided transportation to and from the polling stations for those who needed it.

Compared to Kalaycıoğlu, Sayarı (1996) takes a much wider perspective on grassroots activism. According to Sayarı, the WP's dedicated grassroots activists were one of the most important factors in its growing popularity:

> Refah owes its increasing electoral support to an efficient, disciplined, highly motivated, and well-financed organisation. The

> Islamists have the largest number of party workers among all Turkish political parties. Refah's grassroots organisations are staffed with dedicated cadres, male and female, who work with a missionary zeal and benefit from advanced technology, such as computers with voter registration data. Tightly organised in cell-like units in each neighbourhood, Refah relies less on the media for disseminating its views and more on face-to-face contact with the voters (Sayarı, 1996, p. 36).

One of the best-known Turkish writers on political Islam is Ruşen Çakır. Çakır, with his objective approach, has become the most celebrated writer on the Islamic movement. He believes that the main part of the strategy of the WP's membership organisation was focused on the elections. It aimed to mobilise all of the party's members for election campaigning and to recruit a quantity of new members equivalent to the party's votes at the last elections. The WP's model of organisation was unique: known as *tesbih* (rosary), it appointed representatives to every single neighbourhood and these representatives would in turn appoint other representatives to every street, quarter and every building. 'Teachers' educated party members. In the sub-districts there were 'head teachers'. In the district and larger regions 'general inspectors' and 'head teachers' were responsible for educating members. In parallel with its main organisation, mobilised the Hanım Komisyonları (ladies' committees). Right after each election, the WP's highly motivated grassroots organisations started to campaign for the next election as if it were to be held tomorrow (Çakır, 1994, pp. 51–9). The way that a party organises itself is very important for an effective and successful election campaign. Alongside the men's and youth organisations, women turned out to be very effective campaigners. They went street-to-street in their respective neighbourhoods and canvassed building-to-building, apartment-to-apartment, door-to-door. They met people – mostly women in their private living spaces – in a friendly manner. They organised house meetings where a *hatip* – a good speaker or agitator – male or female, would speak to 30 to 50 people at once.

In a similar vein, Sencer Ayata (1997, p. 52) emphasises two key aspects of the WP/VP's party organisations that were crucial to its unprecedented rise. The first of them are the strong, well-organised and militant characteristics of grassroots organisations. And the second is what these organisations were offering to potential voters.

The WP's organisational strength has been underlined by other writers as well. For instance, Ziya Öniş (1997, p. 755), after highlighting the WP's great organisational strength, stresses how, in an age of TV-oriented communication, the WP concentrated on grassroots organisations and face-to-face contact with the electorate. The WP's representatives applied a step-by-step mobilisation strategy at the local level. Computers were employed to great effect for campaigning purposes. In his analysis he finally emphasises that material benefits were offered to the poor – potential voters – in the *gecekondu* areas (Öniş, 1997, pp. 755–6). Although Öniş approaches the question of the rise of the WP from an economic determinist perspective, he ultimately recognises the importance of the WP's organisational strength, which is no less important than the economic conditions. Finally, Margulies and Yuldizoğlu (1997, p. 151) also point out that the WP was the only party with a local grassroots organisation among the Turkish political parties.

Some Western commentators have also emphasised the outstanding role of grassroots activists in the rise of political Islam in Turkey. Henri Barkey (1996) points out that the success of the Islamist WP on 24 December 1995 was due in part to efficient utilisation of the party's capabilities and the complete failure of the other mainstream parties to maintain consistent messages. For him, the WP had one distinctive aspect: it had a nationwide grassroots party organisation.

> The Welfare Party did as well as it did because it had been labouring for years to build a nationwide grass-roots party organisation. Its local cadres have worked their respective districts street-by-street and building-by-building ... With its claimed 4 million registered members, Refah is Turkey's only mass-based political organisation (Barkey, 1996, p. 45).

A *New York Times* journalist also wrote:

> No political machine can beat the Welfare Party when it comes to grass-roots organisation. Women wearing headscarves go door to door in the slums proselytising and meet intercity buses to take new arrivals in hand (Darnton, 1995).

Islamists in Turkey combine their community work – with charities, schools, clinics and cooperatives – with electoral canvassing. Other political parties concentrate on high-powered media campaigns and enlisting celebrities to support them in public meetings, but they are far more deficient in campaigning and canvassing at the grassroots level. The WP also made use of media events and high-profile personalities, but they mainly operated through local party machines involved in clientelistic networks at the grassroots level (Zubaida, 1996, p. 11).

> In its grassroots approach, the [WP] fields a devoted body of cadres from all walks of life. In Istanbul one is impressed by the enthusiasm, friendliness and optimism of the many young men and women who have established networks in the localities and work through them. Candidates accompany local cadres on home visits. They offer advice on how to deal with complicated bureaucracies, provide support during family celebrations and crises, such as weddings and funerals ... Women cadres play particularly important roles in gaining access to homes and establishing female networks (ibid., 1996, pp. 11–12).

Contrary to the general trend in America and Europe, the WP/VP maintained its large party organisations. And through its well-organised, highly committed, militant grassroots organisations, the WP/VP made considerable electoral gains. In the following section of this chapter, I will be introducing my empirical data and interpreting it in relation to grassroots activism.

Not Like Any Other Party: Grassroots Activists in Perspective

> We are not like seasonal workers, we don't get in touch with people every 5 years but we are always among the people. As a representative of the neighbourhood I attend the neighbourhood's committee meetings regularly each week. I send flowers or visit if there is a wedding.[1]

As explained above, among the mainstream parties only the Welfare Party, the predecessor of the Virtue Party, came near to being classified as a mass-membership party in Turkey. The rest showed the characteristics of a cartel party (see Özbudun, 2000). As mass political parties the WP and VP maintained rather large grassroots organisations consisting of very active, devout, highly informed, highly motivated, ideologically oriented members. There was a group of people within the VP's rank-and-file members, whom I call the grassroots activists, who were highly distinct from the rest: they were well educated, highly skilled, better paid, of a higher social status and with high ideological conviction. Above all, this group had better resources at their disposal for political purposes (see chapter 6).

Throughout the 1990s and early 2000s the party organisation of the pro-Islamist WP/VP and later the AKP, with its electoral and campaigning qualities, was acknowledged and admired by many of its opponents.[2] Before moving on to grassroots activism it is important to re-emphasise that in Turkey, since the 1980s, election results have been decided by big metropolitan cities.[3] In this context the characteristics of the population in the metropolitan cities needs to be remembered. As discussed in chapter 4, the population of the metropolitan cities is highly heterogeneous. There are large gulfs in income and living standards within city populations. As the Turkish media frequently point out, there are two Turkeys. The first group is a small minority which has the living standards of major Western European countries. The 'other Turkey', as it is called, lives at the standard of developing countries. In these big cities the two Turkeys live side by side. The 'other Turkey' lives in the *gecekondu*s and accounts for over 50 per cent of the population in Istanbul, Ankara and İzmir. As I also pointed out in chapter 4, the bulk of the WP/VP's popular support came from *gecekondu* areas. Thus the *gecekondu* and grassroots activism in these areas deserve special consideration.

It needs to be established how grassroots activists worked on the ground and how active they were. How much time did they spend on party business on average in a month? How much contact did they have in a week? Where did they meet with potential voters, supporters or their own constituencies? What strategies and tactics were used? What tools were used? What were the methods of their activism? For example, what did they do before, during and after the election campaigning? What were the main patterns of election campaigning? Where did they get the money needed for campaigning? Did they raise money during their campaign?

How Often did the Activists Meet the Voters?

In answer to the question 'As a grassroots activist, how often do you meet with those people who are potential voters, supporters or could be persuaded to join the party?', one-fifth (19 per cent) of my informants said they always had plenty of opportunities to meet people (Table 7.1). Another fifth (19 per cent) of them met with their constituencies every evening but more often during the election campaigns, while 10 per cent met potential voters and supporters every day. Forty per cent of them did so at least once a week while 7 per cent canvassed 3 or 4 times a week. Five per cent of them – which is a very active section – met 20 to 25 people every day. Table 7.1 indicates that the VP's grassroots activists were highly active in their respective neighbourhoods. The majority (60 per cent, if aggregated) said they interacted every day with someone for canvassing purposes.

It must be noted that the way in which social life is organised in the *gecekondu* is a very important determinant for campaigning. The organisation of a community, its main characteristics of social relations, and socioeconomic and demographic factors are all important variables in the electoral process and are equally so in terms of election

Table 7.1 Frequency of meetings with potential voters by VP activities

How often do you meet?	No. of people	%
There are always plenty of opportunities to meet people	8	19
Every evening (but more often during the election campaigning)	8	19
Every day	4	10
At least once a week	17	40
At least 3 to 4 times a week	3	7
I see approximately 20 to 25 people every day	2	5
Total	42	100

Source: Fieldwork.

campaigning. Social life in *gecekondu*s is a form of primary relations.[4] The sense of community, unity and solidarity is consistent and strong. The majority of people in a neighbourhood know each other very well.[5] They know each other's name, occupation, place of birth, family, kin relations, income and political inclination. All is common knowledge in the *gecekondu*.

In most cases *gecekondu*s were established as a result of chain migration from the same district. What Turkish sociologists refer to as *hemşehrilik* (see chapter 4) has provided a strong communal identity for those migrants who are surrounded by a totally alien city full of 'others'. Some writers point out that in the big cities the *hemşehrilik* ties provide the basis for extensive social solidarity networks in poor urban areas.[6] It has been part of a survival strategy for the *gecekondu* population. Although these neighbourhoods are not always populated by people from the same ethnic, religious or district background, there are other issues that bring them together; usually the sense of 'us' as opposed to 'others'. Sharing the same socioeconomic conditions, facing the same problems regarding the lack of services, etc., brings people closer. Given the close community ties in *gecekondu* areas, party campaigning would be carried out in a direct and informal way. Some of my informants talked about their canvassing activities. A representative from Bahçeleriçi neighbourhood described his canvassing activities as follows: 'Every evening I go on visits in the neighbourhood. This is a *gecekondu* area so everyone knows each other and, for this reason, there are always plenty of opportunities to meet people.' A similar point was made by Yılmaz Doğan from the neighbourhood of Türközü: 'We live side by side with our people and always interact with the local party organisation as well as the local people.' Mehmet Arı of Hürel neighbourhood described how he met people: 'Almost every evening, after work, I would come together with people in the neighbourhood.'

On the other hand, some of my informants made a distinction between the election campaign period and normal campaigning:

> Since the election campaign began I see people on a daily, even hourly basis. In normal times we have meetings every week. Our routine activities continue whether it is election time or not. After the election too we will carry on our activities in the same way. With God's permission we have political or normal social meetings in our neighbourhood (Remzi Özcan, representative of Misket neighbourhood).

Most of the informants I talked to saw themselves as a part of the community and spent most of the time doing community work without even realising it. It was apparent from their accounts that their campaigning took an informal style. As such, the way in which a community lives is very important. The way the *gecekondu* neighbourhoods have developed, socially as well as physically, is very conducive to political activism.

The second group, another 19 per cent of my informants, said they met at least one person in their neighbourhood every evening: 'I meet people from our neighbourhood almost every evening after work' (M. Arı, Hürel neighbourhood). Another activist said: 'During the election campaign I canvass 3 to 4 hours every evening.' The reason that this group was active during the evening was that they were working during the day and met people after dinner in their immediate neighbourhoods.

Social life in Turkey, as in many other Mediterranean countries, is predominantly organised outdoors within a community rather than indoors. For this reason, it is much easier for activists to get in touch with the people, not only in the daytime but in the evening or sometimes at night as in the case of house meetings.

Activists usually met people in teahouses – which are a very important part of Turkish community life. In addition to teahouses, these activists would visit houses to canvas. In facts many said they preferred the house meetings. Usually, they asked a VP supporter, member or voter to invite some people from the neighbourhood to their home for a meeting in the evening. It was common to have around 10 to 15 people in these meetings where the host would serve tea or coffee and the speaker would make a speech. In these house meetings, politics was the dominating factor. Communal demands at the local level were raised and proposals discussed.

Some 10 per cent of the activists carried out political activities every day. This group consisted of retired workers, civil servants, shopkeepers or self-employed people who had free time during the day and spent some of it on political activities.

The largest group consisted of 40 per cent of all informants. This group attended the weekly meetings that took place in every neighbourhood's committee, and canvassed someone at least once a week. Melih Demir from General Zeki Doğan neighbourhood explained: 'I do meet people at least once a week but it depends on the situation; if someone is ill or there is a funeral then I visit those households.'

We observed that for a VP activist to attend weekly meetings was the minimum. As Mustafa Şenyurt explained:

> The neighbourhood committee, which consist of 17 members, gathers once a week. If there are ill people in the neighbourhood or someone has died then a delegation from the committee will go and visit these households to offer condolences. Then come the street activities where we go and visit different streets. Before we do that we clearly know who votes for which party in these streets – it is all in our computers.

In some cases my informants said they attended one formal meeting a week but at the same time they said there could be several face-to-face individual meetings in a week. One said, 'As I don't work much during the wintertime I spend some of my time going to the neighbourhood committee and giving some help and training to them'. In addition, there were some activists who reported meeting 15 to 20 people every day. These were usually party administrators, secretaries or other full-time party workers.

So far I have tried to find out how often my informants met with people from their local constituencies and people who were potential voters. Table 7.1 indicates that the VP's activists were highly engaged. The majority of them met someone every day or every evening, and the rest met at least one person a week.

Time Spent on Activism

It can be argued that the amount of time devoted by party activists to party activities is one of the key indicators of the influence of grassroots activism on electoral outcomes. The primary purpose of grassroots activism is to increase the influence and strength of a particular political party. Therefore, I believe that it is very important to establish how often and for how long an activist undertakes that activity in his or her local branch or at constituency level. To this end I asked the following question: 'How much time do you normally devote to political activism in an average month?'

There was an uneven distribution of political activism among the VP's activists (Table 7.2). More than one-quarter (26 per cent) of my informants devoted between five and ten hours to party activism in an average month during the 'normal times'. 'Normal times' are exclusively outside of the election campaign period. During the election campaign, many of them stressed that this time would increase as much as fourfold. Some 15 per cent of them spent 11 to 15 hours a month working for their party, while another 13 per cent devoted up to 20 hours to political activism. Some 15 per cent of my informants dedicated 20 to 30 hours in an average month. The largest group,

Table 7.2 Time spent on party activism per month by VP activists

Hours	**No. of people**	**%**
5 to 10	10	26
11 to 15	6	15
16 to 20	5	12
20 to 30	6	15
35 and +	12	31
Total	**39**	**100**

Source: Fieldwork.

comprising around one-third (31 per cent) of respondents, devoted more than 35 hours a month to activism. Giving up this much time was an impressive testimony to the activists' devotion and the strength of the VP's influential grassroots organisations.

Since almost 60 per cent were highly committed and ideologically driven they did not see party activism as a costly activity, as many scholars describe it (see Seyd and Whiteley, 1992, p. 86), but as something that was integral to their ideological beliefs and social values. As explained in chapter 5, many of them joined the VP in order to support what they called the *İslami dava* (Islamic cause).

As stated above, almost every one of my informants made a distinction in terms of the time they normally devoted to party activism. The intensity changed from actual election campaigning to the post-election period. For example, 33 per cent of them said that their activity would normally increase fourfold during the election campaigns. If one said that he spent up to ten hours a month, this meant he would spend as much as 40 hours during the election campaign. Indeed, in my own experience the majority put long hours and a lot of energy into campaigning. It was expected that the activists would take days off work or use their annual holiday during the campaign period. I witnessed people, like Süha Çelik from the *ilçe* of Keçiören, say they were closing their shop for the best part of two months in order to participate in the campaigning. Hasan, from the youth committee of Mamak *ilçe*, had to find someone to keep his shop open while he was doing errands as a member of a youth committee. There were even people who were workers in Western European countries such as Holland, Germany and France who came back to Turkey on their annual holiday for the purpose of campaigning with their Islamic brothers. I met such people, though not as many took part as had during previous election campaigns.

By now it is a well-known fact that Islamists are very well organised among the Turkish workers in European countries. The *Milli* Görüş Teşkilatı (Organisation of National View) is the motor of these organisations. It has been reported over the years by the media that the National View has organised an army of canvassers and political activists with the latest cars and considerable financial resources. In addition, it organises charter flights and sends thousands of guest workers to Turkey to vote for the WP/VP, providing cheap or free tickets for them.[7] These activities organised by the National View abroad show the scope and extent of organised election activities. Otherwise, the bulk of the election campaigns are run by local party organisations throughout the country.

I observed committed, devout and hard-working activists in every neighbourhood throughout the election campaign. They turned every occasion and every place into an arena for political activity. The activists appeared very competitive, well informed, energetic and ready to work long hours. You would see them organising house or teahouse meetings until very late at night. Members of the youth committee would be out until 2 am or later putting up party flags all around the neighbourhood, pasting party posters on all available walls and electricity and telephone poles, and hanging massive portraits of the candidates on cotton banners.

I shall now move on to the question of how these activists met the people, the potential voters, on the ground. It had been assumed that as the VP was a pro-Islamic party it must have been utilising religious institutions such as mosques for propaganda and as a recruitment ground. But my data showed that this was not the case at all. Instead, they preferred house meetings, which they successfully utilised for their political activism. My findings were as follows.

Where Did They Meet with Potential Voters?

VP activists canvassed people in diverse ways. Perhaps this diversity reflects the militant characteristics of their political activities in their constituency. Table 7.3 shows that 23 per cent of VP activists met people for political activism at the weekly meetings held by the neighbourhood committee.

These neighbourhood committees were the backbone of the local party organisation and numbered from 14 to 17 members. As mentioned above, they had weekly activity programmes prepared, implemented and assessed by these same committees in cooperation with the *ilçe* party organisation.

Salih Bağcı said of these meetings:

> There are weekly meetings, usually on Thursdays. The neighbourhood committee meets to discuss the agenda, assess the last week's activities and prepare next week's plan. And above all members are called on to make visits and canvass in the neighbourhood.

Around 18 per cent of my informants met people for political activism in a peculiar way that has not been developed as a means of canvassing

Table 7.3 VP activists' meeting places for grassroots activism

	%
Weekly meetings in neighbourhood	23
Visits for various occasions: weddings, engagements, celebrations, visiting sick or elderly, funerals, etc	18
House meetings	16
In mosques and after Friday prayers	11
Wherever there is an opportunity	11
In the teahouses	9
Workplace	7
At face-to-face meetings	5
Total	**100**

Source: Fieldwork.

in Western European countries at all. This form is more sociable than political, at least at the outset. Activists regularly and persistently attended any occasion for celebration or mourning, or any kind of social gathering. They visited ill or elderly people either in their home or in hospital. İdris Erdoğru, the representative Uyanış neighbourhood, explained how, through active campaigning, he increased party membership by seven and a half times in his neighbourhood:

> I go every day. I am the representative of the neighbourhood of Uyanış. While I am visiting I recruit new members and visit the ill. I wish them well, whoever they are, whether our neighbour or friend or someone totally unknown. I go to their weddings or funerals. So they accept us. More correctly, we go there to introduce ourselves, e.g. 'I am X from the VP's Uyanış neighbourhood party committee. We are here to congratulate your wedding. May God bless it.' If there is a funeral we go there and read the Koran, make friends with them. So they like it because we are there in their bad or good, easy or difficult days. This way I increased the number of members from 200 to 1,500. At least ten times I have won the award of high achievement in the neighbourhood.
>
> I think the best way to meet people to talk politics is during engagement and wedding celebrations. There you can talk one to one. Then I would visit those houses where there is someone who is ill or has died. You cannot talk politics, especially at funerals, but it gives us a chance to get publicity, and to talk about some non-political issues. When we go to this kind of occasion we usually take a present, nothing too expensive, but it is just good to take something with you. Our people like it if you turn up to their parties and celebrations to share their joy or problems.[8]

Community ties are much stronger in the *gecekondu* areas. One of the reasons for this is that the majority of the *gecekondu* settlers came originally from rural parts of the country. Thus political activism in these areas has to take a social or an informal form. The visits organised by the local party organisation functioned on several levels. Sharing the lives of people in the neighbourhood is certainly an effective form of political activism.

The exchange of gifts is of course a worldwide cultural phenomenon and it has been studied by many anthropologists. It has a very important role in community life. The VP leadership seemed to be aware of this fact, because in the VP handbook *Halkla İlişkiler Nedir?* (What is Public Relations?) party activists were strongly advised not to turn up empty-handed on their visits.[9]

Some 16 per cent of respondents said they met people at house meetings. As the representative of Aşağı Ayrancı neighbourhood explained:

> We have house meetings every week. In there everyone talks one by one. Also, there are meetings once a week in the neighbourhood, in the *ilçe* (sub-district) and in the *il* (district), and all the problems are discussed there.

These house meetings varied in the form they took. Most were arranged through family, kinship, *hemşehrilik* or ethnic ties. The activists usually visited such houses and if the host was willing they would ask him to invite some people from the same neighbourhood as an audience. Sometimes he would visit a particular household for tea. In other cases he would invite a group of people to his own home for tea and he would talk with them there. These house meetings were sometimes attended by middle-ranking politicians such as the candidate for the municipality or local parliament, or the chairman of the VP's *ilçe* (sub-district) organisation might be invited as a speaker. This kind of house meeting was usually organised during election campaigns.

Where else did party activists meet the people? Over one in ten (11 per cent) of them said they met people in mosques or after Friday prayers. In this case, as one would expect, religious institutions provided a fertile ground for canvassing. But more importantly this religious arena was open to the VP on unequal terms, as no other party would utilise mosques or Friday prayers as the VP did. Therefore it can be argued that the VP had a monopoly over the use of religious institutions to canvass. In this respect, religious ideology, rhetoric and religious institutions were important assets of the VP. However, it is important to keep in mind that only a small minority (11 per cent) of VP activists chose to meet people in mosques or at Friday prayers. The vast majority (89 per cent) preferred non-religious arenas.

Another 11 per cent of the informants said they met people wherever they found the opportunity. This group was a very interesting one and must have been the most dynamic of the grassroots activists because, theoretically speaking, there must have been immense possibilities for such opportunities. As one activist put it: 'Even on the bus, or while waiting in the queue for a doctor, no matter where I am, I explain our political ideas to other people.'[10] M. Balcı of the Şenlik neighbourhood took the same attitude on canvassing: 'Wherever I find people I talk politics.' M. Karaağaç from the Kutlu neighbourhood also practised his political activism whenever there was an opportune moment. He answered the same question with 'wherever I get an opportunity I talk to people'.

Many of the activists seemed outgoing and confident, were good communicators and highly informed on current political issues. With these qualities they were able to bring political dialogue into many occasions. They interpreted current political issues from their own perspective as a way of informing others. Moreover, they usually showed no hesitation in talking to people they didn't know.

There was another group consisting of 9 per cent of the activists that preferred to meet people in the *kahfehane* (teahouses) of the neighbourhood. As mentioned above, the teahouses play a central role in Turkish community life. It is very common for Turkish men to spend on average 4 to 5 hours every day in teahouses discussing everything from daily events to economics and from football to politics.[11] The teahouses are centres where the majority of men congregate to chat, play cards watch football, listen to the news and reflect, or, especially during the election campaigns, to host political candidates for discussions. They are usually open very late every day, including weekends, and serve as a platform for politics.

During my fieldwork I attended, as part of my research, many of the teahouse meetings organised by neighbourhood party branches and usually the candidates were asked to make speeches. Teahouse meetings are the commonest way of canvassing during election campaigns in Turkey and candidates have the chance to meet an audience of around 40 to 50 people – for a small teahouse – or 60 to 100 people in a large teahouse.

Around 7 per cent of the activists canvassed in their workplace, while 5 per cent said they met people one to one in different environments. Workplace canvassing was very important, as unlike most VP activism it took place outside the boundaries of the immediate community, sometimes beyond the *ilçe* boundaries. Party activists that canvassed in the workplace therefore carried the ideology and policies of the VP much further than many of their colleagues in the local party branches. Such activity was also valuable because of the heterogeneous community structure the workplaces in contrast with the neighbourhood's homogeneous community, so the ideas, policies and political messages of the VP were spread to much wider audiences via this group of activists.

The last group, who preferred to meet people one to one, was very influential too. Although their numbers were much lower – 5 per cent – because of their special tactics they reaped much better results from their activism than their colleagues in the local branch. As has been pointed out by many political scholars, face-to-face meetings are always a highly effective way to influence someone's voting behaviour (see Milbrath and Goel, 1977, p. 37).

What Perceptions Did Activists Have about Their Activities?

The majority of the VP's grassroots activists believed that their political activism was vital to the party's electoral performance; 74 per cent of them viewed their role as 'very important'. This is no surprise at all, as activists would not put in so much effort on behalf of the party if they did not feel that what they did was good for the party and essential for its success. As one party worker pointed out: 'The local party branches are the central pillar of the party.' Another activist noted: 'Without local organisations no party can stand up on its feet nor survive. Local organisations keep the party running.' Many of my informants acknowledged the crucial role of party activists at local level. One of them, Melih Demir, was a member of the executive committee of General Zeki Doğan neighbourhood. He believed that local organisations were so important that without them nothing would happen. At most, he said, the party would only exist on election posters. It would not reach out to people. To reach out it must have an organisation behind it. About one in five (19 per cent) of the informants regarded party activism as 'important'. This group believed that their activities were an important variable for the party's success but that there were other issues, such as party policies, leadership and nationwide campaigns, that were important as well. The number of those who did not think that grassroots activism was significant for the party's performance was very small. Just 2 per cent of the informants assessed their role as 'not so important' and another 4 per cent put forward alternative arguments for party performance other than party activism. After hearing their opinions on the effects of grassroots activism, I wanted to find out how they thought they affected the electoral chances of the VP.

How Did the Activists Improve Their Party's Electoral Fortune?

The informants had few doubts about the role and effect of their own activities on the fate of the party. As Mustafa Şenyurt from Mamak *ilçe* explained:

> From 1984 to 1991, because of their conformist approach the WP's neighbourhood representatives could not reach out to the people at all. As the WP developed and improved its *ilçe* organisations, extended its organisations in the *mahalles* (neighbourhoods) as well as into the streets as street representatives, its share of the vote increased. After 1989 the WP started to visit teahouses and *meyhaneleri* (pubs) so it increased its share of the vote. We would go there to greet them and sit at the tables of those who were drinking or gambling. So they saw that we are not what the media reports say and they voted for us. We have adopted the tactic of 'shameless politicians'. I mean, if someone turned one of us down another would go there to canvass him.

> If that did not work then we would find someone close to him, a relative or sometimes his wife through our lady activists.[12]

He continued:

> The main point is not to win extra votes. This problem is secondary. But we have developed solidarity. Trade cooperations like KOMBASAN, YİMPAŞ, GİYDAŞ, have been growing on the basis of this spirit of solidarity. In addition to that, there have been small funds established to provide credit for small-size investments like the Yutong firms in Yozgat ...

Mustafa Şenyurt drew my attention to the relationship between party organisations and campaigning: meeting or reaching the people. He correctly pointed out that between 1983 and 1991 the WP could not reach people because of two factors. First was the conformist approach of party organisations, and second was the lack of local organisations. From 1991 onwards the WP expanded its organisation networks vertically as well as horizontally. It extended its branches to the neighbourhood level and appointed representatives to every street and apartment block. In terms of its canvassing strategy and tactics, it developed a twin-headed strategy. On the one hand, its local organisations turned into social care units providing material benefits like food, fuel, clothing, bursaries for poor students, networking for jobs and hospital beds for patients, and helped out in a crisis such as in organising funerals. On the other hand, it used very assertive canvassing and propaganda tactics, like the 'shameless salesman' who tries to sell goods to an uninterested household. A good party organisation needs consistency between these two elements of its activities.

A party may have a great programme and the right policies, but if it is not consistent and coherent then it will not have credibility in the public eye. A representative of the Bahçeleriçi neighbourhood raised this issue:

> That is exactly where the difference between our party and the others lies ... The other parties are only active for one or two

> months from election to election but our party is active for 12 months. Our party activities are not bound to the election campaigns but are a year-round event. We listen to everyone, whether our member or not. At house meetings we go and listen to people then report the problems up to the *ilçe* branch. In contrast with our attitude, other parties forget people right after the election campaign.

The representative from Bahçeleriçi neighbourhood noted the consistency of their activities as opposed to other parties' activism, which was concentrated a round election time. He stressed that the VP's activists undertook year-round activity.

VP activists were seen to be very conscious of their own role and influence. When I asked what my informants thought about their contributions, one replied:

> Actually the election result decides our contributions. At the last election our party [WP] became the number one party by obtaining 33 per cent of the votes in our neighbourhood, Yeşiltepe. That time we didn't even have an election bureau but this time we have got one and that is a sign of our success. If you work hard you will get the prize. You won't be paid if you did not go to work (Fazlı Dalkıran, Yeşiltepe neighbourhood).

Perhaps the best answer to my question about whether grassroots organisations make any difference or not came from Fazlı Dalkıran. As he put it, the proof of the effectiveness of local party campaigning lies in election success. In other words, what counts is deeds not words. He also emphasised the basic principle of 'no pain no gain', showing how aware he was of his role as a political activist. He was especially proud because this time the party had an election bureau that they used as a base during the election campaign. He added:

> We play a very important role here. We are the mirrors of the party at the local level. As the people at the bottom end of the

> party we take the biggest share of the responsibility during election campaigns (Fazlı Dalkıran).

The VP's activists worked voluntarily with great passion, knowing that theirs was the only party that had a well-structured party organisation:

> Other parties lack this [organisation]. In the past the TTP tried it but failed, the NAP also tried and failed, because our activities are voluntary. Today some of our friends have no money in their pockets for the bus fare but they walk here every day. If they were not volunteers, you would not get them here even if you paid for them. The secret behind this commitment is the ideals that people [party activists] share. These people [activists] say, 'We are here for the service of the community'. It is for everyone regardless of their party affiliation whether they are from the Motherland Party or Republican People Party (representative of Aşağı Ayrancı neighbourhood).

What we see here is a strong sense of commitment to one's ideals among the activists and the significance of doing it voluntarily. İdris Erdoğru asserted that party activists can be described as the foundation of the party, because the activities in a neighbourhood depend on the representative:

> İE: I mean our activities are very important. Representatives follow events, go around to register new members and so on. Everyone, including our leaders at the top, knows that our work is valuable. Because, first of all, nobody but us goes around in the neighbourhoods.
>
> Q: What can you say if you compare your activities with other parties?
>
> İE: Yes, we have got our special methods. Other parties cannot work like us.
>
> Q: Why not?

İE: I do not know. This is a matter of belief and a method of working so no other party would work as much as we do.

Aydın Yürür, the representative of Çaldıran neighbourhood, pointed out that:

> the activities of the neighbourhood organisation play an important role in the rise of the VP. We are the party here. If our activities were not approved of by the people no one would vote for us. We are in constant contact with people. Whatever the occasion, first we run to the help of the needy; because of our closeness and genuine friendship people trust us.

In the same vein Mehmet Arı (Hürel neighbourhood) stressed the direct connection between the local and national level:

> Since the days of the WP we are the most active party in Mamak. We organise weekly meetings. If you are not successful in the local elections you are not going to succeed in the national elections either. So we explain ourselves to the people in greater detail. We do correct the wrongs that are said about us. We are putting in great effort to pre-empt the media's attacks on our party.

The connection between local and general election came up time and time again. This was not without good reason. The local area is where the grassroots organisations exist and carry out daily activities. They were all well aware that whatever they did in their particular locality would have an impact at the national level. M. Arı's view reflected how he perceived his role in his locality. He, rightly and consciously, equated his effort in the neighbourhood with the nationwide electoral success of the VP. He also emphasised another vital aspect of party activism that is, propaganda and counter-propaganda in the neighbourhood. Propaganda was the prime objective of the campaigns but up until then it had not been brought up by my informants. The reason for this may be the negative connotations that the concept of propaganda carries or it may be that they saw their activities as more effective than propaganda itself.

Şuaip, a member of the youth committee in Mamak, saw their role as very important for the VP's success in elections. He emphasised that:

> Via our activities the leadership holds the 'pulse of the public'. They get feedback about the people's needs and feelings. In addition, our youth committee organises activities designed for young people in the neighbourhood. By doing this we recruit young people into our ranks.

It was very interesting to see how Şuaip, despite his young age, saw his position between the party and the public. For him the local party organisation was a kind of organ that communicated between the party and neighbourhood community. It operated something like a nerve, passing the demands and feelings from community to party. He also pointed out the activities designed especially for young people. Indeed, at the previous general election the VP had developed some very clever tactics and strategies to attract the young, especially unemployed young people. The VP set up teahouses in every neighbourhood where they provided free facilities such as table tennis or snooker. The tea was very cheap and those who had no money were entitled to free tea (see *Milliyet,* 23 January 1999). Naci Tunalı from Ekin Başak neighbourhood also emphasised that some of their activities, such as football, were directed at the youth in their locality.

Yılmaz Doğan, from Türközü neighbourhood, described their role and duties as follows:

> Our duties are: providing ready information to the *ilçe* branch and organising coffee-house and house meetings and the like. There are 62 neighbourhoods in Mamak and there is no way the administrative committee of the sub-district, which consists of 24 people, could cope with all 62 neighbourhoods. There simply are not enough people to do that. So without us they would not

> know what was going on here. However, when we as neighbourhood committees have each got 14 people, that makes 900 in all 62 neighbourhoods.

In fact the numbers were much higher than he thought. Neighbourhood organisations, mainly the executive committees, were organised in the image of the *ilçe* organisations. The *ilçe* executive committees consisted of 30 people. A chairman and his deputy headed them. Fourteen of them were also chairpersons of various sub-groups such as election affairs, public relations, and so on, and equal numbers of their deputies held similar offices. There was also a ladies' committee and a youth committee. I observed that the neighbourhood committees usually consisted of between 20 and 30 members, which means that in the Mamak committee there were 1,240 to 1,860 party members. If we add the ladies' committee and youth committees, this figure goes much higher. I am not suggesting that every part of the neighbourhood had an active ladies' committee but most parts of it had youth committees that were actively involved. When added to the Keçiören *ilçe*, which had 43 neighbourhoods, and between 860 and 1,290 members in the executive committees, the total number (2,100–3,150) of grassroots activists in Ankara's two sub-districts was a considerable figure. Plus, there were many other activists who were not necessarily members of these committees. This all amounted to a considerable number of people who played a very constructive and influential role in their localities 'every hour of every day', as they would say.

The Main Points Emerging from the Interviews

It appears that grassroots activists perceived the role and the effects of political activism as very important for the party's electoral success: they saw themselves as messengers of the party, reaching out and spreading the party's messages across society. As well as carrying the party messages to the voter, they also functioned like a nerve relaying information from their particular community to the upper levels. For some, the success of the WP during the 1990s was due to the expansion of the local party branches at the sub-district, neighbourhood and street levels. This point is especially important because it was this expansion of the grassroots organisations from top to bottom that made the WP/VP the only mass-membership party.

For some of my informants, continuity was the key aspect of their activities. Many stressed that their activity was a year-round campaign. They carried on their tasks routinely, regardless of the election campaigns. Unlike the other parties in Turkey, many of my informants said they were active in the community continuously, and that in turn helped to build public trust in them.

Another common recurring factor was that the activists were working voluntarily. Often the VP's activists were all volunteers. Of course there were some who expected some gain, material or otherwise, out of their activism, but this was not the driving force for the majority of the VP's activists.

Aside from their political volunteering they also carried out a lot of community work. The notion of being at the service of the community or society was one of the defining characteristics of the WP/VP. This is especially important because politics in Turkey has been dominated by an elite that sees itself not as serving society but as dictating to or governing society.

As previously argued, no party could match the size and quality of the WP/VP's grassroots organisations. The grassroots organisations were given real meaning and an open space to perform on the ground. This situation was closely connected to the party structure as well. The membership and local organisations of the cartel parties carried little weight. But because the VP was a mass-membership party the local party organisations did the bulk of campaigning.

The last pattern that emerges is of the special tactics and strategies that the WP/VP developed. On one hand, it could be said that because the VP was the only mass-membership party its campaign strategy and tactics must have been different from the rest of the political parties. This is true to a degree, but other parties also have party activists and local organisations. However, from the beginning of the 1990s the WP introduced different and highly creative tactics such as utilising the ladies' committee as one of its main campaigning forces.

Initially this looked very unlikely given the party's attitude towards women in general and the status of Muslim women in particular. It was unthinkable to have women as one of the main campaigning forces in a male-dominated religious conservative party. Until 1999 the party did not even have a woman candidate for parliament. Despite this, it successfully integrated women into its rank and file and returned women MPs to parliament.

What Did the Activists Do, and How Did They Do It?

'How can I vote for you while I am eating bread provided by the WP/VP?'

This section discusses the different dimensions and methods of the VP. As noted earlier, from the early 1990s the WP and later the VP displayed a wide range of political activism. Surprisingly many of those activities took place outside the political sphere, such as charity work and visiting people socially for occasions from wedding ceremonies to funerals.

Various kinds of activities were carried out by local party organisations. These activities were as diverse as distributing roses in the more affluent non-VP neighbourhoods – as in Tıp Fakültesi Caddesi – to organising charity work such as handing out clothing, food, coal or even bursaries for poor schoolchildren in *gecekondu* areas (such as Hürel or Türközü). The VP concentrated especially on the poor *gecekondu* areas where high levels of unemployment and poverty, low-quality housing, low income, low-quality public services, etc., were the defining characteristics.[13] This concentration of WP/VP activities in the *gecekondu* areas did not go unnoticed among Turkish political writers and the media in general.[14]

Besides its political activities, the VP's local organisations provided various kinds of material aid for the poorest sections of the *gecekondu*. From my observations and interviews I can say that most of the time these activists saw themselves as charity workers who were there to help the poor, ill, elderly, disabled, orphans and widows. When asked what kind of activities they carry out as neighbourhood organisations,

Table 7.4 Activities carried out by VP grassroots activists

	%
Charity work (providing material aid (food, clothing, fuel, etc.) and social services)	37
House visits (house meetings)	19
Attending weekly meetings of local party organisation	15
Visits for any social occasions (weddings, funerals, patient visits)	12
Developing and maintaining good relations in the neighbourhood	10
Educating people (propaganda, counter-propaganda, putting up posters, etc.)	8
Total	100

Source: Fieldwork.

the majority of them would speak about this charity work. Here we will examine exactly what sort of charity work they undertook.

Nearly four in ten (37 per cent) of my informants reported that their political activism was dominated by charity work: provision of some material and non-material commodities, guidance and other kinds of assistance (Table 7.4). One in five (19 per cent) said house visits or meetings were most favourable for them, while 15 per cent said the weekly meetings in the neighbourhood branch were the most common form of activism they performed. Some 12 per cent preferred social visits to households, usually when there was some sort of celebration or a death had occurred. They often attended wedding celebrations, visited the ill, attended funerals and so on. For 10 per cent of the informants, developing and maintaining good relationships with the voters was the most positive type of political activism.

Charity work in particular was an invaluable instrument for the activists. For example, Halis from Aktepe neighbourhood explained:

> We help those health workers who come to our quarter to carry out medical checks. We lend a hand with the distribution of meals,

coal or coats for school children aged between 9 and 12. This year there were a lot of coats given to children. The meals have stopped now but bread is coming from the metropolitan municipality. We give some help to those poor people who cannot pay their rent, regardless of their party inclinations. Also this year there have been large quantities of dried food given away in the neighbourhood. One of my neighbours told me what he said to an activist from another party who was canvassing in our quarter: 'How can I vote for you while I am eating bread provided by the VP?' We also visit the sick and give a lot of support if there is a funeral.

What we see from Halis's activities is that party activists were actively involved with very diverse elements of social work from helping and guiding health professionals through the neighbourhood to distributing food or clothing aid from the municipality. Remzi Özcan also described a wide variety of activities undertaken by activists in his locality, Kutlu:

RÖ: For instance, we try to help those needs in material form as well as in non-material (spiritual) ways. If someone were very poor you would not do anything spiritually. First you must feed him. At this moment in our neighbourhood bread has been distributed. The *halk ekmek* (people's bread) continues. It is not just for the election. It was there before the election campaign as well. What we are doing is searching for those poor people to provide them at least with bread and a hot meal. While we give this it is not that we are expecting anything from anyone. It is because they are human beings. If he gets food he can then think.

Q: What else are you doing?

RÖ: We organise food giveaways every year a round Ramadan. There are those who want to give their alms, so we collect from them and pass them on to the poor who are our brothers. Plus, this year there are some bursaries for schoolchildren. They can be given from primary to university level. They are around 3 million TL for primary,

4 million TL for elementary, 6 million TL for high school and 7 million TL for university.

Q: How about fuel: coal and wood?

RÖ: Yes around half a ton of coal and ten sacks of wood per household.

As Özcan noted, their activities in the neighbourhood committee consisted of providing some material benefits – food, fuel, clothing and bursaries – as well as non-material benefits such as helping people find jobs and solving problems with the government offices. In a similar vein, M. Karaağaç, from the same *İlçe*, pointed out that:

> As VP devotees we meet like-minded people in our neighbourhood, hold discussions. Then those who have got some need come to us, because the metropolitan municipality, governed by the VP, comes to us. Our neighbourhood is a very poor one. Most of its population are labourers. At least 50 per cent of them are day labourers. People usually do not want to ask for help because they feel embarrassed, but we know them and try to help them in whatever way we can.

The location of Kutlu is not far from the wealthiest district of Çankaya with its presidential palace and where the high-ranking bureaucrats reside. Despite this physical closeness, these districts might as well be on different planets. In contrast to Kutlu's third-world standards, Çankaya has the living standards of major developed countries. As Karaağaç stressed, high unemployment, low income and bad housing are common in Kutlu. He explained how, using the resources of the metropolitan municipality, he and his friends organised charity work to ease the situation a little bit.

Q: Approximately how many households received fuel (coal and wood) in Kutlu?

MK: Last year it was approximately 50 families but I do not know for this year. This year the head men are giving more than the neighbourhood executive committee. Our neighbouring quarter of Mutlu received a lot of it this year. It all comes from the metropolitan municipality. At least 90 per cent of this material – coal, wood, food – comes from there.

Q: How about the food?

MK: The food packages include pasta, margarine, sugar, chick-peas, baked beans, rice, bulgur and tomato puree. In last year's list there were 13 different items including Omo [detergent] listed. The food bags usually weigh around 30 kg or so. I gave them to people with my own hands last year. They would be enough for a month for a family, maybe more.

Also we got some bursaries and winter coats for children last year. For example, I myself registered 50 people alone last year. I gave 15 of them in this school and also gave the rest of the forms to school. Poor people benefited from them a lot. The metropolitan municipality gave 20,000 bursaries last year. This year, too, students will start to receive them. It was said that up to 75,000 students will be involved but I do not know for sure. The amount of bursary will be 7.5 million TL for university, 5 million for high schools and 3 million for primary schools.

Q: It is very good that the municipality can afford it.

MK: Yes, as I said the pious Muslims will find resources. If you employ 19,000 workers instead of 26,000, so [the municipality] will use the money that previously paid for the extra 6 to 7,000 workers. This amounts to a lot of money. He [the mayor] says I will use that money for this kind of service. It has been said that there are around 1,000 people that are paid but never come to the workplace. When you cut out this wasted money it will go directly to the municipality's coffers. Plus there are businessmen who are good Muslims and want to help ...

The local organisations carried out extensive and expensive charity work throughout Ankara's *gecekondu* areas. The above three cases covered both sub-districts: Keçiören and Mamak. As stated previously, the charity work is the highest-scoring activity among the VP's political activists. The provision of certain goods – food, fuel, clothing, bursaries – and other non-material services and assistance seemed to be unified across Ankara's many *gecekondu* areas.[15]

The welfare state is very weak in Turkey and provision of basic services from education to health, electricity, roads, water, etc. has been further hampered by neoliberal policies. As a result of rapid urbanisation starting in the early 1980s, cities expanded beyond their physical boundaries. The influx of mass migration exhausted the cities' industrial and services sectors. Already scarce resources for housing, health, education and so on were overwhelmed by these waves of migration.[16]

In addition to this, with the implementation of the IMF's restructuring policies, immigration from rural to urban areas accelerated. At the same time, as if things were not bad enough, the state reversed its traditional role in the economy in general and made huge cutbacks from its social policies. Everything was left to the mercy of 'market forces'.[17] But we need to ask to what extent the VP grassroots's charity work was effective. Was it really significant and did it benefit the poor, as well as contributing to the VP's electoral success?

A 'Messiah in the Making'?

By organising charity work the VP showed that it was interested in people's daily problems. As Fazlı Dallı, an activist from Keçiören, put it:

> Our approach to people is to make friends and show compassion. As a neighbourhood organisation we get some goods for charity, and distribute them regardless of party affiliations. Usually we get coal, food, bursaries and clothing for the students and bread to distribute here. In our neighbourhood there are currently 300 families, which get four loaves bread per family a day. So that makes 1,200 loaves of bread per day. There are many people who wait for a long time in the cheap bread queue. It shows that

> those people need to buy bread cheaper than they normally do elsewhere. Now if it were the ANAP (Motherland Party) not us who were distributing this aid, they would vote for them not for us. But by doing this you show that at least you are interested in their problems.

The impact of these acts of charity could be interpreted in many different ways. The material benefits – food, fuel, medical aid, etc. – must carry a variety of values within. This charity work did of course carry basic material values, such as use-value and exchange value, but part of its worth lies in its 'social use value'.[18] Also, charity work was valuable for the VP itself because the party would gain votes in return. First and foremost, those material benefits contributed to easing the daily struggle of poor households for a while, however small and palliative they might have been. In addition, they showed that there was someone who cared about the lives of these poor families.

This involvement with charity work also credited the VP with being the party of the poor. It created a future vision where the VP, which was already helping and seemed to be concerned with the problems of the poor, would bring the justice, equality and prosperity that had been denied to the people for so long. What the opponents of the VP were doing, at most, was proposing a free-market economy that was not addressing the pressing economic problems of large sections of society. But the VP had not only its charity work but also its unique *Adil Düzen* (Just Order) economic programme. The rhetoric of the Just Order appealed to the millions of the lower-middle and lower classes from right and left. With this programme the VP managed to get the support of the traditionally leftist voters who had been disillusioned with leftist parties since the mid-1980s.

It can be argued that social solidarity is seen as one of the most precious aspects of social life and that it is always regarded as the first condition of a 'good society'. As societies change, and advance from one form to another, the aspects of solidarity change too; but interestingly enough there is always a common and constant desire for more of it. In the case of the VP, solidarity took material as well as non-material forms.

The source of the WP's and later the VP's financing has been much discussed and speculated on. It must be said that one of the main financial sources of funding for political parties is the state itself. According to the Turkish constitution (1982) and article 69 of the law of political parties (2820), parties are entitled to receive state funding. The conditions and the amount of financial aid that parties would be entitled to and granted have changed considerably over time; however, it is usually those parties, that received at least 7 per cent of the total votes that are eligible to receive the money. It has been calculated that between 50 and 90 per cent of the parties' total income comes through state funding.[19]

Another significant source of funding arose from the transformation of the traditional Anatolian bourgeoisie; this had a massive impact on the rise of the WP via financial as well as political support. Throughout the 1980s Turkey developed a much closer connection with Muslim countries that it had long neglected. In particular, Arab countries such as Saudi Arabia, Kuwait, UAE and Qatar became a source of funding for investment in various sectors. Islamic banks such as Al Baraka Turk (a Saudi–Turkish financial venture) started to operate.

The second phase in the rise of the Islamist bourgeoisie was the well-managed flow of the savings of Turkish migrant workers in various European countries via various religious groups, brotherhoods and Islamic business associations. The 'petrodollar' connection with rich Arab countries and the savings of Turkish migrant workers were two crucial external contributing factors to the rise of Islamist capital. At the same time during the 1980s and 1990s there were internal factors that also contributed to the transformation of some elements of the Anatolian bourgeoisie.[20]

What can be said finally is that the charity work carried out by VP activists was also an indication of the widespread networking that took in the metropolitan municipality, district municipalities, Islamic business groups, various political and non-political groups, brotherhoods, Islamic trusts, trade unions and associations. Through these networks the VP helped finance its activities as well as its charity work.

Around one-fifth (19 per cent) of my informants said that they attended house meetings or visits. Although my findings showed otherwise, house-to-house or door-to-door visits were actually the most common and most reported type of canvassing by the VP. Obviously door-to-door canvassing results in face-to-face contact, which is the most effective way of affecting someone's party preferences. As Metin Toker, one of Turkey's most prominent political commentators, observed during the 1999 election campaign: 'The most effective election campaign activity of a candidate in Turkey is still to go around shop-to-shop, door-to-door, teahouse-to-teahouse to shake voters' hands.'[21]

The house meetings were valued as a more intimate, informal and private way of meeting potential voters. As mentioned above, in its public relations booklet the party encouraged activists to make visits and organise house meetings. The neighbourhood representatives or members in the neighbourhoods usually arranged them. The number of house meetings increased considerably before the elections. On occasion I attended four such meetings in one night from 7 pm to 12 pm. Especially during election campaigning these meetings were attended by the candidates for various posts and each candidate made a speech explaining policies and appeals for support. In return, those who attended would ask a variety of questions about the candidate's policies, employment opportunities in the municipality, the needs of particular *gecekondu* settlements, roads, water supply, etc. The meetings sometimes turned into a kind of negotiation between the candidate and the residents of the neighbourhood over the services that would be provided if he was elected.

But this type of meeting was more common during election campaigns. During normal times these house meetings were more educative. Generally they were like a sermon where a *hatip* (preacher/good speaker) would be invited to talk about current political or economic issues. He would start off with religious matters and explain some issues if asked by the audience. In addition to attending house meetings, the VP's activists were very keen to make social visits and attend mourning gatherings.

Fifteen per cent of my informants said that most of their political activism took the form of weekly meetings. These were the meetings that the neighbourhood executive committee held every Thursday or

Sunday. Each meeting lasted about two and a half hours. All members of the neighbourhood committee were expected to attend these meetings, where the previous week's action plan was assessed. Daily issues were discussed and the following week's action plan was prepared. After the plan and assessment, the urgent tasks, for example visiting the sick, attending funerals, weddings, etc., were allocated among the members.

Some 12 per cent of my activists said the commonest form of activism for them was through social visits. If there was a wedding or engagement celebration, a young boy's circumcision celebration, if someone entered military service, or if someone was sick or there was a funeral, they would visit these households to join the celebration or share the grief. As Yahya Konuk (representative of the Mutlu neighbourhood) pointed out, activities such as visiting the sick, attending weddings or visiting households where someone is going to join the army to say goodbye are 'things that people like'. As the *gecekondu* population consists of new migrants from rural areas, they are used to close communal ties and seek to simulate these relations in *gecekondu* areas. The *gecekondu* population is more like a rural community (*Gemeinschaft*) than an urbanised community. Most *gecekondus* are in transition, and for some commentators they are 'in-between – neither villagers nor urbanites' (Erman, 1998, pp. 552–3).

The VP's grassroots activists were well aware of the centrality of traditional rural values for *gecekondu* dwellers and the importance of following rural traditions and costumes. When they attended these gatherings they usually took a gift for the bride and groom, even if just a flower. If they visited a patient they took something with them: some flowers or cologne, for example. Most importantly, when someone died their help with organising the funeral was much appreciated by families. None of the other parties were as well armed to cope with death and its rituals as the VP's grassroots. In fact, most of the centre-right and leftist parties are secular and their activists do not have any ritual coping mechanism. Some of the activists interviewed mentioned the importance accorded to a proper burial. Nowadays, it is difficult to find a convenient and inexpensive grave in Ankara. It costs at least half a billion TL (USD 1,150) and most people are unable to pay. With the help of friends and the metropolitan municipalities, the activists arranged gravesites and assisted with funeral expenses and transport, as well as feeding the crowd afterwards. 'People say, "you are closer to me than my brother"', said the representative of Şehit Kubilay neighbourhood.

The fact is that the activists were themselves from rural Anatolia, and had usually come to the city at a young age and never left the *gecekondu* communities. This may have made it much easier for them to appreciate the importance of traditional, cultural and religious customs in their own surroundings. Being familiar or growing up with the same customs, traditions and certain regional codes gave them an advantage compared to other party activists.

Ten per cent of my informants gave priority to developing and maintaining good relations with potential voters. This aspect is very important for many reasons. Having a good relationship is itself a very effective means of influencing people's attitudes. As already mentioned, the *gecekondu* communities have predominantly rural characteristics and first-group relations and close community ties are still the dominant form. In this context developing good, close, friendly relations is a prerequisite for a successful local party organisation.

The VP built its success through its skilful approach to voters. To do this the community leaders and neighbourhood representatives were often chosen through examination. Those who were known for their qualities of seriousness, trustworthiness and religious devotion were encouraged to come forward as neighbourhood representatives. The members of the executive committees were also chosen from among respected members of the community. In addition, the VP paid special attention to winning the hearts of people before winning their minds and possibly votes. Its strategy was to build bedrock of good relationships with the electorate, slowly but steadily.

A good relationship is more difficult to achieve than it sounds for a political party competing with many others. In order to develop a good relationship in a community the activists had to have very good communication skills, be good at observing, be caring and be willing to volunteer, devoting much time and energy to political activities.

Some 8 per cent of my informants gave priority to educating people as a political activity. This method of campaign activism is more in line with modern methods of campaigning, consisting of propaganda, counter-propaganda, displaying posters, hanging party flags, distributing leaflets, etc., all around the sub-district.[22] The activists concerned were predominantly from the party's youth committee and these activities required more energy than others. The other neighbourhood committees also carried out these tasks when needed. These activities intensified during the election campaign.

After the election the youth committee focused more on community activities. As one young activist stated: 'In two years the numbers in the youth committee increased from ten to 450. They organised charity work worth 7 billion TL (USD 16,099) in eight months. There is no street that they have not been to in all of the 62 neighbourhoods in Mamak' (Hasan, member of Mamak youth committee). This itself shows how the youth committee was active and engaged in similar activities to the other activists outside election times.

To make sense of this data we need to compare it with similar material from other countries and with other academic studies. Unfortunately there is no single Turkish study of grassroots activism or a study of the effects of party organisation on the electoral process. Given this practical difficulty, I must compare my findings with studies from Britain and America.

Comparing Activism: British, American and Turkish Activists in Perspective

A study on the British Labour Party revealed that only 44 per cent of the Labour Party's activists said they frequently had contact with each other. Some 10 per cent did not do anything at all while 17 per cent did and 29 per cent met people occasionally. Another criterion for party activism is the frequency of attendance at party meetings. Compared to their level of activism in their local branch or constituency, Labour Party activists attended far fewer party meetings. Some 36 per cent of the activists said they had not attended any Labour Party meeting in the last year, while only 30 per cent said they attended frequently. Twenty per cent said they attended these meetings occasionally and the other 14 per cent replied that they did so rarely (Seyd and Whiteley, 1992, p. 89).

Again, when asked 'how much time do you devote to party activities in the average month?' 50 per cent of them replied none, fewer than one in three (30 per cent) said up to five hours, while 10 per cent replied between five and ten hours. Only 4 per cent said they spent ten to 15 hours, while as few as 2 per cent said 15 to 20 hours. Just 4 per cent spent more then 20 hours on party activities in the average month (ibid, 1992, p. 88). However, Labour and Liberal Democrat (Lib Dem) party activists recorded much more time on party activities during the 1997 UK general election campaign.

Both Labour and Lib Dem activists were involved in various sorts of campaign activities. Some of them were highly active. Over three-quarters of both parties' activists displayed an election poster and around 70 per cent donated money to their party (see Table 7.5). But when it came to more costly activities in terms of time, the rate fell

Table 7.5 Activities carried out by Labour and Liberal Democrat activists during the 1997 general election campaign

'Thinking about the 1997 general election, we would like to ask you about your activities during the campaign. Did you:

	Percentage of respondents saying 'Yes'	
	Labour	Lib Dems
Display an election poster	78	70
Donate money to party election funds	64	71
Help to run an election-day committee room	17	19
Drive voters to the polling station	17	19
Take numbers at the polling station	26	36
Remind voters to vote on polling day	45	27
Attend the count/celebration party	12	22

Source: Whiteley and Seyd, 1999, p. 30.

Table 7.6 Level of activity during the 1997 election campaign

'Again, thinking about the 1997 general election, did you:

	Not at all		once or more	
	Labour	Lib Dem	Labour	Lib Dem
Telephone canvass voters	90	94	10	6
Canvass voters door-to-door	76	76	24	24
Help with a fund-raising event	80	74	20	26
Deliver party leaflets	52	46	48	54
Attend a party rally	78	78	22	22
Help organise a street stall	91	96	9	4
Help with party mailings	79	75	21	25
Help with telephone fund-raising	98	98	2	2

Source: Whiteley and Seyd, 1999, p. 30.

to one-quarter or below. For example, a fifth of activists from both parties drove voters to the polling station.

Ten per cent of Labour activists and six per cent of Lib Dem activists telephone canvassed voters once or more (Table 7.6). In the case of door-to-door canvassing, the figure rose to a quarter. Some 24 per cent of activists from both parties canvassed voters by going door-to-door, which is a very effective way of influencing people's political preferences, while 20 per cent of Labour and 26 per cent of Lib Dem activists had helped with a fundraising event. More than half (52 per cent) of Lib Dem and 48 per cent of Labour activists delivered party leaflets, while 22 per cent of both party's activists had attended a party rally. Another 21 per cent of Labour and 25 per cent of Lib Dem activists helped with party mailings. There were also activities that attracted very low levels of attendance: 9 per cent of Labour and 4 per cent of Lib Dem activists had helped to organise a street stab.

It seems that except for 'delivering party leaflets', three-quarters of party activists from both parties stayed inactive, while 25 per cent of them were active. Nevertheless, this 25 per cent comprised thousands of party activists who, as shown in Tables 7.5 and 7.6, were highly active. For this reason, as Whiteley and Seyd (1999) argued, they had a considerable impact on Labour's landslide election victory in the 1997 general elections. Nevertheless, while in the British context they seem very active, compared to the VP's activists they lagged far behind.

In the USA most parties are not bureaucratic or hierarchically run organisations. Their leaders and activists are part-time volunteers; there are no permanent headquarters or paid staff. Unlike the VP's activists in Turkey, their activity is not a year-round phenomenon, but rather cyclical and concentrated around the campaign season. However, contrary to the common belief that parties have been declining or may even be dead, case studies of local parties have proven otherwise:

> A case study of Cuyahoga County (Cleveland), Ohio, showed that party activists were at least as active in 1981 in attending meetings, registering voters, distributing literature, and getting out the vote as they had been in the mid-1970s. Similarly in Middlesex County, New Jersey, two-thirds of the district leaders reported that they worked at least six hours a week for the party during campaigns and over 40 percent indicated that they often engaged in voter registration, telephone canvassing, and door-to-door canvassing (Bibby, 1987, pp. 104–5).

While these figures are higher than conventional wisdom would suggest (Seyd and Whiteley, 1992, p. 90), they are not as impressive as the level of political activism carried out by the VP's grassroots activists. If we compare the amount of work carried out by party activists in Britain, the USA and Turkey, it is clear that the VP's activists in Turkey were far more active than their British and American counter parts.

Conclusion

In this chapter I examined the effects of grassroots activism on electoral outcomes. The first half of the chapter was devoted to the theoretical arguments. It was argued that there are two distinct, competing approaches. According to the proponents of the 'counter argument', political parties have lost their historical role as the means of electoral canvassing. Many explained the decline of party organisation as the result of technological television – candidate-centred campaigns built on the polls and run by the media and public relations experts (Crotty and Jacobson, 1980). However, many political scientists have challenged this approach. They argue that contrary to the counter-argument, party organisations have continued to be very influential on the parties' electoral fortunes (see Crotty, 1971; Huckfeldt and Sprague, 1992). In line with the theoretical explanations, there is substantial empirical evidence supporting claims of the continuing effectiveness of party organisations. For example, Whiteley and Seyd (1998) discovered that Labour's landslide election victory in the previous general election (1997) was in fact the work of Labour's renewed energetic militant grassroots activists.

I have reviewed other case studies from Canada (Clarke et al., 2000) and the United States (Crotty, 1971; Huckfeldt and Sprague, 1992). In addition to these studies from different Western countries, my own observations have led me to think that there is a strong correlation between a party's electoral fortunes and its grassroots activism. As discussed already, having a large membership organisation would only contribute to the strength of that party – not the other way around. The argument that it is too expensive to maintain a larger membership is unconvincing.

Wherever it is fought and whatever technologies are available, every election campaign needs manpower to canvass door-to-door, deliver party leaflets, post the party mail, attend party rallies, telephone canvass voters, drive voters to polling stations and the like. Every party needs party activists to do door-to-door canvassing, recruit new members, and listen to people and report back, to spread the party's message, policies and ideology. All this requires active members prepared to dedicate long hours and energy to party causes.[23]

The influence of local party organisations is especially enhanced under certain conditions: declining partisan attachments, declining party loyalties, and increased electoral swings. In other words, if there are many people leaving their parties for one reason or another, they will choose other parties. In this case a party with a large grassroots organisation will be in a better position to persuade new voters through face-to-face encounters. We know that those who are personally contacted are inclined to be more active and change their party preferences (see chapter 5).

Returning to the central issue of the effects of the VP's grassroots activists on the party's electoral outcomes, I will start with levels of activity. Turkish activists tend to be more active than British and American activists. Although there are differences of technique, it is possible to gauge the frequency, duration and effectiveness of political activism.

Why were the VP's activists more active? In chapter 5, I examined the most important reasons why activists become members of the VP. It was observed that 62 per cent of them gave religious and ideological reasons. These findings suggest that the majority of them were ideologically radical. For many it was actually a way of serving their ideological goals, and for others it served the Islamic cause. So this conviction made them more active than ordinary members or other party activists.

It has already been established that they were very active, but was this enough to boost the party's electoral fortunes? The answer is no, not by itself. What was also important was what they did and how they did it in their respective constituencies. It has been argued that the VP's activists combined different methods and strategies to win people's hearts, minds and then their votes. Indeed, this order of events is very important. As some of my informants asserted, they were not like other parties that knock on people's doors once every four or five years, but were always with the people. Their activism was a year-round activity rather than occuring merely during the election periods. They visited households on many social occasions, offered help in times of crisis and showed solidarity, compassion and sympathy.

It seems that social work and political activism go hand in hand. The VP's grassroots activists effectively combined social work and political activism. They were well balanced and complemented one another. Due to their community work they were viewed as compassionate, really caring about the problems of the community. Activists visited government offices, solved bureaucratic problems and improved services through the municipality and other agencies. Furthermore, because of this social work and its caring image the VP was elevated to the level of the messiah: 'a messiah in the making'. If the VP representative were a professional social worker he might have done a lot better for the welfare of the poor and needy, but he would not be the same person who would possess, via elections, the governmental power needed to create a better society and a better future. After all, a social worker is a social worker, but a VP activist is a social worker as well as someone who can change things by political means. So he is in fact, up to a point, 'a would-be messiah in the making'.

Finally, one of the most unusual characteristics of the VP's party organisation was that it combined both the 'modern' and the 'traditional'. In very few arenas has the mixture of modern and traditional been used so well to create such a positive and effective outcome.

CHAPTER 8

CONCLUSION: FUNDAMENTALISM DEMYSTIFIED

Islamic Fundamentalism: A Misplaced Categorisation

The last two decades of the twentieth century witnessed an unprecedented rise in religious movements. As argued, this phenomenon is prevalent in all faiths of the world (Juergensmeyer, 1993, pp. 11–18; Kepel, 1994, pp. 6–7). Among them Islamic fundamentalism occupies a very special place (Halliday, 1996). For many, Islamic revivalism poses a multiple threat; from political to military, cultural to demographic and, because of the oil reserves concentrated in the Middle East, an economic threat as well. For some other writers, these fundamentalist movements are anti-modernist, living in a bygone age and wanting to turn the clock back to AD 700 – the time of the Prophet Muhammed. According to postmodernist students of political Islam, Islamist movements are the product of postmodern conditions (Akbar, 1992; Gülalp, 1995).

However, many of these approaches and studies in the late twentieth century misinterpreted the reactions that these movements embodied and totally neglected the circumstances in which they arose by focusing entirely on the 'imagined threat' that they pose. In other words, the majority of writers and the Western media portrayed these movements as 'extremist', 'terrorist', 'intolerant', or 'irrational' without paying any attention to the sociological realities and conditions in which they emerged. Mostly readers are informed again and again about religious zealots, intolerant villains, or Islamic fundamentalists, without having a glimpse of the conditions that bred these movements or what their aims and ideologies are. As area specialists Halliday (1996) and Esposito (1995) pointed out, they are often not a threat to anyone or to Western civilisation and the Western way of life, nor they made up of extremist, intolerant zealots, but are mostly a reaction to their own often anti-democratic, corrupt and incompetent governments. They are also a reaction against the foreign domination and influence that Muslim societies have been subjected to for a long time (Demirer, 1998, pp. 66–9).

This book does not suggest that the rise of political Islam has been entirely independent of the trend of religious revivalism across the Muslim world. It is not, but in connection with the unprecedented rise of political Islam in Turkey the effect of religious revivalism has been much smaller compared to the effects of grassroots activism on the electoral success of WP/VP and later (from 2002 onwards) that of the AKP.

There are many scholars who disagree with mainstream Western approaches and suggest that Islamic movements have not simply engaged with re-Islamisation or the restoration of religious fundamentalism. Rather they view these movements as emerging in the context of economic and social crisis, unemployment, poor income dispersal among the lower and lower-middle classes, the growing gap between poor and rich, rapid urbanisation, and inadequate government services (see Bulliet, 1993; Caplan, 1987; Keddie, 1981; Roy, 1994; and Salt, 1995). In addition, these countries are notorious for their oppressive, corrupt, anti-democratic nature and bad human rights records.

It was argued in chapter 1 that the majority of the Turkish elite failed to correctly identify the underlying causes of the rise of political Islam. Instead they labelled political Islam as Islamic fundamentalism and concentrated on its supposedly 'extremist', 'irrational', 'intolerant', 'anti-modern', 'anti-secular', 'anti-Kemalist', or 'anti-positivist' characteristics. I argued that the majority of the Turkish elite, of all political persuasions – Kemalists, secularists, radicals, socialists, liberals and even the conservatives – have misconceptualised and misdiagnosed the rise of political Islam as purely Islamic revivalism.

From the mid-1990s until very recently, the discourse of political Islam in Turkey revolved around the axis of *laicism–anti-laicism* (secularism–anti-secularism), modernism–anti-modernism, positivism versus idealism; this axis had its roots in Enlightenment philosophy and the French Revolution.

The foundations of the Turkish secularists' arguments come mainly from Kemalist ideology and its positivist philosophy, limited to a few basic principles such as the dismissal of the existence of God and holding religion responsible or blaming Islam for the underdevelopment of Turkish society and economy. It envisages a simple continuation of the historical contention between progressivism and traditionalism. Turkish leftists and socialist writers take a similar line and fail to contribute a new dimension to this old discourse (Akçam, 1994, pp. 7–8).

For example, Server Tanilli (1996, p. 9), a prominent intellectual of the left, views the ascension of the WP in the context of the rise of Islamic fundamentalism occurring in many other Muslim countries. For him some of these movements are refusing to compromise on their principles to live in peace with the secular republican regime. So, he says, the time has come for an ideological battle to save not only the institutions of the secularist republic but also all of the values of the 150-year-old Turkish Enlightenment movement, because they are under threat from Islamic movements.

For many other radical secularist intellectuals, the rise of the WP in the 1990s and the AKP in the early 2000s represented nothing but the threat of Islamic fundamentalism. One of the most common causes of the rise of political Islam, for this group, was the promiscuous policies of consecutive right-wing governments towards Islam since the 1950s and 1960s. It is argued that these governments nurtured, protected and even encouraged Islamic ideology for electoral purposes and political manipulation. The argument is that for decades right-wing parties dominated the Turkish polity and they all compromised the principle of secularism for the sake of votes (see Çetinkaya, 1996, pp. 91–2; Ekşi, 1995, p. 15; Tuşalp, 1994, p. 23). It is true that right-wing governments, especially after the 1960s, gave some concessions to the Islamists' demands, such as opening İmam-Hatip (religious) schools and allowing Koran courses, but such actions can be interpreted as the reason for rather than a result of an ongoing process.

Traditionally, Turkish 'progressive' intellectuals, comprising a wide range of radical secularists, liberals, socialists of various tendencies, and radicals, have regarded religion merely as a relic of the past. In doing so they have underestimated the historical, cultural, political and social importance of Islam as one of the key elements of society in Turkey. Perhaps this dismissive attitude prevalent among the Turkish elite was a result of the militant secularism of the state itself since the 1920s.

At this juncture it is important to recall that the Turkish modernist approach or radical secularist approach towards political Islam has been shared by most sections of the ruling classes: the influential military and bureaucratic elites and upper classes.

In many ways Turkish modernist interpretations share the same wisdom as the Western modernist approaches to political Islam. Both have failed to correctly diagnose the nature of political Islam, or to grasp the underlying causes behind its increasing popularity. The first problem they face is their lack of understanding of the modern character of political Islam. Second, they fail to see the causes of the discontent of the masses with the present establishment. In other words, they defend the values of modernity and secularism and the principles of Atatürk's revolution but fail to discuss the particular socioeconomic and political preconditions of the rise of political Islam (Delibaş, 1996, p. 27).

Another common characteristic in their writing has been a visible, blunt sense of fear, anxiety and shock due to the unprecedented success of the WP in the local elections of 1994 and in the general elections of 1995, 2002 and 2007. Again, instead of conducting a critical analysis of the conditions in which this widespread disillusionment of large sections of society with the current political parties of centre-right and centre-left arose, the discourses have concentrated on distrust, fear and a confrontation between modernist secularism and Islamic fundamentalism.

As Heper (1997) points out, radical secularists in Turkey view Islam as the antonym of enlightenment, and have adopted a hostile attitude towards it. But for him 'not only have the radical secularists in Turkey failed to realise the significance of Islam for the people – inter alia, as a source of belief, ethics, identity and/or consolation – but they have also exaggerated the Islamist threat to the Turkish secular democratic state' (1997, p. 42).

Perhaps the most significant result of this attitude was that the rise of the WP/VP throughout the 1990s and 2000s was seen as an exaggerated Islamic threat to the secular republic. As this view was prevalent among radical secularists, the bureaucratic and military elite and other elements of the ruling classes, it caused one of the deepest political crises of recent history in Turkey. Due to a largely unfounded fear of Islamic fundamentalism, the secularist elite reacted fiercely to the Islamist-led coalition government and this confrontation caused a serious political crisis that ended with the 28 February process, which was described as a postmodern coup.

The concept of fundamentalism does not explain much about the movements itself, but demeans them as fanatics, extremists or reactionaries. As Frank Furedi (1995, pp. 18–19) points out:

> The uncritical acceptance of the term fundamentalism by conservative, liberal and radical commentators is symptomatic of the way in which a 'them' and 'us' outlook on the world has become intellectually plausible. At its most banal, this outlook proposes that they are irrational while we are rational or that they are intolerant while we are permissive. The fundamentalist label provides a moral and cultural condemnation of millions of people ... At its simplest, the fundamentalist label helps to recycle the old Orientalist stereotypes about fanatical, frustrated people.

First, the usage of the concept of 'fundamentalism' itself is highly contentious. While scholars such as Bruce Lawrence, Henry Munson, Leonard Binder and Bernard Lewis have used 'fundamentalism' as a key descriptive concept, these scholars, as Campo (1995) argues, are not in agreement about the precise meaning of the term. Moreover, those who have been using the term fundamentalism, and applying it to 'Islamic fundamentalist' movements, have so far been unable to produce a satisfactory answer to the major criticism about using a term that originated in the 1920s American Protestant fundamentalist movement (see Campo, 1995, p. 169; Munson, 1995, p. 152).

What Purpose Does Labelling Serve?

Labelling political Islam, one of the main political movements in the country, as Islamic fundamentalism or as the threat of Sharia, has taken away any 'legitimacy' that these movements may have and has put them under the spotlight. Labelling such an important political opposition confused the people, creating unjustified suspicion and tension in society.

At best it distracted attention from the real social economic and political problems that were crippling the country. In other words, the whole issue of the 'threat of Islamist fundamentalism' hijacked real politics for almost ten years. It artificially dominated the political agenda by pushing away basic problems such as high inflation, the high unemployment rate, increasing inequalities, deepening poverty, lack of provision of basic services and elusive democratisation.

It seems that labelling such movements as Islamic fundamentalist, communist, nationalist, separatist or extremist made it easier for the authorities to deal with them. In a way, labelling them as such stripped them of their socioeconomic or political bases and reduced them to a security matter, and their followers to suspects, criminals or convicts. It can be argued that, usually, by demonising a movement the authorities acquire legitimacy to use force against it. The Islamic fundamentalist threat of the 1990s mirrored the 1960s and 1970s preoccupation with the communist threat, when the left was perceived as the major threat to the country's security and leftist groups were demeaned. Ironically, at that time the Islamists played the same card and in the 1970s attacked the left for being communists under Moscow's command, without realising that one day they would be targeted in the same manner.

Despite the fact that there was general disagreement about the categorisation of political Islam as fundamentalism, it had often been regarded as a major threat to the Western world and to stability in the Middle East (Esposito, 1995, p. 4). There were also commentators who equated political Islam with 'terrorism', 'extremism', 'irrationalism', 'intolerance' and so forth.[1] The long-term consequences of this uncritical acceptance of the term fundamentalism caused an unjustified harsh treatment of anything to do with Islam whether political, social, cultural or religious in the West as well as in Muslim countries. As Frank Furedi argued, in the long term more and more authoritarian measures would be introduced to deal with this new plague of Islam, as the West sees it, and this would have repercussions both in the West and outside. It was very likely that Western governments would demand that Muslim governments keep a close eye on the 'imaginary Muslim enemy' and make sure it was kept at bay (Furedi, 1996, p. 13). It was clear that this stigma attached to Islam would lead to certain complications in the West and elsewhere. That said, it is important to add that there were and always have been Islamist groups and movements involved in radical, extremist politics and terrorist activities – such as Al-Qaeda or Hizbullah and other extremist Islamist groups in Turkey and elsewhere. However, it must be questioned whether or not those separate groups and activities justify generalisations about all movements with an Islamic tone.

For some scholars like Esposito (1995) and Furedi (1996, p. 12), they were often neither a threat to Western civilisation nor extremist, or they were intolerant zealots who were reacting to their own governments, which were often anti-democratic, corrupt and incompetent. For others like Roy (1994), these movements can be seen as third-world movements rising against foreign domination in their countries. The Islamist movement in question in Turkey (the WP/VP) in the 1990s and early 2000s as well as current Islamist movements that have risen against the dictatorships and paved the way for the Arab Spring in Tahrir Square in Egypt (2011), in Tunisia (2011) in Libya (2012) and elsewhere in the Middle East have been symptomatic of a globalised modern world. In fact, this process has been dialectical, affected by politics as well as affecting politics.

Contrary to common wisdom, the militants were and to this day still are rarely mullahs; they have been young products of the modern educational system, and are university educated. They are often raised in migrant families or impoverished middle classes from the fringes of the big cities. Islamist intellectuals gave a new dimension to Islam. Since the early 1980s Islam has become an ideology as well as a religion. Islamist intellectuals are heavily influenced by militant Marxists in universities and have often borrowed concepts from them. They did not seek to return to what existed before but wanted to reappropriate society and modern technology based on politics (Roy, 1994, p. 3). As the latest political developments and so-called Arab Spring in the Middle East have shown, Islamist movements tend to follow a similar pattern from one country to another. It has been interesting to see that what happened a decade ago in Turkey – the rise of the pro-Islamic AKP – happened in many Arab/Muslim countries but with one difference: the former came through elections (the ballot box) and the latter through popular uprising.

Despite the fact that many of the emergent Islamist political parties in Egypt and other countries have been following different patterns in terms of strategy and tactics, organisational style, ideological position, main cultural or political priorities and the like, after the Arab Spring it seems that many will follow the Turkish path. This close association between the Islamic brotherhood and Turkey's AKP is not restricted to Egypt's Islamists (Schenker, 2012). Major Islamist groups, such as the Justice and Development party of Morocco; the Ennahda party of Tunisia; Al-Islah, the main Islamist opposition party of Yemen; and Justice and Development of Libya, have recently indicated that they intend to take Turkey's AKP as a role model (Beaumont, 2011).

It could be suggested that there is not one but several Islams. In a general sense the Muslim world is divided into three geographic and cultural spheres: the Sunni Arab Middle East, the Sunni Indian subcontinent, and Irano–Arab Shi'sm. Turkey is totally different from the Arab world and has its own organisations. These groups are different from each other geographically and politically. Therefore it is not plausible to talk about an Islamic union (Roy, 1994, p. 2). The great diversity of Islamic parties and movements has been another factor that challenges the myth of a unified Islamic fundamentalism. As Karabell (1996, pp. 78–9) argued, these Islamist groups – from Hamas in Palestine, to Hizbullah in Lebanon, the Welfare Party (Refah) in Turkey, the armed Islamic Group (GIA) in Algeria and the Jemaat-i-Islami in Pakistan – have been very different from each other in many aspects. Therefore it is not realistic to conjecture about a unified, universal, aggressive Islamist fundamentalist threat.

The above debate shows that despite widespread suspicion and anxiety, and the perception of an Islamic fundamentalist threat, such groups were not in a position to pose much danger to the West and its institutions. Nor, necessarily, should their rise be interpreted in that way. In general they were rising as a reaction to their own governments, out of long-term dissatisfaction with corruption and the inadequacy of government policies in preventing poverty, unemployment and falling living standards, not to mention foreign domination.

As Esposito (1995, p. 5) argued, unfortunately American policy-makers have too often proven to be myopic, seeing the Muslim world and Islamic movements as a monolith and viewing them only in terms of extremism and terrorism. For him (1995, p. 77) 'the term "Muslim fundamentalist" had become a convenient but misleading way for the Western media and Western governments to identify wide-ranging Islamist groups in Muslim countries as well as a ready "bogey" for Muslim regimes wishing to degrade and demean their opposition'.

In light of this, it can be argued that the fundamentalism categorisation in this case appears to be misplaced. Although the rise of the WP/VP has been overwhelmingly viewed as the rise of Islamic fundamentalism, neither the WP/VP's leading cadres or the majority of its voters seemed to be religious extremists or fundamentalists.

In contrast with many Islamic movements in the Muslim world, the leaders of the Turkish Islamic parties (Erbakan and his close associates) were not clergymen but had professional or business backgrounds (Heper, 1997, p. 35). For instance, Erbakan was not an Islamic thinker; he was a professor of engineering graduated from a German university. In this respect his close aides and long-term followers Recep Tayyip Erdoğan and Abdullah Gül of the Milli Görüş movement (National View), which was founded by him, followed the same path. Erdoğan, the founder and leader of the AKP (in 2001) who has led the country since 2002, and Abdullah Gül, the president of the Turkish Republic since 2007, have followed quite a pragmatist, liberal–conservative democratic path. Furthermore, in contrast to some other Islamic movements, the tradition of the WP/VP and later AKP has not been able to produce original Islamic thinkers like Jamal al-Din al-Afghani, Abul A'la Mawdudi, Sayyid Qutb, Ali Shariati or Ayatollah Khomeini (Çakır, 1994, pp. 126–7).

Some liberal authors have seen Islamic movements as 'not solely a reaction to a given situation of class and cultural domination, but also present a counter-cultural model of modernity, and a new paradigm for self-definition that has led to the formation of Islamic counter-elites' (Göle, 1997, p. 53). For Göle, 'Islamism, both in its ideological formations and sociological practices, has created new hybridisations between tradition and modernity, religion and secularism, community and religion' (ibid., p. 54). She argues that these new agents of change represented the move of Islam 'from the periphery of the system to its centre, and yet were themselves a product of that centre, of its educational institutions and its urban life' (ibid.). What this hybridisation process actually meant was that the identification of the leaders of the WP/VP (Erbakan and his associates) and, since 2002, the leading figures of the AKP as Islamist fundamentalists was not an accurate one. However, it is important to recognise that they were not truly modernist elites either. This is why they could easily be charged with having an ambivalent attitude towards important issues – Islamist ideology, democracy, secularism, etc. – since the early 1990s. For instance, democracy and Islam, and especially the Islamists' attitude towards democracy, has been one of the most hotly discussed topics in this respect. Despite people's mistrust and its authoritarian approach over the past few years, the AKP government has passed several reform packages in an attempt to democratise the country.

Turkey's involvement with the European Union dates back to the early sixties (1963). At the Helsinki summit in 1999 Turkey was recognised as a full candidate for membership, but substantive talks on EU membership could only begin once political and economic conditions – known as the Copenhagen criteria – were met. The parliament enacted revolutionary reforms by ending the death penalty, lifting restrictions on the use of Kurdish language and sweeping away constraints on free speech to fulfil the Copenhagen criteria on 3 August 2002. With this, the pro-European politicians won a landmark victory in Turkey (Dymond, 2002). From 1999 onwards the country's progress towards EU membership was significant and the new AKP government enthusiastically fostered already flourishing relations.

When the party came to power in 2002 the AKP leaders developed good relations with the US and the EU, and even strengthened their ties with Israel.[2] EU membership was declared to be of primary importance to the country. In order to expand civil rights and democracy, several changes in the constitution and legal system were made; freedom of thought, press freedom, freedoms of peaceful assembly and of association, the judicial system and minority rights improved. Furthermore, many restrictions on associations as well as cultural, ethnic and religious rights were lifted. For a variety of reasons, external support for the AKP was paramount in its first years in office (see Barkey, 2005, p. 8). Hence these reforms also secured the external support the party needed.

However, back in the 1990s and early 2000s, the WP/VP's views on democracy were somewhat ambivalent.[3] The WP/VP called the Turkish system in those years a 'fraud', a 'guided democracy', and a 'dark-room regime' and announced the WP's intention to create a 'real democracy' (Özbudun, 2000, p. 87). What the party meant by a 'real democracy' remains unclear. In the past the WP/VP (and later the AKP) failed to show strong democratic instincts (see Çakır, 1994, p. 129; Özbudun, 2000, pp. 87–8). But then the credentials of Turkish democracy in general and other parties' democratic instincts have not been well developed either.

In terms of party activists, even though they seem to be more radical than ordinary WP/VP voters, the difference appears slight.[4] The ideological attitudes of the local or 'middle elites', as they have been called by some students of politics, or as I preferred to call them throughout this book, the 'grassroots activists', have always been an important consideration. It was noted in chapter 5 that, compared to the WP/VP's voters, grassroots activists' involvement in the party seems to be motivated more by religious and ideological reasons than in the case of the voters. Some 40 per cent of activists were motivated by religious reasons, while 21 per cent joined the party for ideological reasons. Although they wanted Islam to be given some sort of place in everyday life, in the public sphere the majority of them wanted separation of state and religion. Very few opposed the principle of secularism altogether. Equally, however, the overwhelming majority of them wanted a Western-style, Anglo-Saxon model rather than the French model of secularisation.

Behind its radical rhetoric, the WP often showed signs of pragmatism and flexibility (Özbudun, 2000, p. 89). This pragmatism and flexibility were reflected in its electoral bases as well as throughout its years of power in office since 2002. It can be argued that the general characteristics of a political party cannot be separated from its social bases:

> [In terms of] political Islam and support for the WP/VP in the 1990s and the AKP throughout the 2000s, surveys showed that the WP and AKP combined both religious and class appeals. A survey in December 1996 revealed that 60.6 per cent of WP voters favoured including some Islamic principles in the constitution. However, when the voters were asked why they voted for the WP only half gave ideological reasons, such as the WP's defence of religious values (20.9 per cent), its promise of a 'just order' (13.4 per cent), and its respect for 'national and moral values' (12.5 per cent). Some 29.6 per cent of them voted for the WP because they believed it was an honest and reliable party (Özbudun, pp. 89–90). My findings showed that there was a strong religious appeal and between one-third and one-half of the WP's voters had been voting for non-ideological reasons

The fact that half of the WP voters voted for the WP for reasons other than ideological/religious reasons was a very important indicator that the WP/VP cannot be defined solely in religious terms. Other surveys indicate far less religiously motivated voting among the WP's voters. For example, according to a 1994 survey only one-third of the WP's voters chose the party because it was an Islamic party (Heper,

1997, p. 35). What was common in those survey findings was that the WP/VP's social and electoral supporters were far from being religious extremists or radicals.

Secularisation and the Threat of Political Islam

Why then did the 1994 and 1995 election results cause such a reaction among the Turkish elites? And why did the WP/VP continue to be seen as an Islamic fundamentalist party, to be closed down by the high court in 1998? Why wasn't it viewed as a pragmatist mass party? How can this overstated reaction of the Turkish civilian and military elites which led to the 28 February process be justified?

It seems this situation can be explained in terms of two different but related dimensions. The first was the almost mystical notion of secularisation that had been embedded deep into the public consciousness, the political and popular culture, while the second was the very special and central role of secularisation in Turkish politics since the early 1920s. Both dimensions are extremely important in explaining how Turkish elites made sense of the threat of Islamist fundamentalism throughout the 1990s.

The perception of political Islam's ascendancy as a threat to secularism, modernity and democracy was closely associated with how the concept of secularism was defined in the first place. The definition and implementation of secularisation was an ambivalent process, profoundly underscored in the popular culture and official ideology. This ill-defined concept of secularism led in time to some mystification. The application of this concept in politics proved to be problematic, as could be seen in Turkish politics throughout the 1990s.

Turkey's political crisis has shown how a social myth could continue to distract from the development of a healthy, stable democracy. The confrontation between secularists and Islamists began with the 1994 local elections. In these elections the Welfare Party gained an unprecedented result by winning the majority of the municipalities, including Istanbul and Ankara. This trend continued in the general election of 24 December 1995. The pro-Islamist WP/VP emerged from these elections as the largest group in the parliament, achieving 158 seats out of 550. This trend would continue throughout the 2000s. There was a brief period between 1998 and 2002 when the military intervened in politics (the so-called 28 February process). Otherwise a successive line of Islamist parties came to dominate Turkish politics.

In many ways the process of 28 February provides the best example of the mythification of a concept and its long-term consequences upon political life. First of all, it created an illusion among the influential military and bureaucratic elites, the intelligentsia, and the secularised and modernised strata of a 'purely and completely secularised' society, which never existed. It seemed that once political Islam – that is, the WP/VP – became visible in politics, the illusion was triggered automatically because the purely secularised modern society was coming under attack from the rise of political Islam.

As the rural masses moved to the cities in their hundreds of thousands every year as a consequence of restructuring policies, and as they seized the opportunity for political participation with the WP, the dogma of secularism was challenged by politically emancipated masses. However moderate this challenge, there was a very serious counter-attack to destroy its social and political foundations. Immediately after the elections in 1995 the country was shaken by the growing electoral support for the pro-Islamist WP. The principle of secularisation as sacrosanct was seen to be threatened. The headlines read: 'Shariat is coming'; 'Şeriat Tehtidi' (threat of Islamic fundamentalism)'; 'Religious threat against the contemporary, modern and *laik* (secular) republic'; 'Fundamentalism is the enemy of democracy and contemporary civilisation', and so on.

Needless to say there have been very few issues in Turkish history that have united political and social organisations of all different political persuasions. However, all parties of the centre-left and centre-right, various civil society organisations, the military, trade unions, major universities, various pressure groups, women's organisations, political commentators and columnists all rallied around the issue of fighting the threat of Islamic extremism.

The military, which views itself as the ultimate guarantor of the secular establishment, stepped in to press the Islamist-led government to step down. The threat of Islamic fundamentalism reached a point where for the first time, according to a leading Turkish daily, the military assessed an internal threat as more pressing than any external one (*Milliyet*, 30 April 1997). This was a historical turning point. The internal threat was, of course, the rise of political Islam or Sharia, namely the Welfare Party.

After openly naming the WP as the biggest threat to the secular republic, the military, via the NSC, increased its pressure to a point intolerable to the Islamist-led government, which soon decided to step down. However, the tension between the pro-Islamist WP and secularist elites did not stop there. Erbakan, the leader of the WP, was not about to lose just the government but his party too. The largest party in the Turkish parliament was closed down by the Supreme Court for its actions against the principles of the secular republic. Although the Islamist party was not a newcomer to Turkish politics, the electoral successes of the WP triggered a flood of suspicion and paranoia among Turkey's secularist elites. The WP's narrow success with 21.3 per cent of the vote created shockwaves not just at home but abroad too (Sayarı, 1996, p. 35). Islamophobia (*Irtica fobisi*) came to dominate the daily reports. Some urged an immediate action against the *seriatci yukselis* (the rise of fundamentalism) while others urged the military to intervene to restore the principles of the secular republic. All this anxiety confirms a deep confusion over the concept of *secularisation*, a term used for so long without a proper understanding of its meaning. Furthermore, it indicates a deep-rooted phobia of Islam among certain groups, fed by the media throughout the 1990s.

It is argued that there have been four phobias that shaped official ideology throughout the Republican political history, namely Islamism, Kurdish identity, leftist ideology and liberalism. They also constitute the biggest obstacle to the development of civil society (Göle, 1996, p. 20). Two of these ideologies, Islamism and Kurdish identity, challenged the new regime in the first years of the Republic, so the modernist secular elite has legitimate grounds for this fear. But, it can be argued that the response to the Islamist challenge was disproportionate. This suspicion about religion's position and potential in the political sphere meant that the process of secularisation automatically became an ideological issue and an instrument in the hands of modernist secularist elites. This point brings us to our second dimension: the very special role of secularisation.

A Very Politicised Form of Secularisation

The second dimension behind the apparent over-reaction by the Turkish establishment to the rise of Islamist political parties is the overly politicised interpretation of secularisation. In the late 1990s very few commentators challenged the basic assumption that political Islam constituted an immediate threat to the secular order. However, there were a few, such as Demirer (1998), Göle (2000) and Özdalga (1997) who questioned whether this widespread fear of Sharia was well founded or not. For instance, Özdalga (1997, p. 21) asked: 'Does the fact that this political movement scored little more than one fifth of the votes in the last elections (December 1995) constitute a threat to the very foundation of the secular republic?' The answer to this question, she suggested, was very much related to how the concept of secularism was defined. It was evident that it was the very definition of the concept of 'secularisation' that really created the problem. And it often brought the country to a standstill, creating a political crisis that caused the collapse of the Islamist government in 1997. The problem did not stop there: the parliament, political parties and elites lost public trust.[5]

Özdalga (1997, p. 23) argued that the propaganda put forward by those groups seeking to curb the growing influence of Islamic groups, which claimed that the secular nature of the Turkish regime was being threatened, was untrue. Hence the characterisation of the present situation was based on false consciousness in the Marxist sense. She added: 'A secular and relatively stable regime has been presented as if it were on the verge of collapse, due to a heavy onslaught by radical Islamists' (ibid., p. 23).

The first half of Özdalga's assessment of the stability and strength of the secular regime in Turkey is commencing, and it is true that it was presented as if the regime were about to collapse due to the rise of the WP. It is also correct that this presentation resembled scare-mongering and created mistrust, suspicion and social tension. However, the assumption that the situation played out in this way because of the power ambitions of the military and bureaucratic elite with the leftists should not be accepted as a full explanation of the phenomenon. What I would argue instead is that, more than their ambitions for power, it was the notion of 'mystical secularisation' that caused such a reaction from the military and bureaucratic elite and other modernised secularised sections in society, leading Turkey to the 28 February process.

Undoubtedly, this kind of intervention in politics was a serious blow to the country's fragile democracy. In this sense democratic stability and civil initiative had once more gone down the drain. The biggest losers in that crisis were democracy and the people of Turkey.

It seemed, throughout the 1990s, that the paradox of putting secularisation before democracy continued to fuel political conflict in the country. As Göle (1996, p. 19) argues, the modernist elite has always feared that if religious values were allowed to be represented freely in the public sphere it may someday become too influential in politics and threaten the principle of secularism. To prevent this from happening, the principle of secularism was upheld while democratic representation was restricted. Thus state authoritarianism, 'enlightened despotism' or single-party regimes often become the only choice for secular Westernised elites.

In fact, in the general elections of 1995 the WP was the largest party yet it received less than one-quarter of the votes. This means that the majority of the electorate did not support the WP's politics. And the majority of people who voted for the WP/VP did not do so for Islamic reasons.[6] Also, the pro-Islamic parties had been part of the Turkish polity since the late 1960s and until that time there was no compelling evidence that the radicals were the stronger faction of this Islamist movement. Individuals such as Şevki Yilmaz who were the strongest proponents of Sharia law appeared to remain marginal or had been expelled for various reasons while the majority of Islamists were in favour of the present constitutional order.[7] How, then, do we make sense of the expression of religion and religious values in the public arena? One could view it as part and parcel of the expansion of the civil society, rather than a reason for interrupting the democratic process.

So if it was not motivated by religious reasons or fundamentalism, what were the driving forces behind the rise of political Islam in Turkey? What the above analysis indicates was that the rise of the WP can be understood not necessarily as the rise of Islamic fundamentalism but as the estrangement of significant sections of Turkish society from the mainstream political parties. It was argued in chapter 2 that throughout the 1990s parties faced a real problem due to the erosion of public confidence in them. According to a survey, political parties are the least trusted institutions in Turkey.[8]

Can we exclude the possibility that religious reasons were behind the rise of the Welfare Party, as well as more practical socioeconomic reasons? The answer is 'yes' and 'no'. It is 'yes' in the sense that the WP more or less preserved its core of ideological voter support from the early 1970s to the late 1990s. For example, throughout the 1970s the WP's predecessor, the National Salvation Party, had around 10 per cent of the vote. The NSP had received 11.8 per cent of the vote in its first election in 1973 and 8.1 per cent in the 1977 general elections. Although it received 4,000 more votes (1,269,918) in the 1977 elections compared to the 1973 elections, due to an increased rate of voter participation, its share dropped to 8.1 per cent (Çaklr, 1994, pp. 216–17). After the military coup of 1980 the WP had a slow start, but in the 1987 general elections its share increased to 7.16 per cent, taking it near to its core/ideological voter support. The period from 1973 to 1987 shows that traditionally the NSP/WP/VP had around 10 per cent of the hard-core support.

However, from the early 1990s onwards the situation changed. The WP changed its main policies such as 'just economic order', changed its organisational structure, strategy and tactics, and adopted a new rhetoric that managed to combine religious and class appeal (Özbudun, 2000, p. 87). Thus, the WP/VP expanded its electoral support considerably among the newly migrated urban poor in the big cities.

From the 1991 general election onwards, the WP's support bases began to change. Studies indicate that between one-third and one-half of the WP/VP's voters voted for the party for religious or ideological reasons, but the other half did so for reasons other than religion or ideology (see Özbudun, 2000, pp. 90–91). When this figure is compared with the WP/VP's share of the vote, which was 21.4 per cent in 1995 and 15.5 per cent in 1999, it shows that there had not been much change in its traditional, hard-core religious/ideological support, but this was not true for the other half of its electoral support base. These voters were not supporting the WP/VP for religious or ideological reasons but because of its 'just economic order' policies, its clean image and its protection of the poor and other similar policies.

It is undeniable, however, that the rising tide of religious revivalism also played some role in the rise of the WP/VP in Turkey. As argued in chapter 1, throughout the 1990s and to the present day religious movements were on the rise all around the world. Although Islamic revivalism has been most extensively discussed and attracted enormous media attention, all forms of religious revivalism had been rising across the globe. From Hindu fundamentalism in India to Jewish fundamentalism in Israel, and from Christian fundamentalism in the US to Islamic fundamentalism in the Muslim world, religious fundamentalism is thriving in all faiths (Esposito, 1995, p. 11).

Although it is logical to argue that the rise of religious revivalism across the Muslim world must have contributed to a certain extent to the rise of the WP/VP during the 1990s in Turkey, there is little empirical evidence available to test this relationship. What seems to have happened throughout the 1990s and early 2000s was that the WP/VP retained its traditional strong 10 per cent of religious/ideological support and added another 10 per cent from non-religious/ideological voters in 1995, 1999 and much more in 2002. Nevertheless, we cannot altogether rule out any impact of this rising tide of religious revivalism on the rise of the WP/VP. It might have assisted in other ways, such as helping the WP to retain its core support of 10 per cent religious voters. It is plausible that if religious revivalism had not been rising steadily, as it had been doing since the 1970s, the WP/VP might have lost some of its religious/ideological support since then.

Islamic Fundamentalism Demystified

The Role of Party Organisations

At the start of this book it was hypothesised that the rise of political Islam could not be described simply as religious revivalism or Islamic fundamentalism, but, rather, that other 'worldly reasons' – social problems – were responsible for its popularity. If not Islamist fundamentalism, then to what does the WP/VP owe its electoral success?

The success of political Islam has resulted from a combination of various factors, none of which, apart from grassroots activism, individually dominates the others. It is a combination of various factors in which the local party organisations and grassroots activists play the role of a catalyst to activate the process. And if the mixture were lacking one of its several elements, it might not produce the same result.

In this section, I intend to demonstrate that the rise of the WP/VP throughout the 1990s was not the rise of fundamentalism as such but was something the pro-Islamic WP/VP achieved through hard-working, highly committed, resourceful grassroots organisations. In this context, perhaps the most important factor was the decline of the political party system – which caused a significant process of estrangement of large sections of voters away from the mainstream political parties.

I have argued that from the 1980s onwards the Turkish political party system has experienced high levels of party fragmentation, electoral volatility and ideological polarisation. Individual parties have suffered a decline in organisational capacity, party identification and public support (see Özbudun, 2000 and Delibas, 2011). Turkish politics has endured a long-term impasse and the state of the Turkish political parties has been responsible for this situation.

Especially from the late 1980s onwards, more and more people have become disillusioned with their political parties and started to look elsewhere for a better alternative.

Fragmentation and volatility has been much higher in Turkey compared with Western European countries. It was estimated that between 1954 and 1999 the average volatility was 21 per cent from one election to the next (TESEV, 2000, p. 12). There have been several sociological reasons for this ongoing political alienation of the masses from mainstream Turkish parties.

Throughout the 1980s and the 1990s, Turkish politics was shaken by a series of disturbing factors that redefined the spectrum of the traditional party system as well as party loyalties and values (Kalaycıoğlu, 1998, p. 1). The first major event was the military coup of 12 September 1980 which effectively banned all political activities. All parties were closed down and all leaders and cadres in the higher echelons of the parties were interrogated and imprisoned for several months, or years in some cases. It meant a total breakdown in politics and nothing was going to be the same ever again.

Following the September 1980 coup the military wanted to reshape the Turkish polity by introducing new electoral laws and political agents – political parties – and vetoing some of the old elements. The aim was to discredit the multiparty politics of the 1970s and return to the two-party systems of the 1950s. It was thought that the multi-party polity was causing the political disarray and that two-party systems would prevent high fragmentation and volatility. For this reason all pre-1980 parties or their successors were banned or vetoed by the military government. Two parties, the PP and the NDP, were prepared to take part in the first elections of 1983 and a third party, the Motherland, was also given permission to take part. After three years in power the military wanted to redesign the political as well as the party system. In order to do this, 'the military under Evren supported the new National Democracy Party under a leader of military provenance, Turgut Sunalp, and allowed a respected left of centre Populist Party to emerge as the major opposition. It was a curious and artificial attempt to replay the immediate past, but with new actors' (Dodd, 1990). However, it did not work. The third party, the Motherland, won the elections in 1983. While the NDP and PP were perceived to be supported by the military, the Motherland party under the leadership of Turgut Özal managed to portray itself as the free-market-oriented, independent and liberal alternative.

In fact, the military wanted to establish a two-party political system politics for the post-1980 period in Turkey. However, this ambitious plan did not work. In fact, it was effectively over with the return of pre-1980 political leaders such as Demirel, Ecevit, Erbakan and Türkeş to politics in 1987. The Turkish party system became much more fragmented and the restrictions led to a process of 'party duplication' on the centre-left and centre-right. This duplication of the centre parties has been one of the most significant factors in the high level of fragmentation.

Increased electoral volatility and organisational decline have played an important role in the process of declining party attachment and identification among the electorate. The military's intervention and subsequent restrictions were partially responsible for the institutional decline of the Turkish party system. Along with the frequent closure of political parties this meant that none of the parties enjoyed the support of more than two generations. So there were constant interruptions and breakdowns, creating a cycle of discontinuity in the social and electoral bases, organisational structure, membership, party identity, policies and party ideology. In a sense the system started from scratch whenever there was an intervention from outside of politics. However, these interventions are not the only cause of the decline of the Turkish party system.

The organisational structure and characteristics of the mainstream political parties have always been an important factor. With the exception of the WP, Turkish political parties have been 'described as cadre or catch-all parties with strong clientelistic features'. Many of them developed features of cartel parties with strong sultan-like authoritarian leaderships (Özbudun, 2000). When this current state of affairs for political parties is combined with Turkey's long-term, ongoing, multiple socioeconomic problems, it provides a perfect recipe for more party fragmentation, electoral volatility, party organisational decline and lessened party identification and loyalty among the voters.

Over the last 15 years, except for the WP/VP, all Turkish parties have suffered a decline in their party organisations and a weakening of party identification. The demise of party identification has been a problem in developed countries and new democracies alike (see Crotty and Jacobson, 1980; Özbudun, 2000, p. 79; TESEV, 2000). Nonetheless, the Turkish case has been significantly different in many ways. It is distinct because electoral volatility has been very high. More than one in five of the electorate has been voting for a different party from one election to the next. For this reason a different party came out top in the each of the four elections between 1995 and 2002. In the search for a better alternative the electorate swung from one party to another, but the situation continued deteriorating. A survey at the time showed that on the whole no party seemed to be appealing to more than 10 per cent of voters in the country (see chapter 2).

The organisational decline is rooted in the characteristics of the Turkish political parties. Apart from the WP/VP they are not mass-membership parties but mostly cadre or catch-all parties with common clientelistic characteristics. Therefore the major Turkish parties of the centre-left and centre-right have not developed widespread party organisations throughout the country. Instead of cultivating well-organised horizontal party networks, their organisational network is based on vertical, clientelistic ties.

Party-directed patronage was the main characteristic of pre-1980 parties, and despite the breakdown of the political system in 1980 the situation has not changed. Even the new parties of the post-1983 period like the MP, which governed the country for two terms, did not want to develop modern, effective, vibrant and horizontally organised party organisations. Instead it chose to use pork-barrel patronage to sustain its electoral support.

The organisational weakening of parties and party identification ties was closly connected to the disillusionment of millions with political parties. In addition, widespread political corruption involving many party leaders caused disappointment and anger among citizens (see Özbudun, 2000, p. 79). In many ways the economic problems of the late 1970s were worsened by the neoliberal restructuring policies of the 1980s and 1990s. What was intended to be a solution led to far more serious socioeconomic problems. The high rate of inflation, unemployment, social inequalities and poverty had become far more prevalent.[9]

The fact is that after 1983 all of the political parties on the centre-right and centre-left were tested more than once and none of them achieved the smallest success in alleviating any of the country's burning problems. In addition, their clientelistic structures made them much more vulnerable to losing party attachments and party identification among their followers.

The Welfare Party escaped this trend of increasing fragmentation, electoral volatility, party realignment, declining party identification and party loyalty and the declining role of local party organisations. On the contrary, the WP/VP emerged as the main beneficiary of this process.

In answering the following question we can help to understand another part of the mystery that surrounds the unprecedented rise of political Islam in Turkey: how did the WP/VP buck the trend of party decline in Turkey and become the largest party, while the other political parties were disintegrating and losing their electoral support? The answer must be the WP/VP's organisational strength and efficient, highly committed and informed grassroots activism.

Despite the general trend away from party-centred politics to candidate-centred politics, the party organisations proved to be significantly influential in contributing to the party's electoral successes. If the party organisation is the first condition for a successful election campaign, the second condition must be grassroots activism.[10]

Political parties are the bridge between society and governmental power and are a key component of representative democracy. As they are the means of acquiring or influencing governmental power they need sufficient public support behind them. To achieve this support, parties need to mobilise voters through party organisations and party activists. Although there are various methods of election campaigning to mobilise social support and canvass votes, my findings show that the local party organisations and grassroots activists have proven to be very influential on election results. From its foundation to its closure, the WP developed nationwide membership organisations and, thanks to its mass grassroots activism, won unprecedented election victories.

The Foundation Stones: Role of Grassroots Activists

One of my main objectives was to find out whether or not grassroots activists and party organisations had any effect on the increase of the WP/VP's share of votes during the 1990s. As argued above, despite the current trend, political parties still need members for the traditional electioneering functions of canvassing and leafleting voters, and persuading supporters to go out and vote. Grassroots activists are elected representatives of the party and carry out electioneering. More than that, they are often the key opinion-formers in the neighbourhood. They provide a voice in the community and help to set the political agenda, legitimising certain opinions above others (see Seyd and Whiteley, 1992, pp. 219–20).

One of the major findings was that the effect of the local party organisations on election results was highly significant. It is observed that becoming mass-membership party organisations can prevent the major problems suffered by contemporary political parties. As the WP/VP showed, with its mass-party characteristics, strong local branches and committed, active party members it was possible to distinctively buck the trend of party decline that was severely undermining all other mainstream parties in Turkey.

Except for the WP/VP, none of the parties had active membership organisations or membership activities. A survey in 1996 showed that 12.1 per cent of the voters were party members, but membership in Turkey, as Özbudun (2000, p. 80) argued, was often little more than being a party supporter. In contrast with the rest of the Turkish parties, the WP/VP had a very large grassroots organisation. Especially after the 1994 local elections, the WP launched a massive recruitment campaign and it reached 4.5 million members before its closure in 1998 (see Çakır, 1994, pp. 51–2).

Some have said that technological and social innovations have significantly reduced the role of party membership and grassroots organisations. But the role of party membership is not limited to the election campaign only. Grassroots organisations and party activists fulfil many other important functions essential for political parties and the electoral process.[11]

Grassroots activists act as a mediator between the neighbourhood – the constituency – and the *ilçe*. As an organisation they carry the opinions, demands and expectations of the local people. As influential agents of the party on the ground, grassroots activities are very powerful. They influence and form opinion in their localities and are the pillars of the party, holding it together in especially difficult, turbulent times. As the arms and the muscles of the party, they carry out day-to-day party activities.

Chapters 5 and 6 illuminated some important aspects of the grassroots activists and activism. In chapter 5, as well as patterns of participation, significant determinants of activism such as regional disparities and family were also identified. It revealed that the majority (76 per cent) of informants came from less-developed regions while 79 per cent of them had at least one person in their family who was also a member or supporter of the VP. Around 40 per cent expressed religious and 21 per cent ideological incentives as the most important factor for their membership. The remaining 38 per cent joined the VP for non-religious or ideological reasons. Some 14 per cent said it was the best party for the country, while 16 per cent saw it as trustworthy, and the other 7 per cent joined the VP as a reaction to other parties.

The portrait of the VP's activists is examined in chapter 6, and the picture is very interesting and important in many respects. It indicates striking similarities between the VP's grassroots activists and activists elsewhere. Despite the fact that the WP/VP was viewed as an Islamic fundamentalist party by many commentators, my findings illustrate that its activists had a lot in common with political activists from around the world. They came from similar socioeconomic and demographic backgrounds as their counterparts in Western Europe and North America: they had better educational qualifications than average, were doing better jobs and earning more money. They were in the same (40–50) age group (average was 43 years old), married with 3.07 children on average.

Chapter 7 examined the effects of grassroots activists on the VP's electoral successes. It looked closely at what the VP's activists did and how they did it. It was discovered that the most common (37 per cent) type of party activism they undertook was charity work. They provided material and non-material benefits: food, coal, clothing and bursaries for the needy in the neighbourhoods. On the basis of our field observations and data it appears that this kind of grassroots activism was the most effective way of canvassing. Because of their community work, they were viewed as people who genuinely cared about the poor and therefore about the community's problems. Also via this social work and caring image, the WP/VP was elevated to a messiah-like position.

Besides charity work, the grassroots activists met people on an almost daily basis, showing sympathy, friendship and appreciation. They shared the worries and problems of the ordinary people, and shared the joy and sorrow of their neighbours. The WP/VP, a mass-membership party, distinguished itself from other parties by its structure, its efficient nationwide network of local party organisations, and its highly committed, ideologically orientated, resourceful and militant-like grassroots activists.

It must be kept in mind that the WP/VP did not totally neglect high-tech, media-led nationwide election campaigning methods, either. Instead it employed both 'labour-intensive' and 'capital-intensive' campaigning methods, although the former to a lesser extent than the latter.[12] In other words the VP didn't just concentrate on grassroots activism and door-to-door or face-to-face canvassing in isolation. It carried out nationwide, centrally organised election campaigns through the media, television and radio as well. The VP's election campaigns were planned, organised and monitored rigorously by a computerised Centre of Election Issues set up in every district centre.

There is now sufficient evidence to claim that being the only mass-membership party gave the WP/VP the edge over other parties. While all the other parties of the centre-right and centre-left lost touch with the people and their electoral support, the WP/VP increased its public support by utilising its membership organisations, youth and ladies' committees.

If that was the case, what made the WP/VP so distinct? As illustrated in chapter 7, the WP/VP's grassroots activists were more engaged than activists of other parties. They were also more active than British or US party activists. On the whole, they spent many hours a month canvassing. Their party activities were not only geared towards election campaigns but were a year-round activity. They seemed to be with the people on the ground talking to them, listening to their problems and grievances. The way they connected with people and the activities that they organised were unique in many ways. They behaved like a social security organisation in the neighbourhoods, providing material and non-material aid for the *gecekondu* poor. Maintaining close relationships, they regularly visited households for social gatherings, celebrations or wakes. They were active residents within their communities, organising charity works, political meetings to spread the party's message, but mostly forming opinion in the community.

Hybridisation of Party Activism: Blending the Modern with the Traditional

It seems there are very few areas where the mix of modern with traditional can generate such a positive, creative and effective outcome as the WP/VP's campaigning strategies did. To mix modern with traditional has often been seen as too difficult and confusing, or as an obstacle to progress in any area of social life, but the WP/VP's strategy and tactics proved the opposite. The ability of the WP/VP's cadres and grassroots activists to tap into historical, traditional and religious networks, existing relationships, cultural and local customary codes and local common knowledge, utilising the linguistic richness of Islam, Islamic knowledge and culture in the service of daily politics – all of these rather clever creative combinations – provided a leading edge to the WP/VP in electoral competition. They ingeniously combined traditional and local relationships and networks with nationwide modern communication technologies, methods and strategies in their day-to-day party activities.

The WP/VP employed both very sophisticated campaigning methods and traditional aspects of community work: on the one hand, the VP's party organisations staged a fully fledged modern election campaign using various experts for public relations, opinion polling, media professionals, fundraising and image promotion. The VP made extensive use of computers and opinion polling, and used mass-media techniques, TV, radio and numerous newspapers at local as well at national level. The VP combined all the latest campaigning methods, techniques and strategies with the most traditional human relations. Grassroots activists utilised traditional culture, religious rhetoric and centuries-old religious networks very successfully in their daily political activities. In other words, the WP/VP developed a style that melded modern with traditional, producing a hybrid campaigning method that was very effective. It was also a unique style that was predominantly local without neglecting the national.

The Extraordinary Ability of Political Islam to Tap into Popular Culture

Another factor in the success of the WP/VP, in addition to the innovative approach of its leading cadres and grassroots activists in tapping into readily available local, traditional and religious networks and using them in daily politics, is the fact that the religion of Islam is also highly adaptable and can be used to tap into popular culture and has become a political ideology to *mobilise the masses* in many Muslim countries.

In Islam, religion and politics are not separate spheres, as some writers may think. Although there are traces of such separation between the religious authority and the secular ruler, this separation has been very thin in many cases and non-existent in others. As Lewis (1988, p. 2) argued, in classical Islam there was no distinction between church and state. Throughout the history of Christendom, he argued, there have been two powers – God and Caesar, representing the church and state in this world – but in Islam there is no such separation.

From its birth to the present century, Islam has occupied an important place in the ideology of the state and in Muslim politics. Therefore, the present revival of Islam in Muslim politics should not be all that unexpected (Esposito, 1983, p. 3).

> The Islamic state is a community of believers. Allah is the ultimate sovereign of the state and, indeed, of all creation. Political and religious leadership was vested in Muhammad, God's messenger on earth, who served as both Prophet and political leader of the Islamic community/state. (ibid., p. 4)

After Muhammad's death, this political and religious leadership persisted under the caliphate. But, within time, especially under the Ottoman Empire, a duality of religious and political leadership emerged. However, this duality was never meant to be a withdrawal of Islam from politics or any other aspects of socioeconomic or cultural life.

From the mid-nineteenth century onwards, modernisation started to take place in some Muslim countries as a result of Western influence and colonial rule. In a general sense these countries followed a path of Westernisation and secularisation as they increasingly adopted Western models in politics, law and education. Nevertheless, during the twentieth century religion re-emerged in the politics of the Muslim world, inspiring anti-colonial, nationalist movements and their struggle for independence (Esposito, 1983, pp. 5–6).

For more than two decades, Islamic movements have been on the rise throughout the Muslim world and the role of Islamic ideology has become ever more important. In many cases, Islamic rhetoric provides a whole set of ideological objections to secular nationalism and Westernisation in Muslim countries like Turkey. As stated above, politics in Muslim countries has been dominated by Islam and in some cases, such as Shi'ism in Iran, the tradition of *struggle against oppression* is embedded into the very heart of religious ideology. As Juergensmeyer (1993, pp. 50–1) suggested, nowhere in Islam is struggle more a part of its tradition than in Shi'i society. Struggle against oppression is part of Shi'ism.

It is well known that religion has been one of the most successful predictors of political preference.[13] Islam in particular exerts a far-ranging influence on politics. As several students of Islam have pointed out, '"Islam" constitutes the language of politics in the Muslim world' (Eickelman and Piscatori, 1996, p. 12). It is much more than simply a vocabulary, as it is made up of both symbols and mediators – those who modify and rework the symbols in specific circumstances and for particular purposes (ibid., p. 13).

The 'language of Islam' is one of the most developed and effective means of communication, packed with symbols and mediators that are universally recognisable across the Muslim world. In addition to its universally (in the Muslim world) recognised linguistic abilities, the religion of Islam is for many millions in the Muslim world a way of life, an ideology, and a belief that covers every aspect of life – not just in this world but also beyond. This has been confirmed by my findings on the ground.[14]

As Esposito (1995, p. 249) noted, 'political economy is essential in understanding the rise of Islamic movements. However, the force of political Islam cannot be simply reduced to the socioeconomic failures of society'. For many of the activists I interviewed, 'Islam was a motive force, a source of guidance for this life as well as the next'. It seems there are similarities between Esposito's observations and my findings in Turkey. The majority (62 per cent) of VP activists joined the party for religious (40 per cent) and ideological (21 per cent) reasons. The WP and the VP have been described as the religiously oriented or pro-Islamist, party and this fact, it seems, played a very significant role in the process of membership (see Kalaycıoğlu, 1998, p. 15). Religion, as the most eminent feature of culture, also inspires political ideologies.[15] 'It has acted as a source for various political ideologies. In this sense Turkey is not an exception' (Turan, 1994, p. 42).

It has been observed that the stronger the ideological conviction, the more effort the individual puts into party activities. A strong ideological incentive is very likely to lead an individual to take the initiative to join a party rather than waiting passively for a call from the party: 'Ideological radicalism should motivate party members to become more involved than the voters or inactive members' (Whiteley, 1995, p. 222).[16] The empirical evidence also shows that the rate of political participation is positively influenced by the degree of political sophistication (Klingemann, 1979, p. 281). It can be concluded that the high level of ideological sophistication and ideological conviction that the VP's activists possessed led to a high level of political activism.

Not Like Any Other Party: Setting Itself Apart

Throughout the 1980s and 1990s the WP had a rather clever, effective strategy of creating a clear line between itself and the rest of the political parties in Turkey. It was a very deliberate and conscious campaign to lump the other parties together under the label of *taklitciler* (imitators) of the West, while portraying the WP as the genuine adherent of national and sacred values, and the true representative of Turkish society.

In many ways the WP/VP seemed to succeed in this strategy of labelling and degrading others and distinguishing itself from the rest. One of the most significant reasons for this was the anti-system rhetoric of the WP until its fourth congress in 1994. Along with this rhetoric it opposed Kemalist ideology, such as the principle of secularism and close relations with the West in the form of membership of NATO and the EU.

In terms of economic policies too, the WP distinguished itself from the rest. As mentioned in chapter 2, there was a policy convergence among the mainstream political parties. All became staunch proponents of global capitalism, restructuring policies and the free-market economy. The WP put forward a different social and economic policy called *Adil Düzen* (Just Order). As expected, the promise of a just society and just economic order attracted considerable support from the lower classes, the poorest sections of society and traditional centre-left voters as well. The process of convergence meant that the parties of the centre-right and the centre-left began to resemble each other. This convergence of policies helped the WP immensely in distancing itself from other parties as well.

Differentiation from the other parties occurred in many other areas too. The issue of widespread political corruption in which many of the other parties were deeply involved was one area from which the WP distanced itself. Throughout the 1990s, corruption become a very common part of Turkish politics. When combined with political clientelism, the corruption, nepotism and bribery scandals, it melted away the public trust in the Turkish parties. As pointed out in chapter 2, since 1983 all of the mainstream parties – the MP, TPP, SDPP and later the RPP – that have come into government have been rocked by corruption scandals as well as by their incompetence in solving the country's acute problems.

As the WP/VP was the only mass political party, it successfully survived the irresistible trend of party decline that effectively wiped out all centre-right and centre-left parties in the 1990s. The VP escaped from this process of party fragmentation, electoral volatility and organisational decline, as well as declining party attachment and party identification among voters, by developing effective nationwide party organisations and attracting a very well-informed, highly committed, militant-like party membership who were actively engaging with politics in their localities.

An Urban Based, 'Anti-Neoliberal/Globalisation' Movement, under an Islamic Veil?

The urban roots of the Islamic movements were examined in chapter 4. It was argued that, contrary to the common perception, Islamic movements are part and parcel of the modernisation process influenced by the rapid phase of urbanisation. They emerged as a reaction against the failures of a modernising, secular state, perceived as corrupt, unable to solve socioeconomic problems, and often dictatorial. In addition, these movements emerged as a reaction to the problems of over-urbanisation, unemployment and foreign domination in Muslim countries. It seems that Islamic movements have no problem whatsoever in adapting their ideology and organisational structures to contemporary conditions.

As observed, grassroots activists were educated in modern schools, raised in recently urbanised families, and came from the impoverished middle class. From the early 1990s onwards, the WP/VP elite adopted traditional leftist policies, slogans and campaign techniques. The majority of WP/VP supporters were not 'traditional' or 'traditionalist', either. By and large they lived with the values of modern city life, which has adopted the current trend of consumerism.

In Turkey the process of urbanisation started in the 1950s, but this process accelerated with the IMF-designed restructuring programmes introduced in the 1980s. This process triggered a massive influx of migrants from rural to urban areas and this led to a rapid and uneven urbanisation in the last two decades. From the 1970s many other Muslim countries including Algeria, Egypt, Iran and Pakistan witnessed, as did Turkey, a rapid growth of urban populations beyond the cities' capability to absorb them into mainstream urban life (Kepel,

1994, pp. 6–7). The vast majority (76 per cent) of the VP's activists had themselves migrated to Ankara (see Table 6.1).

Not only did rapid urbanisation facilitate more political participation, but it also deepened the dissatisfaction of the urban masses. As the millions were driven by the 'push factors' of rural Anatolia into a few metropolitan cities, the *gecekondu* areas expanded enormously. It is estimated that at the turn of the century around ten million people lived in *gecekondu* areas – in other words, 35 per cent of the total urban population (Kongar, 2000, p. 566). This ratio was even higher when the five largest cities were taken into account. In Ankara, for example, 58.4 per cent of the population lived in *gecekondus* (see Table 4.4). These new migrants faced unemployment, poverty, a lack of housing and insufficient basic services such as health centres and schools. Against this background, the WP/VP developed particular socioeconomic policies (e.g. the *Adil Düzen*) that voiced the concerns of the urban under classes, lower and lower middle classes, artisans, merchants and shopkeepers. Also, through its nationwide grassroots organisations the WP/VP carried out charity work, providing material and non-material help for the most needy in every neighbourhood.

As mentioned previously, the WP/VP successfully tapped into existing traditional, religious and cultural resources. From the early days of its establishment the WP and later the VP made ingenious use of traditional religious networks, relationships, associations, groups and cultural resources as well as utilising traditional, deep-rooted forms of solidarity organisation that had been around for centuries. It also creatively reconfigured the old, traditional political culture, especially in relation to religious issues, social justice and equality, for example through the rhetoric of *Adil Düzen*, greater emphasis on Islamic brotherhood, and the like. The WP/VP, in its political campaigning, drew upon a certain type of language and phrasing that most people identified with, and it was very effective in yielding results at the level of recruitment of new members and for electoral support.

The WP/VP voiced the demands for equality, justice and democracy of the millions of urban poor who had been badly affected by the globalisation process. Growing income disparity, unemployment, deepening poverty, long-term high inflation, a sharp decline in the income of millions of wage and salary earners and the decline of state welfare provisions have been the most defining characteristics of the last two decades in Turkey.

Globalisation has significantly eroded the functions and the borders of nation-states. As a result national-level governance has become ineffective.[17] In this process, nation-states 'have become the local authorities of the global system. They can no longer independently affect the level of economic activity or employment within their territories: rather that is dictated by the choices of internationally mobile capital. The job of nation-states is like that of municipalities within state heretofore' (Hirst and Thompson, 1996, p. 176). This process has inescapably weakened the functions of governments and of political parties once they are in office. It is observed that international corporations have increasingly been taking over the nation-states' space by pushing them out of the economic and political sphere as well. Today, many of them are more powerful than many nation-states and are able to force their will upon governments, dictating policies relating to taxation, privatisation and a flexible labour market that most suit their interests.

Globalised neoliberal policies deepened the problems of inequality, injustice, poverty and misery for millions, as well as exacerbating dissent and dissatisfaction among them. As a result, the majority of the urban poor in many Muslim countries turned away from politics.

However, my findings suggested a different story in Turkey. As the neoliberal restructuring policies obliterated everything in their path the urban poor of the *gecekondu*s areas became increasingly politicised and raised their voices against this process. By voting, supporting the WP/VP or becoming party activists, the urban poor actually made a strong statement in fighting opposition to global capitalism. The *gecekondu* communities displayed their dissatisfaction with the whole process and showed their desire for an alternative politics by throwing their own leaders into the political arena and uniting around the WP/VP. The party had showed its opposition to the current political system by offering a kind of 'third way'[18] economic model that it called Just Order. According to Özbudun (2000, p. 88), the WP's Just Order was an Islamic-inspired economic policy that it conceived as a third way. But it lacked a coherent theoretical base and demonstrated the party's confusion over economic policies. The Just Order policy and its contradictions are discussed in full in chapter 3.

The policy of Just Order was mostly used in rhetorical terms; it was not defined by the party or debated properly, and it had no chance of being implemented while the WP was in government (see chapter 3). Its content and meaning were never clear. Nevertheless, it was the crown jewel in the WP's programme, attracting attention and voter support. Perhaps it owed its success to its complexity, as well as seeming to offer something to everyone.

Neoliberal restructuring policies increased migration massively. In less than a decade, millions moved to the peripheries of megacities, where they became even more disappointed and disillusioned with the mainstream political establishment. As a result of the alienation of the urban masses, voting patterns changed. It is known that at times of crisis, especially among those newcomers, there is a tendency to turn to extremes, both on the right and the left (Shmuelevitz, 1996, p. 168). The urban lower-middle and lower classes of the *gecekondu* sought an alternative to the incompetent, corrupt elite of mainstream politics.

So the Islamist WP/VP emerged as the party of social justice and prosperity, as its name implies. Its Just Order policy filled the gap left by the decline of the centre-left RPP. Islamists strengthened their position among the urban poor and disadvantaged masses by expressing their grievances, concerns and identity problems. The VP's social policies were supported by a massive and very active grassroots organisation which was in action not only at election time but all year around. As one of my informants said: 'We are not "seasonal workers" like the other parties' activists. We are permanent workers in our neighbourhoods.'

Since the Social Democratic party, the RPP, like many in Europe, has lost its belief in its core ideology of freedom, equality and social justice and has failed to put forward an alternative ideology against the rising new right but rather has become an awful imitation of it, it has lost its traditional working-class support. In contrast, the Islamist WP/VP has continued to enjoy the support of the urban poor. In fact, the mass support that the WP/VP attracted could in many ways be classified as an urban squatter movement, unique in its mobilisation strategies under the VP's flag.

What the analysis of the role of party organisations and grassroots activism has shown is that it was the profound role of the grassroots activists rather than religious fundamentalism that led to the ascendancy of political Islam into power for the first time in 1995, and for the second time in 2002 under the AKP, which has been in power since then. The WP/VP as a modern mass party made its way into government not by simply being 'Islamic fundamentalist' or exploiting religious values and rhetoric, but by winning the hearts and minds of millions of voters with its very effective and efficient election campaigns, carried out by its local party organisations. One of the key findings of this study is the fact that party organisations and grassroots activists are highly influential in increasing the party's electoral fortunes.

Finally, what the lesson of the pro-Islamist parties (WP/VP and AKP) since the 1990s has shown is that party decline and the apparent political impasse in Turkish politics could have been prevented by the adoption of mass-party systems by other mainstream political parties in Turkey. Given the current trend of party decline, declining party attachment and declining party identification among citizens in Western Europe and North America, the mass-party strategy might be a viable alternative to revitalise the political engagement of the wider citizenry as well as politics itself in these rather troublesome times.

APPENDIX

The Organisational Structure of the VP

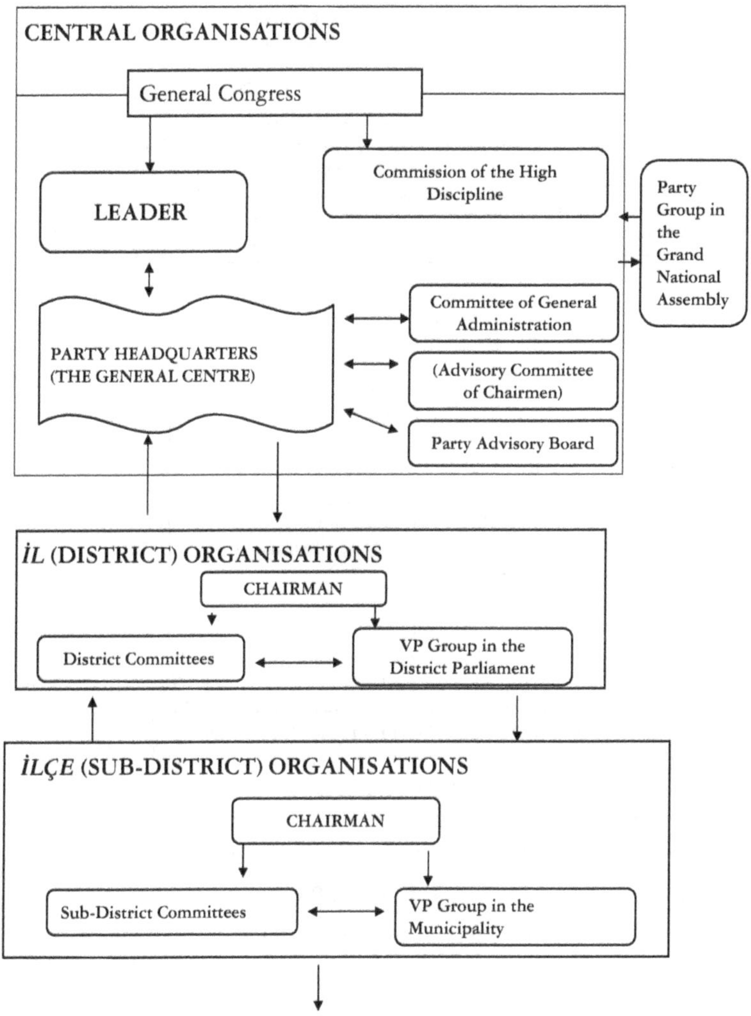

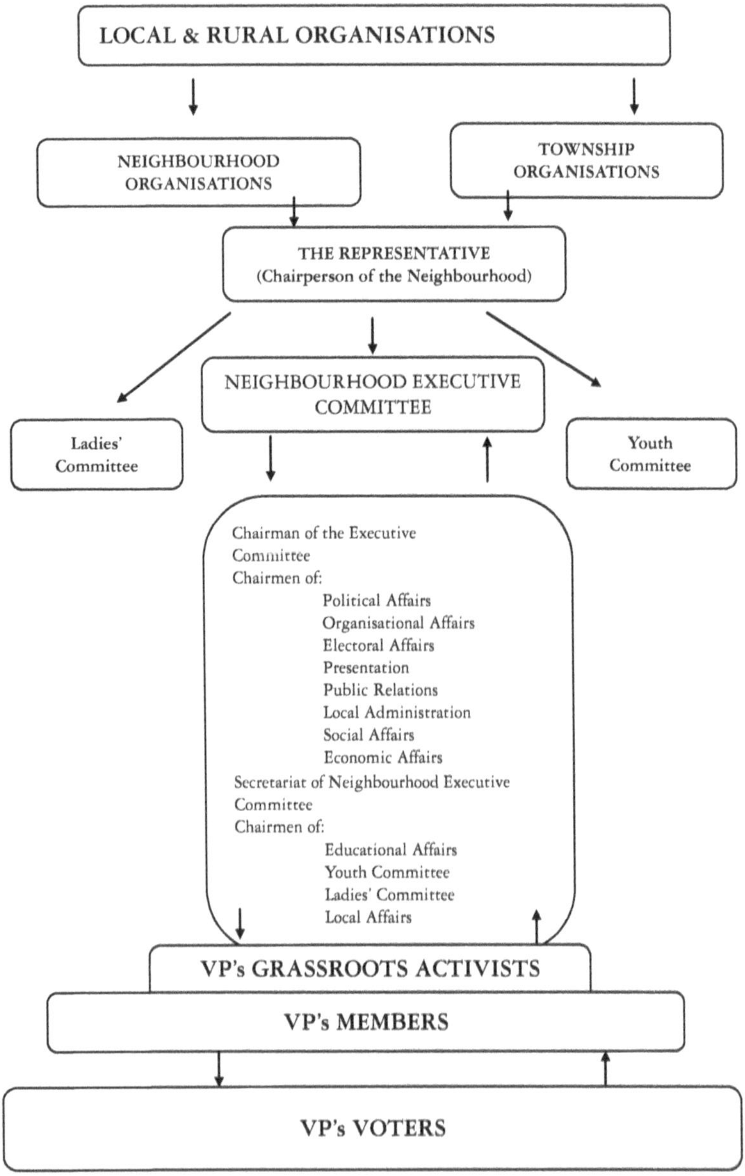
LOCAL & RURAL ORGANISATIONS
NEIGHBOURHOOD ORGANISATIONS
TOWNSHIP ORGANISATIONS
THE REPRESENTATIVE (Chairperson of the Neighbourhood)
NEIGHBOURHOOD EXECUTIVE COMMITTEE
Ladies' Committee
Youth Committee
Chairman of the Executive Committee
Chairmen of:
Political Affairs
Organisational Affairs
Electoral Affairs
Presentation
Public Relations
Local Administration
Social Affairs
Economic Affairs
Secretariat of Neighbourhood Executive Committee
Chairmen of:
Educational Affairs
Youth Committee
Ladies' Committee
Local Affairs
VP's GRASSROOTS ACTIVISTS
VP's MEMBERS
VP's VOTERS

NOTES

Prelims

1. See Eickelman, 2002; Eisenstadt, 2000; Göle, 2002.
2. For further details on Turkish political developments, see http://timelines.ws/countries/TURKEY_B.HTML (last accessed 5 August 2014).

Chapter 1. Political Islam in Turkey: Grassroots Activists and Their Effect on the Rise of Pro-Islamic Parties

1. Seçim Sonuçları 24 December 1995 – Results of Elections of Representatives – State Institute of Statistics, Printing Division, November 1996, Ankara.
2. For the term 'postmodern coup' see daily Radikal, 15 Ocak 2001, *Özkasnak: 28 Şubat post modern darbeydi* (Özkasnak: '28 February was postmodern coup') (15 January 2001).
3. See *Milliyet*, 29 June 2000, 'Komutandan Savaş Uyarısı' ('Warning of War from Commandant') and 30 June 2000, 'Askerden Iknici Cikis' ('Military's Second Warning').
4. Quoted in Darnton, 1995.
5. Ibid.
6. Following the WP's electoral success in general elections in 1995 there was an atmosphere of widespread anxiety and fear. This was reflected by several commentators and news articles. See Atabek, 1996, 'Refah Sendromunu Aşmak ...' ('Overcoming the Syndrome of Welfare'), Istanbul daily *Cumhuriyet* 8 January 1996; Ateş, 1996 *'Refah Korkusu'* ('Fear of Welfare'), *Cumhuriyet* 4 January 1996; Çetinkaya, 1996; 'RP den Korkulurmu' ('Should we be Scared of WP?'), *Cumhuriyet* 30 January 1996.

7. Esposito, 1995, p. 4; see also 'A declaration of war', *Guardian* 12 September 2001.
8. See Fukuyama, 1989, pp. 3–18 and Fukuyama, 1992, p. 66.
9. See Çetinkaya, 1996, p. 80; Ekşi, 1995, p. 9; Kongar, 2000, p.40.
10. See Huntington, 1994, pp. 22–49; Lewis, 1990, pp. 47–60; Miller, 1993, pp. 43–56; Munson, 1995, pp. 151–66.
11. According to Fred Halliday (1995a, p. 48) the 'contingent' approach emphasises modernity and contingency in these 'fundamentalist' movements. He argues that the rise of 'fundamentalisms' in many developing countries is a reaction against the failures of the modernising, secular state.
12. In the area of political participation I must mention studies like: Deutsch (1970), Di Palma (1970), Duverger (1964), Verba and Nie (1972), Barnes and Kaase (1979), Ashford (1972), Marsh (1990), Milbrath and Goel (1977). On the party organisations I found these studies useful: Crotty (1971), Crotty and Jacobson (1980), Herrnson (1986), Huckshorn (1984), Katz and Mair (1995), Parry, Moyser and Day (1992) and Scarrow (1996).
13. See, for example, an article in *The Economist* titled 'Islam and The West' (6 August 1996). This article took Huntington's ideas as an intellectual framework.
14. See Çetinkaya, 1996, p. 80; Kongar, 2000, p.40; Poyraz, 1996, p. 85; Selcuk, *Cumhuriyet*, 20 January 1996; Tanilli, 1996, p. 212.
15. Also see Tuşalp, 1994; Poyraz, 1996, p. 85.
16. A portrait of the grassroots activists of the VP is given in chapter 6.
17. See Caplan, 1987, p. 5; Halliday, 1995a, p. 49; Keddie, 1981, pp. 244–5; Bulliet, 1993, p. 39; Salt, 1995, p. 24; Roy, 1994, pp. 48–53.
18. The term *gecekondu*, translated literally as 'houses which land in the night', is used to describe a type of housing which is hastily erected in a single night if possible, usually with low-quality materials, and grouped together for security reasons (Danielson and Keleş, 1985, pp. 162–6).
19. From this point onwards, I will refer to this period as the 'second phase of rapid urbanisation'. This issue will be discussed in detail in chapter 4.
20. The Gini index measures the extent to which the distribution of income (or, in some cases, consumption expenditure) among individuals or households within an economy deviates from a perfectly equal distribution. Gini index of zero represents perfect equality and 100, perfect inequality (see http://stats.oecd.org/glossary/detail.asp?ID=4842). The Gini coefficient was developed by the Italian statistician and sociologist Corrado Gini and published in 1912.
21. For detailed account see the weekly *Nokta*, 26 June – 2 July 1994.
22. For details see Erder, 1999, pp. 25–6.

23. See Clarke et al., 2000; Frendreis et al., 1990; Huckfeldt and Sprague, 1992; Whiteley and Seyd and Richardson, 1994 and 1999.
24. See Barkey, 1996, p. 45; Çakır, 1994, pp. 216–32; Darnton, 1995; Kalaycıoğlu, 1994; Margulies and Yildizoglu, 1997, p. 151; Özbudun, 2000, pp. 73–93; Şen, 1995, pp. 82–91.
25. Also see Butler and Kavanagh, 1992; Crotty and Jacobson, 1980; Kavanagh and Jones, 1998; Herrnson, 1986; Huckshorn, 1984; Jones et al., 1998.
26. See Clarke et al., 2000; Crotty, 1971; Frendreis et al., 1990; Huckfeldt and Sprague, 1992; Kramer, 1970; Seyd and Whiteley, 1992; Whiteley and Seyd and Richardson 1994 and 1999.
27. Berry, 1970, p. 34; MacAllister et al., 2001, pp. 41–59.
28. For an analysis of 'old politics' and 'new politics' see Dalton and Kuechler, 1990; Pakulski, 1991, pp. 25–51; Dalton, 1988, pp. 151–76.
29. For more details see chapter 6.
30. See http://www.ankararehberi.com/ankara-genel-bilgiler/nufus-demografi.html (last accessed 5 September 2014).
31. These figures were given by Gazi Sahin, the candidate mayor (presently mayor of Mamak) from Virtue Party during his interview on a local TV channel called Kanal A, 8 April 1999.
32. The word *varoş* (plural form *varoşlar*) is another term for *gecekondu* and has been widely used by Turkish writers. Its literal meaning is 'destination', as the *gecekondu* have been the primary destination of millions of migrant workers since the 1950s.
33. I am using the term 'ethnographic' in the same way as Atkinson and Hammersley (1994, p. 248) used it. See also Fielding, 1994, pp. 154–7.
34. The fact that part of my field research took place during the general election campaign provided a rare opportunity to observe the party activists in a real situation, in their day-by-day party activities. Not surprisingly the political activities increased considerably during this time, as my informants acknowledged.
35. Systematic selection means that 'all elements of the population are listed and a fixed sampling interval is used to select sample members. The sampling interval is the reciprocal of the sampling fraction. For example if 50 small businesses are to be selected from a population of 400, the sampling fraction would be 1/8 and the sampling interval would be 8. Every eighth small business on the list is selected after a random start between 1 and 8' (Arber, 1994, p. 79).

Chapter 2. The Decline of the Turkish Political Party System, 1980–2002

1. See Sakallıoğlu, in Tosun, 1999, p. 150.
2. See Istanbul daily *Sabah* (17 Temmuz/17 July 2001) *'Vegıı gelirinin hepsi faize gitti'* ('All tax revenues went to interest repayments').
3. According to a Standard & Poor's report dated 20 August 2001: 'Turkey's public sector debt burden [is] approaching 110 per cent of GNP ... In addition, Turkey has the highest rates of inflation and real interest rates recorded in recent years among its peers. This puts Turkey's high public sector debt burden on an explosive spiralling course' (see *Milliyet,* 24 May 2002).
4. According to TESEV (2000, p. 6), in 1994 the richest 20 per cent of the population received 54.9 per cent of GDP while the poorest 20 per cent received only 4.9 per cent of GDP.
5. According to the Istanbul daily *Milliyet* (24 July 2001), *'Beş kişiden birinin karnı doymuyor'* ('One in five goes hungry'), the income gulf had widened enormously. The richest 5 per cent of the population earned US $32,000 a year while the poorest 5 per cent (7 million people) earned around US $481 a year, meaning that the rich earned about 66 times as much as the very poor.
6. Birand (2001) 'Washington, Ankara nın gözyaşına bakmıyor' ('Washington does not pity Ankara's weeping') in Istanbul daily *Milliyet* 21 Temmuz/ 21 July 2001.
7. I am using the term 'structural adjustment' as Walden Bello defined this concept in his book *Dark Victory* (1994, p. 140).
8. According to some economists the IMF was primarily responsible for this crisis by insisting on inappropriate policies (Ercan Kumcu, 'The IMF's blunder in Turkey' *Financial Times*, 12 March 2001). Also, Sonmez pointed out in 2001 that due to the IMF's disastrous policies the Turkish economy had lost US $120 billion dollars since 1999. Sönmez daily *Hürriyet*, 'IMF bize kişi başına 1500 dolar borçlu' ('IMF owes US $1500 to each of us') 28 July 2001.
9. Istanbul daily *Sabah*, 18 July 2001, 'Piyasalar cildirmis olmali' ('Markets must be crazy').
10. See some of the media reports from following daily papers: *Hürriyet*: 7 July 2001, 'Ecevit: 'IMF ile çok duyarlı bir dönemdeyiz' ('Ecevıt: we are in a delicate position with the IMF'); Turgut, 13 Temmuz 2001 'Ara dönem hükümeti gerekiyor' ('Turkey needs a transition government'); Cihan, 2001, *'Borçlu değil ALACAKLISINIZ'* ('you are not debtor but the CREDITORS').
11. The phrase 'lords of the horizons' comes from Jason Goodwin's 1998 book *Lords of the Horizons: a history of the Ottoman Empire*, (Chatto & Windus, London, 1998).

12. Compared to the average volatility score for the OECD countries of 12.6 per cent in the 1990s (Dalton et al., 2000, p. 40), 21 per cent volatility can be classified as high volatility.
13. 28 February 1997 saw a postmodern coup, an intervention in politics was staged by the army on account of the unexpected election results of 24 December 1995. In this general election the WP attained 21.4 per cent of the total vote and gained more seats (158 out of 550) than any mainstream secularist party. It heightened the tension between *laicists* (secularists) and Islamists (fundamentalists) to a degree where the Islamic-led government was forced to resign in 1997 after just 11 months in office.
14. The positive influence of the local party organisations and grassroots activism on the electoral process is explored in chapter 7.
15. For a detailed discussion on party members and party organisations, see chapters 6 and 7.
16. There are differences between a party supporter and a party member. Apart from voting for a certain party, the party supporter by and large remains inactive. A party member on the contrary pays a membership fee and is ready to spend their time, energy and resources for the party (Seyd and Whiteley, 1992).
17. See chapter 5.
18. For an account of the military coup of 27 May 1960 see Ahmad, 1977, pp. 147–77; Hale, 1994, pp. 53–79; Tosun, 1999, pp. 87–92; Kongar, 2000, pp. 154–6.
19. Kongar, 2000, p.146; also, for the DP see Sarıbay, 1991, pp. 119–33; Dodd, 1969, chapter IX.
20. Sherwood, 1967/8, pp. 54–65, cited in Levi, 1991, p. 148.
21. For example see Özbudun, 1976, pp. 134–6; see also Tachau, 1991, pp. 108–9.
22. I am not suggesting that clientelism in a party system would inevitably lead to fragmentation, electoral volatility or organisational decline. But what has happened in Turkey since the late 1980s has changed the basic mechanism that clientelism maintained. Especially as a result of neoliberal restructuring policies the state has been withdrawn from many economic activities. This shift has severely undermined the ability of governmental parties to create spoils to distribute to their supporters. It is clear that any clientelist party can only retain its clients if it can continue to provide rewards, and the lower these rewards the less loyalty it can expect from the client. The decline in the spoil-generating mechanism meant a decline of party attachment, identification and party support among the party supporters, leading to fragmentation, volatility and organisational decline.

23. See Güneş-Ayata, 1994; Kalaycıoğlu, 1998 and Özbudun, 2000.
24. For example, political commentator Hasan Cemal described how HADEP works as follows: 'Here the HADEP has been canvassing one-to-one, house-to-house like the WP did. Other parties need to come and work like this' (*Milliyet* 14 June 2001). For more details about the grassroots activism of the WP/VP see chapters 5, 6, and 7.
25. The 'Banker Yalçın affair' refers to the financial scandals which became a characteristic of the 1980s in Turkey. In an atmosphere of market liberalisation, but a lack of regulatory bodies, firms and groups would set up bank-like companies and collect money from people by offering really high interest rates that were not sustainable. Many people lost all their earnings, pensions or even homes by investing in these companies.
26. See chapter 4 for some detail on *gecekondu*s, and the living conditions of the *gecekondu* population.
27. For the data on economic variables see chapter 4.

Chapter 3. From Movement to Political Party: The Changing Contours of Political Islam in Turkey

1. For a short review of social movements see Castells, 1976, p. 151; Diani and Porta, 1999; Rootes, 1990; Rucht and Porta, 1999; Pakulski, 1991, 1995, pp. 55–87; Pickvance, 1976, 1995, pp. 123–146 and Touraine, 1981.
2. For a detailed account of the competing ideologies in the last quarter of the nineteenth century see Berkes (1964).
3. *Meşrutiyet* literally means Legitimacy or rule of Law. In the long history of Ottoman reform attempts the Constitution of 1876, which is also known as the first Constitution, was proclaimed on 23 December 1876. It provided for separation of powers much more in form than fact, and the institutional changes reflected evolution rather than a radical departure from past practices. Despite all its shortcomings, however, it was a significant step forward in terms of granting equal rights to all Muslims and non-Muslim Ottoman subjects. However its implementation was postponed for another 30 years until the second proclamation of Constitution in 1908 (Second Mesrutiyet) (Shaw and Shaw, 1978, pp. 174–267).
4. The regional disparity and party preferences are examined in detail in chapter 5. The NSP had 11.8 per cent of the total votes in 1973 elections across Turkey but its electoral support rose as high as 33.0 per cent in less developed districts.
5. The term 'mason' used by Necmettin Erbakan in his speech refers to a small group of people, a business community related usually to Freemasonry

groups. In the 1970s these so-called masons were often accused of being semi-secret, pro-Israel and powerful in business circles.

6. For a detailed account of the social base of the WP/VP see chapter 4.
7. The role of religion in politics is explained in chapter 5. See also Toprak, 1987, p. 219.
8. Çakır, 1994, p. 21. Also see Çalışlar, 1995, pp. 25–6; Şaylan, 1992, pp. 154–8; Yalçın, 1999.
9. The Nurcu movement takes its name from Said Nursi (1876–1960), an Islamist thinker and opponent of the Kemalist republican ideals. Nurcu groups have become one of the most influential Islamist movements in Turkey. Since the early 1950s this group has been active in Turkish politics and it has been defined in many different ways. For those professionals who write for Istanbul's big circulation daily newspapers they are a *tariqa*, a Sufi 'religious order' in new, modernist clothing. For the militant (and often military) secularists who view the community's dead namesake as the 'very incarnation of backwardness. They are dangerous fundamentalists, bent on submerging Turkey in a rising religious tide and taking over the government and the regime (Reed, 2003, p. 35). Some saw them as an identity-based movement: In order to safeguard the Islamic religious and cultural underpinnings of Turkish identity this movement has responded to the search for identity which has been a salient characteristic of Turkish politics since the collapse of the Ottoman Empire (Yavuz, 2003, p. 151).
10. For a detailed account of the 'Green Belt' project, see Çalışlar, 1995; Çakır, 1994; Hunter, 1995, p. 21; Kürkçü, 1996; Tuşalp, 1994; Yalçın, 1999.
11. For a detailed analysis of Saudi connections, see Mumcu, 1996, p. 138.
12. There have been numerous articles and books written on Turkish–Islamic synthesis. See Güvenç et al., 1994; *Türk İslam Sentezi* [Turkish–Islam Synthesis], Sarmal Yayınevi, İstanbul; Şaylan (1992, p. 111).
13. See Milli Nizam Partisi Kuruluş Beyannamesi, Ankara, 1970, p. 34 (quoted in Sarıbay, 1985, p. 100).
14. See MSP Genel Başkanı Süleyman Arif Emre'in I. Büyük Kongreyi Açış Konuşması, Ankara, 1973, s. 5/ 6 (quoted in Sarıbay, 1985, pp. 110–11).
15. See Erbakan, 1975, pp. 29–40, quoted in Sarıbay, 1985, pp. 111–13.
16. Ibid., p. 127.
17. For some elaboration see chapter 2.
18. See RP Tüzük ve Programı (WP's Program and Principles), Ankara, 1985, pp. 35–6.
19. Ibid, p. 36.
20. Ibid.
21. See 20 Ekim 1991 Seçim Beyannamesi (The Election Manifesto 20 October 1991), Ankara (1991, p. 73).

22. In this election, fearing they would not achieve the 10 per cent national threshold the WP's leadership devised an alliance with two right-wing parties: the ultra-nationalist Milliyetçi Çalışma Partisi (Nationalist Work Party, which later became the NAP) and Islahatçı Demokrasi Partisi (Reformist Democracy Party, RDP).
23. The WP's well organised grassroots activism has been noted by many students of Turkish politics. For some of them see Ayata, 1997; Barkey, 1996; Çakır, 1994; Darnton, 1995; Kalaycıoğlu, 1994.
24. For a comparison see tables in Çakır, 1994, pp. 218, 220, 222.
25. See Nizam Demir's interview.
26. Erbakan, 1991, pp. 11–12, quoted in Çakır 1994: 133–4; *Adil Ekonomik Düzen* ('Just Economic Order'), Ankara.
27. Also, for an Islamic perspective on the WP's foreign policies see Akgül, 1997a.
28. The emphases are the author's.
29. Istanbul daily *Hurriyet*, 20 Nisan (April), 1999.
30. For the result of the 18 April 1999 elections see webpages: www.belgenet.net/ayrinti.php?yil_id=13 (link no longer working).
31. (1998: 1) Fazilet Partisi TÜZÜK (Virtue Party Book of Code of Practices) Ankara.
32. The division emerged before the WP closed down but it became most visible in the first and only general party congress of the VP on 18 May 2000. At that congress for the first time ever there were two candidates for the leadership: R. Kutan, the acting leader, who had been appointed by N. Erbakan and challenged Abdullah Gül, the representative of the 'progressives' group that later became the AKP.
33. The pro-Islamist Welfare Party (WP) (1983–1998) was established by the former cadres of Islamist NSP of the pre-1980s. The Welfare Party tripled its share of votes between 1987 and 1995: from 7 per cent to 21 per cent at the general elections. This gain in support caused political turmoil, eventually leading up to the postmodern coup of 28 February process in 1997. Islamist parties from the NOP to the WP, VP and the AKP have been following the same path and representing the Islamist movement in Turkey. The latest of these – the AKP – has been ruling the country since 2002. (Çarkoğlu and Kalaycıoğlu, 2007; also see Sayarı and Esmer, 2002).
34. See Donat (1998) 'Fazilet te "orta yol" arayışı' ('The VP searches for "middle way"' (*Sabah* 11 July 1998)).
35. Özgürel, 1998 'Fazilet Partisi nde rota Değişikliği' ('The change of direction in the VP'), Istanbul daily *Radikal* (23 Eylül/ September 1998).

36. Donat, Istanbul daily *Sabah*, 11 July 1998.
37. For the concept of 'theo-democracy' see Esposito and Voll (1996, p. 24).

Chapter 4. The Urban Roots of Political Islam

1. See, for example, Huntington, 1994, pp. 22–49; Lewis, 1990, pp. 47–60; Miller, 1993, pp. 43–56; Munson, 1995, pp. 151–66.
2. See also Keddie, 1981, pp. 239–49.
3. For further elaboration see chapter 3.
4. See Özbudun, 1973 cited in Sarıbay, 1985, pp. 143–4.
5. See Table 4.1.
6. See chapter 3. In a 1999 interview, the leader of the VP Recai Kutan also said that the majority of the party's voters and supporters lived in towns and urban centres. See Recai Kutan's interview by Melih Birsel, *Gündemdekiler*, NTV, 28 October 1999.
7. See Ayata, 1993, pp. 51–67; Kalaycıoğlu, 1996, pp. 403–24; Öğütcü, 1994, p. 826; Özbudun, 2000, pp. 87–91; Sarıbay, 1985, p. 45.
8. For detail see Danielson, and Keles, 1985, p. 26. Also for the urban and rural population and their ration to total population see Table 4.2.
9. Turkish Statistical Institute, http://www.turkstat.gov.tr/PreTablo.do?alt_id=39 (last accessed, 26 January 2013).
10. See 1990 census of Population, 1993, p. 28.
11. http://www.worldbulletin.net/?aType=haber&ArticleID=61970(last accessed 5 August 2014).
12. Pye quoted in Danielson and Keleş, 1985, p. 3.
13. Shmuelevitz (1996, p. 175) argued that 'There is no doubt that the continued waves of immigrants to the big cities and the continued socioeconomic crisis, which the coalition governments of the centre-moderate right and the left of centres parties have not yet managed to solve, only strengthened the trends which appeared in the elections of 1991 towards extremism, especially towards the religious right as the most promising option to solve the crisis.'
14. For an analysis of 'old politics' and 'new politics' see Dalton and Kuechler, 1990; Pakulski, 1991, pp. 25–51; Dalton, 1988, pp. 151–76.
15. The socioeconomic characteristics of Ankara are described in brief and those of the sub-districts of Keçiören and Mamak in some detail in chapter 1. I shall not repeat the facts here.
16. 'Over-urbanisation' as one of the key concept of urban studies has been discussed by many Western as well as Turkish writers. See for example Danielson and Keles, 1985, pp. 38–9; Castells, 1977, pp. 41–3.
17. See 1990 Census of Population, 1993, p. 28.

18. For the term 'push' factors see Castells (1977, p. 41).
19. See http://www.die.gov.tr/nufus_sayimi/02012002T3.jpg (last accessed 5 August 2014).
20. The fall in the ratio of *gecekondu* housing from 72.4 per cent in 1980 to 58.4 in 1990 in Ankara is unlikely to indicate a slowdown in the rate of urbanisation/squatterisation in the 1990s in general, but it might be an indication of the rapid transformation of old *gecekondu* areas, while new *gecekondu* areas are growing, into authorised apartments in Ankara (Özdemir, 1999).
21. For a detailed analysis of the structural adjustment programme and its impacts see the collection of essays in Eralp et al. 1993; Boratav, 1990, pp. 199–230; Öniş and Webb, 1993, pp. 128–84. See also Öniş, 1997, pp. 743–76 and Ramazanoğlu, 1985.
22. For accounts of the military rule of 12 September 1980, see Dodd, 1990; Yetkin, 1995; also see Hale, 1994.
23. For an account of the economic politics of the military regime, see Tosun, 1999, pp. 145–8.
24. *Cumhuriyet*, 26 Ocak/January 1982, quoted in Tosun, 1999, p. 146.
25. See Danielson and Keles, 1985, pp. 101–10; Karpat, 1975, p. 89–199; Hale, 1981, pp. 117–27; Özbudun, 1976, pp. 200–5; Shmuelevitz, 1996, pp. 162–93.
26. See Ayata, 1993, pp. 51–67; Çakır, 1994, p. 223; Kalaycıoğlu, 1996, pp. 403–24; *Milliyet* (Istanbul daily) 22 January 1999; Özbudun, p. 88 and Shmuelevitz, 1996, p. 168.
27. See 'General election turnout 1945–2010', http://www.ukpolitical.info/Turnout45.htm (last accessed 5 September 2014).
28. The WP/VP, as argued in chapter 2 and 3, was the only modern mass-based political party and opposed neoliberal economic policies. It proposed a set of broadly social democratic economic policies called *Adil Düzen* (Just Order). Also see Özbudun, 2000, p. 88.
29. See *Milliyet*, 22 January 1999.
30. The term 'seasonal worker' takes its meaning from an employment practice common in Turkey. There are thousands of people who work for the government on seasonal contracts, e.g. in the agricultural sector seasonal workers usually work for three or four months a year in the summer.
31. For a detailed account of the Susurluk event see chapter 5.

Chapter 5. Explaining the Meaning of Party Membership: Routes to and Reasons for Party Membership

1. See Verba et al., 1993, p. 310; Leighley, 1995, pp. 181–209; Whiteley, 1995.
2. See Appendix.

3. The biggest reflection of the gap between the regions might be in terms of the direction of migration dependant on social and economic development. Since the 1950s, certain regions and provinces have experienced out-migration well above the national average, such as Ağrı, Amasya, Bingöl, Çorum, Kars, Malatya, Mardin, Muş, Niğde, Ordu, Sinop, Tokat, Tunceli and Yozgat. These cities are mainly situated in the eastern regions with a high proportion of rural inhabitants, high birth rate and low level of agricultural income (see Peker, 1996, chapter 1).
4. For a detailed account of the neoliberal economy policies and impact of the restructuring programme on the lower and lower-middle classes see chapter 4.
5. In 1995 there were an estimated two million *gecekondu* housing units with ten million inhabitants. Altogether 35 per cent of the urban population lives in the *gecekondu* areas (Kongar, 2000, p. 566).
6. The word *hemşehrilik* describes a presumed tie between people from the same village, town or province (Kalaycıoğlu, 1998, p. 18). The *hemşehri* networks have been one of the widespread forms of solidarity among newly migrated families in the metropolitan areas. It was developed as an informal coping strategy among migrants from the same regions. The phenomenon has been studied by many Turkish social scientists; see Ayata-Güneş 1991; 1994, p. 326; Schüler, 1998; Şenyapılı, 1978; Tekeli, 1982.
7. This point is discussed further in chapter 7.
8. A similar observation was made by Seyd and Whiteley, 1992, p. 100.
9. There is a sizeable body of literature concerning ideology and political participation and it is impossible to cite all relevant references here. For a selected literature see Ashford, 1972; Barnes and Kaase 1979; Dowse and Hughes, 1986; Milbrath and Goel, 1977; Marsh, 1990; Verba and Nie, 1972.
10. Dowse and Hughes, 1986, especially chapter 8
11. According to Kalaycıoğlu (1998, p. 9) since the 1950s, traditionalists, including the centre-right and religious right, have maintained the upper hand in electoral contests. He argues that they tried to carry out policies that were geared to accomplishing their version of a good society in Turkey. He argued 'in the very core of that exercise rests the role of religion in socio-economic relations and politics of country'.
12. This point was discussed in chapter 4.
13. See Barkey, 1996, p. 45; Çakır, 1994, pp. 216–32; Özbudun, 2000; Sayarı, 1996, p. 36.
14. Various studies on public trust in indicate a constant lack of trust in politicians. A study in 2001 found that political parties and parliament (the Grand National Assembly) were the least trusted group among Turks. The degree of

trust for parliament was 3.2 out of 10, and political parties received just 2.1 out of 10. See TESEV's study Türkiye de Yolsuzluklar Hane Halkı Araştırma Sonçları ('The Results of The Study of Corruption in Turkey') 28 February 2001. TESEV's web address: www.tesev.org.tr (last accessed 5 September 2014); World Economic Forum 2006 'Full Survey: Trust in Governments, Corporations and Global Institutions Continues to Decline' (Accessed 1 April 2006) http://www.weforum.org/site/homepublic.nsf/Content/Full+Survey per cent3A+Trust+in+Governments per cent2C+Corporations+and+Global+Institutions+Continues+to+Decline (last accessed 5 September 2014); See also Delibas, 2011, pp. 171–89.

15. Susurluk is a small town near to Balikesir, but after this famous traffic accident it was transformed and came to describe a phenomenon in Turkish politics. On 3 November 1996, a Mercedes car collided with a lorry four miles away from the town of Susurluk-Balikesir. At first it seemed a very ordinary accident, nothing unusual on Turkish roads, but soon it became clear that a high-ranking police officer, Hüseyin Kocadağ, a fugitive criminal, mafia leader Abdullah Çatlı; and a parliamentarian, the leader of the Kurdish tribe of Bucak Sedat Bucak were in the same car. And even more extraordinary, the car was packed with guns, explosives, long-range assault rifles, and so on. This accident gave a picture of the relationship between the state, the mafia and the security forces which developed over a decade and was fuelled by the low-intensity war against the PKK in the south-east of the country.
16. For a detailed account of Susurluk, see http://ilef.ankara.edu.tr/susurluk (link no longer working). Also, a keyword search (on 22 January 2001) through Google.com found 8,910 news items and articles on the Susurluk. This figure itself indicates the massive debate and importance of the Susurluk event in Turkish politics.
17. Kutlu Savaş, a state prosecutor, was appointed by the government to investigate the Susurluk event and produced a 400-page report. This report was important because it was the first time a state-appointed prosecutor had investigated such a corruption case and by and large it pointed objectively to the relations between the mafia-criminal gangs, politician/bureaucrat and the some elements within state. For a summary of it see Hürriyet, 13 Ocak 1998, 'İşte tarihi rapor' ('Here is the historic report', 13 January 1998).
18. I am using the concept of 'relative deprivation' as defined by W.G. Runciman (1966). He (1966, pp. 10–11) argued that: 'Relative deprivation should always be understood to mean a sense of deprivation; a person who is "relatively deprived" need not be "objectively" deprived in the more usual sense

that he is demonstrably lacking something. In addition, relative deprivation means that the sense of deprivation is such as to involve a comparison with the imagined situation of some other person or group. This other person or group is the "reference group", or more accurately the "comparative reference group".'

19. Kalaycıoğlu (1998, p. 12) argued that: 'The Turkish party system is not only plagued by fragmentation, and the volatility of the electorate. Furthermore, in the 1990s a realignment of the vote seems to be happening, as the centre-left-right spectrum rapidly diminishes, while the far-right increases with leaps and bounds.'
20. The PP, which later became SODP (SDPP) joined the government with Demirel's TTP following the general elections of 1991. Upon the sudden death of President Özal in 1993, Demirel left the government to become president, but the coalition government continued under T. Çiller and M. Karayalçın until 1995.
21. In the local elections of 1989 the PP (later SHP (SDPP)) won many municipalities including the metropolitan cities Istanbul, Ankara, Kayseri and Mersin, but due to the widespread corruption scandals it lost them in the following 1994 local elections. In this period scandals involving the large publicly owned municipality companies İSKİ in Istanbul and ASKİ in Ankara were very high profile.
22. See Cord et al., 1974, p. 184; Dawson and Prewitt, 1969, pp. 5–6, 105.

Chapter 6. The Grassroots Activists: The Making of Islamist Activism

1. For example, TÜSES 1999, a study of the social structure and the electorates/supporters of political parties in Turkey. This study represents all of Turkey and deals with various aspects of the electorate. The second one was by Ahmet Yücekök (1997); Dinin Siyasallaşması (The Politicisation of Religion) was carried out in Istanbul. It has a large sample of 15,683 and deals with politics as well as issues of identity. At the end of this chapter data are compared with the findings of these studies. Other relevant studies include Özbudun's (2000) study on contemporary Turkish politics and TESEV (2000).
2. See also Blondel, 1958, p. 40.
3. As Berger (1994, p. 88) noted: 'In many places the SDP managed to install itself within working-class communities as a creditable alternative to other political parties. It did so by developing into a neighbourhood-based party that became meaningful to the everyday lives and struggles of the workers in a particular locality. Party members were given a strong sense of cohesion

and belonging by simple organisational innovations such as the introduction of uniform membership booklets after 1907 or the weekly (sometimes monthly) payment of their membership fees.'

4. *Guardian*, Monday 28 February 2000.
5. For a detailed account of the party decline and policy convergence in Turkey see chapter 2.
6. For a debate on the effects of grassroots party organisations on electoral outcomes see chapter 7.
7. For a debate about the neighbourhood effect on voting behaviour see MacAllister et al., 2001; see also Savage, 1987, pp. 53–76; Warde and Savage, 1988, pp. 339–51.
8. See Giles and Dantico, 1982, pp. 144–9; Kenny, 1992, pp. 259–67.
9. For an analysis of 'old politics' and 'new politics' see Dalton and Kuechler, 1990; Pakulski, 1991, pp. 25–51; Dalton, 1988, pp. 151–76.
10. These figures were given by Gazi Sahin mayoral candidate the (later mayor of Mamak) of the Virtue Party, during his interview for a local TV channel called *Kanal A*, 8 April 1999.
11. For more detail see chapters 1, 3 and especially 7.
12. This is definitely not an attempt to deny or underestimate the existence and importance of Hanım Komisyonları (ladies' committees) within the grassroots organisation but we must note that in Turkey grassroots activism is still predominantly a male vocation.
13. There is a growing body of literature on these schools. See Akşit, 1994; Ayata, 1993; Lapidot, 1995.
14. For population by gender and occupation in Ankara see the webpage http://www.ankara.bel.tr/AbbSayfalari/ABB_Nazim_Plani/rapor/5-sosyodemografi.pdf (link no longer working).
15. Derviş was a former deputy president of the World Bank who was brought in by the Ecevit government to handle this worst-ever economic crisis.
16. See http://arsiv.ntvmsnbc.com/news/254830.asp (last accessed 27.11.2012).
17. Data collected during my fieldwork in Ankara between February and May 1999 (US $1 = 381,000 TL on 16 April 1999).

Chapter 7. Not Like Any Other Party: The Effects of Grassroots Activism on the Electoral Outcome

1. See the interview with a representative of the Şehit Kubilay neighbourhood.
2. The Istanbul daily *Milliyet* (28 January 1999) reported that the Motherland Party drew its campaigning strategy and tactics during the campaign for the general elections in April 1999 from the WP's past election campaign

strategies. This report was highly significant in that it showed how the WP/VP's campaigning style was emulated even by its staunchest opponents.

3. See Istanbul daily *Cumhuriyet*, 'Birinciyi varoslar belirleyecek' (16 April 1999) (Squatters will decide the winner); Also see Istanbul daily *Milliyet* 7 Ocak 1999 (7 January 1999); Istanbul daily *Milliyet,* 20 Nisan 1999 (20 April 1999).
4. The American sociologist Charles H. Cooley coined concepts of primary and secondary groups. A primary group refers to a typically small social group whose members share close, personal, enduring relationships. The family is an example. A secondary group, on the contrary, is a number of people who meet regularly, but whose relationships are mainly impersonal and formally defined (Giddens, 1993, p. 285).
5. For information on social relations and living conditions in *gecekondu* see Acar, 1994, pp. 313–24; Ayata, A., 1994, pp. 325–40; Demir, 1994, pp. 357–66; Kurdoğlu, 1994, pp. 367–84; Gökce, 1994, pp. 283–94 and Özer, 1994, pp. 303–12.
6. For the socioeconomic and demographic characteristics of *gecekondu* see research by Devlet Planlama Teşkilatı (1991) (State Planning Organisation on Gecekondu Population), DPT Matbaası, Ankara; also see Istanbul daily *Miliyet*, 'Gecekondu 1999', (31 March 1999) and 'Bütün umutları çocuklari', ('All their hopes are their children') 1 April 1999.
7. See *Milliyet,* 24 March 1999 'Seçmen Havayolları' ('Voter Airlines'). In this article it was reported that the Kombassan Holding group was organising charter flights from various European countries to bring around 4,500 voters to support the VP in the general elections of 18 April 1999. In another article in the same newspaper it was reported that National View was the most influential organisation among the Turkish workers and their supporters would come to Turkey to vote. It continued, 'At the 1999 general election the Organisation of National View raised around 2 million DM to send to the WP'.
8. See interview with Mustafa Şenyurt, member of the municipality's parliament in Mamak *ilçe.*
9. See Fazilet Partisi Halkla İlişkiler Başkanlıg, Halkla *İlişkiler Nedir?* (Virtue Party Chairman of PR Affairs, What is Public Relations?), Ankara, 1998.
10. See the interview of representative of Şehit Kübilay neighbourhood.
11. See Istanbul daily *Milliyet* 1 Nisan 1999 (1 April 1999). Before the general elections in April 1999 *Milliyet* looked at various aspects of the social life in the *gecekondu* areas and the writer made similar observations about teahouses.
12. There were some media reports with titles like: 'Faziletin Seçim Taktiği: Kovulduğunuz Kapıya Mal Satın' ('Virtue party's Election Tactic: Selling goods where you've already been turned down'). Before the general and local

elections in 1999 the VP organised a preparation camp in Antalya. During the camp the delegates were lectured about some new election tactics. It was stressed that a good salesman is one who succeeded in selling goods to the household that had already turned him away from its door. See Istanbul Daily *Radikal* 26 Ekim 1998 (26 October 1998); Sabah 26 Ekim 1998 (26 October 1998).

13. For a detailed analysis of the *gecekondu* areas see chapter 4.
14. See Ayata (1997, p. 52); Çakır (1994, pp. 51–9); Kalaycıoğlu (1997); Öniş (1997, pp. 755–6); Özbudun (2000); Sayarı (1996, p. 36); Şen (1995, pp. 82–91). Also see media report 'VP Gecekondularda Devlet Baba', *Milliyet* 23 Ocak/ January 1999 ('The VP is the Father State in Squatter areas').
15. 'The unemployment rate in cities reached 13 per cent in April 1994; in October 1995, it was 10 per cent', *State Institute of Statistics, Statistical Yearbook of Turkey 1996* (Ankara: SIS Publications, 1997, p. 280); 'many of the unemployed live in squatter settlements. In metropolitan cities, the wealthiest one-fifth of the population receives 57.2 per cent of the national revenue, whereas the poorest one-fifth of the population receives only 4.8 per cent of the national revenue' (*State Institute of Statistics, Statistical Yearbook of Turkey 1996*, quoted in Erman, 1998, p. 561).
16. For a detailed account of migration from rural to urban areas and its socio-economic and political consequences see chapter 4.
17. There are writers who saw a very strong connection between the neoliberal restructuring in Turkey in the post-1980 era and the rise of the Welfare party to power. See for example Öniş, 1997.
18. For the concept of 'value' and its varieties, see Marx, *Capital*, Vol. 1, p. 131.
19. See http://www.tesev.org.tr/projeler/siyasi_parti_metin_teblig24.php, p. 64 (link no longer working).
20. Among these factors were the relatively succesful integration of the Turkish economy into the global markets, economic liberalisation and structural adjustment programmes in period following the military coup of 1980 (Öniş 1993; Keyder, 1999).
21. See *Milliyet*, 13 Nisan/April 1999 'El sıkmanın 1001 fazıleti' ('The 1001 virtues of the handshake').
22. See interviews with Remzi from Şirintepe neighbourhood and Hasan member of the Mamak *ilçe* youth committee.
23. As the closely fought Presidential elections since 1990s in the USA have shown, however developed a country is and whatever sophisticated campaigning technology is available, without the hard work of the active party members the election will not be won.

Chapter 8. Conclusion: Fundamentalism Demystified

1. See Huntington, 1995, pp. 22–49; Lewis, 1990, pp. 47–60; Miller, 1993, pp. 43–56.
2. But this close relationship deteriorated later on. The deterioration of relations between two friends began with 'the one-minute incident in Davos' and hit rock bottom after the deadly Israeli commando raid on a Turkish flotilla, *Mavi Marmara,* in 2010.
3. See Özbudun, 2000, p. 87; Çakır, 1994, pp. 127–30; Heper, 1997, p. 35.
4. This point was discussed extensively in chapter 5.
5. For a detailed account of how parties lost public trust see Delibas, 2011.
6. See the survey results in chapter 5 for reasons why people voted for the WP/VP.
7. Özdalga, 1997, p. 22. Also, my own observations from the field confirm Özdalga's claims that the majority of voters and 40 per cent of political activists voted for or joined the WP/VP for other reasons than religious or ideological incentives. See chapter 5.
8. See Strateji MORI 1998, p. 35 (cited in TESEV, 2000, p. 16).
9. For a detailed account of the neoliberal economy policies and their long-term consequences in Turkey see chapter 4.
10. Although there are writers who doubted the benefits of grassroots activities on the parties' electoral fortunes, there is compelling evidence from case studies done in different countries that party organisations and grassroots activism are very influential on the parties' electoral fortunes. For both views see chapter 7.
11. The functions of the party membership are discussed in chapters 5 and 6.
12. For definition of the term 'capital-intensive' party organisations see Mair, 1997, p. 11.
13. See for example Jennings et al., 1979, p. 463; Verba and Nie, 1972, pp. 97–101; Dalton, 1988, p. 148.
14. For elaboration see chapter 5.
15. For this, see Dijik and de Groot, 1995; Çakır, 1995; Çalislar, 1995; Lewis, 1974; Price, 1999, chapter 2; Tapper, 1993 chapters 1–7; Yücekök, 1997.
16. Also see Ashford, 1972; Barnes and Kasse, 1979; Dowse and Hughes, 1986; Marsh, 1990.
17. See Hirst and Thompson, 1996, pp. 175–195; see also Hague et al., 1998, pp. 36–7.
18. Although the term 'third way' was revitalised by Giddens in the late 1990s, various political movements and various political persuasions have long used the idea of 'third way' as a political ideology. In this sense the Islamist leader

N. Erbakan coined his economic policies as *Adil Düzen* (Just Order) and claimed that it benefited from the good sides of communism and capitalism and left their undesired sides out. There are some parallels between the 'third way' as Giddens (see 1998, 2000) described it and the WP's *Adil Düzen* as Erbakan formulated it. But the differences are definitely more numerous than similarities. Erbakan's *Adil Düzen* exhibited some confused thinking and had very little chance to be implemented. The reader may wish to consult Giddens, 1998 and 2000 for the 'third way' and Akgül, 1997a and 1997b and Çakır, 1994, pp. 131–49 for *Adil Düzen* and its critique.

BIBLIOGRAPHY

Abrahamin, E., 1991, 'Khomeini: Fundamentalist or Populist?', *New Left Review*, 186, pp. 102–19.

Abramson, J.B., Arterton, F.C. and Orren, G.R., 1988, *The Electronic Commonwealth: The Impact of New Media Technologies on Democratic Politics*, Basic Books Inc, New York.

Acer, F., 1994, 'Bireyleraras Iliskiler ve Cinsiyet Rolleri', in *Dunya'da ve Turkiye'de Guncel Sosyolojik Gelismeler* (1. Ulusal Sosyoloji Kongresi, Sosyoloji Dernegi Yayinleri III, Ankara), pp. 313–24.

Ahmad, F., 1977, *The Turkish Experiment in Democracy 1950–1975*, C. Hurst & Company, London.

—— 1993, *The Making of Modern Turkey*, Routledge, London.

Akbar, A., 1992, *Islam, Globalisation, and Postmodernity*, Routledge, London.

Akçam, T, 1994, *Islam'da Hosgoru ve Siniri* [Tolerance and its Limits in Islam], Basak Yayinlari, Ankara.

Akgül, A., 1997a, *Adil Düzen ve Türkiye nin Geleceği* [Just Order and Turkey's Future], Burak Yayıncılık, Elazığ.

—— 1997b, *Dünyanın Değişimi ve Erbakan Devrimi* [The Changing World and Erbakan's Revolution], Burak Yayıncılık, Elazığ.

Akşit, B., 1991, 'Islamic Education in Turkey: Medrese Reform in Late Ottoman Times and Imam-Hatip Schools in the Republic', in R. Tapper (ed.), *Islam in Modern Turkey*, I.B.Tauris, London.

Almond, G.A., 1974, *Comparative Politics Today: A World View*, Little, Brown and Company, Boston.

Alpay, S., 1999, 'West to the Left, Turkey to the Right', *Milliyet*, 20 April, p. 20.

ANKARA, 1991 (Türk Hava Kurumu Basımevi İşletmeciliği, Ankara).

Arber, S., 1994, 'The Research Process', in N. Gilbert (ed.) *Researching Social Life*, Sage Publications, London.

Ashford, D., 1972, *Ideology and Participation*, Sage Publications, London/Beverly Hills.

Atabek, E., 1996, '*Refah Sendromunu Aşmak*...' [Overcoming the Syndrome of Welfare Party], *Cumhuriyet*, 8 January 1996.

Ateş, T., 1995, *Ne oldu bize?* [What Has Happened to Us?], Çınar Yayınları, Istanbul.

Atkinson, P. and Hammersley, M., 1994, 'Ethnography and Participant Observation', in N.K. Denzin and Y.S. Lincoln (eds), *Handbook of Qualitative Research*, Sage Publications, London.

Ayata, A., 1994, 'Geleneksel ve Modern Dayanışma' [Traditional and Modern Solidarity], 1. Ulusal Sosyoloji Kongresi (Sosyoloji Derneğ yayıları III, Ankara), pp. 325–41.

Ayata, S., 1993, 'The Rise of Islamic Fundamentalism and Its Institutional Framework' in A. Eralp et al. (eds), *The Political and Socioeconomic Transformation of Turkey*, Greenwood Press.

—— 1997, 'Patronage, Party, and State: The Politicisation of Islam in Turkey', *Middle East Journal*, 51(1), pp. 40–57.

Baharoğlu, D., 1993, 'Forced Moves and Chosen Moves: Residential Mobility in Ankara, Turkey', unpublished PhD thesis in Urban Studies, University of Kent at Canterbury.

Barkey, H., 1996, 'Turkey, Islamic Politics, and the Kurdish Question', *World Policy Journal*, Spring, pp. 43–52.

Barkey, J.H., 2005, 'Turkey and Iraq: The Perils (and Prospects) of Proximity', United States Institutes of Peace Special Report 14 July 2005, available at www.usip.org/publications/turkey-and-iraq-perils-and-prospects-proximity, (accessed 10 April 2014).

Barnes, S. and Kaase, M., 1979, *Political Action: Mass Participation in Five Western Democracies*, Sage Publications, London/Beverly Hills.

Barnes, S., Farah, B. and Heunks, F., 1979, 'Personal Dissatisfaction', in S. Barnes and M. Kaase (eds), *Political Action: Mass Participation in Five Western Democracies*, Sage Publications, London/Beverly Hills, pp. 381–409.

Beaumont, P., 2011, 'Political Islam Poised to Dominate the New World Bequeathed by Arab Spring', *Guardian*, 3 December 2011.

Bell, W. and Boat, M.D., 1957, 'Urban Neighbourhoods and Informal Social Relations', *American Journal of Sociology*, LXII, pp. 391–398.

Bello, W., 1994, *Dark Victory*, Pluto Press, London.

Benin, J. and Stork, J., 1997, *Political Islam: Essays from Middle East Report*, I.B.Tauris, London.

Berberoğlu, E., 1999, '28 Şubat blokları ve MHP nin Şansı' [The Blocs of 28 February and NOP's Chance], *Hürriyet*, 29 April 1999.

Berger, S., 1994, *The British Labour Party and the German Social Democrats, 1900–193*, Clarendon Press, Oxford.

Berkes, N., 1964, *The Development of Secularism in Turkey*, McGill University Press, Canada.

Berry, D., 1970, *The Sociology of Grass Roots Politics*, Macmillan, St Martin's Press, London.

Bibby, J.F., 1987, *Politics, Parties and Elections in America*, Nelson-Hall, Chicago.

Bina, C., 1994, 'Towards a New World Order: US Hegemony, Client States and the Islamic Alternative' in H. Mutalib and T. Hashmi (eds), *Muslims and the Modern State*, St Martin's Press, New York.

Birand, M.A., 2001, '*Washington, Ankara' nın gözyaşına bakmıyor*' [Washington Does Not Pity Ankara's Weeping], *Milliyet*, 21 July 2001.

Blair, T., 2000, Speech marking the Labour Party's 100th anniversary. Quoted in the *Guardian*, Saturday 26 February 2000.

Blondel, J., 1978, *Political Parties: A Genuine Case for Discontent?*, Wildwood House, London.

Boratav, K., 1990, 'Inter-Class and Intra-Class Relations of Distribution under "Structural Adjustment": Turkey during the 1980s', in T. Aricanli and D. Rodrik (eds), *The Political Economy of Turkey*, Macmillan/St Martin's Press, London, pp. 199–230.

Bulliet, R.W., 1993, 'The Israeli–PLO Accord: The Future of the Islamic Movement', *Foreign Affairs*, 72(5), pp. 38–44.

Burke, E. and Lapidus, I.M. (eds), 1988, *Islam, Politics and Social Movements*, I.B.Tauris, London.

Butler, D., 1952, *The British General Elections of 1951*, Macmillan, London.

Butler, D. and Kavanagh, D., 1992, *The British General Elections of 1992*, Macmillan, London/Basingstoke.

Butler, D. and Stokes D., 1974, *Political Change in Britain: Evolution of Electoral Choice*, Macmillan, London.

Çakır, R., 1990, *Ayet ve Sologan: Türkiye de İslami Oluşumlar*, Metis Yayınları, Istanbul.

—— 1994, *Ne Şeriat Ne Demokrasi*, Metis Yayinlari, Istanbul.

—— 1998a, 'FP Gerçekten değiştimi?' ['Has the VP really changed?'], *Milliyet*, 3 September 1998.

—— 1998b, 'The NAP after Türkeş', *Milliyet*, 29 September 1998.

Çalışlar, O., 1995, *RP Nerden Nereye* [WP From Where to Where], Pencere Yayınları, Istanbul.

Çam, S., 1999, 'Job Security, Unionisation, Wages and Privatisation: A Case Study in the Turkish Cement Industry', *The Sociological Review*, 47(4), pp. 695–714.

Campo, E.J., 1995, 'Hegemonic Discourse and the Islamic Question in Egypt', *Contention*, 4(3), pp. 167–94.

Caplan, L. (ed.), 1987, *Studies in Religious Fundamentalism*, State University of New York Press, Albany.

Çarkoğlu, A. and Kalaycıoğlu, E., 2007, *Turkish Democracy Today Elections, Protest and Stability in an Islamic Society*, I.B.Tauris, London.

Castells, M., 1976, 'Theoretical Propositions for an Experimental Study of Urban Social Movements', in C.G. Pickvance (ed.), *Urban Sociology: Critical Essays*, Tavistock Publications, London, pp. 147–73.

—— 1977, *The Urban Question: A Marxist Approach*, Edward Arnold Ltd, London.

Çetinkaya, H., 1996a, *Din Baronuunun Kazları* [The Goose of the Baron of Religion], Çağdaş Yayınları, Istanbul.

—— 1996b, 'RP den Korkulurmu' [Should We Be Scared of WP?], *Cumhuriyet*, 30 January 1996.

Clarke, H.D., Kornberg, A., Ellis, F. and Rapkin, J., 2000, 'Not For Fame or Fortune: A Note on Membership and Activity in the Canadian Reform Party', *Party Politics*, 6(1), pp. 75–93.

COGİTO, 1994, *Laiklik* [Secularisation], Summer 1994.

Collins, 1992, *Softback English Dictionary*, HarperCollins Publishers, Glasgow.

Cord, R.L. et al, 1974, *Political Science: An Introduction*, Appleton-Century-Crotts, New York.

Crewe, I., 1985, 'Introduction: Electoral Change in Western Democracies: A Framework For Analysis', in I. Crewe and D. Denver (eds), *Electoral Change in Western Democracies: Patterns and Sources of Electoral Volatility*, Croom Helm, London.

Crotty, J. William, 1971, 'Party Effort and Its Impact on the Vote', *American Political Science Review*, 65, pp. 439–50.

Croty, 1973 *Political Parties and Political Behavior*, Allyn & Bacon, Boston.

Crotty, W. and Jacobson, G., 1980, *American Parties in Decline*, Little, Brown and Company, Boston.

Cumhuriyet (Istanbul daily), 1982, 26 January.

Dalton, R., 1988, *Citizen Politics in Western Democracies*, Chatham House Publishers, New Jersey.

Dalton, R., Beck, P.A. and Flanagan, S.C., 1984, 'Electoral Change in Advanced Industrial Democracies', in R. Dalton, P.A. Beck and S.C. Flanagan (eds), *Electoral Change in Advanced Industrial Democracies*, Princeton University Press, New Jersey.

Dalton, R. and Kuechler, M., 1990, *Challenging the Political Order: New Social and Political Movements in Western Democracies*, Oxford University Press, New York.

Dalton, R., MacAllister, I. and Wattenberg, M.P., 2000, *Parties Without Partisans: Political Change in Advanced Industrial Societies*, Oxford University Press, Oxford.

Danielson, N. and Keleş, R., 1985, *The Politics of Rapid Urbanisation: Government and Growth in Modern Turkey*, Holmes & Meier, Teaneck, NJ.

Darnton, J., 1995, 'Uneasy Crossroads – A Special Report; Discontent Seethes in Once-Stable Turkey', *New York Times*, 2 March.

Dawson, R.E. and Prewitt K., 1969, *Political Socialization*, Little, Brown and Company, Boston.

Delibaş, D., 2011, 'The Collapse of the Turkish Party System and Its Effects on the Perceptions of Citizenship and the Legitimacy of Governance in Turkey', in I. Pardo and G.B. Prato (eds), *Citizenship and the Legitimacy of Governance in the Mediterranean Region: A Comparative Anthropology*, Ashgate Publishers, Aldershot.

Delibas, K., 1996, 'Socio-economic Analysis of Islamic Movement in Turkey: The Emergence and Rise of Islamic Movement', unpublished MA thesis, submitted to the University of Kent at Canterbury, Department of Sociology.

Della Porta, D., H. Kriesi and D. Rucht, 1999, (eds.), *Social Movement in a Globalizing World*, Macmillan, New York.

Demir, E., 1994, '1980 Sonrasi Turkiye'de Uygulanan Ekonomik Politikalarin Kent Emekci Ailelerinin Gecim Stratejileri Uzerine Etkisi', in *Dunya'da ve Turkiye'de Guncel Sosyolojik Gelismeler* (1. Ulusal Sosyoloji Kongresi, (Sosyoloji Dernegi Yayinleri III, Ankara), pp. 357–67.

Demirer, Y., 1998, *Türkiye İslamını Anlamak* [Understanding Turkey's Islam], Öteki Yayınevi, Ankara.

Denzin, N.K. and Lincoln, Y.S., 1994, *Handbook of Qualitative Research*, Sage Publications, London.

Deutsch, K.W., 1963, 'Social Mobilisation and Political Development', in H. Eckstein and D.E. Apter (eds), *Comparative Politics*, Free Press of Glencoe, New York, pp. 582–603.

—— 1970, *Politics and Government*, Houghton Mifflin Company, Boston.

Devine, F., 1995, 'Qualitative Methods', in D. Marsh and S. Gerry (eds), *Theory and Methods in Political Science*, Macmillan Press.

Di Palma, G., 1970, *Apathy and Participation*, The Free Press, New York.

Diani, M. and Porta, D., 1999, *Social Movements: An Introduction*, Blackwell Publishers, Oxford.

DIE, 1993, Genel Nufus Sayımı (Census of Population) 1990, State Institute of Statistics, Printing Division, October 1993, Ankara.

DIE, 1994, *Türkiye Istatistik Yıllığı* (1994 Statistical Yearbook of Turkey), State Institute of Statistics, Printing Division, February 1995, Ankara.

Dıjık, C. van and Groot, A.H. de, 1995, *State and Islam*, Leiden: Research School CNWS publications, v.31.

Dodd, C.H., 1969, *Politics and Government in Turkey*, Manchester University Press, Manchester.

—— 1990, *The Crisis of Turkish Democracy*, The Eothen Press.

Donat, Y., 1998, '*Fazilet 'te 'orta yol' arayışı*' [The VP Searches for 'Middle Way'], *Sabah*, 11 July.

Dowse, E.R. and Hughes, J.A., 1986, *Political Sociology*, John Wiley & Sons, UK.

Drummond, A., 2002, 'Electoral Volatility and Party Decline in Western Europe: 1970–1995', *The Centre for the Study of Democracy Research Paper Series in Empirical Democratic Theory* CSDO2–02, available at http://escholarship.org/uc/item/30m7720n#page-5, (last accessed 10 April 2014).

Dülger, I., 1987, 'Turkiye'de Sehirde Yasayan Kadinin Siyasi Haklarini Kullanma Egilimleri', DPT, Ankara.

Duman, D., 1997, *Demokrasi Sürecinde Türkiyede Islamcılık* [Islamism in the Process of Democracy in Turkey], Dokuz Eylül Yayınları, İzmir.

Duverger, M., 1964, *Political Parties: Their Organisation and Activity in the Modern State*, Methuen & Co. Ltd, London.

Dymond, J., 2002, 'Pro-European landmark victory in Turkey' *The Observer*, Istanbul Sunday August 4, 2002.

Ecevit, B., 1979, *Democracy and Development in Turkey*, The Eothen Press.

—— 1999, *'14.* Kuruluş Yıldönümü nedeniyle 28 Kasım 1999'da yaptıkları konuşmanın metni [Ecevit's speech for the 14th anniversary of the DLP on 28 November 1999], available at www.dsp.gov.tr/tarihcemiz_htm, page no longer available.

The Economist, 2001, 'Turkey's Real Crisis', 15 May, available at www.economist.com/node/623158, (last accessed 18 February 2014).

Eickelman, D. and Piscatori, J., 1996, *Muslim Politics*, Princeton University Press, Princeton.

Ekşi, A., 1995, *Din Devletleri* [States of Religion], Ümit Yayıncılık, Ankara.

Epstein, L., 1967, *Political Parties in Western Democracies*, Pall Mall Press, London.

Eralp, A., Tünay, M. and Yeşilada, B., 1993, *The Political and Socio-economic Transformation of Turkey*, Praeger, London.

Erbakan, N., 1975, *Milli Görüş* [National View], Dergah Yayinlari, Istanbul.

Erder, N., 1999, *Turkiyede Siyasi Parti Secmenleri ve Toplum Duzeni* [The Social Structure and Electorates of the Political Parties in Turkey], TÜSES Vakfı, Boyut Matbaacılık, Istanbul.

Ergüder, Ü., 1991, 'The Motherland Party, 1983–1989', in M. Heper and J.M. Landau (eds), *Political Parties and Democracy in Turkey*, I.B.Tauris, London.

Erkan, A., 2008, Siyasi Partiler ve Hazine Yardimlari, Bütçe Dünyası, Cilt 3 Sayı 28 Kış, available at www.butce.org/Html/dergi/28/aerkan.pdf, (last accessed 30 May 2012).

Erman, T., 1998, 'Becoming "Urban" or Remaining "Rural": The Views of Turkish Rural-to-Urban Migration on the "Integration" Question', *Int. J. Middle East Studies*, 30, pp. 541–61.

Esposito, J., 1983, *Voices of Resurgent Islam*, Oxford University Press, Oxford.

—— 1995, *The Islamic Threat: Myth or Reality?*, Oxford University Press, Oxford.

Esposito, J. and Voll, J.O., 1996, *Islam and Democracy*, Oxford University Press, Oxford.

Farrell, D.M and Webb, P., 1999, 'Political Parties as Campaign Organizations', available at http://195.130.87.21:8080/dspace/bitstream/123456789/564/1/Political%20Parties%20as%20Campaign%20Organizations.pdf, (last accessed 10 April 2014).

Farah, B., Barnes, S. and Heunks, F., 1979, 'Political Dissatisfaction', in S. Barnes and M. Kaase., *Political Action: Mass Participation in Five Western Democracies*, Sage Publications, London/Beverly Hills, pp. 409–49.

Fazilet Partisi, 1998, *TÜZÜĞÜ* [The VP's Constitution], Semih Ofset Matbaacılık Yayıncılık, Ankara.

Fazilet Partisi, 1998, *Halkla İlişkiler Nedir* [Public Relations?], Ankara.

Feroz, A., 1977, *The Turkish Experiment in Democracy, 1950–1975*, Hurst, for Royal Institute of International Affairs, London.

Fielding, N., 1994, 'Ethnography', in N. Gilbert (ed.), *Researching Social Life*, Sage Publications, London, pp. 154–72.

Flanagan, S.C., 1987, 'Value Change in Industrial Society', *American Political Science Review*, 81, pp. 1303–19.

Fontana, A. and Frey, J.H., 1994, 'Interviewing. The Art of Science', in N.K. Denzin and Y.S. Lincoln (eds), *Handbook of Qualitative Research*, Sage, Thousand Oaks/London.

Frendreis, J.P., Gibson, J.L. and Vertz, L.L., 1990, 'The Electoral Relevance of Local Party Organizations', *American Political Science Review*, 84(1), pp. 225–35.

Frey, F.W., 1965, *The Turkish Political Elite*, The M.I.T. Press, Massachusetts.

Fukuyama, F., 1989, 'The End of History?', *The National Interest*, 16 (Winter), pp. 3–18.

—— 1992, *The End of History and the Last Man*, Penguin Books, London.

Füredi, F., 1995, 'The Moral Condemnation of the South', Presented to BISA Conference, Southampton.

—— 1996, 'The Panic about Islam', *Impact International*, 26(2), February, pp. 12–13.

Gellner, E., 1992, *Postmodernism, Reason and Religion*, Routledge, London and New York.

General election turnout 1945–2010 (UK), available at www.ukpolitical.info/Turnout45.htm, (last accessed 10 April 2014).

Geyikdağı, M.Y., 1984, *Political Parties in Turkey: The Role of Islam*, Prager, New York.

Giddens, A., 1993, *Sociology* (2nd edn), Polity Press, Cambridge.

—— 1998, *The Third Way: The Renewal of Social Democracy*, Polity Press, Cambridge.

—— 2000, *The Third Way and Its Critics*, Polity Press, Cambridge.

Giles, M.W. and Dantico, M.K., 1982, 'Political Participation and Neighbourhood Social Context Revisited', *American Journal of Political Science*, 26(1), pp. 144–9.

Gologlu, M., 1982, *Demokrasiye Geçiş 1946–1950* [Transition to Democracy 1946–1950], Kaynak Yayınları, Istanbul.

Gökçe, B., 1994, 'Gecekondularda Ailelerarası Geleneksel Dayanışmanın Çağdaş Organizasyonlara Dönüşümü' [The Transformation of Traditional Interfamily Solidarity into the Contemporary Organisations in the *Gecekondus*] 1. Ulusal Sosyoloji Kongresi (Sosyoloji Derneğ yayıları III, Ankara) pp. 283–8.

—— 1996, *Türkiyenin Toplumsal Yapısı ve Toplumsal Kurumlar* [Social Institutions and The Structure of Turkish Society], Şavaş Yayınevi, Ankara.

Göle, N., 1991, *Modern Mahrem* [Modern Veil], Metis Yayinlari, Istanbul.

—— 1996, 'Authoritarian Secularism and Islamist Politics: The Case of Turkey', in A.R. Norton (ed.) *Civil Society in the Middle East*, E.J. Brill, New York.

—— 1997, 'Secularism and Islamism in Turkey: The Making of Elites and Counter-Elites', *Middle East Journal*, 51(1), pp. 46–57.

—— 2000, *İslam ve Modernlik Üzerine Melez Desenler*, Metis Yayınları, Istanbul.
Gülalp, H., 1995, 'Islam and Postmodernism,' *Contention*, 4(2) (Winter), pp. 59–70.
Gün Dem, 2001 *Cumhuriyet Halk Prtısı Haftalık Yayın Organı (The Weekly News Bulletin of the RPP)* 51–2, 22 January 2001.
Güneş-Ayata, A., 1984, 'Participation and Organisation in Local Politics: A Comparative Study of Class and Clientele in Two Small Towns [in Turkey]', unpublished PhD thesis, University of Kent at Canterbury.
—— 1990, 'Class and Clienteles in the Republican People's Party', in A. Finkel and N. Sirmen (eds), *Turkish State, Turkish Society*, Routledge, London.
—— 1991, 'Gecekondularda Kimlik Sorunu ve Dayanışma Örüntüleri ve Hemşhrilik' [Problem of Identity and Organisations Solidarity in Shanty Towns and Hemşhrilik], *Toplum ve Bilim* 1991 51–2.
—— 1994, 'Roots and trends of clientelism in Turkey', in L. Roniger and A. Günes-Ayata (eds), *Democracy, Clientelism, and Civil Society*, Lynne Rienner Publishers, Boulder.
Günışığında Türkiye, 1999, 18 *Nisan Seçim Beyannamesi* [Turkey under Sunlight, The Election Manifesto of 18 April 1999], pp. 38–9.
Güvenç, B., Şaylan, G., Tekeli, İ. and Turan, Ş., 1994, *Türk İslam Sentezi* [Turkish Islamic Synthesis], Sarmal Yayınevi, Istanbul.
Hadar, L.T., 1993, 'What Green Peril?', *Foreign Affairs*, 72(2), pp. 27–42.
Hague, R., Harrop, M. and Breslin, S., 1998, *Comparative Government and Politics*, Macmillan Press Ltd, London.
Hale, W., 1981, *The Political And Economic Development of Modern Turkey*, Croom Helm, London.
—— 1994, *Turkish Politics and the Military*, Routledge, London.
Hall, D. and Hall, I., 1996, *Practical Social Research*, Macmillan.
Halliday, F., 1995a, 'Fundamentalism and the Contemporary World', *Contention: Debates in Society, Culture, and Science*, 4(2), pp. 41–58.
—— 1995b, 'Review Article: The Politics of "Islam"– A Second Look', *British Journal of Political Science*, 25, pp. 399–417.
—— 1996, *Islam and the Myth of Confrontation*, I.B.Tauris, London.
Hamel, P., 1995, 'Collective Action and the Paradigm of Individualism', in L. Maheu (ed.), *Social Movements and Social Classes*, Sage, London.
Hart, W.M., 1969, *Zeytinburnu Gecekondu Bölgesi*, Istanbul Ticaret Odası Yayınları, Istanbul.
Hasan, C., 2001, 'Siyasette Tayyip Erdoğan rüzgarı' [The Wind of Tayyip Erdoğan in Politics], *Milliyet*, 21 July.
Haynes, J., 1993, *Religion in Third World Countries*, Open University Press, Buckingham.
Heper, M., 1982, 'The Plight of Urban Migrants: Dynamics of Service Procurement in a Squatter Area', in Ç. Kagıtcıbaşı (ed.), *Sex Roles, Family and Community in Turkey*, Indiana University Turkish Studies 3 USA, pp. 249–67.

—— 1985, *The State Tradition in Turkey*, The Golden Press.

—— 1997, 'Islam and Democracy in Turkey: Toward a Reconciliation?' in *Middle East Journal*, 51(1), pp. 32–45.

Heper, M. and Demirer, T., 1996, 'The Press and the Consolidation of Democracy in Turkey, *Middle East Studies* (Special Edition: Turkey: Identity, Democracy, Politics), pp. 109–23.

Heper, M. and Keyman, F., 1998, 'Double-Faced State: Political Patronage and the Consolidation of Democracy in Turkey' *Middle Eastern Studies*, 34(4), pp. 259–77.

Heper, M. and Landau, J.M., 1991, *Political Parties and Democracy in Turkey*, I.B.Tauris, London.

Herrnson, P.S., 1986, 'Do Parties Make a Difference? The Role of Party Organisations in Congressional Elections', *The Journal of Politics*, 48, pp. 589–615

Heywood, A., 1997, *Politics*, Macmillan.

Hinderik, J. and Kiray, M., 1970, *Social Stratification as an Obstacle to Development*, Praeger Publishers, London.

Hirst, P. and Thompson, G., 1996, *Globalisation in Question*, Polity Press, Cambridge.

Huckfeldt, R. and Sprague, J., 1992, 'Political Parties and Electoral Mobilization: Political Structure, Social Structure, and the Party Canvass', *American Political Science Review*, 86(1), pp. 70–86.

Huckshorn, R.J., 1984, *Political Parties in America*, Brooks/Cole Publishing Company, California.

Hunter, S., 1995, 'Turkey at the Crossroads: Islamic Past or European Future?', CEPS Paper No. 63, Centre for European Policy Studies, Brussels.

Huntington, S., 1994, 'The Clash of Civilisations?' *Foreign Affairs* (Summer), pp. 22–49.

—— 1998, *The Clash of Civilizations and the Remaking of World Order*, Touchstone Books, London.

Hürriyet (Istanbul daily), 1999, 'The Big Success Surprised the NAP too', 21 April.

İnalcık, H., 1993, *The Middle East and the Balkans under the Ottoman Empire: Essays on Economy and Society*, Indiana University, Bloomington.

Inglehart, R., 1977, *The Silent Revolution*, Princeton University Press.

—— 1997, *Modernization and Postmodernization: Cultural, Economic and Political Change in 43 Societies*, Princeton University Press, Princeton: New Jersey.

Inglehart, R., and Klingemann, H.D., 1979, 'Ideological Conceptualisation and Value Priorities' in S. Barnes and M. Kaase, *Political Action: Mass Participation in Five Western Democracies*, Sage Publications, London/Beverly Hills.

Isleyen, E., 1999, '*Yeni secmenin yarisi MHP ye oy atti*' [Half of the New Electorate Voted for the NAP], *Sabah*, 19 April.

Jacobson, G., 1997, *The Politics of Congressional Elections*, Longman, New York.

Jennings, M.K, Allerbeck, K.R. and Rosenmayr, L., 1979, 'Generations and Families: General Orientation', in S. Barnes and M. Kaase, *Political Action:*

Mass Participation in Five Western Democracies, Sage Publications, London/ Beverly Hills, pp. 449–78.

Jones, B., Kavanagh, D., Moran, M. and Norton, P. (eds), 1998, *Politics UK*, Prentice Hall, London.

Juergensmeyer, M., 1993, *The New Cold War*, University of California Press, Berkeley.

Kabasakal, M., 1991, *Turkiyede Siyasal Parti Orgutlenmesi* [Political Party Organisation in Turkey] (1908–1960), Tekin Yayınevi, Istanbul.

Kahveci, E., Nadir, S., Nichols, T., 1996, *Work and Occupation in Modern Turkey*, Mansell, London.

Kalaycıoğlu, E., 1994, 'Elections and Party Preferences in Turkey: Changes and Continuities in the 1990s', *Comparative Political Studies*, 27(3), pp. 402–24.

—— 1996, 'Turkey's New Beginning Turns into a False Dawn', *Guardian*, 7 August.

—— 1997, 'The Logic of Contemporary Turkish Politics', *Middle East Review of International Affairs*, 1(3), September.

—— 1998, 'The Changing Party System in Turkey: Party Preferences, Parties and the System in Transition', Paper presented in London, as part of a lecture series organised by SOAS. University of London, 20 March.

Karabell, Z., 1996, 'Fundamental Misconceptions: Islamic Foreign Policy', *Foreign Policy*, 105 (Winter 1996–97), pp. 77–91.

Karpat, K., 1975, 'The Politics of Transition: Political Attitudes and Party Affiliation in the Turkish Gecekondu', in E.D. Akarli and G. Ben-Dor (eds), *Political Participation in Turkey*, Bogaziçi University Publications, Istanbul, pp. 89–119.

—— 1991, 'The Republican People's Party, 1923–1945', in M. Heper and J.M. Landau (eds), *Political Parties and Democracy in Turkey*, I.B.Tauris, London.

Katz, R.S. and Mair, P., 1995, 'Changing Models of Party Organisation and Party Democracy: The Emergence of the Cartel Party,' *Party Politics*, 1, pp. 15–28.

Kavanagh, D. and Jones, B., 1998, 'Political Parties', in B. Jones, D. Kavanagh, M. Moran and P. Norton (eds), *Politics UK*, Prentice Hall, London.

Keddie, N.R., 1981, *Roots of Revolution*, Yale University Press, New Haven & London.

Keleş, R., 1971, *Eski Ankara'da Bir Şehir Tipolojisi* [The Old Ankara: A Typology of the Urban], Ankara Universitesi Siyasal Bilgiler Fakültesi Yayınları, Ankara, No. 314.

—— 1993, *Kentleşme politikası*, İmge Kitabevi, Ankara.

Kenny, C.B., 1992, 'Political Participation and Effects from the Social Environment', *American Journal of Political Science*, 36(1), pp. 259–67.

Kepel, G., 1994, *The Revenge of God*, Polity Press, Cambridge.

Keyder, Ç., 1987, *State and Class in Turkey*, Verso, London.

—— 1999, *Istanbul Between The Global and The Local*, Rowman & Littlefield, New York.

Kıray, M., 1982, 'Gecekondu: Azgelişmiş Ülkelerde Hızla Topraktan Kopma ve Kentle Bütünleşememe [Gecekondu: Rapid Displacement from the Land and Urban Integration in Underdeveloped Countries]', in M. Kıray (ed.), *Toplumbilim Yazıları*, G. Üniversitesi yayınları, Ankara.

Kışlalı, A.T., 1995, *Kemalizm, Laiklik ve Demokrasi* [Kemalism, Secularism and Democracy], Imge Kitapevi, Ankara.

Kitschelt, H, 1989, 'The Internal Polity of Parties: The Law Of Curvilinear Disparity Revisited', *Political Studies*, 37, pp. 400–21.

Klingemann, H.K., 1979, 'Ideological Conceptualisation and Political Action' in S. Barnes and M. Kaase, *Political Action: Mass Participation in Five Western Democracies*, Sage Publications, London/Beverly Hills.

Köker, L., 1990, *Modernlesme, Kemalizm ve Demokrasi*, Iletisim Yayinlari, Istanbul.

Kongar, E., 2000, *Demokrasi ve Laiklik* [Democracy and Secularisation], Remzi Kitapevi, Istanbul.

—— 2000, *21. Yuzyilda Turkiye* [Turkey in the 21st Century], Remzi Kitapevi, Istanbul.

Koray, M., 1995, *Turkiye'de Kadin*, Turkiye Sosyal Ekonomik Arastirmalar Vakfi.

Kramer, G., 1970, 'The Effects of Precinct-Level Canvassing on Voter Behaviour', *Public Opinion Quarterly*, 34, pp. 560–72.

Kriesi, H., Rucht, D., Porta, D. (eds), 1999, *Social Movements in a Globalizing World*, Macmillan/St Martin's Press, New York/Basingstoke.

Kumcu, E., 2001a, *'Çabalama kaptan bu gemi gitmiyor'* ['Leave It Captain: This ship Is Not Moving'], *Sabah*, 19 July.

—— 2001b, 'The IMF's blunder in Turkey', *Financial Times*, 12 March.

Kurdoğlu, A., 1994, 'Istanbul'un Nufus Kompozisyonu ve Hemsehrilik Dernekleri: 1944–89', in *Dunya'da ve Turkiye'de Guncel Sosyolojik Gelismeler* (1. Ulusal Sosyoloji Kongresi, Sosyoloji Dernegi Yayinleri III, Ankara), pp. 367–84.

Kürkçü, E., 1996, 'The Crisis of the Turkish State', in *Middle East Report*, Spring, pp. 2–9.

Kutan, R., 1998a, 'İlk Adım ... !' Toplantısı Açılış Konuşması [Opening speech of the 'First Step ... !' meeting), 14 May, Ankara.

——1998b *Fazilet Partisi Kızılcahamam Toplantıları* [Virtue Party Kizilcahamam Meetings], Semih Ofset Matbaacilik, Yayincilik, Ankara.

Laakso, M. and Taagepera, R., 1979, 'The "Effective" Number of Parties: A Measure with Application to West Europe', *Comparative Political Studies*, 12(1), pp. 3–29.

Landau, J., 1991, 'Political Parties and Democracy in Turkey', in M. Heper and J.M. Landau (eds), *Political Parties and Democracy in Turkey*, I.B.Tauris, London.

Lapidot, A., 1995, Islam and Nationalism: A Study of Contemporary Islamic Political Thought in Turkey, unpublished PhD thesis, University of Durham.

Leighley, J.E., 1990, 'Social Interaction and Contextual Influences on Political Participation', *American Politics Quarterly*, 18(4), pp. 459–75.
—— 1995, 'Attitudes, Opportunities and Incentives: A Field Essay on Political Participation', *Political Research Quarterly*, 48, pp. 181–209.
Leiserson A., 1958, *Parties and Politics: An Institutional and Behavioral Approach*, Alfred and Knopf, New York.
Lerner, D., 1958, *The Passing of Traditional Society: Modernising the Middle East*, The Free Press, New York.
Levi, A., 1991, 'The Justice Party, 1961–1980', in M. Heper and J.M. Landau (eds), *Political Parties and Democracy in Turkey*, I.B.Tauris, London.
Lewis, B., 1974, *Islam: Politics and War* Vol. I, Harper Torchbooks, New York.
—— 1988, *The Political Language of Islam*, University of Chicago Press, Chicago.
—— 1990, 'The Roots of Muslim Rage', *Atlantic Monthly*, September, pp. 47–60.
Lijphart, A., 1984, *Democracies: Patterns of Majoritarian and Consensus Government in Twenty-One Countries*, Yale University Press, New Haven.
Lipset, S.M. and Mair, P., 1994, 'Party Organizations: From Civil Society to the State', in S.K. Richard and P. Mair, *How Parties Organize*, Sage Publications, London.
MacAllister, I., Johnston, R.J., Pattie, C.J., Tunstall, H., Dorling, D.F.L. and Rossiter, D.J., 2001, 'Class Dealignment and Neighbourhood Effect: Miller Revisited', *British Journal of Political Science*, 31, pp. 41–59.
Mair, P., 1994, 'Party Organizations: From Civil Society to the State', in R. Katz and P. Mair, *How Parties Organize*, Sage Publications, London.
—— 1997, *Party System Change, Approaches and Interpretations*, Clarendon Press, Oxford.
Mango, A., 1991, 'The Social Democratic Populist Party, 1983–1989', in M. Heper and J.M. Landau (eds), *Political Parties and Democracy in Turkey*, I.B.Tauris, London.
Maor, M., 1997, *Political Parties and Party Systems*, London: Routledge.
Mardin, Ş., 1973, 'Centre–Periphery Relations: A Key to Turkish Politics?', *Daedalus*, 102(1), pp. 169–91.
—— 1982, *Ideoloji*, Turhan Kitapevi, Ankara.
—— 1991, *Turkiye'de din ve siyaset* [Religion and politics in Turkey], *Makaleler 3*, İletişim, Istanbul.
—— 1995, Turkiye'de din ve siyaset [Religion and politics in Turkey], Makaleler 3, İletişim, Istanbul.
Margulies, R. and Yıldızoğlu, E., 1997, 'The Resurgence of Islam and the Welfare Party in Turkey', in J. Benin and J. Stork (eds), *Political Islam*, I.B.Tauris, London.
Marsh, A., 1990, *Political Action in Europe and the USA*, Macmillan Press, Hong Kong.
Marsh, D. and Stoker, G., 1995, *Theory and Methods in Political Science*, Macmillan Press.

Marty, M.E., 1995, 'Comparing Fundamentalisms', *Contention*, 4(2), pp. 19–39.

Marty, M.E. and Appleby, R.S., 1993, 'Introduction: A Sacred Cosmos, Scandalous Code, Defiant Society', in M.E. Marty and R.S. Appleby (eds), *Fundamentalism and Society*, University of Chicago Press, Chicago.

—— 1994a, *Fundamentalism Observed*, University of Chicago Press, Chicago.

—— 1994b, *Accounting for Fundamentalism: The Dynamic Character of Movements*, University of Chicago Press, Chicago.

Marx, K., 1976, *Capital* Volume 1, Penguin Books.

May, D., 1973, 'Opinion Structure of Political Parties: The Special Law of Curvilinear Disparity', *Political Studies*, 21, pp. 135–51.

Metiner, M., 1994, "RP'nin Yeni Söylemi üzerine," [On the New Discourse of the WP] Yeni Zemin sayi 11, Kasim [number:11 Nowebmer] 1994.

Micaud, A.C., 1975, 'French Political Parties: Ideological Myths and Social Realities', in S. Neumann (ed.), *Modern Political Parties*, University of Chicago Press, Chicago/London.

Michael, G. et al., 1982, 'Political Participation and Neighbourhood Social Context Revisited', *American Journal of Political Science*, 26(1), February, pp. 144–49.

Milbrath, L.W. and Goel, M.L., 1977, *Political Participation*, Rand McNally College Publishing Company, Chicago.

Miller, J., 1993, 'The Challenge of Radical Islam', *Foreign Affairs*, 72(2), pp. 43–56.

Milliyet, 1999, *'Secime metropoller damga vuracak'* [The Elections Will Be Decided by the Metropolises], 7 January, Ersan Atar, Ankara.

Milliyet, 1999, *Varoşlarda seçim savaşı-1 Varoşa özel' taktikler* [Election war at the shanty towns 'Special tactics for shanty towns'], (22 January, 1999), Murat Sabuncu.

Milliyet, 2002, *Erken Seçimin maliyeti daha az,* 24 May.

Minkenberg, M. and Inglehart, R., 1992, 'Neoconservatism and Value Change in the USA', in J Gibbins (ed.), *Contemporary Political Culture Policies in a Post-modern Age*, Sage, London.

Moussalli, A., 1998, *Islamic Fundamentalism, Myths & Realities*, Ithaca Press, Lebanon.

Muller, C.W., 1994, 'The Development of Austrian Party Organisation in the Post-war Period', in S.K. Richard and P. Mair, *How Parties Organize*, Sage Publications, London.

Mumcu, U., 1996, *Rabita*, um:ag Vakfi Yayınları, Ankara.

Munson, H. Jr, 1995, 'Not all Crustaceans are Crabs: Reflections on the Comparative Study of Fundamentalism and Politics', *Contention*, 4(3), pp. 151–66.

Nelson, J.M., 1979, *Access to Power: Politics and the Urban Poor in Developing Countries*, Princeton University Press, Princeton.

Neumann, S., 1963, *Modern Political Parties: Approaches to Comparative Politics*, University of Chicago Press, Chicago.

Nichols, K., 1996, 'Introduction', in E. Kahveci, S. Nadir and T. Nichols (eds), *Work and Occupation in Modern Turkey*, Mansell, London.

Orren, G.R., 1982, 'The Changing Styles of American Party Politics', in Joel L. Fleishman (ed.), *The Future of American Political Parties*, Englewood Cliffs, Prentice Hall.

Öğütcü, M., 1994, 'Islam and the West: Can Turkey Bridge the Gap?', *Futures*, 26(8), pp. 811–29.

Öniş, Z., 1997, 'The Political Economy of Islamic resurgence in Turkey: the rise of the Welfare Party in perspective', *Third World Quarterly*, 18(4), pp. 743–66.

Öniş, Z. and Webb, S.B., 1993, 'Turkey: Democratisation and Adjustment From Above', in S.B. Webb and S. Haggard (eds), *Voting for Reform: Democracy, Political Liberalisation and Economic Adjustment*, pp. 128–84, Oxford University Press, New York.

Özbudun, E., 1976, *Social Change and Political Participation in Turkey*, Princeton University Press, New Jersey.

—— 1996, 'Turkey: How Far From Consolidation?', *Journal of Democracy*, 7(3), pp. 123–38.

—— 2000, *Contemporary Turkish Politics: Challenges to Democratic Consolidation*, Lynne Rienner Publishers, London.

Özdalga, E., 1997, 'A Secularism in Need of Secularisation', *TASG News*, November, pp. 21–3.

Özdemir, N., 1999, 'The Transformation of Squatter Settlements into Authorised Apartment Blocks: A Case Study of Ankara, Turkey', unpublished PhD thesis submitted to the University of Kent at Canterbury, Urban Studies.

Özer, I., 1994, 'Kentlilesme ve Kent Yasami', in *Dunya'da ve Turkiye'de Guncel Sosyolojik Gelismeler* (1. Ulusal Sosyoloji Kongresi, Sosyoloji Dernegi Yayinleri III, Ankara), pp. 303–13.

Özgürel, 1998, *Fazilet Partisi nde rota Değişikliği* [The Change of Direction in the VP], *Radikal*, 23 September.

Pakulski, J., 1991, *Social Movements*, Longman, Cheshire.

—— 1995, 'Social Movements and Class: The Decline of the Marxist Paradigm', in L. Maheu (ed.), *Social Movements and Social Classes: The Future of Collective Action*, Sage Publications, pp. 55–86.

Parry, G., Moyser, G. and Day, N., 1992, *Political Participation and Democracy in Britain*, Cambridge University Press, Cambridge.

Pattie, J.C., Johnston, J.R. and Fieldhouse, A.E., 1995, 'Wining the Local Vote: The Effectiveness of Constituency Campaign Spending in Great Britain, 1983–1992', *American Political Science Review*, 89(4), pp. 969–83.

Pedersen, M.N., 1979, 'The Dynamics of European Party Systems: Changing Patterns of Electoral Volatility', *European Journal of Political Research*, 7, pp. 3–27.

Peker, M., 1996, 'Internal Migration and the Marginal Sector', in E. Kahveci, S. Nadir, and T. Nichols (eds), *Work and Occupation in Modern Turkey*, Mansell, London.

Pennings, P. and Lane, J.E., 1998, *Comparing Party System Change*, Routledge, London.

Pickvance, C.G., 1976, 'On the Study of Urban Social Movements', in C.G. Pickvance (ed.) *Urban Sociology: critical essays*, Tavistock Publications, London.

—— 1995, 'Social Movements in Transition from State Socialism: Convergence or Diversity', in L. Maheu (ed.), *Social Movements and Social Classes: The Future of Collective Action*, Sage Publications, pp. 123–46.

Piscatori, J., 1999, *Islamic Fundamentalism and the Gulf Crisis*, The Fundamentalism Project, American Academy of Arts and Sciences, Chicago.

Poyraz, E., 1996, *Refah ın Gerçek Yüzü* [The True Face of Refah], Poyraz Yayınevi, Ankara.

Price, D.E., 1999, *Islamic Political Culture, Democracy, and Human Rights: A Comparative Study*, Praeger, Westport/London.

Pulur, H., 1999, 'MHP'nin Oylari Nerden Geliyor?' [Where Do NAP's Votes Come From?], *Milliyet*, 21 April.

Pulzer, P.G.J., 1967, *Political Representation and Elections in Britain*, George Allen and Unwin Ltd, London.

Radikal (Istanbul daily), 2001, 'Özkasnak: 28 Şubat post modern darbeydi' [Özkasnak: 28 February Was Postmodern Coup], 15 January.

Rae, D.W., 1967, *The Political Consequences of Electoral Laws*, Yale University Press, New Haven.

Ramazanoğlu, H., 1985, *Turkey in the World Capitalist System*, Gower Publishing Company Ltd.

Ray, L., 1999, '"Fundamentalism", Modernity and the New Jacobins', *Economy and Society*, 28(2), pp. 198–221.

Reed, Fred A., 2003, 'In the Footsteps of Said Nursi,' *Islam at the Crossroads: On the Life and Thought of Bediüzzaman Said Nursi*. Ed. Ibrahim M. Abu-Rabi. Albany: SUNY Press, 33–44.

Riddell, P., 1998, 'State of the Parties', in B. Jones, D. Kavanagh, M. Moran and P. Norton (eds), *Politics UK*, Prentice Hall, London.

Roberts, B.R., 1995, *The Making of Citizens: Cities of Peasants Revisited*, Arnold, London.

Rootes, C., 1990, 'Theory of Social Movements: Theory for Social Movements?', *Philosophy and Social Action*, 16(4), pp. 5–17.

Rose, R., 1980, *Do Parties Make a Difference?*, Macmillan Press, London.

Roy, O., 1994, *The Failure of Political Islam*, I.B.Tauris, London.

Runciman, W.G., 1966, *Relative Deprivation and Social Justice: A Study of Attitudes to Social Inequality in Twentieth-Century England*, Routledge & K. Paul, London.

Rustow, D., 1991, 'Political Parties in Turkey: An Overview', in M. Heper and J.M. Landau (eds), *Political Parties and Democracy in Turkey*, I.B.Tauris, London.

Sabah, 2001, 'Vegiı gelirinin hepsi faize gitti' [All tax revenues went to interest repayments], 17 July.

Said, E., 1993, *Culture and Imperialism*, Random House, New York.
Salt, J., 1995, 'Nationalism and the Rise of Muslim Sentiment in Turkey', *Middle Eastern Studies*, 31(1), pp. 12–27.
Sarıbay, A.Y., 1985, *Türkiye de Modernleşme Din ve Parti polıtıkası 'MSP örnek olayı'* [Modernization, Religion and Party Politics in Turkey: 'Case of NSP'], Alan Yayincilik, Istanbul.
—— 1991, 'The Democratic Party, 1946–1960', in M. Heper and J.M. Landau (eds), *Political Parties and Democracy in Turkey*, I.B.Tauris, London.
Sartori, G., 1976, *Parties and Party Systems: A Framework for Analysis*, Cambridge University Press, Cambridge.
Savage, M., 1987, 'Understanding Political Alignment in Contemporary Britain: Do Localities Matter?', *Political Geography*, 6s, pp. 53–76
Sayarı, S., 1977, 'Political Patronage in Turkey', in E. Gellner, J. Weterbury (eds), *Patrons and Clients in Mediterranean Societies*, Duckworth, London.
—— 1996, 'Turkey's Islamist Challenge', *Middle East Quarterly*, September, pp. 35–43.
Sayarı, S., and Esmer, Y., 2002, *Parties and Elections in Turkey*, Lynne Rinner Publishers, London.
Scarrow, S.E., 1996, *Parties and their Members*, Oxford University Press, New York.
Standard & Poor's, 2001, Analysis Turkey (Republic of) Rationale 'The ratings on the Republic of Turkey are constrained by...', 20 August, available at www.standardandpoors.com.
Şaylan, G., 1992, *Türkiye de İslamcı Siyaset* [Political Islam in Turkey], V. Yayınları, Ankara.
Schenker, David, 2012, 'Arab Spring or Islamist Winter?', *World Affairs Journal*, January/February 2012, available at www.worldaffairsjournal.org/article/arab-spring-or-islamist-winter, (last accessed 10 April 2014).
Schüler, H., 1998, *Türkiye'de Sosyal Demokrasi Particilik Hemşehrilik Alevilik* [Social Demokracy, Partisanship, Hemşehrilik Alevilik in Turkey], İletişim Yayınları, Istanbul.
Scott, R. and Hrebener, R., 1984, *Parties in Crisis: Party Politics in America*, John Wiley & Sons, New York.
Selçuk, İ., 1996, *Cumhuriyet* (Istanbul), 20 January 1996.
Şen, S., 1995, *Refah Partisinin Theory ve Pratiği* [The Theory and Practice of Welfare Party], Sarmal Yayinevi, Istanbul.
Şenyapılı, T., 1978, *Bütünleşmemiş Kentler Nufus* [Un-integrated Urban Population], ODTÜ Yayını, Ankara.
—— 1982, 'Economic Change and the Gecekondu Family', in Ç. Kagıtcıbaşı (ed.), *Sex Roles, Family and Community in Turkey*, Indiana University Turkish Studies, USA, pp. 237–48.
Şerif, M., 1991, *Türkiye de Din ve Siyaset* [Religion and Politics in Turkey], İletişim Yayınevi, Istanbul.
Seyd, P. and Whiteley, P., 1992, *Labour's Grass Roots: The Politics of Party Membership*, Clarendon Press, London.

Seyyed Vali, R.N., 1995, 'A Re-examination of the Origins of Islamic Fundamentalism', *Contention*, 4(2), pp. 121–39.

Shankland, D., 1999, *Islam and Society in Turkey*, The Eothen Press.

Shaw, S., and Shaw, E.K., 1978, *History of the Ottoman Empire and Modern Turkey* (Vol. II), Cambridge University Press, Cambridge.

Shmuelevitz, A., 1996, 'Urbanisation and Voting for the Turkish Parliament', *Middle Eastern Studies*, 32(2), pp. 162–76.

Sidahmed, A.S. and Ehteshami, A., 1996, *Islamic Fundamentalism*, Westview Press, Boulder.

Soner, Y., 1999, *Milli Nizam'dan Fazilete Hangi Erbakan?*, [From National Order to Virtu [Party] Which Erbakan?], Su Yayınları, Istanbul.

Szyliowicz, J.S., 1966, *Political Change in Rural Turkey: Erdemli*, Mouton & Co, Paris.

Tachau, F., 1991, 'The Republican People's Party, 1945–1980', in M. Heper and J.M. Landau (eds), *Political Parties and Democracy in Turkey*, I.B.Tauris, London.

Tanilli, S., 1996 *İslam çağımıza yanıt verebilir mi?* [Can Islam Be the Answer for Our Century?], Çağdaş Yayınlerı, Istanbul.

Tapper, R., 1993, *Islam in Modern Turkey: Religion, Politics and Literature in a Secular State*, I.B.Tauris, London.

Taşar, M., 1997, *Refah Partisi Gerçeği* [The Reality of Welfare Party], Irmak Matbaacılık, Ankara.

Tekeli, İ., 1982, *Türkiye de Kentleşme Yazıları* [Urban Writing in Turkey], Turhan Kıtapevı, Ankara.

—— 1997, "Türkiye Bağlamında Modernite Projesi ve İslam" (ed. in) *Türk İş Yıllığı, 1990'ların Bilançosu*, Ankara, Türkiye İşçi Sendikaları Konfederasyonu.

Tekeli, Ş., 1990, 'Women in the Changing Political Associations of the 1980s', in A. Finkel and N. Sirman (eds), *Turkish State, Turkish Society*, Routledge, London.

TESEV, 2000, *Türkiye de Yeni Bir Parti Sistemine Doğru* [Towards a New Party System in Turkey], Türkiye Ekonomik ve Sosyal Etüdler Vakfı Yayinlari, Istanbul.

Toprak, B., 1987, 'The Religious Right', in I. Schick and A. Tonak (eds), *Turkey in Transition*, New York University Press, New York.

Tosun, T., 1999, *Türk Parti Sisteminde Merkez Sağ ve Solda Parçalanma* [Fragmentation at the Centre-Right and Left in the Turkish Party System], Boyut Kıtapları, Istanbul.

Totten, J.M., 2012, 'Arab Spring or Islamist Winter?', *World Affairs Journal*, January/February, available at www.worldaffairsjournal.org/article/arab-spring-or-islamist-winter, (last accessed 21 July 2012).

Touraine, A., 1981, *The Voice and the Eye. An Analysis of Social Movements*, Cambridge University Press, Cambridge.

Tunçay, M., 1981, *Türkiye Cumhuriyeti'nde TEK-PARTİ YÖNETİMİ'nin Kurulması* [The Establishment of Single Party Rule in Turkish Republic] (1923–1931), Yurt Yayınları, Ankara.

Turan, I., 1994, 'Religion and Political Culture in Turkey', in R. Tapper (ed.), *Islam in Modern Turkey*, I.B.Tauris, London.

Turan, S.G., 1995, *Koktenrefah* [Welfare Fund], Utku Yayinlari, Istanbul.

Türkiyede Kentleşme, 1971, [Urbanisation in Turkey], Mimarlar Odası Ankara Şubesi Yayını, Ankara.

Tuşalp, E., 1994, *Şeriat Aş* [Fundamentalist Co], Bilgi Yayınevi, Ankara.

TÜSES, 1999, *Türkiyede Siyasi Parti Seçmenleri ve Toplum Düzeni* [Social Structure and Political Party Voters in Turkey], Türkiye Sosyal Ekonomik Siyasal Araştırmalar Vakfı Veri Araştırma, Boyut Matbaacılık A.Ş, Istanbul.

Verba, N. and Nie, N., 1972, *Participation in America, Political Democracy and Social Equality*, Harper & Row, New York.

Verba, N., Nie, N. and Kim, J.O., 1978, *Participation and Political equality: A Seven-Nation Comparison*, The University of Chicago Press, Chicago.

Verba, N., Nie, N. and Kim, J.O., 1980, *Participation and Political Equality*, Cambridge University Press, Cambridge.

Verba, S., Schlozman, K.M., Brady, H. and Nie, N., 1993, 'Citizen Activity: Who Participates? What Do They Say?' *American Political Science Review*, 87(2), pp. 303–10.

Voll, J.O., 1994, 'Fundamentalism in the Sunny Arab World: Egypt and Sudan', in M.E. Marty and R.S. Appleby (eds), *Fundamentalism Observed*, University of Chicago Press, Chicago/London.

Walker, A., 1987, 'Fundamentalism and Modernity: The Restoration Movement in Britain', in L. Caplan (ed.), *Studies in Religious Fundamentalism*, State University of New York Press, Albany.

Walton, J. and Seddon, D., 1994, *Free Markets & Food Riots: The Politics of Global Adjustment*, Blackwell Publishers, Oxford.

Warde, A. and Savage, M. et al., 1988, 'Class, Consumption and Voting: An Ecological Analysis of Wards and Towns in the 1980 Local Elections in England', *Political Geography Quarterly*, 7, pp. 339–51.

Waterbury, J., 1977, *Patrons and Clients in Mediterranean Societies*, Duckworth, London.

Wattenberg, M., 1991, *The Rise of Candidate Centred Politics*, Harvard University Press, Massachusetts.

Weiker, W.F., 1973, *Political Tutelage and Democracy in Turkey: The Free Party and its Aftermath*, E.J. Brill, Leiden.

Whiteley P., 1995, 'Rational Choice and Political Participation – Evaluating the Debate', *Political Research Quarterly*, 48(1), pp. 211–33.

Whiteley P., Seyd P. and Richardson J., 1994, *True Blues: The Politics of Conservative Party Membership*, Clarendon Press, Oxford.

Whiteley, P. and Seyd, P., 1998, 'The Dynamics of Party Activism in Britain: A Spiral of Demobilization?', *B. Journal of Political Science*, 28, pp. 113–37.

—— 1999, 'How to Win a Landslide by Really Trying: The Effects of Local Campaigning on Voting in the British General Elections of 1997', paper presented at the panel on 'Political Parties and Democratic Choice' at the

Annual Meeting of the American Political Science Association, Atlanta Marriot Marquis and Atlanta Hilton Towers, 2–5 September 1999.

—— 2001, 'Party People', *Guardian*, 27 March 2001.

World Economic Forum, 2006, 'Full Survey: Trust in Governments, Corporations and Global Institutions Continues to Decline', available at www.weforum.org/site/homepublic.nsf/Content/Full+Survey%3A+Trust+in+Governments%2C+Corporations+and+Global+Institutions+Continues+to+Decline (last accessed 1 April 2006).

Yalçın, S., 1999, *Hangi Erbakan?* [Which Erbakan?], Su Yayınları, Istanbul.

Yalman, N., 1973, 'Some Observations on Secularism in Islam: The Cultural Revolution in Turkey', *Daedalus*, 102(1), pp. 139–69.

Yavuz, M.H., 1997, 'Political Islam and Welfare (Refah) Party in Turkey', *Comparative Politics*, 30(1), pp. 63–82.

—— 2003, *Islamic Political Identity in Turkey*, Oxford University Press, Oxford.

Yeni Evrensel (daily), 2001, 'Davosun Ardindan' [After Davos], 1 February.

Yeni Safak (daily), 2002, [Faiz Turkiyeyi bitirdi], 26 May.

Yetkin, Ç., 1995, *Türkiye'de Askeri Darbeler ve Amerika* [Turkey's Military Coups and America], Ümit Yayıncılık, Ankara.

Yılmaz, S., 2001, 'Dervişi sıkıştırırsanız batarsınız' [You Will Go Bankrupt if Dervish Is Given Hard Time], *Milliyet*, 19 July.

Yücekök, A., 1971, *Türkiye de Örgütlenmiş Dinin Sosyo Ekonomic Tabanı* (1946–1968), [The Socioeconomic Bases of Organised Religion in Turkey, 1946–1968], Sevinç Matbaası, Ankara.

—— 1997, *Dinin Siyasallaşması: Din-Devlet İlişkilerinde Türkiye Deneyimi* [Politicisation of Religion: Turkish Experience in Religion and State Relations], AFA Yayıncılkı ve TÜSES Vakfı, Istanbul.

Zubaida, S., 1996, 'Turkish Islam and National Identity', *Middle East Report* (April–June), pp. 10–15.

INDEX

Numbers in **bold** refer to tables; numbers in *italic* refer to photographs; n. after a number refers to an endnote